Springer Studies in Law & Geoeconomics

Volume 3

The series 'Springer Studies in Law & Geoeconomics' is devoted to analyzing the role of law in conditioning the use of geoeconomic power and the role of geoeconomic power in conditioning the formation, enforcement, and systematic variation of laws and (public and private) norms. The series specializes in the application to these problems of insights developed across scientific disciplines, not only law and IR, but also geography (economic and political), economic sociology, economic anthropology, comparative politics, epistemology, history, economics and game theory, probability theory, negotiation theory, cognitive science, and social psychology. The range of disciplinary approaches dealt with by the series is virtually unlimited, in line with its commitment to transcending disciplinary boundaries.

The series welcomes contributions from distinguished legal scholars working in international, comparative, or domestic law, empirical legal studies, or different "law and . . ." areas, as well as IR scholars, political economists, and political scientists with an interdisciplinary focus. The series also strives to offer a forum for contributions to legal theory by scholars working in disciplines outside of law. For thematic issues, particular issues are commissioned and a call for papers is distributed. The series also publishes open issues that provide publication possibilities for uncommissioned manuscripts intended to stimulate submissions by talented master students and Ph.D. candidates.

The series publishes contributions following a substantive review by the editors and rigorous double-blind peer-review by external experts as appropriate. The series editors have published extensively in the field of law and geoeconomics. They are supported by an international board of advisory editors consisting of established scholars of the highest reputation.

Jens Hillebrand Pohl • Thomas Papadopoulos •
Janosch Wiesenthal
Editors

National Security and Investment Controls

Springer

Editors
Jens Hillebrand Pohl
Finnish Institute of International Affairs
Helsinki, Finland

Thomas Papadopoulos
Law Department
University of Cyprus
Nicosia, Cyprus

Janosch Wiesenthal
University of Lüneburg
Lüneburg, Germany

ISSN 2948-1899 ISSN 2948-1902 (electronic)
Springer Studies in Law & Geoeconomics
ISBN 978-3-031-68018-2 ISBN 978-3-031-68016-8 (eBook)
https://doi.org/10.1007/978-3-031-68016-8

This Springer imprint is published by the registered company Springer Nature Switzerland AG
The registered company address is: Gewerbestrasse 11, 6330 Cham, Switzerland

Preface

The notion of national security, an existential concept for all States, constitutes a ground for justifying and thus allowing various restrictions on foreign direct investments (FDI) in the EU and on free movement in the internal market. National security possesses a central role and constitutes an essential tool in investment control, an emerging area in EU and international law during the current period of global geoeconomic challenges. More specifically, national security is one of the cornerstones of the investment screening mechanisms introduced or strengthened especially during the last years by EU Member States as well as by third countries. Various foreign direct investments are screened on the basis of national security.

While international bibliography has analyzed before generally the notion of national security in the context of EU internal market law and international investment law, this collection of chapters constitutes an effort to discuss in detail various aspects of this notion specifically in the context of investment screening. In the era of multiple geoeconomic challenges, the analysis of the concept of national security as tool of screening foreign direct investments is essential. This collection of essays aims at providing original analysis and at shedding light on intriguing and previously unexplored aspects of national security and investment controls. Nevertheless, the topics analyzed in this book are not strictly restricted to national security and investment control, but various other relevant legal issues of investment screening are also scrutinized in the light of law and geoeconomics of foreign capital. There are chapters discussing many interesting legal developments and underexplored topics in the area of investment screening.

National security and investment controls constitute in two volumes a selection of original research papers on national security in the context of investment screening as well as on other topical and challenging issues on investment screening and geoeconomic conundrums. These next two volumes are published in the new book series of Springer with the title *Springer Studies in Law & Geoeconomics*, which seeks to cover a gap in international bibliography by promoting the research in this evolving interdisciplinary area of law. These two volumes continue the research and the exploration of topics analyzed at volumes I and II of *Weaponising Investments*, which were published previously in the same book series and which are laying an analytical foundation and are providing a framework for the emerging research field of foreign investment control.

This volume contains 12 pioneering, original, and thought-provoking chapters examining current topics on national security, screening of foreign direct investments and law & geoeconomics issues in the context of EU, domestic, international, and comparative law. The purpose of this edited book is to contribute to the evolution and development of the emerging interdisciplinary research area of investment control. Preliminary drafts of the papers were presented at Uppsala University, Faculty of Law, on 1–6 June 2022 at the CELIS Forum on Investment Screening organized by Prof. Dr. Steffen Hindelang and Jens Hillebrand Pohl.

The first chapter with the title "Inward Foreign Investment Screening in Australia: Development and Implications," which was written by *Philipp McCalman, Laura Puzzello, Tania Voon,* and *Andrew Walter,* outlines political, legal, and economic aspects of Australia's inward foreign investment screening regime, taking account of the historical development of the legislative framework and its practical implementation to date. Australian screening is characterized by high levels of discretion in the Treasurer, within broad policy parameters regarding the meaning of 'national interest' and 'national security'. The impact of the most recent changes as of 2021 is difficult to assess, but they have clearly increased the number of investment proposals that are subject to review. Although most applications are approved, approval with conditions is common, while other applications may be withdrawn following informal feedback, obviating the need for formal rejection.

In the second chapter, *Wolf Zwartkruis* is seeking to explore the link between FDI and the security interests of the State and to identify the problem. If a foreign company takes over a major domestic firm, this often sparks concerns in the public opinion of the country of the acquired entity. He explores how FDI is part of the State-firm dynamic, drawing on literature in the field of economics and international political economics. He also sketches a framework that makes it possible to determine whether a given FDI transaction creates a risk for State security. He uses the framework to assess whether such a risk exists in the controversial Midea-KUKA takeover that dates from 2016 and at the end he reaches some conclusions.

The next chapter written by *Jochem de Kok* focuses on foreignness in EU Investment Screening Law. Concerns regarding FDIs from China have played a central role in the adoption and development of the EU framework for FDI screening. The official discourse regarding these concerns initially focused on economic interests but shifted to security following the introduction of the FDI Screening Regulation. Because the precise security threats posed by FDI were largely unspecified, there is a lack of meaningful indications in the law and the legislative history regarding the definition of security and public policy, as well as the broader objectives of the EU FDI Screening Regulation. Since its adoption, the official discourse on FDI screening has emphasized the importance of European strategic autonomy, which is used as a wide umbrella term for various industrial political interests.

Manu Misra analyzes the subject matter of foreign investment screening and trust in international relations. A greatly consequential, if not decisive, underlying factor affecting both the expansion and usage of investment screening mechanisms has been the level of trust between States. Trust, or the lack of it, has been at the heart of the recent cluster of State activity related to investment screening mechanisms. Accepting foreign investment proposals, especially in critical sectors and/or involving State-controlled entities, naturally increases the host State's potential vulnerability and thus requires a higher level of trust toward both the investor and its governing home State.

Next, the topic of international legal framework for foreign investment control is scrutinized by *Pascale Accaoui Lorfing*. The provision on security interest inserted in an international investment agreement allows the State to take regulatory measures without compensating the foreign investor whose rights are affected, provided that the specific conditions inserted in the provision or the general principles of customary international law are met. Art. XXI GATT (1994) provides for such a security exception. The way it is drafted has been interpreted along lines that are of great interest as they open the way to a possible approach that could be adopted by arbitral tribunals assessing the same type of provision. A harmonized approach to interpretation can be ensured by a multilateral investment court with interpretation guidelines and an institutional structure for their implementation.

Georgios Dimitropoulos contributed a chapter with the title "Regulating Sovereign-Driven Investments in International Trade and Investment Agreements: The Role of Investment Screening Mechanisms." The chapter discusses the principles that govern sovereign-driven investments in different areas of international economic law. First, it discusses ownership neutrality. Subsequently, it discusses the sovereign power of States to regulate market access and elaborates on how changes in national law impact international economic law. The open-ended nature of international trade and investment agreements has allowed for domestic law to jump-start a process of reforming international law. New investment screening mechanisms bring about changes in the overall structure of the international investment regime, and the way it deals with sovereign investments.

A comparative analysis of the definition of foreign investors and protected investments is provided by *Yarik Kryvoi*. This chapter identifies shortcomings concerning the definitions of "foreign investor" and "foreign investment" found in the legislation of some States. It then proceeds to develop specific recommendations for improvement of these definitions. More specifically, the chapter analyzes bilateral and multilateral investment treaties, the legislation of different countries, awards of investment tribunals, and recommendations of international organizations and experts concerning the definition of "foreign investor" and "protected investments."

Yulia Levashova and *Niccolò Zugliani* discuss in their chapter investor obligations through the prism of the EU foreign investment screening framework. This paper examines two applications for possible enforcement of investor obligations in the context of the EU foreign investment screening framework. The first application concerns the role of investor obligations; it is explored from the perspective of various Member States' screening mechanisms and relevant investment agreements concluded or negotiated by the EU. The second application considers several exemptions to capital transfer provisions that may also facilitate the enforcement of investor obligations. Finally, the implications of international investment agreements' exemptions of public policy and public security grounds that may restrict capital transfer under the EU foreign investment screening regulation are discussed from the perspective of investor obligation to comply with the national law of the host State.

The next chapter with the title "Facilitating and Scrutinizing National Security Measures: Analysis of an Investment Screening Case in the European Union" is written by *Bálint Kovács*. The reasons for adopting new regulations for the screening of foreign direct investment, and the particular context, have been extensively discussed, both in academic circles and in the mainstream media. Nevertheless, this paper reiterates some of this, with the purpose of illustrating changes in attitude toward economic relations, in particular foreign direct investment, in a context in which open economies are becoming increasingly suspicious and have started to pay more attention to the security risks posed by economic actors whose intent – as is often claimed – is not purely commercial. The EU FDI Screening Regulation is scrutinized in this context. The Hungarian authorities' decision to veto a takeover in case of AEGON Group and VIG is also examined. Issues on investment screening and arbitration are also discussed.

The next chapter analyzes a domestic investment screening mechanism in the context of the EU legal framework. More specifically, the Italian investment screening regime is examined by *Sara Pugliese* in her chapter with the title "Toward a Multilevel System of Investment Control oriented to Crisis Management: Italian Golden Power in the Framework of the EU FDI Screening Mechanism." This chapter examines the evolution of Italian special power regulation, Italian government reforms in light of the recent crises, and their influence on establishing an EU system of control over foreign direct investment and other transactions. Its ultimate aim is to assess the effectiveness of this system in promptly identifying and countering risks to national and EU strategic interests without disincentivizing foreign investors to enter the domestic and EU internal markets.

The negotiation of mitigation agreements is the focus of *Dominik Eisenhut*'s chapter. This chapter gives an overview of agreements to mitigate national security concerns between the concerned State, on the one hand, and the acquiring company and the target company, on the other hand. Through such mitigation arrangements, States seek to alleviate their national security concerns. The acquiring and target companies, in turn, are willing to make certain undertakings to obtain an – albeit conditional – clearance of the transaction. Mitigation actions have become increasingly popular with screening authorities, allowing them to preserve at the same time the security interests of the State and a general investor-friendly business environment, important to attract foreign capital. The chapter looks at typical types of security undertakings and at the different legal means to implement these undertakings.

The last chapter written by *Fabien Gehl* deals with the international coordination of national screening procedures with emphasis on the case of the EU cooperation mechanism. This chapter identifies the main challenges at the crossroad of international cooperation and investment screening, which are confidentiality, reconciling international cooperation with national interest, ensuring efficiency and adding value. It then argues that the EU cooperation mechanism has addressed those challenges successfully, even if not perfectly. Finally, the chapter offers a glimpse into the flagship international cooperation initiative at European level: the EU-US Trade and Technology Council Working Group on investment screening.

Helsinki, Finland
Nicosia, Cyprus
Lüneburg, Germany

Jens Hillebrand Pohl
Thomas Papadopoulos
Janosch Wiesenthal

Contents

About the Contributors

Georgios Dimitropoulos is an Associate Professor of Law, as well as Associate Dean for Research and S.J.D. Programme Coordinator at HBKU College of Law. He is also an Adjunct Associate Professor at Georgetown University in Qatar and a Research Associate at the University College London Centre for Blockchain Technologies (UCL CBT). He serves on the editorial boards of the Journal of World Investment & Trade (JWIT) and the Asia Pacific Law Review (APLR). Before joining HBKU he was a Senior Research Fellow at the Max Planck Institute Luxembourg and a Hauser Research Scholar at New York University (NYU) School of Law. He has held visiting positions at the Athens Public International Law Centre (AthensPIL), Singapore Management University (SMU), University College London Centre for Law, Economics and Society (UCL CLES), the Université Catholique de Lyon (UCLy) and the Jigme Singye Wangchuck (JSW) School of Law in Bhutan. His work has appeared in journals such as the *Washington Law Review*, the *Cornell International Law Journal*, the *University of Pennsylvania Journal of International Law*, the *Northwestern Journal of International Law & Business*, the *World Trade Review*, and the *Journal of International Economic Law*. He studied law at the University of Athens, and holds an LL.M. and J.S.D. from Yale Law School, as well as an LL.M. and Ph.D. *summa cum laude* from the University of Heidelberg.

Dominik Eisenhut is a Senior Legal Counsel at Airbus, located in Toulouse, France. In his current role, Dominik advises on EU law matters, with a particular focus on public procurement law, offset agreements, and issues related to investment screening. Before joining Airbus, he worked as a corporate attorney in Munich and served at the Chair of International and European Law at the University of the Bundeswehr. Dominik holds a Ph.D. from Augsburg University, where his research concentrated on the applicability of EU law in the areas of defence and security. He also earned an LL.M. from University College London. His academic journey included studying law in Freiburg, Grenoble, and Munich, and he was admitted to the Munich bar in 2007. In addition to his role at Airbus, Dominik is a lecturer in European Law at the Bundeswehr University. He has contributed to several TEU/

TFEU commentaries and authored numerous articles focusing on Article 346 TFEU and other aspects of EU law related to security and defence. Dominik's work is characterized by his extensive expertise in commercial contracts, EU law, and dispute resolution, making him a key figure in the legal and regulatory landscape of the aerospace and defence sectors.

Fabien Gehl is Deputy Head of Unit for South and South East Asia, Australia and New Zealand at the Directorate General for Trade of the European Commission. He has worked for over 15 years in trade policy, with a focus on Trade and Security, Services, Investment and Digital Trade. As a negotiator for the European Union, he participated in various trade negotiations with key trading partners and at the World Trade Organization (WTO). Fabien previously worked with the Mission of the European Union to the World Trade Organization in Geneva and with the WTO Unit of DG TRADE where he worked on the reform of the WTO. He started his career in trade with the Belgian Ministry for Foreign Affairs and External Trade where he represented Belgium in the EU Council's Trade Policy Committee (services and investment). Prior to that, Fabien was teaching European Affairs at the Swiss Graduate School of Public Administration (IDHEAP) in Lausanne. Fabien graduated from the University of Liege (Belgium) in Public Administration, from the College of Europe in European Political and Administrative Studies and holds a Ph. D. in law from the University of Bern (Switzerland).

Jochem de Kok is a Senior Associate at A&O Shearman and a Ph.D. Candidate at the University of Amsterdam. He is specialized in foreign investment screening, competition, and regulatory law. He has notable experience advising clients on complex multi-jurisdictional investment screening and merger control proceedings, behavioural antitrust, and compliance. He regularly represents clients in proceedings before the European Commission, the Dutch Competition Authority, the Dutch Ministry of Economic Affairs and Dutch and European courts. He has also published various articles on investment screening and competition law in international and national law journals and lectures at the University of Bonn. He previously completed the Blue Book Traineeship at the European Commission, DG Competition and worked at the Competition Law and Policy team of Maersk on secondment. Jochem holds LL.M. degrees from the University of Groningen (cum laude) and the University of Cambridge (First Class Honours).

Bálint Kovács is Assistant Lecturer of International Economic Law at the University of Szeged and Researcher at the Ferenc Mádl Institute of Comparative Law in Budapest. He will soon earn his Ph.D. from the University of Debrecen with a thesis focusing on small- and medium-sized investors' access to investor-state dispute settlement. He is Visiting Lecturer at the University of Miskolc teaching International Commercial Arbitration and at Sapientia Hungarian University of Transylvania teaching International Economic Law. In 2022–2023, he spent a year at American University Washington College of Law as a Visiting Scholar. His interests include international investment law and dispute settlement, regional economic integration, the legal accommodation of economic security, and the human rights of minorities.

Yarik Kryvoi is the Senior Fellow in International Economic Law and Director of the Investment Treaty Forum at the British Institute of International and Comparative Law. He is also an Of Counsel at Keidan Harrison in London and a co-founder of the Arbitration Lab. Prof. Kryvoi's expertise is primarily in international dispute resolution, international public law and comparative law. He has managed major law reform projects and assessments around the world related to commercial courts, investment climate, arbitration, and international investment law. Prof Kryvoi has practiced international dispute resolution with Freshfields Bruckhaus Deringer in London, Morgan Lewis & Bockius in Washington, DC and Baker & McKenzie in Saint Petersburg. He has also worked an extern at the US Court of Appeals for the District of Columbia Circuit. He was admitted to the Bar in New York, holds a doctorate from the University College London, an LL.M. degree from Harvard Law and other degrees from England, the Netherlands and Russia.

Yulia Levashova is Associate Professor in International Investment Law and International Arbitration at Nyenrode University in the Netherlands and an arbitration legal practitioner with a background in Russian and Dutch law. Yulia has extensive experience in international dispute resolution, business law, public law and legal aspects of ESG. Yulia is serving as a Director of Dispute Prevention of the Asia Pacific FDI Network (APFN). Yulia has been appointed as arbitrator in international commercial disputes and served as an expert consultant to the Dutch Ministry of Economic Affairs and Climate Policy in the RWE v. the Netherlands case. She is a member of CIArb, the LCIA, the Dutch Arbitration Association, and Arbitral Women. Yulia consults for international organizations like UNCTAD and UNECE, providing advice and contributing to reports on ISDS and trade law issues. She also has vast experience in complicated projects in the private sector involving ESG, due diligence, sustainability, and CSR. Since 2023, Yulia is a delegate observer to the United Nations Commission on International Trade Law (UNCITRAL), and she is currently participating in the UNCITRAL Working Group III: Investor-State Dispute Settlement Reform. Yulia has published extensively on commercial and investment arbitration topics, including a monograph on fair and equitable treatment and the right to regulate (Wolters Kluwer), and has organized numerous international conferences with UNCITRAL, UNCTAD, CIArb and in collaboration with various international law firms.

Pascale Accaoui Lorfing is Associate Researcher at CREDIMI—Univ. Burgundy, and Affiliated Professor at ESCP Business School—Paris. Her research focuses on international contracts (hardship, force majeure, and other related doctrines) and investment contracts (the right of the State to regulate and the protection of investors). She contributes to Lamy International Contracts on Investment Contracts, on Key clauses in international contracts and investment contracts (stabilization clauses, balancing clauses, force majeure clauses), and the Jurisclasseur (Investment

Contract). She is a regular contributor to International Law Reviews and is the author of several publications on international contracts and investment contracts. She is co-editor of *Balancing the Protection of Foreign Investors and States' Responses in the (Post) Pandemic World*, Kluwer (2022) and published a book on *The Renegotiation of the International Contracts*, Bruylant (2011). She is also a member of the ICC Institute of World Business Law and the ICC Commission on Arbitration and ADR. She co-leads the chronicle on Investment of the International Business Law Journal (IBLJ) and is a member of several working groups including the Working Group on International Contracts (International Arbitration Institute (IAI), *Groupe de Travail sur les Contrats Internationaux*), the Society of Comparative Legislation (*Société de législation comparée*), and the International Law Association (French branch).

Philip McCalman is a Professor of Economics at the University of Melbourne specializing in international economics. He was previously a Peter B. Kenen Fellow at Princeton University and a Resident Scholar at the International Monetary Fund.

Manu Misra is a Lecturer in Law at the University of Exeter, U.K. He was previously a Postdoctoral Global Fellow at the FGV School of Law in Sao Paulo and a Visiting Fellow at the BRICS Policy Centre, Institute of International Relations, Pontifical Catholic University of Rio de Janeiro, Brazil. Specializing in foreign investment law, policy, and politics, he received his Ph.D. in Legal Studies from Bocconi University, Milan, Italy and an LL.M. in Law & Economics from the University of Hamburg, Germany. He has also been a Visiting Scholar at the Max Planck Institute for Procedural Law in Luxembourg and the Max Planck Institute for Comparative Public Law and International Law in Heidelberg. He has previously worked for the Department of Economic Affairs, Ministry of Finance within the Government of India where he contributed to the drafting of India's 2015/16 Model Bilateral Investment Treaty.

Thomas Papadopoulos is an Associate Professor of Business Law at the Department of Law of the University of Cyprus. He received his DPhil in Law from the Faculty of Law, University of Oxford, UK (2010). He received a degree of Magister Juris-MJur (2006) and a degree of MPhil in Law (2007) from the Faculty of Law, University of Oxford, UK. He also received his LL.B. with Distinction (ranked 1st) from the Department of Law, Aristotle University of Thessaloniki, Greece (2005). Previously, he was a Visiting Researcher at Harvard Law School, USA (2009–2010). He is also a Visiting Professor at University of Trento and at International Hellenic University, a Teaching Fellow at Open University of Cyprus and an Attorney at law (Greece). Additionally, he was a Visiting Researcher at King's College London and at Max Planck Institute Luxembourg. Moreover, he is a member of the editorial board of European Company Law (ECL) Journal published by Kluwer and a member of the editorial board of European Company Case Law (ECCL) Review published by Nomos. He is a country reporter-legal expert for Cyprus at the European Model Company Act (EMCA) Group, the Common European Law on Investment Screening (CELIS) Institute, the Covid-19 Litigation

Project of the University of Trento, Italy and research projects of the European Trade Union Institute (ETUI). He is also a member of the academic board of European Banking Institute (EBI). He was awarded the "Cyprus Research Award-Young Researcher (2014)" of the Research Promotion Foundation of the Republic of Cyprus (category of "Social Sciences & Humanities"). His articles were published in many top international law journals. He is also the author of the following monograph published by Kluwer: *EU Law and the Harmonization of Takeovers in the Internal Market, 2010, Kluwer*. Moreover, he is the editor of the following book published by Springer: *Cross-Border Mergers: EU Perspectives and National Experiences, 2019, Springer*. In February 2023, his 1280 pages book on *Cyprus Company Law* was published in Greek by Nomiki Vivliothiki publications.

Jens Hillebrand Pohl is a legal scholar, geographer, and political scientist writing and lecturing at the intersection of law and geoeconomics. An experienced attorney having practiced before U.S. federal and state courts in New York and for EU institutions, Jens researches the (geo)politicization of the legal order. His Ph.D. in law at Maastricht University concerns judicial deference to executive power in national security cases and his second Ph.D. in political science at Tampere University analyses "lawfare" and the (mis)use of the legal system as an instrument of geostrategic power. Jens is an adjunct professor (docent) at Maastricht University and the United Nations University, a doctoral fellow of the Institute for Globalization and International Regulation (IGIR), a doctoral research scientist at Tampere University, and an Associate Fellow at the Royal Geographical Society. He is the founding series editor of Springer Studies in Law & Geoeconomics, an advisory editor of the Yearbook of Socio-Economic Constitutions, and a former article editor of the Harvard International Law Journal. He has held visiting appointments at the Max Planck Institute for Procedural Law, T.M.C. Asser Institute, and the World Trade Institute. He holds an LL.M. from Harvard Law School and an MSc in Economics and Business from the Stockholm School of Economics.

Sara Pugliese is Associate Professor of EU Law at the "Parthenope" University of Naples. She has authored articles and contributions concerning several issues (EU environmental and cultural policy, EU defence policy, EU economic governance, EU agencies, protection of minorities, Special Economic Zones, joint procurements, EU energy policy, investment screening) and the volume "*Il rischio nel diritto dell'Unione europea tra principi di precauzione, proporzionalità e standardizzazione*". The Universidad de Jaén hosted her as an "Invited Researcher" and within the Erasmus teaching mobility scheme. She has been invited to hold virtual lessons at the Politehnica University of Timisoara. She was Visiting Professor at the Nicolas Copernicus University in Toruń. She has lectured on several degree and postgraduate courses at her university. She has also participated in numerous research projects, conferences, and editorial boards. She is the Associate investigator responsible for the Local Research Unit "Parthenope" in the Project of National Interest (PRIN) 2022 "Towards Stricter Rules on Transparency and Liability for

Online Platforms in the European Digital Single Market", funded by Italian Research Ministry in the ambit of the Programme Next Generation EU.

Laura Puzzello is an Associate Professor in the Department of Economics at Monash Business School, Monash University, specializing in International Economics. Her research tackles policy-relevant questions in international trade, currently focusing on the economic implications of trade and investment policies. Laura has consulted for leading international organizations, including the World Bank and the Asian Development Bank.

Tania Voon is Professor and former Associate Dean (Research) at Melbourne Law School. She was previously a Legal Officer in the WTO Appellate Body Secretariat. She has practised law with King & Wood Mallesons and the Australian Government Solicitor and taught law at the National University of Singapore, Chinese University of Hong Kong, Georgetown University, the University of Western Ontario, the University of British Columbia, and several Australian universities. Tania undertook her LL.M. at Harvard Law School and her Ph.D. at the University of Cambridge. She is on the WTO Indicative List of Panelists and the Roster of Panelists for the Energy Charter Treaty. She is also on the list of chairpersons for arbitrations under the EU's trade agreements with third countries and the list of arbitrators under Article 304(4) of the Trade Agreement between the EU, Colombia, Peru, and Ecuador. She was Editor of the Oxford University Press Series on International Economic Law from 2013 to 2024. She is the author of Cultural Products and the World Trade Organization (CUP 2007) and currently lead CI on an interdisciplinary ARC Discovery Project investigating the global causes and consequences of foreign investment screening.

Andrew Walter is Professor of International Relations and Co-Chair of Politics in the School of Social and Political Sciences, University of Melbourne. He obtained his BA (Economics) from the University of Western Australia and his MPhil and DPhil degrees (International Relations) from Oxford University. His previous academic positions were at Oxford University and the London School of Economics and Political Science. He has published widely on the political economy of international money, finance, wealth, and investment. His last book, The Wealth Effect: How the Great Expectations of the Middle Class Have Changed the Politics of Banking Crises (Cambridge University Press, 2019, with Jeffrey Chwieroth), won the XXVth Stein Rokkan Prize for Comparative Social Science Research and the Best Book award in International Political Economy by the International Studies Association. His current research is on the politics of wealth inequality and crises, investment and national security, and finance in the energy transition.

Janosch Wiesenthal is a Ph.D. candidate and research assistant at the University of Lüneburg (Chair for Public Law, Public International Law and Comparative Law) currently working on a thesis which focuses on Foreign Investment Screening. He holds a Ph.D.-scholarship from the German Academic Scholarship Foundation

(*Studienstiftung des deutschen Volkes*). Janosch is also Deputy Assistant Director of the CELIS Institute, an independent nonprofit, nonpartisan research enterprise dedicated to promoting better regulation of foreign investment in light of security and public order concerns. He co-founded the CELIS Early-Career Scholars' and Practitioners' Network on the Law and Practice of Economic Warfare (CELIS NOW) and the CELIS Blog. Janosch completed his law studies at Humboldt-Universität zu Berlin by passing the first state examination (*Erstes Staatsexamen*). He also studied at the Université Paris II Panthéon-Assas, where he specialized in international law and obtained both the *Licence en droit* and the *Maîtrise en droit*.

Niccolò Zugliani is a postdoctoral research fellow in International Law at the Department of Legal Studies of Bocconi University (Italy) and an adjunct professor at the University of Milan (Italy). He holds an LL.M. from the University of Vienna (Austria) and a Ph.D. from the University of Verona (Italy). He was Visiting Researcher at the Grotius Centre for International Legal Studies (the Netherlands), at the University of Ottawa (Canada), and at the Amsterdam Centre for International Law (the Netherlands). He has published in leading international journals and edited books on issues of public international law, international economic law, humanitarian law, and jurisdiction of domestic courts.

Wolf Zwartkruis is currently the Lead Strategist at the Dutch Ministry of Economic Affairs and Climate Policy. He has been with the Ministry since 2021, previously serving as a Coordinating Policy Advisor. Wolf is also a Ph.D. candidate at Leiden University, where his research focuses on the interplay between EU law and geoeconomics, specifically in the area of foreign direct investment (FDI) screening. His academic and professional work is highly regarded in the field of international economic law, where he combines his expertise in policy, strategy, financial markets, and law to address critical issues related to economic security and regulation. Wolf's background includes positions at the Dutch Central Bank and the Ministry of Finance, where he advised on financial markets and policy. He has also contributed to significant academic and policy discussions on the EU's FDI screening regulation, highlighting its impact on the European internal market and global economic relations.

Inward Foreign Investment Screening in Australia: Development and Implications

Phillip McCalman, Laura Puzzello, Tania Voon, and Andrew Walter

Contents

We thank Clementine Girard-Foley, Diane Hu, and Dean Merriman for their research assistance in the preparation of this chapter. We also gratefully acknowledge the support of the Australian Research Council pursuant to the Discovery Project DP200100639. All opinions expressed here and any errors are ours and do not necessarily reflect those of any employer or other entity.

P. McCalman
University of Melbourne, Faculty of Business and Economics, Melbourne, VIC, Australia
e-mail: mccalman@unimelb.edu.au

L. Puzzello
Monash University, Department of Economics, Melbourne, VIC, Australia
e-mail: Laura.Puzzello@monash.edu

T. Voon (✉)
University of Melbourne, Melbourne Law School, Melbourne, VIC, Australia
e-mail: tania.voon@unimelb.edu.au

A. Walter
University of Melbourne, School of Social and Political Sciences, Melbourne, VIC, Australia
e-mail: andrew.walter@unimelb.edu.au

J. H. Pohl et al. (eds.), *National Security and Investment Controls*,
Springer Studies in Law & Geoeconomics (2024) 3: 1–26,
https://doi.org/10.1007/17280_2024_33, Published online: 23 February 2024

Abstract This chapter outlines political, legal, and economic aspects of Australia's inward foreign investment screening regime, taking account of the historical development of the legislative framework and its practical implementation to date. Australian screening is characterised by high levels of discretion in the Treasurer, within broad policy parameters regarding the meaning of 'national interest' and 'national security'. The impact of the most recent changes as of 2021 is difficult to assess, but they have clearly increased the number of investment proposals that are subject to review. Although most applications are approved, approval with conditions is common, while other applications may be withdrawn following informal feedback, obviating the need for formal rejection. The increasing restrictiveness of Australia's approach and its continuing differentiation between investors from different countries create risks of violating one of Australia's 30+ international investment agreements in force, the majority of which include investor–state dispute settlement mechanisms. The economic and diplomatic rationale for such restrictiveness and differentiation (particularly in the form of higher screening thresholds for some but not all of Australia's preferential trade agreement partners) is unclear.

1 Introduction

Although Australia touts itself as an 'open ... economy',[1] the Organisation for Economic Co-operation and Development (OECD) places Australia 37th out of 44 OECD countries in its 2020 index of restrictiveness of Foreign Direct Investment (FDI), at 0.15 in comparison with the OECD average of 0.06 (with 1 being maximum restriction).[2] Since 2010, while the OECD average has dropped slightly, Australia's measured restrictiveness to FDI has only increased.[3] The major component of Australia's FDI restrictiveness takes the form of screening and approval of foreign investment proposals, and in that regard, only New Zealand shows a higher level of restriction.[4] Even while tightening foreign investment screening in recent years, as discussed in this chapter, the government continues to insist that the economy welcomes foreign investors. Indeed, Australia's foreign investment policy explicitly states that the 'Australian Government welcomes foreign investment for the significant benefits it provides'.[5]

[1] DFAT (2022d).

[2] OECD (2020). The OECD FDI Restrictiveness Index is a composite index measuring four kinds of restrictions on FDI. One of these is screening and approval mechanisms. The three others are foreign equity restrictions, foreign personnel restrictions and operational restrictions (such as branching, profit repatriation and land ownership).

[3] OECD (2020).

[4] OECD (2020).

[5] FIRB (2022a), p. 1.

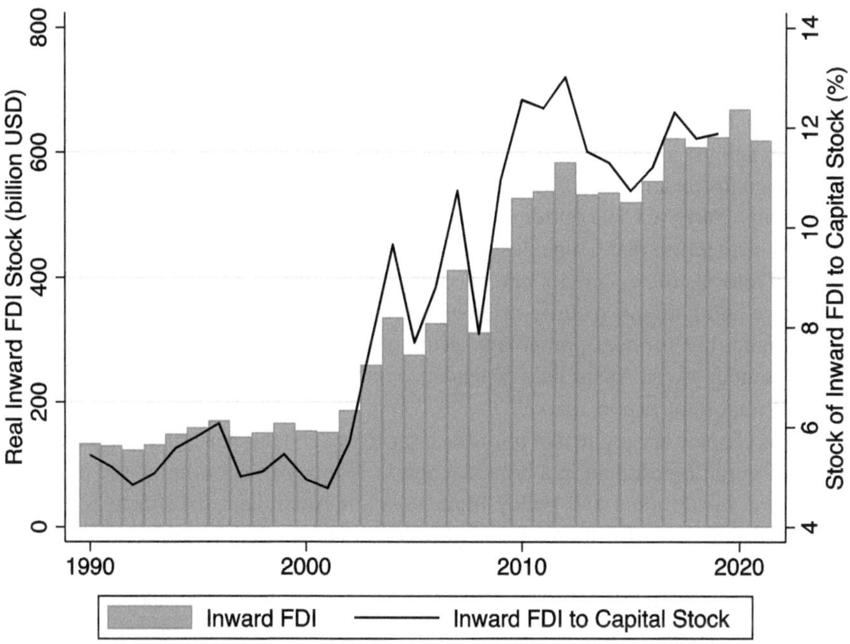

Fig. 1 Australia Inward FDI, 1990–2021. *Note*. Data on the stock of inward FDI, CPI and capital stock are from UNCTAD, World Development Indicators, and the Penn World Tables 10.0. Data on capital stock are available only until 2019

The success of Australia in attracting foreign capital is evident from Fig. 1, which shows a nearly fivefold increase in the stock of inward FDI between 1990 and 2021. This growth, particularly pronounced since the early 2000s, has translated into higher reliance on foreign investment in the accumulation of capital, with FDI accounting for approximately 12% of the total stock of capital by the end of 2019—double the level of the early 2000s.

Australia's inward foreign investment screening mechanism (ISM) has evolved substantially in recent years. First introduced in 1976, the Foreign Investment Review Board (FIRB) was given a broad and undefined remit to screen inward investment for transactions deemed 'contrary to the national interest'. For decades, FIRB served as a means of resisting periodically resurgent protectionist interests. It was granted only an advisory role and limited resources and was situated within the Department of the Treasury, the dominant economic policy department with a strong interest in encouraging foreign investment inflows.[6] During the resource boom that emerged in the years before the global financial crisis (GFC) of 2007-9, Chinese investment in the Australian resources sector began to displace investment from more traditional sources such as the United Kingdom, the United States and Japan.

[6]Drysdale and Findlay (2009), Drysdale (2011), p. 56.

Australia briefly became the largest single destination of Chinese outward foreign investment.[7]

Initially, the screening of Chinese inward investment was limited, and FIRB seemed to be playing its traditional role as a means of resisting a protectionist backlash against a surge of inward foreign investment. However, the predominance of state-controlled investors in this investment surge, the reassertion of Chinese Communist Party (CCP) control over the corporate sector under Xi Jinping, and the growing perception that China posed a unique security threat ultimately prompted a series of reforms to Australia's ISM. Together, these factors have moved it in a more protective and national security-oriented direction. This development is not unique to Australia, but it poses particularly acute challenges for foreign policy and economic strategy given Australia's dependence on foreign investment and on China as its most important export market.

In this chapter, we argue that it is necessary to understand Australia's screening of inward foreign investment in a broader context. We begin by outlining the political, legislative, institutional and policy framework for Australian investment screening (Sect. 2) and then the more recent developments in that framework since the beginning of the COVID-19 pandemic (Sect. 3). In Sect. 4, we analyse the operation of the screening mechanism in practice by considering trends and statistics in applications and approvals and the limited evidence of economic incentives for the preferential treatment granted by Australia to some of its trading partners in the context of screening. Finally, in Sect. 5, we identify the potential for an investment treaty claim to be brought against Australia with respect to its screening regulations or actions, concluding that such a claim by a Chinese or other investor remains possible (particularly following the recent regulatory reforms), despite the inclusion of various safeguards in Australia's investment treaties. We conclude that the variation in Australia's approach to screening investments from different countries and the growing restrictiveness of Australian screening have uncertain and untested economic, political and legal benefits.

2 Development and Implementation of Foreign Investment Screening in Australia

In this section, we introduce the political background and legislative framework governing Australia's foreign investment screening mechanism (including the different screening thresholds applicable to different forms of investment) before turning to the relevant institutions and policy (specifically the national interest test). Australia's major political parties have differed over how to balance the country's high export dependence on the Chinese market with rising concerns about the potential negative consequences of Chinese investment. All have found

[7] Scissors (2022).

it challenging. This section also highlights the complexity of the system and transparency difficulties as a basis for understanding post-COVID developments addressed further below.

2.1 *Domestic Politics of Inward Foreign Investment and Screening*

On the centre-left of Australia's political system, the Australian Labor Party has prioritized employment and, in government from 2007–2013, was generally welcoming of Chinese investment, despite Prime Minister Kevin Rudd's personal concerns. Its 2007 National Platform recognized 'the importance of maximising trade and investment opportunities for Australia in a rapidly changing world', noting the need for 'educating Australians about the contribution that trade and investment make to our living standards'.[8] In October 2007, two months before Labor won the election, Rudd stated that 'managing an influx of Chinese investment would be "an interesting challenge" for whoever won the election, but he was inclined to take a "market-based approach"'.[9] Once in office, Rudd asked the Treasury to prepare a position paper on how to deal with a takeover bid from a major Chinese government-owned resource company, but this was not provided by officials, who were seen as disengaged on the issue.[10] The onset of the GFC and the accompanying global downturn reinforced the government's incentive to maintain an overall stance of openness.

Although this stance was becoming politically sustainable, the Labor government's 2013 election platform celebrated 'a huge flow of mining investment' as one of its achievements.[11] During this election, several smaller political parties demanded more restrictions on the sale of agricultural land and resources. This included the National Party, the conservative rural party that with the Liberal Party constitutes the centre-right 'Coalition'. This group committed to 'dropping the Foreign Investment Review Board trigger to scrutinise rural property from $244m to $15m' and 'set[ting] up a register for rural land to keep track of foreign ownership in the agricultural sector'.[12] Labor opposed changing the rules governing FIRB, criticizing the Coalition's 'populist approach on the issue'.[13] Labor's trade minister argued that 'any tightening of foreign investment rules would ruin Asian markets for Australian farmers'.[14]

---

[8] ALP (2007) [6], [27].

[9] Garnaut (2007).

[10] Uren (2012), p. 43.

[11] ALP (2012), p. 13, 19, 51.

[12] Chan (2013).

[13] Ibid.

[14] Ibid.

The Coalition won the 2013 election and began to elaborate a more restrictive approach to inward investment, especially from China. Since approximately 2015, it has increasingly framed foreign investment from China as a national security issue, indicating an intention to modernize Australia's ISM to meet this threat. This was also consistent with a foreign policy that aligned closely with that of the United States, including during the Trump administration, which, as noted earlier, modified its own approach to investment screening in 2018. The Coalition government's response was encapsulated in the 2021 legislation discussed below, which Treasurer Frydenberg hailed as follows:

> the most significant reforms to the *Foreign Acquisitions and Takeovers Act 1975* in nearly 50 years ... [which] ensures that our foreign investment framework keeps pace with emerging risks and global developments, including similar changes to foreign investment regimes in comparable countries.[15]

The Labor Party's election manifesto in 2021 (preceding its 2022 federal election win) continued to emphasize the need to promote investment in Australian infrastructure and, especially, in renewable energy and manufacturing. Some of its members continued to argue that Australia's screening laws had become too strict, with serious economic costs for the country.[16] However, the manifesto also indicated an acceptance that the changed regional political and security environment required a more cautious approach towards foreign investment:

> Labor recognises that foreign investment is important for jobs and the Australian economy but believes these investments must be in the national interest. Labor will ensure investments are properly scrutinised in the national interest and any conditions are properly enforced.[17]

2.2 Legislative Framework

As in the United States, foreign investment screening began in Australia in the 1970s with the enactment of the Foreign Acquisitions and Takeovers Act 1975 (Cth) (FATA), which continues as the primary relevant legislation today. Restrictions on foreign investment have been added and removed over the years by successive Australian governments.[18] Other key pieces of legislation now governing screening are the Foreign Acquisitions and Takeovers Regulation 2015 (Cth) (FATR) and the Foreign Acquisitions and Takeovers Fees Impositions Act 2015 (Cth), developed in conjunction with significant amendments to FATA in 2015.[19] Additional legislation (which we do not regard as 'foreign investment screening') imposes requirements or restrictions on foreign investment in various specific sectors, such as

[15]Treasurer (2020a).

[16]McIlroy (2022).

[17]ALP (2021).

[18]Hanratty (1996).

[19]Treasury (2015).

telecommunications, banking, air transport, shipping, broadcasting, water entitlements, and agricultural land.

Proposed foreign investments in Australia are generally subject to screening only above certain monetary thresholds, depending on the nature and origin of the investor and the type of investment. Zero dollar thresholds currently exist for the national security-targeted reviews introduced in 2021, as discussed in Sect. 3.2 (e.g. for national security businesses and national security land), residential land, vacant commercial land, and foreign government investors.[20] For private (non-government) investors in agricultural land, developed commercial land, mining and production tenements, agricultural land entities, and non-agricultural land entities, the threshold depends on the nationality of the investor (being the 'immediate acquirer').[21] Higher thresholds apply for both land and non-land investments to investors from some but not all countries with preferential trade agreements (PTAs) with Australia: currently Canada, Chile, China, Hong Kong, Japan, Mexico, New Zealand, Peru, Singapore, South Korea, the United States, and Vietnam.[22] For example, for investments by investors from those countries in businesses other than agribusinesses and national security businesses, the threshold is A$1,250 million for non-sensitive businesses and A$289 million for sensitive businesses (e.g., media, communications, military), whereas for investments by investors from other countries (e.g., Thailand, Malaysia and Indonesia, despite their PTAs with Australia), the threshold is A$289 for both sensitive and non-sensitive businesses.[23]

2.3 Screening Institutions

The primary body assisting the Treasurer in making decisions with respect to foreign investment screening in Australia is FIRB, a non-statutory body established in 1976, as noted in Sect. 1 above. This means that its composition is entirely at the discretion of the Treasurer. FIRB has adapted over time, responding to changes in policy and perceived risks. As Fig. 2 indicates, in its first decade, FIRB was dominated by government appointees with non-security backgrounds. Appointments from the government sector have continued to dominate FIRB, but members from the general business and finance sectors have been the second most important constituency. Generally, the board has comprised fewer than 10 members, most of whom are part-time. It includes one full-time executive member (the First Assistant Secretary of the

[20] FIRB (2022a), pp. 14–16.

[21] FIRB (2022a), pp. 14, 16.

[22] Ibid. See Foreign Acquisitions and Takeovers Regulation 2015 (Cth) s 5 (definition of 'agreement country or region') (FATR). Thailand also benefits from some lower thresholds with respect to certain land investments.

[23] FIRB (2022a), pp. 15–16. See FATR s 51.

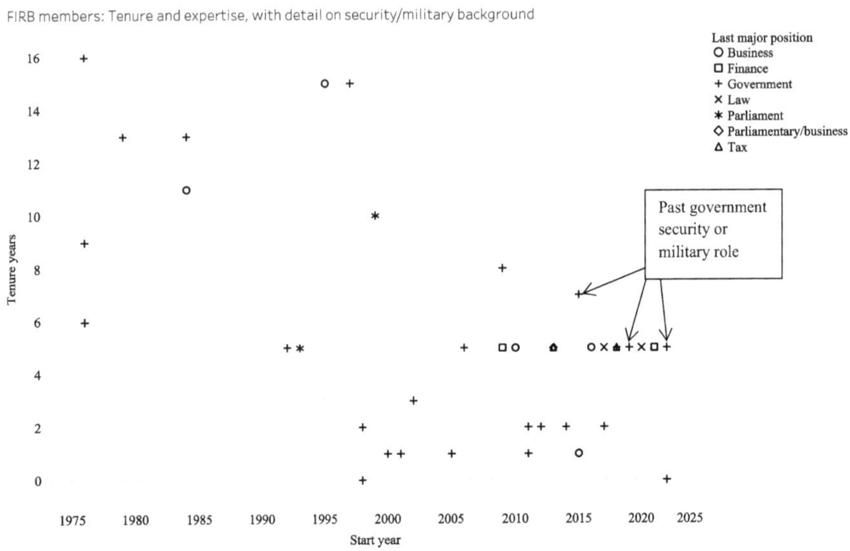

Fig. 2 Foreign Investment Review Board Members, 1976–2022: Tenure and Previous Expertise, with National Military or Security Detail (3 members only)

Treasury's Foreign Investment Division)[24] and is supported by a secretariat (the Foreign Investment Division) located in the Department of Treasury (Treasury) and by the Australian Taxation Office (ATO). The Treasury is responsible for administering business, agricultural land and sensitive commercial land proposals, while the ATO administers foreign investment in residential real estate.[25]

From 2015, government appointees with national security expertise were appointed to FIRB. This included David Irvine—the former director general of both the Australian Security Intelligence Organisation and the Australian Secret Intelligence Service—who joined FIRB in 2015 and became chair in April 2017.[26] This development is one indication of the growing national security orientation of Australia's ISM.

Various other federal government agencies may also be consulted in the course of assessing an application, including the Department of Foreign Affairs and Trade (DFAT), national security agencies, the Australian Criminal Intelligence Commission, the Department of Defence, and the Department of Home Affairs.[27] The latter department includes the Cyber and Infrastructure Security Centre, which focuses on critical infrastructure resilience regardless of ownership (foreign or domestic),

---

[24] FIRB (2021), p. 1.

[25] FIRB (2022a), p. 2.

[26] Treasurer (2017).

[27] Parliament (2021), [3.42].

pursuant to legislation including the Security of Critical Infrastructure Act 2018 (Cth).

2.4 *The National Interest Test: Policy Guidance*

Until the 2021 amendments discussed in Sect. 3.2 below, foreign investments subject to screening were considered pursuant to the national interest test, which remains the applicable test in most instances today. This test is 'negative',[28] in that the Treasurer determines whether taking the relevant action 'would be contrary to the national interest'.[29]

The meaning of 'national interest' is not defined in FATA or FATR. However, the surge in Chinese investment around the time of the GFC, especially the highly politicised strategic investment in 2009 of A$19.5 by state-owned Chinalco in Rio Tinto, a major resource company,[30] placed pressure on the then minority Labor government to clarify its approach to investment by state-owned enterprises (SOEs). It did so by clarifying via policy documentation that it would pay attention to non-equity investments that could ultimately entail foreign control and by listing 'six principles' to guide FIRB assessments under the national interest test, namely, (1) whether the investor was independent from its home government; (2) whether the investor was fit and proper; (3) the impact of the investment on competition; (4) the government revenue impact; (5) whether the proposed investment had national security implications; and (6) the impact on the national economy and local community.[31] In retrospect, these six principles mark the beginning of a more prominent role for national security in Australia's ISM, but the multifaceted national interest test remains and distinguishes it from narrower ISMs, notably that of the United States.

Today, the Treasurer/FIRB continues to issue policy guidance on how the national interest test applies. The factors typically considered part of the national interest are national security, competition, other Australian government policies (including tax), impact on the economy and the community, and the character of the investor.[32] Additional considerations apply to investments in the agricultural sector, investments in residential land, and investments by foreign government investors, with the latter including 'if the investment is commercial in nature or if the investor may be pursuing broader political or strategic objectives that may be contrary to Australia's national interest'.[33]

[28] Productivity Commission (2020), p. 83.

[29] E.g. FATA s 67(1)(b).

[30] Reuters (2009).

[31] Treasury (2008).

[32] FIRB (2022a), pp. 8–9.

[33] FIRB (2022a), p. 10.

Compliance by investors with Australia's foreign investment screening regime entails significant costs in terms of time, money and administrative burdens, particularly due to the growing complexity of the regulatory framework.[34] The absence of a legislative definition of national interest, which leads to broad discretion by the Treasurer, enhances uncertainty and reduces transparency, despite attempts by government, commentators and stakeholders since 1975 to clarify its meaning.[35] Limited scope exists for judicial review of screening decisions, and Australian courts are reluctant to interfere in Ministerial decisions about the national interest.

3 Post-COVID Developments in Australian Foreign Investment Screening

The Australian regime for foreign investment screening has undergone various changes since the emergence of the COVID-19 pandemic. Generally, in contrast to the aftermath of the GFC, these were in the direction of tighter screening. We address these changes and their rationales chronologically in the following sections, although, as noted above, most of these also relate to longer-term developments in Australia's economic and political relationship with China that are recognized by all major political parties. Several factors have contributed to this changing relationship, including the revitalization and reassertion of the pre-eminence of the Chinese Communist Party in China's own political economy, its assertion of a right to obtain corporate data from any business located in China, its growing military capabilities and assertiveness in the South and East China Seas, its long-term pursuit of technological parity with the West, its elevation since 2017 of the Military–Civil Fusion policy, and concerns about Chinese infiltration of Australian public institutions. On Australia's side, aggressive demands by the Coalition government for an investigation of China's role in the COVID-19 pandemic contributed to a sharp deterioration in bilateral relations, including a series of trade sanctions implemented by Beijing (as elaborated in Sect. 5 below).

Set in this wider political context, the Australian Coalition government introduced several measures to tighten Australia's ISM to meet perceived escalating risks in the external security environment and in foreign investment. First, in 2020, temporary changes were introduced subjecting all foreign investment to screening. Second, with effect from 2021 (and with respect to actions taken or proposed from 2021), the legislation and regulations were amended to create a new form of review based solely on national security, including the possibility of reviewing an investment that had already been made in Australia. Third, more minor amendments took effect in 2022 following a Treasury evaluation of the 2021 reforms. Future developments following the change of government in May 2022 are currently unknown,

[34] Bath (2018), pp. 154–155.

[35] Esplugues (2018), pp. 364–368; Senate (2013), [4.66]; Senate (2016), [5.2].

but (as discussed below) there is a cross-party consensus that Australia, like other Western advanced countries, faces a rising potential threat from Chinese investment. In Australia's case, this perceived threat has been most apparent in critical infrastructure, widely defined.

3.1 Temporary Changes Responding to the COVID-19 Pandemic

In March 2020, the Australian government announced a temporary reduction to $0 of the screening thresholds for all foreign investment under FATA, 'regardless of value or the nature of the foreign investor'.[36] In other words, in response to the COVID-19 pandemic, all foreign investment in Australia became subject to screening for the remainder of 2020,[37] until FATA and FATR were amended on a more permanent basis from 1 January 2021, as explained in Sect. 3.2.

3.2 Major Changes as of 1 January 2021: National Security Reviews

Major changes were made to FATA and FATR, commencing 1 January 2021. These included the introduction of reviews of foreign investment proposals specifically on the basis of national security (as opposed to the national interest more generally) and 'retrospective' national security reviews of investments that have already been established in Australia. These changes to screening in connection with national security continued a pattern of increasing restrictiveness in the preceding four years.[38] Although the national interest test has long been understood to include national security—made explicit in the six principles of 2009—the changes were intended as a signal to foreign investors and alliance partners of the growing importance of national security considerations in Australia's ISM.

The ongoing reappraisal of Australia's relationship with China was central to this new legislation, although the United States government was also requesting that its allies adopt or strengthen their existing mechanisms for investment screening for national security purposes. The US Foreign Investment Risk Review Modernization Act (FIRRMA), which became law in August 2018, included provisions for exempting investors from countries with similar ISMs from some aspects of FIRRMA's enhanced investment screening; it also encouraged the sharing of

---

[36] Treasurer (2020b).

[37] Treasurer (2020a).

[38] Productivity Commission (2020), p. 113.

investment information with trusted allies.[39] The Australian Coalition government, mindful of Australia's privileged position as a US ally and member of the 'Five Eyes' intelligence sharing group, thus had both economic and foreign policy incentives to align its ISM more closely with that of the United States. The new Australian legislation, like FIRRMA, includes references to investments in critical technology and critical infrastructure,[40] on which national security concerns have become focused.

Foreign investors must now notify the Australian Treasurer of (among other things) a proposed acquisition of a direct interest (e.g., 10 percent) in a 'national security business',[41] defined as a business carried on wholly or partly in Australia that is, for example, a telecommunications carrier, a supplier of critical goods or technology for military or intelligence use, or a storer of information with a security classification or personal information of defence personnel.[42] Also included in the definition of a national security business is an entity that is a 'direct interest holder' in relation to a 'critical infrastructure asset',[43] the definition of which was significantly expanded in separate legislation in 2021 to include assets such as a critical telecommunications asset, broadcasting asset, data storage asset, financial market infrastructure asset, energy market operator asset, hospital, education asset, public transport asset, and defence industry asset.[44] According to FIRB, in the first six months of 2021, almost 60 out of 730 non-residential foreign investment applications were national security-related applications that before the reforms 'would not have been subject to government scrutiny'.[45]

The Treasurer, who already enjoyed extensive discretion in the application of screening policy, now also has both 'call-in' and 'last resort' powers to conduct national security reviews. The call-in power applies to certain actions (such as starting or acquiring a direct interest in an Australian business)[46] that were not previously notified and are proposed or taken from 1 January 2021, for up to 10 years after the action is taken,[47] 'if the Treasurer considers that the action may pose a national security concern'.[48] The last resort power applies to certain actions notified after 1 January 2021, where material changes have arisen in the relevant business, activities, or market circumstances, or the notification contained a material

[39] Black (2019).

[40] See, e.g., FATA ss 4 (definition of 'national security business'), 55B(a)–(c), 67(1A)(a)(i); FATR s 8AA(2)(b), (e).

[41] FATA ss 55B(1)(b), 81.

[42] FATR s 8AA(2)(c)-(e), (g)-(h).

[43] FATR s 8AA(2)(b).

[44] Security of Critical Infrastructure Act 2018 (Cth) s 9.

[45] FIRB (2021), p. 12.

[46] FATA s55E.

[47] FATR s 60A.

[48] FATA s 66A(1) (see also (2), (5)).

false or misleading statement or omission.[49] The Treasurer must in exercising this power 'decide whether a national security risk relating to the action exists' and in so doing have regard to 'advice from an agency in the national intelligence community'.[50] In its annual report for the year ending 30 June 2021, FIRB indicated that the call-in power had not yet been exercised[51] but did not explicitly state whether the last resort power had been exercised.

The current FIRB guidance does not define the content of a national security review, instead stating that '[i]nvestments subject to the national security test are assessed against factors that give rise to national security concerns'[52] and that 'the Government considers the extent to which the investment will affect Australia's ability to protect its strategic and security interests', taking account of 'advice from relevant national security agencies'.[53] Further guidance for investors is provided regarding potential national security concerns with respect to specific sectors, according to which investors may wish to notify the Treasurer voluntarily even in the absence of mandatory notification, in order to avoid later application of the call-in (but not last resort) power.[54] For example:

Voluntary notification

> Foreign persons proposing to undertake a reviewable national security action by investing in a business or entity that manufactures essential medicines or medical devices are encouraged to seek foreign investment approval.[55]

The relevant legislation, regulations, and explanatory statements contain no further details about the content of the national security test in the abstract. This absence of a clear overarching definition is consistent with the general, longstanding approach to defining the national interest, as explained in Sect. 2.4 above. This approach is also consistent with practice in many other jurisdictions. However, the potential outcomes of such a review are clear: these may include the imposition of conditions, prohibition of a proposed action, or divestment of an existing asset.[56] This combination of uncertainty in application and potentially serious consequences for investing parties could have significant negative effects on investment flows.

---

[49] FATA s 79A(1).

[50] FATA s 79A(2).

[51] FIRB (2021), p. 46.

[52] FIRB (2022b), p. 3.

[53] FIRB (2022a), p. 11.

[54] FIRB (2022b), p. 11.

[55] FIRB (2022b), p. 27.

[56] FATA ss 67, 69, 79D, 79E.

3.3 Morrison Government Responses in 2022

In December 2021, the Australian Treasury issued its final report following an evaluation of the 2021 foreign investment reforms.[57] In February 2022 (before the change of government arising from the May 2022 federal election), the Australian government, then led by Prime Minister Scott Morrison of the Liberal Party of Australia, issued its response to this evaluation.[58] The government accepted the seven findings of the evaluation (including that 'It is too early to determine whether the reforms have had a singular impact on foreign investment flows, given the short time period and significant impact that COVID-19 has had on foreign investment flows globally, including into Australia')[59] and committed to reforming the foreign investment framework in two tranches. The first tranche entailed amendments to the FATR that commenced on 1 April 2022. The changes were specific to particular issues but in several instances designed to 'reduc[e] the regulatory burden for [certain] foreign investors'.[60] The public consultation period for the draft regulations was only 12 days in February 2022; not surprisingly, only five submissions were received.[61] Among other things, these amendments narrowed the definition of an Australian media business and the circumstances in which such a business will be generally subject to screening.[62] Other amendments related to, *inter alia*, moneylending, unlisted Australian land entities, and foreign custodian corporations.

In April 2022, the Morrison government issued its response to an earlier Senate Committee report on the regulation of foreign investment in Australia.[63] That report highlighted the 'secretive' nature of Australia's foreign investment regime in comparison to those in other countries such as the United States, Canada and New Zealand (and the practices of other Australian regulators including the Australian Securities and Investment Commission and the Australian Competition and Consumer Commission), echoing similar views expressed by Australia's Productivity Commission in 2020.[64] However, security reasons for not publicly disclosing details such as conditions imposed on approved deals are common throughout the world. In its response, the government rejected several recommendations to enhance transparency in the regime, for example, by publishing details about conditions imposed on investment approvals.[65]

[57] Treasury (2021).

[58] Treasury (2022a).

[59] Treasury (2021), p. 15.

[60] Treasury (2022b).

[61] Treasury (2022b).

[62] Foreign Acquisitions and Takeovers Amendment Regulations 2022 (Cth) pt 2.

[63] Parliament (2021).

[64] Parliament (2021), [5.1], [5.14] (citing Productivity Commission (2020)), [5.17], [5.26].

[65] Parliament (2022).

4 Australian Foreign Investment Screening in Practice

4.1 Analysis of Applications and Approvals to Date

Since the time inward investment took off around July 2001 until June 2021, FIRB approved a total of 233,179 applications (116,495 with conditions) and rejected 448 applications. The number of approved applications varies greatly by year, from a minimum of 4360 in 2004–2005 to a maximum of 41,445 in 2015–2016. This variation is mostly driven by policy changes for investment in the residential real estate sector, which accounts for, on average, 89% of all approved applications since 2001. Indeed, as Fig. 3 shows, over the same period, approved applications in sectors other than residential real estate vary from only 468 to 1296 before jumping to 2266 with the introduction of zero dollar thresholds.

Although applications in sectors other than real estate make up a small percentage of total approved applications, they relate primarily to the main target of Australia's screening policy: mergers and acquisitions (M&A), whose value is much larger than residential real estate purchases/projects. To obtain a sense of the role investment screening plays in the local market for capital control, Fig. 4 shows the distribution

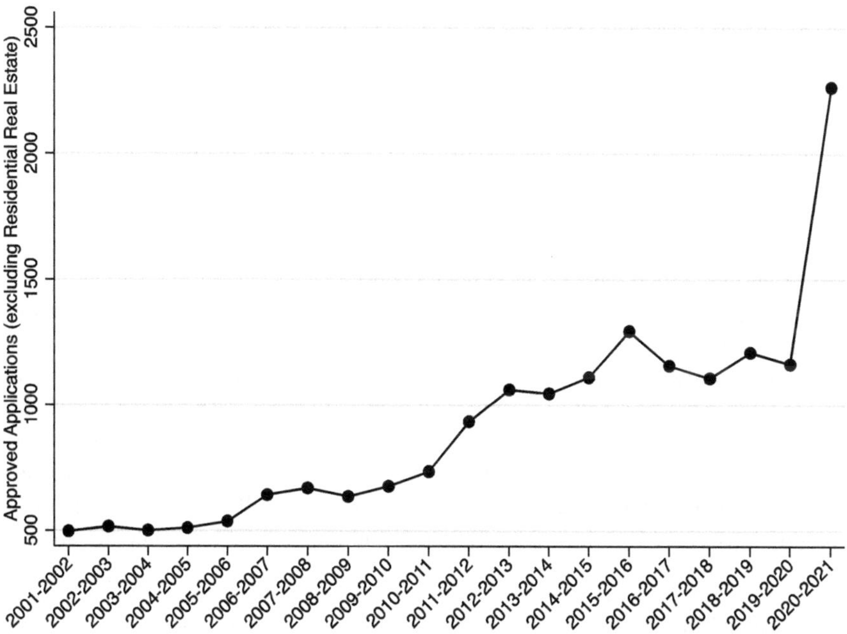

Fig. 3 Applications Approved by FIRB, July 2001–June 2021

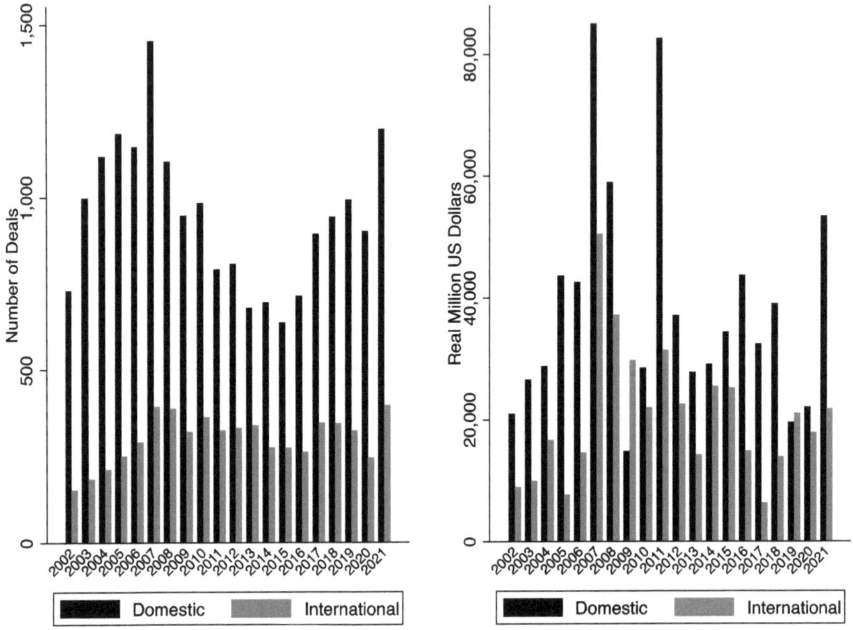

Fig. 4 Australian Screening Policy and the Market for Capital Control

of the number and value of domestic as well as international M&A deals[66] between 2002[67] and 2021, using data from SDC Platinum. While international M&A deals never account for more than one-third of all M&A deals involving an Australian target, in some years, they account for more than two-thirds of the value of all of them. This discrepancy is because, on average, international deals are larger than domestic deals. Put simply, the Treasury and FIRB have oversight over a substantial part of the Australian market for corporate control.

Although the majority of foreign investment proposals are approved in Australia, the approvals are often subject to conditions. For example, in the financial year 2020–2021, only one of the 6650 proposals on which a decision was made was rejected, but more than half were approved with conditions.[68] This number excludes the 891 proposals that were withdrawn and the 72 proposals that were determined to be exempt from screening.[69] Possible reasons for a prospective investor to withdraw a proposal include receiving indications from Treasury/FIRB that the proposal is unlikely to succeed,[70] reducing transparency and the ability to evaluate the impacts

[66]International M&A deals are deals between an Australian target and an acquirer firm not located in Australia.

[67]2002 is the first full year of data in Fig. 3.

[68]FIRB (2021), p. 17, 19.

[69]FIRB (2021), p. 19.

[70]Zhou (2017), p. 423, 425; Parliament (2021), [5.16].

of the screening regime. The potential for rejection may also discourage applications in the first place.[71] With respect to the imposition of conditions on investment approvals, according to the Productivity Commission, '[i]n general, national laws and regulations are a more responsive and proactive way to identify risks, and are likely to be a more effective way to manage risks'.[72]

4.2 *Explanations for Preferential Treatment?*

Monetary thresholds that trigger the review of an investment may be higher for certain PTA partners, as discussed in Sect. 2.2. Table 1 lists the countries, agreements, and year in which this preferential treatment became effective, using the example above of thresholds for businesses other than agribusinesses and national security businesses.[73] Table 1 shows that preferential treatment is a relatively recent phenomenon: with the exception of the United States, all other partners have benefitted from the higher thresholds for under 10 years.

The economic reasons behind this preferential treatment are not obvious. Investor size could explain this result. Investors responsible for a large share of FDI in Australia might be able to leverage their size to negotiate higher screening thresholds. The evidence on this, based on SDC M&A data, is weak. While during 2002–2021, seven (those asterisked in Table 1) of the 12 favoured partners were among the top 10 investors in Australia, their contribution to inward FDI varies greatly, with some of them accounting for very little (e.g., South Korea, New Zealand, see column (4) in Table 1). The timing of preferential treatment is also at odds with this explanation, given that one would expect preferential treatment to boost investment. Figure 5 plots the share of Australian inward FDI accounted for by the top five favoured investors in the four five-year periods between 2002 and 2021. Canada, China, and Singapore benefitted from higher thresholds in 2019, 2016 and 2017, but their share in Australia's inward FDI shrank after 2016. Despite benefitting from higher thresholds since 2005, the United States saw a sharp decline after 2006 in its share of Australian inward FDI that has not yet fully recovered.

An alternative explanation is that preferential treatment is granted to some partners to gain, formally or informally, preferential access to their assets. This could be the case for those partners to which Australia directs a considerable share of its outward FDI. However, only four (those marked with a cross in Table 1) of the 12 favoured partners are among the top 10 destinations of Australian investment, with their share in outward FDI varying between 1.24 and 36.8 percent, as shown in column (5) of Table 1. In addition, these partners would consider granting Australia preferential treatment only if Australia was one of their largest investors. But, with

[71] Parliament (2021) [1.60]; Productivity Commission (2020), p. 12.

[72] Productivity Commission (2020), p. 86.

[73] See above nn 22–23 and surrounding text.

Table 1 Australia's treaty partners receiving preferential treatment in foreign investment screening thresholds

PTA Partner	Relevant Treaty	Year Effective	Share of Australian Inward FDI 2002–2021, %	Share of Australian Outward FDI 2002–2021, %	Australia Share of Partner's Inward FDI 2002–2021, %
(1)	(2)	(3)	(4)	(5)	(6)
Canada*+	CPTPP[a]	2019	12.86	4.98	2.45
Chile	ACLFTA[b]	2015	0.01	0.35	1.32
China*	ChAFTA[c]	2016	8.36	1.04	0.85
Hong Kong*+	HKIA[d]	2020	5.98	1.24	1.75
Japan*	JAEPA[e]	2015	9.74	0.33	0.66
Mexico	CPTPP	2019	3.64	0.48	1.23
New Zealand*+	ANZIP[f]	2013	2.04	8.12	51.16
Peru	PAFTA[g]	2020	–	0.10	0.61
Singapore*	SAFTA[h]	2017	6.16	0.89	1.70
South Korea	KAFTA[i]	2014	1.31	1.20	3.51
United States*+	AUSFTA[j]	2005	21.63	36.80	3.30
Viet Nam	CPTPP	2019	0.02	0.08	1.13

Note. Calculations in columns (4)–(6) are based on M&A data from SDC Platinum. * identifies partners that are among the top 10 investors in Australia during 2002–2021. + identifies partners that are among the top 10 destinations of Australian outward investment during 2002–2021

[a]Comprehensive and Progressive Agreement for Trans-Pacific Partnership (signed 8 March 2018, entered into force for Australia, Canada, Japan, Mexico, New Zealand and Singapore on 30 December 2018, for Viet Nam on 14 January 2019, and for Peru on 19 September 2021)

[b]Australia–Chile Free Trade Agreement (signed 30 July 2008, entered into force 6 March 2009) 2694 UNTS 3

[c]Free Trade Agreement between the Government of Australia and the Government of the People's Republic of China, (signed 17 June 2015, entered into force 20 December 2015)

[d]Investment Agreement between the Government of Australia and the Government of the Hong Kong Special Administrative Region of the People's Republic of China (signed 26 March 2019, entered into force 17 January 2020)

[e]Agreement Between Australia and Japan for an Economic Partnership (signed 8 July 2014, entered into force 15 January 2015)

[f]Protocol on Investment to the Australia–New Zealand Closer Economic Relations Trade Agreement (signed 16 February 2011, entered into force 1 March 2013)

[g]Free Trade Agreement between Australia and the Republic of Peru (signed 12 February 2018, entered into force 11 February 2020)

[h]Singapore–Australia Free Trade Agreement (signed 17 February 2003, entered into force 28 July 2003) (as amended most recently by amendments entering into force on 1 December 2017 and 8 December 2020)

[i]Free Trade Agreement between the Government of Australia and the Government of the Republic of Korea (signed 8 April 2014, entered into force 12 December 2014)

[j]Australia–US Free Trade Agreement (signed 18 May 2004, entered into force on 1 January 2005)

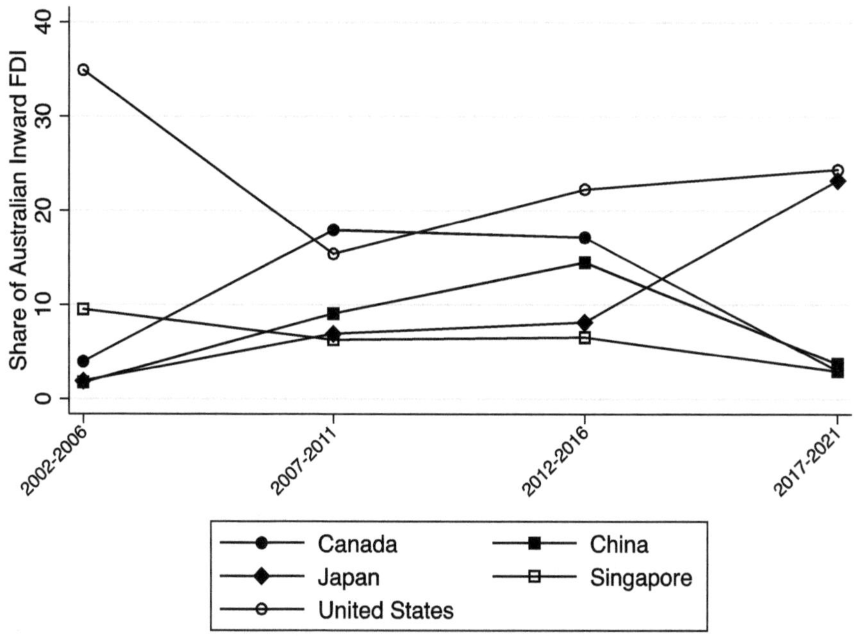

Note. Shares are calculated based on the total value of M&A deals with Australian targets. Five-year periods are considered to smooth the lumpiness in M&A data.

Fig. 5 Share of Australian Inward FDI, Top 5 Preferred Partners. *Note*. Shares are calculated based on the total value of M&A deals with Australian targets. Five-year periods are considered to smooth the lumpiness in M&A data

the exception of New Zealand, Australia is not among the top 10 investors in any of the favoured partners and accounts for at most 3.51% of their inward investment during 2002 and 2021, as shown in column (6) of Table 1.

The weak evidence for the economic incentives behind preferential treatment suggests that there is more at work than the data tell us. From a legal perspective, almost anything might have been 'traded' for preferential investment thresholds in the course of negotiating the relevant treaties. In terms of political drivers, the existence of preferential thresholds still leaves significant discretion with respect to, say, screening of Chinese investments. In particular, as explained in Sect. 3.2, the changes implemented in 2021 to allow for national security-specific reviews have a zero-dollar threshold (for national security land and national security businesses) regardless of the nationality of the investor.

5 Risks of an Investment Treaty Claim against Australia

Investor-state dispute settlement (ISDS) enables investors to bring treaty claims against Australia alleging violations of international investment law. In 2011, Australia's Labor government, led by Prime Minister Julia Gillard, issued a trade policy statement advising that the government would cease the practice of seeking to include ISDS mechanisms 'in trade agreements with developing countries at the behest of Australian businesses'.[74] As noted in Sect. 2.1, the Coalition subsequently formed the Australian government from 2013 to 2022, returning to an ad hoc approach to ISDS.[75] In advance of its success at the 2022 federal election, the Labor Party again indicated that it would seek to prohibit future international agreements including ISDS, 'review ISDS provisions in existing trade and investment agreements and seek to work with Australia's trading partners to remove these provisions.'[76] In November 2022, the Minister for Trade and Tourism Don Farrell confirmed that 'we will not include [ISDS] in any new trade agreements' and that 'when opportunities arise, we will actively engage in processes to reform existing ISDS mechanisms . . . to ensure adequate scope to allow the Government to regulate in the public interest'.[77] This statement suggests the government proposes something short of a systematic review of Australia's existing IIAs, although DFAT appears to be continuing its four-year review of Australia's BITs, commenced in 2020.[78] Whatever happens with Australia's future IIAs, its existing network of IIAs, in the absence of amendment, creates real concerns about the consistency of Australia's foreign investment screening with international investment law, underpinned by ISDS.

Inward Chinese investment has been a focus of Australia's foreign investment screening laws and policy for much of the last decade,[79] notwithstanding the entry into force of the China-Australia Free Trade Agreement (ChAFTA)[80] in 2015[81] and the Regional Comprehensive Economic Partnership in 2022.[82] These are just two of Australia's international investment agreements (IIAs)[83] that raise potential conflicts with Australia's screening regime (on the basis of discrimination, unlawful expropriation, or breach of fair and equitable treatment (FET), for example), particularly due to their variation and overlapping nature.[84] Australia's negotiation of different commitments in different IIAs (including different screening thresholds) increases the complexity of the screening regime and limits the potential for amendments to

[74] DFAT (2011).

[75] See, e.g., Senate (2014), [2.7].

[76] ALP (2021).

[77] Minister for Trade and Tourism (2022).

[78] DFAT (2022b).

[79] Knight and Voon (2020), pp. 117–118, 122–123.

[80] Free Trade Agreement between the Government of Australia and the Government of the People's Republic of China, signed 17 June 2015 (entered into force 20 December 2015) (ChAFTA).

[81] Zhou (2017), pp. 420–426.

[82] Regional Comprehensive Economic Partnership (signed 15 November 2020, entered into force for Australia and China on 1 January 2022) (RCEP).

[83] Mitchell et al. (2017), pp. 17, 27, 35.

[84] Voon and Merriman (2022).

that regime.[85] Similar concerns arise with the intensification and proliferation of inward foreign investment screening around the globe, alongside international investment law requirements.[86]

ISDS would arguably be available to a Chinese investor pursuant to the 1988 bilateral investment treaty (BIT) between Australia and China[87] with respect to Australian screening that allegedly violates the post-establishment expropriation obligation.[88] Both ChAFTA and the Australia-China BIT contain significant protections for Australia against other ISDS claims concerning screening (while RCEP contains no ISDS mechanism). ChAFTA restricts ISDS to post-establishment national treatment claims[89] and explicitly lists Australia's foreign investment policy as a non-conforming measure with respect to both national treatment and most-favoured-nation (MFN) treatment[90] and contains no expropriation or FET clause. The Australia-China BIT restricts the national treatment, MFN treatment and (as remains usual) FET obligations to the post-establishment phase and protects investments and associated activities in this regard (e.g., expansion of investments) subject to its law.[91] However, unlike ChAFTA,[92] the Australia-China BIT does not contain general or security exceptions or a public welfare provision.

The potential for an ISDS claim by a Chinese investor against Australia is heightened by the changes to Australia's foreign investment screening regime in 2021, especially the possibility of retrospective screening as explained in Sect. 3.2 above (applicable post-establishment), given that the FIRB process was already 'a formidable barrier to Chinese investors'[93] before those changes. As part of the broader context for such a claim, tensions in the trading relationship between Australia and China in recent years exacerbate allegations that Australia has been targeting Chinese investments through the screening process.[94] At the time of writing, China is the respondent in two of the three WTO disputes that Australia is pursuing as complainant (with respect to anti-dumping and countervailing duty measures on Australian wine and barley), and China is the complainant in the sole WTO dispute currently continuing against Australia (with respect to anti-dumping and countervailing duty measures on various Chinese products).[95] According to a

[85] Bath (2018), pp. 156–157, 159, 161; Parliament (2021), [2.82]–[2.83].

[86] Voon and Merriman (2023).

[87] Agreement between the Government of Australia and the Government of the People's Republic of China on the Reciprocal Encouragement and Protection of Investments, signed 11 July 1988 (entered into force 11 July 1988) (BIT).

[88] Voon and Sheargold (2018), pp. 220–224.

[89] ChAFTA arts 9.12.1, 9.12.2(a)(i).

[90] ChAFTA annex III, schedule of Australia.

[91] BIT arts I:1(b), (f), II:1, III(a), (b), (c).

[92] ChAFTA arts 9.8, 9.11.4, 16.3.

[93] Huiqin and Zhou (2018), p. 189.

[94] Kehoe et al. (2021).

[95] See DFAT (2022a).

2022 study, Chinese investment in Australia has rapidly declined by value from USD 11,538M in 2016 to USD 585M in 2021.[96]

Nevertheless, a Chinese ISDS claim against Australian foreign investment screening is not necessarily the most likely, nor are the IIAs with China the greatest problems for Australia in this regard. Australia presently has 15 BITs in force (one of which, with Uruguay, entered into force as recently as January 2022 and thus represents more of a modern agreement)[97] plus 16 PTAs with investment chapters or associated investment agreements in force, as well as two new agreements signed but not yet in force: a PTA with the United Kingdom including an investment chapter and an interim agreement with India in advance of concluding a comprehensive agreement with an investment chapter.[98] All of the BITs include some form of ISDS mechanism, as do 10 of the 16 PTAs in force. Although the BITs do not impose obligations in the pre-establishment stage, they all include MFN, expropriation, and FET provisions without explicit exclusions of foreign investment policy or (apart from the new Uruguay treaty) general or security exceptions, as found in Australia's modern PTAs. The PTAs with Chile and ASEAN/New Zealand do not explicitly exclude foreign investment policy from ISDS, while only one of the 11 PTAs signed before 2018 explicitly excludes foreign investment policy from state-state dispute settlement. The PTAs with the United States, Thailand, Chile, and New Zealand all include an MFN obligation covering both pre- and post-establishment, without an NCM for Australia's foreign investment policy.[99]

The potential for inconsistency between Australia's foreign investment screening and its IIAs is complex and depends on the specific substantive and dispute settlement provisions in the relevant treaty, as well as the application of the screening regime in practice. However, due to the variability in the treaty provisions and their evolution over decades, the inclusion of modern-day protections in most of Australia's newer IIAs is not necessarily sufficient to remove the risk of a treaty claim against Australia with respect to screening by a foreign investor or state.

6 Conclusion

Australia's foreign investment screening regime struggles with the tension between the economic benefits of an open economy and the domestic and international politics surrounding inward foreign investment. The Australian government's response to the two deepest downturns in recent decades differed markedly, reflecting a temporal shift in the approach to resolving this tension. While the GFC led to a more open stance in the Australian economy and growth in Chinese

[96]Ferguson et al. (2022), p. 3.
[97]DFAT (2022b).
[98]DFAT (2022c).
[99]Voon Merriman (2022).

investment, reflecting the prioritisation of the presumed economic benefits of increased foreign investment in a global recession, the COVID-19 pandemic prompted a tightening of investment screening measures in the context of increasing suspicion of Chinese investment. The precise nature of and shifts in patterns of rejection and imposition of conditions on investment applications are difficult to track due to the limited transparency of the decision-making process and outcomes, as well as the significant flexibility in the relevant regulations, leaving much to the Treasurer's discretion subject to broad policy guidelines. However, there is little doubt that Australia has become significantly less welcoming of Chinese investment in a range of sensitive sectors over the past decade.

The economic, political and legal rationale for granting higher investment screening thresholds to some but not all of Australia's preferential trade agreement partners is also difficult to discern. Similarly, the economic and political benefits of making it harder to invest in Australia at a time of rising global economic instability and uncertainty are questionable. Greater transparency with respect to the screening process and outcomes would enable better measurement of the impact of changes to Australia's screening regime on the Australian economy. Greater transparency and limits on the perceived politicisation of inward investment could also assist in lowering bilateral diplomatic tensions with important partners such as China.

Potential exists for an investment treaty claim against Australian screening by a state or investor pursuant to one of Australia's more than 30 international investment agreements in force. The risk of such a claim is increased by the recent introduction of national security-specific investment reviews with zero dollar thresholds, including in some circumstances retrospective reviews of existing investments. If the objective of enhanced investment screening is ultimately to reduce risk in the national interest, the Australian government should be taking IIAs into account in considering reforms to Australia's foreign investment screening regime and vice versa.

References

ALP (2007) Australian National Platform and Constitution. Australian Labor Party. https://parlinfo.aph.gov.au/parlInfo/search/display/display.w3p;query=Id%3A%22library%2Fpartypol%2F1024541%22;src1=sm1

ALP (2012) National Platform. Australian Labor Party. https://australianpolitics.com/2012/03/16/alp-national-platform-2012.html

ALP (2021) ALP National Platform As Adopted at the 2021 Special Platform Conference. Australian Labor Party. https://www.alp.org.au/about/national-platform

Bath V (2018) Australia and the Asia-Pacific: the regulation of investment flows into Australia and the role of Free Trade Agreements. In: Morosini F, Ratton Sanchez Badin M (eds) Reconceptualizing international investment law from the global south. Cambridge University Press, Cambridge, pp 146–187

Black L (2019) Remarks in online event, complying with CFIUS and FIRRMA. Director of Policy and Implementation of CFIUS, Department of the Treasury International Trade Administration. 15 Oct. Washington, D.C

Chan G (2013) Foreign Investment Makes Explosive Entry into Election Campaign. The Guardian. https://www.theguardian.com/world/2013/aug/29/foreign-investment-on-election-agenda.
DFAT (2011) Gillard Government Trade Policy Statement: Trading Our Way to More Jobs and Prosperity. Department of Foreign Affairs and Trade, Australian Government. https://web.archive.org.au/awa/20110502020942mp_/http:/pandora.nla.gov.au/pan/126547/20110502-1209/www.dfat.gov.au/publications/trade/trading-our-way-to-more-jobs-and-prosperity.pdf
DFAT (2022a) Summary of Australia's Involvement in Disputes Currently Before the World Trade Organization. Department of Foreign Affairs and Trade, Australian Government. https://www.dfat.gov.au/trade/organisations/wto/wto-disputes/summary-of-australias-involvement-in-disputes-currently-before-the-world-trade-organization
DFAT (2022b) Australia's Bilateral Investment Treaties. Department of Foreign Affairs and Trade, Australian Government. https://www.dfat.gov.au/trade/investment/australias-bilateral-investment-treaties
DFAT (2022c) Australia's Free Trade Agreements (FTAs). Department of Foreign Affairs and Trade, Australian Government. https://www.dfat.gov.au/trade/agreements/trade-agreements
DFAT (2022d) The Benefits of Foreign Investment. Department of Foreign Affairs and Trade, Australian Government. https://www.dfat.gov.au/trade/investment/the-benefits-of-foreign-investment
Drysdale P (2011) A new look at Chinese FDI in Australia. China World Econ 19(4):54–73
Drysdale P, Findlay C (2009) Chinese foreign direct investment in Australia: policy issues for the resource sector. China Econ J 2(2):133–158
Esplugues C (2018) Foreign investment, strategic assets and national security. Intersentia, Cambridge
Ferguson D et al (2022) Demystifying Chinese investment in Australia. KPMG & University of Sydney, Sydney
FIRB (2021) Annual Report. Foreign Investment Review Board, Australian Government. https://firb.gov.au/about-firb/publications/2020-21-annual-report
FIRB (2022a) Australia's Foreign Investment Policy. Foreign Investment Review Board, Australian Government. https://firb.gov.au/general-guidance/australias-foreign-investment-policy
FIRB (2022b) National Security. Foreign Investment Review Board, Australian Government. https://firb.gov.au/guidance-notes
Garnaut J (2007). Should We Sell Out to the Chinese?. Sydney Morning Herald. https://www.smh.com.au/business/should-we-sell-out-to-the-chinese-20071008-gdrabt.html
Hanratty P (1996) Inward Direct Foreign Investment in Australia: Policy Controls and Economic Outcomes. Research Paper 32, 1995-1996, Parliamentary Library. https://www.aph.gov.au/About_Parliament/Parliamentary_Departments/Parliamentary_Library/pubs/rp/RP9596/96rp32
Huiqin J, Zhou W (2018) China's investment in Australia: a critical analysis of Australia's foreign investment review mechanism. Tsinghua China Law Rev 10(2):188–223
Kehoe J et al (2021) Treasurer Blacklists China Investments. Australian Financial Review. https://www.afr.com/politics/federal/treasurer-imposes-informal-ban-on-china-investments-20210112-p56thm
Knight L, Voon T (2020) The evolution of national security at the interface between domestic and international investment law and policy. J World Investment Trade 21:104–139. https://doi.org/10.1163/22119000-12340169
McIlroy T (2022) Australia's Foreign Investment Rules Too Restrictive: Leigh. Australian Financial Review. https://www.afr.com/politics/federal/australia-s-foreign-investment-rules-too-restrictive-leigh-20220405-p5aaxp
Minister for Trade and Tourism (2022) Senator Don Farrell, Australian Government. https://www.trademinister.gov.au/minister/don-farrell/speech/trading-our-way-greater-prosperity-and-security
Mitchell A, Sheargold E, Voon T (2017) Regulatory autonomy in international economic law: the evolution of Australian policy on trade and investment. Edward Elgar, Cheltenham

OECD (2020) OECD Foreign Direct Investment Regulatory Restrictiveness Index. Organisation for Economic Co-operation and Development. https://goingdigital.oecd.org/en/indicator/74
Parliament (2021) Greenfields, Cash Cows and the Regulation of Foreign Investment in Australia. Economics References Committee, The Senate, Parliament of Australia. https://www.aph.gov.au/Parliamentary_Business/Committees/Senate/Economics/Foreigninvestment/Report
Parliament (2022) Australian Government Response to the Senate Economic References Committee Report: Greenfields, Cash Cows and the Regulation of Foreign Investment in Australia. Parliament of Australia. https://www.aph.gov.au/Parliamentary_Business/Committees/Senate/Economics/Foreigninvestment/Government_Response
Productivity Commission (2020) Foreign Investment in Australia: Productivity Commission Research Paper. Productivity Commission, Australian Government. https://www.pc.gov.au/research/completed/foreign-investment
Reuters (2009) Rio Tinto and Chinalco clinch $19.5 billion deal: report. https://www.reuters.com/article/us-riotinto-china-idUSTRE51A5VC20090211
Scissors D (2022) China Global Investment Tracker. American Enterprise Institute and The Heritage Foundation. https://www.aei.org/china-global-investment-tracker/
Senate (2013) Foreign Investment and the National Interest. The Senate, Rural and Regional Affairs and Transport References Committee. https://www.aph.gov.au/Parliamentary_Business/Committees/Senate/Rural_and_Regional_Affairs_and_Transport/Completed_inquiries/2012-13/firb2011/report/index
Senate (2014) Trade and Foreign Investment (Protecting the Public Interest) Bill 2014. The Senate, Foreign Affairs, Defence and Trade Legislation Committee. https://www.aph.gov.au/Parliamentary_Business/Committees/Senate/Foreign_Affairs_Defence_and_Trade/Trade_and_Foreign_Investment_Protecting_the_Public_Interest_Bill_2014/Report
Senate (2016) Foreign Investment Review Framework. The Senate, Economics References Committee. https://www.aph.gov.au/Parliamentary_Business/Committees/Senate/Economics/Foreign_Investment_Review/Report
Treasurer (2017) Media Release: FIRB Chair Appointment. Treasurer Scott Morrison, Australian Government. https://parlinfo.aph.gov.au/parlInfo/search/display/display.w3p;query=Id:%22media/pressrel/5208189%22
Treasurer (2020a) Media Release: Major Reforms to Australia's Foreign Investment Framework Pass the Parliament. Treasurer Josh Frydenberg, Australian Government. https://ministers.treasury.gov.au/ministers/josh-frydenberg-2018/media-releases/major-reforms-australias-foreign-investment-0
Treasurer (2020b) Media Release: Changes to Foreign Investment Framework. Treasurer Josh Frydenberg, Australian Government. https://ministers.treasury.gov.au/ministers/josh-frydenberg-2018/media-releases/changes-foreign-investment-framework
Treasury (2008) Government Improves Transparency of Foreign Investment Screening Process. Treasurer Wayne Swan, Australian Government. https://ministers.treasury.gov.au/ministers/wayne-swan-2007/media-releases/government-improves-transparency-foreign-investment
Treasury (2015) Explanatory Memorandum Circulated by Authority of the Treasurer: Foreign Acquisitions and Takeovers Legislation Amendment Bill 2015; Foreign Acquisitions and Takeovers Fee Imposition Bill 2015; Register of Foreign Ownership of Agricultural Land Bill 2015. https://parlinfo.aph.gov.au/parlInfo/search/display/display.w3p;query=Id:%22legislation/billhome/r5519%22
Treasury (2021) Evaluation of the 2021 Foreign Investment Reforms – Final Report. The Treasury, Australian Government. https://treasury.gov.au/publication/p2022-244363
Treasury (2022a) Enhancing Australia's Foreign Investment Framework: Government Response to the Evaluation of the Foreign Investment Reforms and Discussion Paper. https://treasury.gov.au/sites/default/files/2022-02/c2022-244363-dp.pdf
Treasury (2022b) Explanatory Statement Issued by Authority of the Treasurer: Foreign Acquisitions and Takeovers Act 1975; Foreign Acquisitions and Takeovers Amendment Regulations

2022. Australian Government. https://www.legislation.gov.au/Details/F2022L00465/Explanatory%20Statement/Text
Uren D (2012). The Kingdom and the Quarry: China, Australia, Fear and Greed. Black Inc.
Voon T, Merriman D (2022) Is Australia's foreign investment screening policy consistent with international investment law? Melbourne J f Int Law 23(1):62–113
Voon T, Merriman D (2023) Incoming: how international investment law constrains foreign investment screening. J World Investment Trade 24: forthcoming. https://doi.org/10.1163/22119000-12340253
Voon T, Sheargold E (2018) Australia, China and the Co-existence of successive international investment agreements. In: Picker C, Wang H, Zhou W (eds) The China Australia Free Trade Agreement: a 21st century model. Hart, Oxford
Zhou W (2017) Chinese investment in Australia: a critical analysis of the *China – Australia Free Trade Agreement*. Melbourne J Int Law 18:407–435

Foreign Direct Investment and Security: What is Actually the Problem?

Wolf Zwartkruis

Contents

This paper has benefitted from comments by an anonymous peer reviewer on an earlier version. All errors and opinions expressed in this text remain the sole responsibility of the author.

W. Zwartkruis (✉)
University of Leiden, Faculty of Law, Leiden, Netherlands

J. H. Pohl et al. (eds.), *National Security and Investment Controls*,
Springer Studies in Law & Geoeconomics (2024) 3: 27–58,
https://doi.org/10.1007/17280_2024_29, Published online: 27 February 2024

Abstract This working paper seeks to address head-on the question that is often addressed only fleetingly or indirectly in discussions about FDI screening: what are we actually concerned about? More specifically, how can FDI impact state security? In order to do this, I try to construct an analytic framework that suits different types of FDI and security interests. In doing so, I build on basic legal, economic and international relations concepts. I find that FDI and security are indeed linked, but that this relationship is complex and that any assessment of the security impact of a FDI requires careful examination of the FDI at hand. I also point to the relevance of the overall strategic context and balance of power. The framework is put to the test in case study of the controversial take-over of German robotics manufacturer KUKA. In this case I conclude that there were indeed indications of security risks for the German state involved in this transaction. These were partially mitigated through action of U.S. authorities and a private contract between KUKA and its acquirer.

1 Introduction

This paper will explore the link between Foreign Direct Investment (FDI) and the security interests of the state. If a foreign company takes over a major domestic firm, this often raises concerns in the public opinion of the country of the acquired entity's home country.[1] It is associated with a loss of national prestige but also with more or less articulated security concerns. Why is this so? And to what extent is this based on valid arguments rather than an emotional reflex? The vernacular of "buying" and "owning" dominate our perception of FDI. This is a part of the explanation for publications asking questions such as: "Is China buying the world?".[2] The implication of such questions is that investing is buying, and buying is owning, and owning implies complete control.

[1] Neu and Wolf (1994), p. 44.
[2] See Nolan (2012).

In my view, FDI affects power relations and thus security. However, the real dynamics of FDI are complicated and nuanced. While not much has been written about the details of the FDI-security nexus, a few works such as those of Moran and Oldenski,[3] Graham and Krugman[4] and RAND have provided some useful analysis on this problem. There are also a number of case studies into the geopolitical context of specific FDI transactions.[5] This paper aims to provide a framework to analyse what security implications a FDI transaction may create. The analysis will be based on existing literature as far as possible.

In this paper I assume that security is about protecting essential interests of the state against threats, in particular threats from other states. I assume that such interests include life and health of the population, the functioning of state institutions and the integrity of the territory. Some economic sectors are of particular importance in enabling the state to protect these essential interests. In this regard, one could think of communication, energy, or water supply. These sectors have been recognized by states that identify critical sectors within their economy.[6] Therefore, these sectors deserve specific attention when analysing the impact of FDI on state security. It is on these sectors and related assets that I will focus in this paper.[7]

The rest of this paper is structured as follows: in part (B) I will investigate the impact of FDI on state control over economic assets. In part (C) I will outline a framework for the analysis of security risks emanating from FDI in critical sectors of the economy. In part (D) I will use this framework to perform a case study on a particularly controversial FDI, the take-over of German robotics manufacturer KUKA by Chinese home appliances maker Midea. Part (E) concludes.

2 Preliminary Considerations: The Impact of FDI on State Control Over Economic Assets

Before I turn to the development of the framework, it is necessary to explore the direct consequences of a FDI in terms of control over economic assets. Any impact on security must be connected with those consequences.

---

[3] Moran and Oldenski (2013).

[4] Graham and Krugman (1995).

[5] Libman (2015); Hooijmaakers (2019); Ferchen et al. (2018); Kardon and Leutert (2022).

[6] OECD (2019).

[7] There is a case to be made that security risks may also exists in cases of FDI into non-critical sector. This question is out of the scope of this paper however.

2.1 What Is FDI?

FDI is a cross-border investment in a company that provides the investor with a say in in the companies' decision-making.[8] It is contrasted with "portfolio investment", that is an investment insufficient in size to provide the investor with control over a company.[9] For statistical and regulatory purposes, the threshold determining the controlling element of an investment is often set at 10% of total shares, e.g. by the OECD definition of foreign direct investment.[10]

2.2 What Level of Control Over Economic Assets Is Provided by FDI?

FDI thus provides control over the assets owned by and accessible to the invested company. What these assets are, depends on the nature of the company. If, for example, the company owns intellectual property, the transaction will provide the investor with a degree of control over that intellectual property. If the company owns land, the investor will be granted an opportunity to use that land through its investment, etc. The control is not restricted to assets that are owned by a company. A company can have access to data of its customers, often sensitive data. This does not generally imply that it owns those data, but the access is there as a matter of fact.

The precise level of control over a company provided by a foreign direct investment depends on the shareholder rights circumscribed by the jurisdiction where the invested entity is domiciled. However, there is a common ground shared by most legal systems. Typically, the shareholders have the right to appoint and dismiss board members and vote on certain strategic decisions such as mergers, change of the country of incorporation and (major) acquisitions. The right to appoint board members provides indirect control. The shareholders can appoint a board that will do its bidding. In that way they can ultimately control all board decisions. This includes the nature of the activities that a company pursues, their location, the scale of activities, the choice of suppliers and markets, size and composition of the staff, etc. National law also determines the level of control that any person, including a

[8] According to the OECD Benchmark definition of foreign direct investment: "*Foreign direct investment reflects the objective of establishing a lasting interest by a resident enterprise in one economy (direct investor) in an enterprise (direct investment enterprise) that is resident in an economy other than that of the direct investor. The lasting interest implies the existence of a long-term relationship between the direct investor and the direct investment enterprise and a significant degree of influence on the management of the enterprise. The direct or indirect ownership of 10% or more of the voting power of an enterprise resident in one economy by an investor resident in another economy is evidence of such a relationship.*" See OECD (2008).

[9] Portfolio investments typically purely aim at financial returns and therefore involve spreading the investment over different assets to reduce risk, hence creating a portfolio.

[10] See OECD (2008).

company has over its assets. Think of the law of goods, intellectual property law and other domestic laws applying to different types of assets.

2.3 Instruments of Control of the Host State

The host state is the country where the invested company is located. The fact that the investor with a controlling share has a degree of control over a company, does not mean his control is without limit. The host state specifies what the shareholder's rights are and what the limits are. For instance, under Dutch law, shareholders may be limited in the exercise of their powers by a special Court if they are deemed to use their powers in a way that constitutes negligent administration (in Dutch: "*wanbeleid*").[11] The ultimate limitation of shareholder power is the power that a state can exercise to nationalize a company. It is generally accepted under international investment law treaties that a state can nationalize a company within its territory, as long as it provides adequate compensation for such a measure.

And even to the extent that a shareholder can exercise his powers freely, the room for manoeuvre of a company (as opposed to the shareholder) is also limited by the host state. The jurisdiction of the host state extends also to foreign-owned companies. It includes the power to impose obligations on companies through private and public law. A state typically imposes a wide range of obligations on a company within its jurisdiction. They range from tax obligations and obligations towards employees to requirements on how to process food and separate waste.

But the power of the host state to impose obligations on a company is itself subject to limitations. Firstly, it is limited by its own constitution and by international treaties, including investment treaties, that usually have the aim to provide foreign investor with legal safeguards. Typical clauses include non-discrimination between domestic and foreign-owned companies and safeguards related to the transfer of financial capital.

Secondly, the power of the host state with regard to the right to enact legislation is geographically limited to its own territory. A host state cannot exercise the same degree of control outside its jurisdiction. Even if it imposes obligations that apply to activities outside its own borders, it will have few options to enforce them there, as this right is limited by the sovereignty of other states. For this reason, a host state has no direct control over the board of a foreign-owned company and its decisions.

Finally, the host state's power to legislate is limited to the extent that it has to take into account the risk of a foreign company leaving its jurisdiction. This could be the result if the host state imposes too many requirements that result in the costs of continued presence to exceed the benefits.

---

[11] Article 2:355 of the Dutch Civil Code. Possible measures that can be imposed by the court include transfer of shares to a trustee and nullification of decision of the shareholders' meeting (article 2:356 of the Dutch Civil Code).

2.4 Instruments of Control of the Home State

The home state is the country where the investor is located. The formal control of the home state derives from its jurisdiction control over the board of the Multinational Company (MNC) and its assets within the jurisdiction of the home state. The instruments it may use in order to exercise said control, are comparable to those described for the host state in the previous paragraph. The difference is that the home state is in a better position to control the activities of the MNC as a whole, because it has jurisdiction over persons making up the board as well as the (usually sizeable) assets within the jurisdiction of the home state. A special case is where the FDI provider is a state-owned company or a sovereign wealth fund. In that case, the home state can use its shareholder power to exercise control.

The home state also has informal influence on a company. This translates into influence over the FDI's of such a company. All companies can be expected to have a home bias. As pointed out by Chang, even in the case of MNC's a board mostly consists of nationals of the country where the headquarters is located. American companies have mainly Americans on their board, German companies, Germans and Chinese have Chinese nationals, even though there is no formal reason why this should be so.[12]

Board members are also citizens of their country. They will usually spend most of their life there, their social contacts are cultivated there, their careers will play out there. Additionally, they will often feel a sense of loyalty to their country. Therefore, board members will be likely to take into account the interest of their country when they make decisions for their companies. For example, if they have to cut back activities, they will most probably choose to close down a factory in a foreign country, rather than one in their own, everything else being equal.

As has been argued by Chang, companies (and not just board members) also have solid economic reasons to prefer their home country. Even though companies are usually legally allowed to move their headquarters to another jurisdiction, in practice this is unfeasible because the parts of a company that create most value are hard to move. Chang mentions the people that make up a company, their organization, networks with local companies and institutional surroundings.[13] Thus the fates of a MNC and its home state are tied to a significant degree. This implies that a company has an interest in the welfare of its home state. Called upon by its home state to perform a certain action, the request of the home state will carry a certain weight for a MNC.

[12]Chang (2011), chapter 8.

[13]Chang (2011), chapter 8.

2.5 *Conclusion*

Thus, FDI can be expected to impact the control that a state has over economic assets of a company. The home state of an FDI will generally see its influence increase, while the influence of the host state likely decreases. The host state does retain a significant degree of influence of the activities of a company within its jurisdiction through its ability to legislate the activities of all companies (be they foreign- or domestically-owned) within its borders.

3 Analytic Framework for Security Risks from FDI Into Companies That Own Critical Assets

In the following I shall identify a number of aspects that determine whether the acquisition of a company that has access to critical assets is relevant for the security of a state. Moran argues that three types of security threats relevant in the context of FDI. Moran mentions: (1) denial or manipulation of access; (2) leakage of technology or know-how and (3) infiltration, espionage and disruption.[14] According to Moran, the first reason would be that the goods or services are crucial to the functioning of the domestic economy. This includes but is not limited to, the functioning of the domestic defence industrial base. The second reason would apply, if the acquisition could lead to the transfer of technology or other expertise to a foreign-controlled entity, that the entity or the government of its home state could use in a harmful manner to the host state's interests.[15] The third reason would be that the acquisition would lead to some capability for infiltration, surveillance or espionage into provision of goods and services crucial to the domestic economy including but not limited to the defence industrial base.[16] In my view, these factors are part of a broader framework of factors, as I will seek to demonstrate below. None of these aspects by themselves are conclusive; they have to be assessed and weighted jointly.

[14]Moran and Oldenski (2013).

[15]Ibid., p. 55.

[16]Ibid., p. 55.

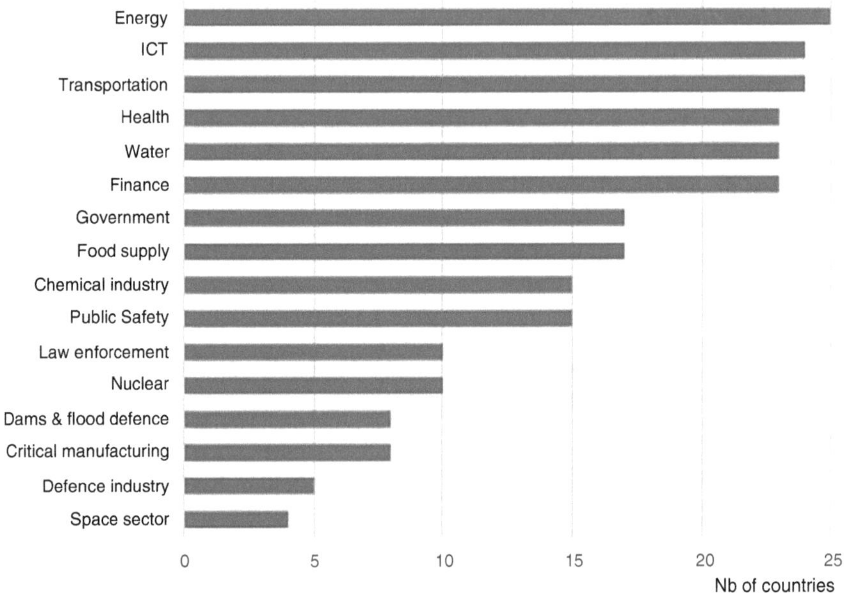

Note: Answers received from 25 OECD countries.
Source: OECD Survey on Critical Infrastructure Resilience and Security (2018)

Fig. 1 Sectors of designated critical infrastructure across OECD country [OECD (2018)]

3.1 Criticality of the Asset for Vital Interests of the State, to be Considered from the Perspective of the Demand Side Market Conditions

Some economic sectors are of particular importance in enabling the state to protect its essential interests. These are often referred to as strategic industries[17] or critical sectors. Classical examples are communication, energy and the water supply. An overview of what sectors states regard as critical for their interests has been assembled by the OECD (see Fig. 1).

Therefore, these sectors deserve specific attention when analysing the impact of FDI on state security.

Criticality is not just determined by the importance of a product for the public interest. It is also determined by the required level of continuity. Some critical supplies, such as water, electricity, communication services, cannot be interrupted for more than a few hours without severe consequences such as threats for human life, the functioning of the state institutions and public order in general. This means that there is little time for improvisation in case the supply is interrupted.

[17] Diesen (2019), p. 16.

On the other side there are products that perform a critical function, but where the temporary supply interruption is unlikely to cause any threats. This applies to many products in the manufacturing industry. If, for example, military equipment production breaks down for a few months, this may hardly impact military readiness. This can be different in case of a sudden spike of demand, for instance if a war breaks out. Also, the production of perishable or one-off goods, such as injection needles for medical purposes, is subject to a different dynamic than durable manufactured goods.

3.2 *The Ability of States to Control a Critical Asset, to be Considered from the Perspectives of Nature of the Asset, the Supply Side Market Structure and State Levers of Control That Are in Place*

It does not only matter whether a company performs critical economic activities, it is also important whether the relevant assets are of fixed or mobile nature.[18] Some assets, such as land for example, are fixed in the sense that they by definition cannot be moved physically. Other assets are not completely immobile but cannot be moved without significant costs or it a considerable amount of time. Think of a factory for example. Fixed assets are much easier to control for the host state than assets that can be moved around easily and duplicated at low costs.

By contrast, data is an asset that can be copied and transferred without any costs. It takes only one email to transfer a dataset to the other side of the world. Since technology is embedded in very different types of receptacles, the situation is more nuanced. Blueprints and software for instance can be duplicated without much cost. Tacit knowledge, that only exists in the minds of experienced staff, is harder to transfer.

The higher the mobility and duplicability of assets, the higher the risk that they can be transferred outside the control of the host state. In that sense mobile assets such as data and technology are associated with higher security risk than fixed assets.

A large firm that enjoys a monopoly or oligopoly is more relevant for security than a firm that has many competitors providing the same goods or services. One example of how a diversified market decreases risks, is food production. This is a market that contains many players both on the domestic and international level. Even though food production is crucial for survival, the risks associated with foreign control of a farm is not that high, as long as many other farms continue to operate independently. Even if national food production would break down, a state that has the means would normally be able to replace domestic production by a wide range of foreign suppliers.

---

[18] Neu and Wolf (1994), p. 44.

Another market factor that might reduce security risks is the possibility to substitute a product. If a critical good or service can be substituted by another product that serves the same need, this has the same effect as the market supply being more diversified. Therefore, both the structure of the relevant market and the substitution options will impact state security connected with a given company.

As we have pointed out above, foreign invested entities are still subject to the legislation of the host state to the extent that they operate there. By way of security safeguards, countries impose a wide range of legal obligations on companies that provide critical goods or services. These range from quality requirements such as food preparation hygiene to continuity requirements for critical economic activities such as payment systems in the financial sector.

However, there are limits to the control that can be exercised through regulation. In general, it is hard to control what stays in the host countries jurisdiction, as companies are generally free to move capital, staff, technology and facilities around to different countries, depending on their preferences. The limit of what a company may transfer outside the borders of the host country is in general determined by export control rules. But the scope of export controls tends to be limited to military and dual-use technology and products.[19]

Even when regulation exist, there are practical limitations as to their enforcement. It is very difficult for a government agency to supervise technology, data and staff moving around between different subsidiaries of a MNC. While it is true that this also applies to domestically owned companies, the board of a foreign controlled company would still be within the jurisdiction of the state, which constitutes a point of leverage over the company as a whole. Also, companies tend to keep most of their assets in their home country, as pointed out above.

Also, in case of a domestically-owned company, a state may often be able to make demands that exceed the legal requirements. For example, if there is a crisis situation that calls for improvisation such as during the COVID-19 pandemic, where manufacturing companies converted their production processes to produce facial protection equipment. This is less likely to succeed in case of a foreign-owned entity. Especially when the interests of the home and host state are not aligned.

As a consequence, an investor will generally not be able to directly disrupt a critical process performed by the invested company. The reason is that home state has means to prevent this, since it has jurisdictional control, with nationalization as the ultimate measure. Indirectly however, the shareholder may be able to influence strategic decisions such as the geographic location of the companies' activities. Such a decision would determine where a critical process takes place, for example the storage of data. Such decisions can impact the existence or removal of strategic

[19] In the case of the EU, important multilateral export control arrangements are the Australia Group, the Wassenaar Arrangement, the Nuclear Suppliers Group and the Missile Technology Control Regime. These are focused on weapons technology and dual-use technology. See: Regulation (EU) 2021/821 of the European Parliament and of the Council of 20 May 2021 setting up a Union regime for the control of exports, brokering, technical assistance, transit and transfer of dual-use items, OJ 2021 L 206/1, Annex I, chapeau.

dependencies or leverage. Legislative safeguards can be used to counter this, for example by demanding local storage of sensitive data. But in many cases, such legislative barriers will be absent.

3.3 The Likelihood of a Critical Asset Becoming Part of a Security Threat, to be Considered from the State Levers of Control and the International Strategic Context

The extent to which the opportunities for influence created by FDI may realistically be seized without prohibitive side-effects, depends on the overall power balance and the strategies that countries employ vis-à-vis each other.

The options that a state has with regard to a foreign-owned company in its territory are not just determined by its own legal system and physical control. It also depends on the relation with the home state of the investing entity. If the overall power balance is asymmetrical to the disadvantage of the host state, this can limit the host state's options. Think of nationalization as the ultimate measure of host state control. Making use of this measure can put a strain on the relationship with the home state. If it impacts the perceived core interests of a more powerful home state, it may not be a viable option. The same applies for the home state if the host state is more powerful.

Additionally, the strategies employed by other states matter. Depending on factors such as geopolitical goals, worldview, and strategic position, some countries will engage in stratagems that involve FDI, whereas many others may not. Some countries perceive their interests to be closely tied to uninterrupted flows of trade and investment. A small trading nation will generally not be inclined to weaponize FDI. A large power in need of foreign technology to reach its economic or military priorities might behave differently.

Thus, it is important to know the intent behind a FDI. Is it purely commercial in nature or also influenced by the home state? And even if it is not, is there a risk that the home state will instrumentalize the assets involved in a later stage? This makes the assessment partly speculative and political.

4 Case Study: KUKA

In this paragraph, the framework developed above will be put to the test. This test serves to determine whether the framework leads to conclusive and plausible outcomes. Further, it will explore the impact of FDI transactions on security in more detail. The acquisition of the German industrial robot maker KUKA by Chinese household appliance maker Midea in 2016 will serve as a case to be studied. The reason is that this was a controversial case, in which it was not immediately obvious if and in what way state security was at risk. In spite of resistance in German public opinion and amongst politicians the transaction was ultimately cleared by the German authorities. It is also the largest Chinese FDI in Germany to date.

It should be noted from the outset that this case study is not intended as the final word on the case. It faces limitations because I can rely only on public information. That said, a considerable amount of information is available. Thus, I am able to state with a reasonable amount of confidence that at least the most important issues and relevant factors are represented here. Also, I can draw a conclusion regarding the question whether security interests of the German state were at stake. This conclusion should be understood as a preliminary one, partially based on assumptions and on less than complete information.

4.1 Context

4.1.1 The World Market for Industrial Robots

Industrial robotics[20] forms one of the main segments of the global robotics market.[21] The other main market segment is professional service robots.[22] In a security context, military robots are also a market segment of importance.[23] Market research companies have estimated the value of the industrial robotics market around USD 16 billion in 2022 although estimates vary considerably.[24]

Globally most industrial robots are used in the automotive and electronics sectors. About 30% of industrial robots in Europe are used in the German car industry.[25] Industrial robots are used for tasks such as welding and painting cars, soldering, assembling, cutting, grinding, gluing, and in semiconductors, moving delicate wafers.[26]

---

[20] A robot can be defined as *"an autonomous system which exists in the physical world, can sense its environment, and can act on it to achieve some goals"*. See Mataric (2007).

[21] McKinsey (2019).

[22] Main segments in the professional service robots are cleaning, agriculture, maintenance and inspection, transportation and logistics, hospitality and medical/healthcare. See IFR (2022), pp. 9 and 39.

[23] In a strict sense of the term, most unmanned vehicles used in warfare are not really robots, because they are often remotely controlled by a human operator. See IFR (2022), p. 6. Nevertheless, the market for unmanned military vehicles will not be fully ignored due to its relevance for security and the similarity to actual robots.

[24] According to Markets and Markets (2023), the industrial robots market was USD 15.7 bn in 2022. According to Fortune Business Insights (2022) the industrial robots market was USD 16.8 bn in 2022. However, McKinsey (2019) valued the market at USD 48 bn in 2017, using a relatively wide definition of industrial robotics.

[25] Charisi et al. (2021), p. 19.

[26] McKinsey (2019) and Aljarboua et al. (2019).

According to the International Federation of Robotics, in 2021 there were 3.5 million industrial robots installed all over the world.[27] The market has shown an upward trend: the compound annual growth rate between 2016 and 2021 was 11%.[28] In 2021, 517,000 new industrial robots were installed worldwide.[29] Of those, 268,000 were installed in China.[30]

Following McKinsey, industrial robots can be divided in four main types. First of all, there are the stand-alone or traditional industrial robots. Such robots are not built to be used in collaboration with humans and often placed in a fenced-off area for safety reasons. Stand-alone robots are the main market segment within industrial robotics with 478,000 units installed in 2021.[31] The main types of stand-alone robots are the Articulated robot,[32] Cartesian coordinate robot,[33] the Selective compliance assembly robot arm (SCARA),[34] and the parallel link or delta robot.[35]

Another main type of industrial robots are collaborative robots (cobots). These operate directly and safely around or with humans. This is a small market with 39,000 units installed in 2021. This is an increase of 50% relative to 2020.[36]

Then there are mobile robots (also known as Automated Guided Vehicles, AGVs). These are used in warehouses and logistical centers (moving boxes, pallets, etc. between machinery, transfer points or storage areas in industrial environments), manufacturing intralogistics, agriculture, domestic use (e.g. vacuum cleaners). Note that mobile robots can also be considered service robots.[37] They are therefore not always included in assessments of the market of industrial robots.

---

[27] IFR (2022), p. 9.

[28] IFR (2022), p. 9.

[29] Ibid., p. 9.

[30] Ibid., p. 16.

[31] Ibid., p. 14.

[32] Articulated robots have a similar mechanical structure to that of a human arm, characterized by highly flexible movement. It features a high degree of freedom, but at the same time controlling the robot is rather complicated. This type of robots is used for various purposes such as welding for automobiles.

[33] This is a robot that performs movements on three dimensions not by rotating but by sliding on its three perpendicular axes.

[34] Selective Compliance Assembly Robot Arm (SCARA): This is a robot specializing in lateral movements, particularly useful for assembly. As all the rotary shafts are vertically positioned, the end effector attached to the arm can move only horizontally. This kind of robots is widely used in many situations, for instance, in handling semiconductor wafers and assembling circuit boards.

[35] The aforementioned articulated robot has serial joint linkages, the parallel link robot has parallel joint linkages. In general, these robots have three arms to control the positioning of the effector and they are usually used in situations such as sorting and selecting food products running along on conveyor belts, in particular when speed is key.

[36] IFR (2022), p. 14.

[37] McKinsey (2019), p. 7.

Table 1 Value chain components of the market for industrial robots (2017) [McKinsey (2019), p. 12]

Value chain component	Annual global revenue
Robot arms without end of arm tooling	USD 14–16 billion
Robot accessories, complementary hardware (e.g. end of arm tooling, vision systems)	USD 12 billion
Installation services to implement and connect robotic hardware	USD 5–8 billion
Software and programming for robots and associated hardware	USD 3–8 billion

A smaller market are exoskeletons. These are robots connected to human body to increase performance. 6,000 of them were estimated to be sold by 2017, mostly for rehabilitation. Prototypes exist for defense, rescue and logistics.[38]

Individual industrial robots are often sold as part of complex automation systems that consist of different parts, such as robotic arms, delivery systems, cell controllers, and safety equipment. Different production cells form a particular line. Robotic manufacturers such as Kuka deliver complete production cells to their customer.

Another way to break down the global market for industrial robots is to consider the different parts of the value chain (Table 1).

The reasons manufacturers use robots include saving labor costs and improving quality.[39] Further growth of the industrial robot market is expected.[40]

In many applications, the demand for standardized robotics is rare. Users tend to need some form of customization. Customization is carried out in systems integration phase with special tools and coupling up of power or production supply feeds and outputs.[41] In industrial robotics, the robot itself may be less than half of the actual applications cost.[42] This need for customization makes it more difficult for customers to switch supplier, as the installation of robots from another brand would require a new customization effort.

The main type of stand-alone robot is the vertical articulated robot. It has typically six axes of movement enabled by joints. One of the key components are the actuators. These are usually a servo motors, i.e. highly functional motors controlling position and speed an allowing for very precise movements, for example 0.01 mm accuracy. Another core part are reduction gears to increase the power of the actuators. Encoders indicate the position (angle) of a motor's rotational shaft. Swappable end of arm tools (EOATs) are used to perform the task at hand, for example hands for lifting up objects, vacuum (suction) types, and tools for welding and painting.[43] Robots also need sensors that allow situational awareness. And there

[38] McKinsey (2019).

[39] Ibid., p. 21.

[40] Ibid., p. 19.

[41] Forge and Blackman (2010), p. 38.

[42] Ibid., p. 39.

[43] Kawasaki Heavy Industries (2018).

needs to be a logical controlling unit containing the programming.[44] The producers of these key components are not necessarily identical with the producers of the final industrial robot. Specialized suppliers exist that focus on software or end of arm tools.[45]

4.1.2 Industrial Policy Context of Robotics

4.1.2.1 German and EU Perspective

Robotics is one of twelve advanced technologies identified by the European Commission as important for the development of the EU industry.[46] Competitiveness of the EU is threatened by the combination of relatively high labor costs in combination with an ageing workforce. Next-level automation presents a welcome opportunity to mitigate this problem. But the relative EU technology position in robotics, measured by the share of global patent applications, is weaker than that of most other major economic powers (Fig. 2).

4.1.2.2 Industrie 4.0

Although industrial robots were already introduced in the 1960s and were thus a part of the third industrial revolution (the first wave of digital automation of production processes), they are also a part of the new generation of advanced manufacturing technology often referred to as *Industrie 4.0* (Industry 4.0). The central idea behind Industry 4.0 is that progress in digital technology enables a fundamental innovation of production technology, through applications such as sensors and the industrial internet, that amount to a fourth industrial revolution. Germany's industrial policy aims at a leading position for German manufacturing at implementing Industrie 4.0., thus sustaining Germany's leading position in global manufacturing.[47]

4.1.2.3 Chinese Perspective

Industrial robots are one of the ten focus areas in the main industrial policy strategy document of the Chinese government, *Made in China 2025*. The aim of this strategy is to build one of the world's most advanced and competitive economies with the help of innovative manufacturing technologies, thus creating a 'manufacturing

[44] Wübbeke et al. (2016), p. 44.

[45] Aljarboua et al. (2019).

[46] Izsak et al. (2021), p. 9.

[47] Smit et al. (2016), p. 20.

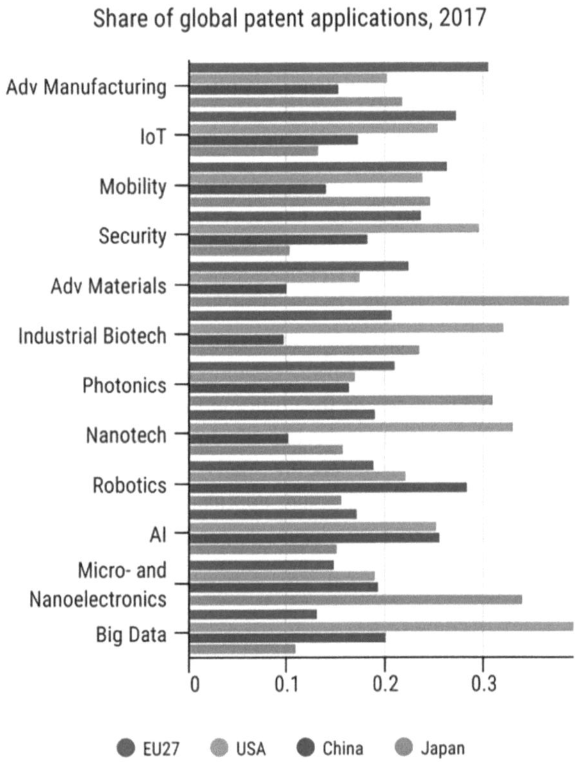

Fig. 2 Share of global patent application by advanced technology [Izsak et al. (2020), p. 5]

superpower'.[48] According to one the official implementing documents of the strategy, Chinese robot makers were to obtain a share of 50% of the domestic market by 2020. Two or three leading companies should be cultivated and five to eight supplementary production sites are to be construed.[49] By 2025, indigenous robot makers should capture 70% of the domestic market. Technology for main components should be at an international level by that time. These targets amount to an import substitution strategy of the Chinese government.[50]

In China, there is more political support and public focus on robotics than on any other manufacturing technology. This translates mainly into funding support. Merics identified robotics subsidy pledges in 21 cities and 5 provinces in China with a total value of CNY 40 billion.[51]

Since the publication of *Made in China 2025* in 2015, Chinese companies have undertaken several FDIs that give access to foreign robot technology. Wanfeng

[48] State Council People's Republic of China (2015).

[49] National Manufacturing Strategy Advisory Committee (2018). For the status of China 2025 see: Zenglein and Holzmann (2019), p. 20.

[50] Wübbeke et al. (2016), p. 14.

[51] Ibid., p. 24.

acquired Paslin, based in the U.S. in 2016; Effort acquired CMA robotics, based in Italy, in 2015.[52] And of course Midea acquired Kuka in 2016, as I will discuss below.

4.2 *Description of the Take-Over*

4.2.1 The Target

KUKA was founded in Augsburg in 1898 as a house and street light enterprise. At the time of acquisition in 2016, KUKA had developed into the largest manufacturer of industrial robots and automated solutions for factories in Germany. In its field it was one of the major companies in the world. The characteristic orange robot arms of KUKA were to be found in many German factories, especially in the automotive industry. Its robots and systems were also used in the aerospace, e-commerce, consumers goods, electronics, metal and energy industries.[53] Further, the KUKA subsidiary Swisslog provided automation systems in the health sector. KUKA was a listed company and still domiciled in Augsburg, Germany. In 2015, KUKA had revenues of EUR 3 billion. Its earnings (after taxes) were EUR 86.3 million. This implies a net profit margin of 2.9%, which is not indicative of a good performance.[54] Its market capitalization was EUR 3.1 billion. It employed 12,300 people at the end of 2015.[55]

4.2.2 The Acquirer

In 2016, the acquirer of KUKA, Midea, was a large manufacturer of home appliances, such as air-conditioners, refrigerators and washing machines as well as smaller appliances. It had no significant expertise in robotics. In 2015 Midea had a total revenue of EUR 19.7 billion and a profit (after tax) of EUR 1.9 billion.[56] It had 93,000 employees[57] and ranked 32nd on the Fortune Magazine's List of China's Top 500 Enterprises.[58] The company was privately owned, being listed on the Shenzhen stock exchange.

---

[52] Ibid., pp. 44–45.

[53] KUKA (2016a), p. 95.

[54] In general a 10% net profit margin is considered average, a 20% margin is considered high, and a 5% margin is low. See Vipond (2023).

[55] KUKA (2016a), p. 36.

[56] Midea (2016), p. 110.

[57] Ibid., p. 97.

[58] Ibid., p. 2.

4.2.3 Chronology of the Take-Over and Its Aftermath[59]

In February 2015 Midea acquired 5.4% of KUKA's shares. The same month of the following year, Midea raised its stake to 10.2% of the total shares. This investment was accompanied by the statement that it intended to further increase its stake over 30%. Since Midea wanted to acquire more than 30% of the shares, it was obliged under German law to submit an offer for the remaining shares. In May 2016, Midea made a public bid offering EUR 115 per share in KUKA. The share closing price on the previous day was EUR 84.41. With its bid, Midea offered a 60% premium compared to February 2016. Midea accompanied its bid with a declaration it would like to have a meaningful stake above 30% and has no intention of concluding a domination agreement or delisting the company.[60]

After May 2016, controversy erupted in German public opinion over Midea's bid. There were concerns that crucial technology could fall into foreign hands and that, particularly with regard to the Chinese market, there was a lack of reciprocity in the admission foreign investments. Furthermore, there was particular concern regarding the impairment of Germany's "Industrie 4.0" ambitions (see above) due the essential role of KUKA in that project. These economic-strategic concerns were more prominent than security-based ones.

In June, Markus Ferber of the European Parliament (European People's Party) was quoted saying: "*We really need to think about whether we want to give such a key enterprise to the Chinese, or try to keep it in European hands.*"[61] That same month, Sigmar Gabriel (German Labour Party), minister of economics and vice-chancellor wrote in German weekly *Wirtschaftswoche*:

"Should it remain the case that government agencies are only allowed to conduct preliminary investigations into investment in areas deemed relevant for security and defense?"[62] He added *"We need to clarify whether we should not create the option to assess the interests of investors against the EU's industrial interests for sectors that can be of existential significance for the strategic future of the European economy."*[63]

Other politicians also called for a counterbid by German or European parties. The German state moved to cap Midea's share at 49% of KUKA. Neither of these goals materialised however. Instead, on 22 June 2016, the board of KUKA expressed a positive sentiment towards the Midea bid.[64] A few days later, on 28 June 2016, KUKA and Midea announced that they entered into a binding investment agreement.[65] The agreement included the promise that there would be no reorganization

[59]This chronology is for the first part largely based on Hooijmaakers (2019), pp. 451–470.

[60]Reuters (2016b).

[61]Chazan (2016).

[62]Reuters (2016a).

[63]Ibid.

[64]Prodhan and Preisinger (2016).

[65]Kuka (2016b).

of KUKA, no delisting, and no domination agreement. As part of this agreement KUKA and Midea signed a "ring-fencing agreement". According to KUKA the ring-fencing agreement describes how industrial property rights and KUKA know-how will be dealt with. Additionally, according to the ring-fencing agreement, databases containing client data are not allowed to be moved by Midea to other locations and are protected against being accessed by Midea or other third parties. The agreement would stay in force until end of 2023.[66]

On August 8, Midea announced that it had acquired 94.55% of shares in KUKA. Mid-August, a spokesman for the German government declared that the German authorities had concluded, after an initial assessment, that they had no powers to block the transaction or even to start an investigation procedure, stating that *"the ministry can only launch a formal inquiry against the sale if crucial German interests such as telecommunications or water and power safety are affected."*[67]

Meanwhile, U.S. authorities, including the Committee on Foreign Investment in the United States (CFIUS) and Directorate of Defence Trade Controls (DDTC), had started their own investigation into the KUKA takeover. The reason behind this was that KUKA had a U.S. subsidiary called KUKA Systems Aerospace North America that was registered under the U.S. International Traffic in Arms Regulations (ITAR). According to the ITAR, Chinese companies were prohibited from owning ITAR-registered entities. The prohibition was part of the sanctions imposed on China by the U.S. after the Tiananmen square massacre in 1989.[68] On 15 December 2016 KUKA announced that it would sell its American subsidiary to Advanced Integration Technology Inc., a U.S. based company specializing in turnkey automation solutions for the aerospace industry.[69] On 29 December 2016 U.S. authorities cleared the takeover of KUKA Systems Aerospace North America.[70] This was the last hurdle to take in order to complete the takeover. It was effectuated early 2017.

Because the take-over was completed years ago, it is possible by now to shed some light on the *fait* of KUKA under control of Midea. After the takeover, KUKA continued to operate with its headquarters in Augsburg. As agreed, no layoffs followed the Midea takeover. Indeed, KUKA's staff has grown from 12,000 at the year-end of 2015 to 14,000 at year-end of 2021.[71] Its financial performance has remained on the same level. Its sales revenue is EUR 3.3 billion in 2021, with earnings after taxes of EUR 49.4 million. KUKA has spent EUR 159.6 million on research and development (R&D) in 2021, while in 2015 it was spending EUR 105.4 million. Overall, these figures indicate that the financial performance and location of

[66] Ibid. (2016b).

[67] Deutsche Welle (2016).

[68] In February 1990, Congress codified the sanctions' prohibition on weapon sales in Public Law 101–246, sec. 902.

[69] Kuka (2016c).

[70] Frankfurter Allgemeine Zeitung (2016).

[71] KUKA, *Annual Report 2021.*

operations of KUKA have not changed at a fundamental level. The point of gravity of KUKA has remained in Germany and investments in R&D have continued.

On a closer look, there have been signs of changes that would enable technology transfer from KUKA towards Midea and its subsidiaries and that Midea is gradually increasing its control over KUKA. On 22 March 2018 Midea, KUKA and KUKA subsidiary Swisslog entered into three joint ventures to produce robots in China.[72] As part of one of the joint ventures, a robot park will be built in South China's Shunde, where Midea is located. It will have a capacity of 75,000 robots (with a total capacity of 100,000 robot units including existing capacities) and AGVs (automated guided vehicles) by 2024. In addition to 6-axis-robots, the robot park will also be used to produce, develop and distribute new robots specifically for the Chinese market.[73] This joint venture is 50% owned by Midea and 50% by KUKA. KUKA chairs the management board.

On 26 November 2018, KUKA announced that its CEO Till Reuter will be replaced before the end of his term that would have ended in March 2022.[74] Media outlet Deutsche Welle reports based on an anonymous source that *"Midea is now trying to speed up the integration of KUKA into its larger business operations and increase its control over the management."*[75] Financial Times reported that the reason behind the early termination was a conflict over the strategy for the KUKA and Midea joint venture, between Reuter and the chairman of the supervisory board, Andy Gy of Midea.[76]

On 23 November 2021 KUKA announced a new "joint growth strategy" with Midea. It involves an increase of investments in R&D by 15% in 2025 compared to 2021 levels. It also includes the delisting of KUKA, by a squeeze-out of the remaining minority shareholders.[77] It is also reported that Midea considers the relisting of KUKA in Asia.[78]

[72] KUKA (2018a).

[73] Ibid.

[74] KUKA (2018b).

[75] Martin (2018).

[76] McGee (2018).

[77] KUKA (2021).

[78] Chan and Baigorri (2021).

4.3 *Application of the Analytic Framework to the KUKA Case*

4.3.1 Criticality of the Asset for Vital Interests of the State, to be Considered from the Perspective of the Demand Side Market Conditions

4.3.1.1 Critical Assets: The Markets Served by KUKA Products

The business model of KUKA is focused on the production of industrial robots and automated systems with robots at the core[79] that are employed in a range of industrial sectors: automotive, automated modular houses, e-commerce, electronics, healthcare, consumer goods, metal industry, entertainment, plastics, energy (e.g. battery packs) and nuclear decommissioning.[80] At the time of its acquisition, aerospace was also an important market for KUKA.[81] KUKA's offering includes articulated robots of different kinds (including stand-alone, delta, cartesian and SCARA robots), mobile robots (AGVs) and collaborative robots. It offers also core components such as logical controllers.[82] The automated systems that KUKA builds for its clients range from individual system components and tools and fixtures to complete turnkey systems.[83] Additional KUKA products are dedicated software to operate the robots[84] and systems and spare parts. KUKA also provides services during the lifecycle of its products including programming, maintenance and software updates (including updates for cybersecurity purposes).

Authorities in different countries have historically in specific cases considered machines for production (of which industrial robots are a sub-category) as relevant for their security because they can enable the production of military goods. A famous example is the illegal provision by Japanese company Toshiba and Norwegian company Kongsberg of a milling machine and logical controller to the Soviet Union in 1981.[85] This machine enabled the Soviet Union to produce low-noise propellers for nuclear submarines which were be difficult to detect for the U.S. Navy. Examples of such machines also surface in the case law of European Court of Justice on export controls for dual-use items.[86]

---

[79] KUKA(2022a), p. 14.

[80] KUKA (2023a).

[81] KUKA (2016a), p. 25.

[82] KUKA (2023b).

[83] KUKA (2016a), p. 23.

[84] KUKA (2016a), p. 23.

[85] Gregory (1987).

[86] Judgement of 4 October 1991, C-367/89, *Richardt*, ECLI:EU:C:1991:376; Judgement of 17 October 1995, C-70/94, *Werner*, ECLI:EU:C:1995:328. In the case of *Richardt*, it concerned a machine for the production of "bubble memory circuits". In the case of *Werner*, it concerned a "vacuum induction and smelting cast oven".

In the case of KUKA, there is evidence of dual-use capability in one specific business line, namely the U.S. subsidiary KUKA Aerospace. According to the KUKA's press release of 2014 the company's manufacturing and assembly solutions included *"state-of-the-art automated systems, from static and mobile robotic drilling and fastening cells to entire assembly lines."*[87] KUKA's project portfolio included orders from some of the world's largest aerospace manufacturers to design and build assembly systems for next generation commercial, business and military fixed wing and rotary aircraft.[88] Aircraft manufacturers Airbus[89] and Boeing,[90] both of which have an important military branch, were customers of KUKA. These facts already suggest that some of KUKA Aerospace's products were of potential dual-use nature. This is confirmed by the requirement of the U.S. authorities that KUKA Aerospace be spun off from KUKA before the Midea take-over, as mentioned above. Furthermore, KUKA's industrial robots are used in a number of other sectors that are considered critical by countries (see above), such as food processing, pharma, semiconductors, logistics, and nuclear dismantlement.

How important are industrial robots in the production in these sectors? Could they be replaced with manual labour, for instance? Industrial robots are not just used to save costs but also for reasons of capability, quality and human safety.[91] And they are used on such a scale that replacement is hard to conceive. At least on the shorter run, skilled manual labour is unlikely to be available on a sufficient scale to replace industrial robots to a sufficient degree to maintain industrial output on the same level. Thus, it is likely that without functioning industrial robots of the type that KUKA produced in 2015, critical economic sectors will be disrupted. This argument is the least persuasive in the case of military aircraft. Here small numbers are produced.[92] Therefore it is conceivable that industrial robots would be more replaceable by human labour in this sector.

Furthermore, the question should be addressed if KUKA's capabilities could be used to make products that can be used against the vital interests of Germany. This does not apply in the case of robots used for logistics, food processing or pharma. This could be different in the case of robots and systems supplied by KUKA Aerospace that can be used to build military-grade aircraft. If such machinery falls in the hands of potential adversaries of Germany, this could be a security risk, depending on whether it increases their existing capabilities. In this case, this was prevented by action from the U.S. authorities. But does not take away the fact that the risk was there at the beginning of the take-over. Additionally, the spin-off erodes the defence industrial base of Germany if not qualitatively and least in size.

---

[87] KUKA (2014).

[88] Ibid.

[89] KUKA (2008).

[90] KUKA (2016a).

[91] McKinsey (2019).

[92] In 2019 for example, Boeing produced 229 military aircraft. See Wikipedia (2023). Airbus has built only 585 of its Eurofighter aircraft in total. See Airbus (2023).

4.3.1.2 Critical Assets: Adjacent Markets

So far, we have considered industrial robots that KUKA currently offers and that can produce critical goods, including military goods. Another question is whether the capacities of KUKA could also be used to build military-grade robots that can be used in warfare, now or in the future, even though KUKA currently does not make such robots.

The market for military robots in the proper sense of the term, that is machines that can operate on their own in a military role, is still in its early stages.[93] Unmanned vehicles used in modern-day warfare tend to be remote-controlled by a human operator. Thus, they are not really robots. Key players in the military robots/ unmanned military vehicles sector are specialized defence companies rather than manufacturers of industrial robots.[94] This suggests that the industrial robot market is different from the military robot market with different requirements. Indeed, compared to industrial robots, military robots have quite different requirements in terms of mobility, vision and programming, to name a few obvious differences that can be inferred from the environment they operate in and their tasks.

This is confirmed by the EU Dual-use Export Regulation, that lists items that are subject to a license requirement because they can be used for military as well as civilian purposes.[95] This regulation suggests that non-military grade robots should be considered civilian rather than dual-use technology. The regulation mentions robots a few times, but only in very specific cases. Cases of dual-use robot technology mentioned by the Regulation are robots that can deal with high explosive materials,[96] radiation-hardened robots,[97] and specific kinds of underwater robots.[98] Industrial robots are not listed but explicitly exempted in the case of robots specially designed for paint-spraying booths.[99] Overall, it seems somewhat far-fetched to argue that KUKA's capability to build some components that a military robot would also require, is a security concern.

[93] Himanshu (2021).

[94] Himanshu (2021) mentions the following key players in the military robotics market: BEA Systems, Elbit Systems, General Dynamics, Israel Aerospace Industries, Lockheed Martin, Rafael Advanced Defense Systems, Rheinmetall, Saab, Thales. Note that Rheinmetall, Saab and Thales are based in the EU.

[95] Regulation (EU) 2021/821 of the European Parliament and of the Council of 20 May 2021 setting up a Union regime for the control of exports, brokering, technical assistance, transit and transfer of dual-use items, OJ 2021 L 206/1 (hereinafter: Regulation (EU) 2021/821).

[96] Regulation (EU) 2021/821, Annex I, 2B207 (b).

[97] Regulation (EU) 2021/821, Annex I, 2B207 (c). KUKA offers robots for nuclear dismantling, but I was not able to assess whether these are radiation-hardened in the sense of the Regulation. If so, they could classify as a dual-use item.

[98] Regulation (EU) 2021/821, Annex I, 8A002 (h).

[99] Regulation (EU) 2021/821, Annex I, 2B207 (b).

4.3.1.3 Critical Assets: Other Assets Controlled by KUKA

Aside from its products that may or may not be critical, KUKA gains access to sensitive customer information in the course of its business. This is revealed by the fact that KUKA and Midea entered into a ring-fencing agreement to protect sensitive customer data, as described above. Such information can be assumed to include procedures for manufacturing of client products, as such information needs to be shared in order for KUKA to be able to perform programming support. Although KUKA software allows customers to program robots themselves,[100] KUKA also offers comprehensive programming services to its clients. This includes planning, implementation and optimization. These services require the client to share data regarding its production process in order for KUKA to adjust robot programming to client needs.[101]

Access to sensitive customer data does of course not automatically involve a security risk for the state. This depends *inter alia* on the nature of the production process involved. In the case of production of military aircraft for instance, the security risk looms clearly. In case of other critical manufacturing, it does not. The leakage of information about production processes such as the processing of pharmaceuticals or food, critical as these processes may be, is unlikely to affect state security interests. The difference with production of military goods is that the leakage of non-military technology is much less likely to be used against the state, in this case Germany. If a foreign power obtains a cutting-edge technology for production of military aircraft, this foreign power can use this information to build aircrafts which can potentially be used against the interests of the state.[102] This is not so with technology for food processing or pharmaceuticals. Even if a foreign power obtains such technology and improves its production of food or pharmaceuticals, this does not harm the state's vital interests.

An exception to the finding above is information related to cybersecurity. If a foreign power would obtain information on weaknesses in software that can be exploited for cyber-attacks, this may create a continuity risk for military as well as non-military critical production, both of which can affect vital interests of the state. In the case of KUKA, cyber-security related to its proprietary software is part of its customer service. This includes assessing and fixing vulnerabilities in software that is used to operate its robots.[103] Thus, cybersecurity related information is an asset controlled by KUKA that involves security risks.

---

[100] KUKA (2023b), p. 160.

[101] KUKA (2022b), pp. 14–15.

[102] That economic assets can include or contain information that is relevant to state security, has been acknowledged in security studies literature. Farrell and Newman have demonstrated that economic networks such as the internet are asymmetric and contain hubs that provide privileged viewpoints over information flows which they call "panopticon points" and which can be weaponized by the state that controls these hubs (Farrell and Newman (2019), p. 30).

[103] KUKA (2023c).

4.3.1.4 Critical Assets: Required Level of Continuity

For the supply of robots and automated systems themselves, a high level of continuity seems not be required. The life span of a robot is around ten years.[104] It is unlikely that a delay of supply of weeks or even months would lead to harm for state interests. This is likely to be different with software updates and maintenance services. In these cases, a more continuous supply would be required than in the case of delivery of the robots and systems. Thus, there is arguably a need for a certain degree of continuity of at least a part of the products provided for by KUKA.

4.3.1.5 Critical Assets: Conclusion

All in all, it seems plausible that KUKA produced and had access to some critical assets at the time of the acquisition by Midea. These consist of production technology and production information related to military aircraft as well as information on vulnerabilities in software that is used to operate robots support the production and processing of critical goods of military and civilian nature.

4.3.2 The Ability of States to Control a Critical Asset, to be Considered from the Perspectives of the Nature of the Asset, the Supply Side Market Structure and State Levers of Control That Are in Place

Now that I have concluded that KUKA produced and had access to some critical assets, it is important to consider to what extent the German authorities are in a position to retain control over this access, in case of foreign ownership of KUKA.

4.3.2.1 Market Structure

In 2016 KUKA was one of the leading industrial robot manufacturers. Data from around that time shows that KUKA had 80,000 robots installed around the world.[105] The International Federation of Robotics estimated that there was a total stock of 2.1 million robots installed worldwide in that period.[106] This is indicative of a market share of around 4% by volume. This may seem relatively small, but as it concerns a competitive market with many players, this is enough to be ranked amongst the top suppliers by market intelligence companies.[107] KUKA is the only EU-based company considered as a leading manufacturer in this sector. The players are mostly

[104] KUKA (2023b).

[105] Figures for 2017, see Frederick et al. (2018), p. 58.

[106] IFR (2018).

[107] Markets and Markets (2023); Mordor Intelligence (2023).

Japanese. It is estimated that 45% of the world's industrial robots are supplied by Japanese companies.[108] These include Fanuc, Yaskawa and Denso. Another major player is Swiss, ABB. Together these Japanese and Swiss and German companies dominated the market.[109]

The consequence of the market structure sketched above is that Germany has multiple sources for the supply of industrial robots. Companies like FANUC and ABB would be able to provide a similar offering as KUKA. But, since the KUKA take-over, there is no leading German- or EU-based industrial robotics company left. Further, switching costs are likely to be considerable since it would involve the expense of new robots or automated systems that have to be interoperable with other company systems as well a new software programming effort. However, given sufficient time, it would be possible for manufacturers based in Germany to find an alternative for KUKA. The take-over means that Germany and the EU lose some capacity in industrial robot production because they lack a leading company within their borders. This loss of control does not mean however that a dependence is created as multiple alternative suppliers remain.

4.3.2.2 The Fixed or Mobile Nature of the Production Assets of the Invested Entity

The main assets controlled by KUKA are production facilities, technology and other information, in particular knowledge of industrial production processes relying on KUKA automation solutions or contained in software for KUKA robots. An indicator of its technological know-how is that KUKA holds 3,454 granted patents as of January 2023.[110]

The production facilities and technology can be moved outside Germany, but not without significant costs and effort. Since the Midea takeover production facilities in Germany have been maintained and the headquarters still remains in Augsburg, Germany. However, in March 2018, Midea and KUKA have created three joint ventures to produce robots in China.[111] KUKA itself already has a subsidiary in China called KUKA China. Therefore, the joint ventures do not seem necessary to enable KUKA's operations in China, but they will enable technology transfer from KUKA to Midea. The intent behind the joint ventures thus could be the transfer of technological know-how from Germany-based KUKA to China-based Midea. Assets in the form of client data and software vulnerabilities could be transferred easily from Germany to any other location in the world. So this information is transferable and hard to control for German authorities.

---

[108] Mordor Intelligence (2023).

[109] Mordor Intelligence (2023).

[110] Bureau Van Dijk (2023).

[111] Kuka (2018a).

4.3.2.3 State Levers of Control Over Industrial Robot Technology and Products

Industrial robots are outside the remit of the EU export control framework.[112] Thus German authorities have few options to assert control over KUKA's technology and information after the take-over. Technology and information can be transferred to the Chinese owner.

To address concerns over protection of sensitive client data, Midea has voluntarily entered into the aforementioned "Ring-fencing Agreement" with KUKA that gives certain assurances for several years after the takeover. To my knowledge, these agreements have not been published. Midea continues to express its commitment to this agreement. However, there are several limitations to the safeguards it provides. Firstly, the agreement expires by the end of 2023. Secondly, the agreement is not concluded between the authorities and Midea, but between KUKA and Midea. If it is violated, KUKA is the one who has to enforce it. However, KUKA is also a subsidiary controlled by Midea. This raises the question how realistic it is that KUKA would take Midea to court in case of a violation of the agreement. Thus, the assurance provided by the "Ring-fencing Agreement" to the German authorities is limited.

4.3.3 The Likelihood of a Critical Asset Becoming Part of a Security Threat, to be Considered from the State Levers of Control and the International Strategic Context

4.3.3.1 Strategic Priorities

As described above, industrial robotics is one of the focus points of China's import substitution and technological dominance ambitions. This increases the likelihood that Midea will use its control over KUKA to serve this ambition by using KUKA's know-how to build up robotic manufacturing capacity in China. Germany, by contrast, is already an advanced manufacturer and does not follow an import substitution strategy. It is however determined to remain a leading manufacturing nation. Germany's Industry 4.0 policy, mentioned above, bears witness of this. From a security strategy perspective, one could argue that Germany's acquiescence to the KUKA take-over was in line with a liberal approach that favours economic integration with the conviction that this prevents conflict. In that sense one may argue that the take-over could be seen as promoting Germany's security interest. In the face of China's strong commitment to an import-substitution based policy, this seems a rather naïve approach, as it is apparent that China rejects the concept of mutual dependencies and aims for independence instead. For that reason, the aforementioned German concerns about reciprocity seem justified.

[112] See the discussion above.

4.3.3.2 Overall Balance of Power

With the KUKA takeover, China has won access to a technology in which it had no major industrial player. From a German and an EU perspective, this has a negative impact on the balance of dependencies between the EU and China. Germany has lost some leverage over China, as it does no longer hold a technology that China lacks but wants access to. Furthermore, China has more leverage over the EU now, as it depends on strategic (investment) decisions made by Midea (which can be influenced by the Chinese home state) to what degree KUKA will remain a major player in the world and in the EU industrial ecosystem.

It is clear that the leverage gained by China through the KUKA take-over should not be overstated. After all, it is hard to imagine that the fate of KUKA would be of such importance to Germany that a threat to its activities in Germany would influence its political decisions in a meaningful way. Also, any explicit threat made by China would be likely to backfire by damaging China's reputation. Therefore, such a political intervention in Midea's management of KUKA seems unlikely. However, this is also a matter of perspective. German political opinion was concerned that KUKA was merely the first important technology company to be taken over by a Chinese company. If China would be allowed to take-over a significant amount of leading German manufacturing companies, the existence of substantial leverage over the German government would become conceivable. If one would only consider the take-over as well as any subsequent one, as one-off events, one would miss this aspect.

4.3.4 Conclusion

Based on the public information considered above, the conclusion seems justified that the KUKA take-over involved some security risks for the German state. These are particularly connected with the U.S. subsidiary of KUKA that was active in the (military) aerospace sector. Arguably, the takeover has also led to an erosion of the EU military industrial base, because it has led to the spin-off of said dual-use subsidiary of KUKA in the U.S. Another, larger part of KUKA is affected by risks to information security related to services that KUKA provides to its customers in areas such as programming and cybersecurity. Also, a leverage point of the Western economies is at risk of being lost, with negative impact on the balance of dependence from their perspective.

This may seem a surprising conclusion, given the fact that the German authorities at the time perceived that they could do nothing to stop the transaction (or even start a full-fledged investigation) as it was not contrary to security interests as defined by German legislation. However, it should also be noted that U.S. authorities did see a reason to act and demanded that the U.S. subsidiary of KUKA be spun off. The answer to the question whether the German authorities could have acted differently than they did, given the definition of security that applied under German legislation in force at the time of the take-over, is not a part of this case study.

This is not to say that the takeover was necessarily conducted in bad faith. Midea has continued investments in research and development in Germany, thus contributing to the German and EU industrial base. There are also risks that one may expect in this case that do not materialize. Given alternative suppliers and fragmented market with limited entrance barriers, there is no clear risk of loss of access of Germany/EU of China to supply of industrial robots (lock-in effects aside). Also, with Chinese control over KUKA, Germany can continue its Industry 4.0 ambitions by installing more, and more advanced, industrial robots in its factories.

Finally, this case study notes that German public opinion seemed more occupied with economic-strategic considerations than hard-core security concerns. China has an import substitution strategy that explicitly includes robots. The take-over can be used to serve that strategy. Can it be expected of Germany to facilitate this by welcoming Chinese take-overs as long as this does not create a security risk? These concerns are out of scope of this study, but the question is valid, in my opinion.

5 Conclusion

Sometimes, a FDI can pose a risk to the security interests of a state. The first key to understanding when this is the case, is the insight that FDI provides a foreign investor and its home state with a degree of control over the domestic companies of the host state and thus over the assets of these companies. These assets can be critical to state interests. However, in itself this does not mean that foreign ownership of a company constitutes necessarily a risk. Further aspects have to be taken into account, in particular the nature of the assets involved and the structure of the market. Furthermore, the security implications of a FDI cannot be assessed well without understanding the strategies of the states involved. This strategic aspect points to the fact that a security assessment of FDI is not a box ticking exercise. It involves also a subjective factor, in the form of the preferred security strategy of the state that hosts the FDI. This in turn depends on factors such as worldview and political aims. Therefore, a country's stance towards foreign investment is also a political question, in general as well as in concrete cases.

The case study of the takeover of KUKA by Midea demonstrates that the framework set out in this paper to assess FDI in companies that own critical assets, can be effectively used to explore the security implications of a FDI. The conclusion of this case study suggests that security risks can be a real issue in case of a takeover of an advanced manufacturing company. Finally, the case also reveals that there can be more problematic aspects of FDI than potential risks to security. The question arises whether a country should be expected to be open to foreign investment if that investment risks to be put in service of an adversarial economic strategy such as import substitution.

References

Airbus (2023) Orders, Deliveries, In Operation Military aircraft by Country – Worldwide. January 31. https://airbus.web.factory.eu.airbus.com/sites/g/files/jlcbta136/files/2023-02/2023-01_MRS_GEN_Ord-Deliv%20by%20country_0.pdf

Aljarboua Z, Santhanam N, Teulieres M, Thomsen J, Tilley J (2019) Industrial robotics: Opportunities for manufacturers of end effectors. McKinsey February 15. https://www.mckinsey.com/industries/industrials-and-electronics/our-insights/industrial-robotics-opportunities-for-manufacturers-of-end-effectors

Bureau Van Dijk (2023) Orbis Database

Chan V, Baigorri M (2021) Midea Considers China Relisting for German Robotics Firm Kuka. Bloomberg. November 23. https://www.bloomberg.com/news/articles/2021-11-23/midea-said-to-mull-china-relisting-for-german-robotics-firm-kuka#xj4y7vzkg

Chang H-J (2011) 23 Things they don't tell you about capitalism. Penguin Books, London

Charisi V, Compano R, Duch Brown N, Gomez Gutierrez E, Klenert D, Lutz M, Marschinski R, Torrecila Salina C (2021) What future for European robotics. Publications Office of the European Union, Luxembourg

Chazan G (2016) Berlin and Brussels wary of Chinese robotics bid. Financial Times June 13. https://www.ft.com/content/acbda1cc-3186-11e6-bda0-04585c31b153

Deutsche Welle (2016) Kuka takeover approved. August 17. Kuka takeover approved – DW – 08/17/2016

Diesen (2019) Russia's geoeconomic strategy for a Greater Eurasia. Routledge, Abingdon

Farrell H, Newman A (2019) Weaponized interdependence: how global economic networks shape state Coercion. Int Secur 44:42–79

Ferchen M, Pieke FN, van der Putten F-P, Hong T, de Blécourt J (2018) Assessing China's influence in Europe through investments in technology and infrastructure: four cases. Leiden Asia Centre, December 2018

Forge S, Blackman C (2010) A helping hand for Europe: the competitive outlook for the EU Robotics industry. JRC Scientific and Technical Reports, Luxembourg

Fortune Business Insights (2022) Industrial Robots Market to Hit USD 35.68 Billion by 2029. At 11.4% CAGR. GlobeNewswire, August 24. https://www.globenewswire.com/news-release/2022/08/24/2503600/0/en/Industrial-Robots-Market-to-Hit-USD-35-68-Billion-by-2029-At-11-4-CAGR.html

Frankfurter Allgemeine Zeitung (2016) Kuka-Verkaug an chinesen nimmt letzte Hürde. December 13. Amerika genehmigt Übernahme: Kuka-Verkauf an Chinesen nimmt letzte Hürde (faz.net)

Frederick S, Bamber P, Cho J (2018) The Digital Economy, Global Value Chains and Asia. Duke GVCC, December. https://www.globalvaluechains.org/wp-content/uploads/DigitalEconomyGVCsAsia2018.pdf

Graham E, Krugman P (1995) Foreign direct investment in the United States, 3rd edn. Institute for International Economics

Gregory J (1987) Controlling the transfer of militarily significant technology: COCOM after Toshiba. Fordham Int Law J 11(4):863–882

Himanshu J (2021) Military Robots Market. Allied Market Research. https://www.alliedmarketresearch.com/military-robots-market-A13130. Accessed 5 Feb 2023

Hooijmaakers B (2019) Blackening skies for Chinese investment in the EU? J Chinese Polit Sci 24: 451–470

IFR (2018) Executive Summary World Robotics 2018 Industrial Robots. https://ifr.org/downloads/press2018/Executive_Summary_WR_2018_Industrial_Robots.pdf

IFR (2022) World Robotics 2022: presentation of the report. https://ifr.org/downloads/press2018/2022_WR_extended_version.pdf

Izsak K, Perez M, Kroll H, Wydra S (2020) Advanced technologies for industry -EU Report. Technological trends and policies. European Commission, Brussels

Izsak K, Markianidou P, van de Velde E, Frietsch R, Kroll H, Wydra S, Glennon M, Garcia JM (2021) Advanced technologies for industry – methodological report. Indicator framework and data calculations. European Commission, Brussels
Kardon I, Leutert W (2022) Pier competitor: China's power position in global ports. Int Secur 46:9–47
Kawasaki Heavy Industries (2018) How are industrial Robots built? A Guide on the Components and the Movement of Robot Arms. May 22 How Are Industrial Robots Built? A Guide on the Components and the Movement of Robot Arms| XYZ | Kawasaki Heavy Industries, Ltd
KUKA (2008) KUKA lands key aircraft order. December 10. KUKA lands key aircraft order | KUKA AG
KUKA (2014) KUKA Aerospace opens Everett, WA facility to support growth. August 11. https://www.kuka.com/en-de/company/press/news/2014/08/kuka-aerospace-opens-everett,-wa-facility-to-support-growth
KUKA (2016a) Annual report 2015. https://www.kuka.com/-/media/kuka-corporate/documents/ir/general-meeting/2015/annual_report_2015_en.pdf?rev=98c2125dcb5d4d90ad06e24ebc878094&hash=52F0D7480F1DFB7A892ED1BB4ED25AB8
KUKA (2016b) KUKA signs investor agreement with Midea and recommends acceptance of the offer. 28 June. KUKA signs investor agreement with Midea | KUKA AG
KUKA (2016c) KUKA sells Systems U.S. aviation section to advanced Integration Technology Inc. December 15. KUKA sells Systems U.S. aviation section to Advanced Integration Technology Inc
KUKA (2018a) KUKA and Midea strengthen cooperation in China. March 2022. KUKA and Midea strengthen cooperation in China | KUKA AG
KUKA (2018b) Till Reuter terminates his office as CEO in December in agreement with the supervisory board – Peter Mohnen takes over and ensures continuity. November 26. Till Reuter terminates his office as KUKA CEO | KUKA AG
KUKA (2021) KUKA expects positive financial year 2021 and jointly with Midea defines long-term growth plan for the company under a private ownership structure -Squeeze-Out process initiated. November 23. Press release KUKA and Midea | KUKA AG
KUKA (2022a) Annual report 2021. annual-report_2021.pdf (kuka.com)
KUKA (2022b) Global. Customer. Services. Our pledge for your robot systems. https://www.kuka.com/-/media/kuka-downloads/imported/9cb8e311bfd744b4b0eab25ca883f6d3/kui_broschuere_customerservice_enus_web.pdf?rev=428fbcddd43d4aecb92536e0711763d8
KUKA (2023a) Industries. Industries | KUKA AG
KUKA (2023b) Product portfolio_09/2023. https://www.kuka.com/-/media/kuka-downloads/imported/87f2706ce77c4318877932fb36f6002d/kuka_rob_product-portfolio_en_screen.pdf?rev=eb5a9009b8694f97bf0fad01a0e941a6&hash=9F4E86CF3DBE97A6F5D792A7BB3E2506
KUKA (2023c) Cybersecurity at KUKA. https://www.kuka.com/nl-be/services/service-voor-robots-en-machines/cybersecurity#protect-yourself
Libman A (2015) Russische Direktinvestitionen in Eurasien. SWP-studie
Markets and Markets (2023) Industrial Robotics Market. https://www.marketsandmarkets.com/Market-Reports/Industrial-Robotics-Market-643.html
Martin N (2018) German robot maker's CEO to be fired. Deutsche Welle. November 24. German robot maker's CEO to be fired – DW – 11/24/2018
Mataric M (2007) The Robotics Primer. MIT
McGee P (2018) Till Reuter faces ousting as chief of German robotics group Kuka. Financial Times. November 25. Till Reuter faces ousting as chief of German robotics group Kuka (ft.com)
McKinsey (2019) Industrial Robotics: Insights into the sector's future growth dynamics. https://www.mckinsey.com/~/media/mckinsey/industries/advanced%20electronics/our%20insights/growth%20dynamics%20in%20industrial%20robotics/industrial-robotics-insights-into-the-sectors-future-growth-dynamics.ashx

Midea (2016) The 2015 Annual Report of Midea Group Co., Ltd. March 26. https://www.midea-group.com/content/dam/mideaco-aem/investors/financial-reports/Midea-Group-2015-Annual-Report.pdf.coredownload.inline.pdf
Moran TH, Oldenski L (2013) Foreign direct investment in the United States: benefits, suspicions, and risks with special attention to FDI from China. PIIE
Mordor Intelligence (2023) Industrial Robotics Market Size & Share Analysis – Growth trends & forecasts (2023–2028). https://www.mordorintelligence.com/industry-reports/industrial-robotics-market?gclid=CjwKCAiArNOeBhAHEiwAze_nKCLP2LBpcxViTUnkXOGIUUlCDiv-RxlrIjzl5DjqvkxxwkXoFuBLuRoCLiwQAvD_BwE
National Manufacturing Strategy Advisory Committee (2018) MIC 2025 Key Area Technology Roadmap
Neu C, Wolf C (1994) The economic dimensions of national security. RAND
Nolan P (2012) Is China buying the world? Polity Press
OECD (2008) OECD Benchmark Definition of Foreign direct Investment, 4th edn. Paris
OECD (2018) Survey on critical infrastructure resilience and security. Paris
OECD (2019) OECD Review of Risk Management Policies, Good Governance for Critical Infrastructure Resilience, revised version. Paris. https://www.oecd-ilibrary.org/sites/02f0e5a0-en/index.html?itemId=/content/publication/02f0e5a0-en
Prodhan G, Preisinger I (2016) Kuka's robotics boss sees benefits of Chinese ownership. June 22. Kuka's robotics boss sees benefits of Chinese ownership | Reuters
Reuters (2016a) Germany's Gabriel seeks EU rule to block foreign takeover of key technologies. June 9. https://www.reuters.com/article/us-kuka-m-a-mideagroup-germany-idUSKCN0YV147/
Reuters (2016b) Midea says size of Kuka stake will depend on shareholders. June 14. https://www.reuters.com/article/us-kuka-m-a-midea-group-stake-idUKKCN0Z010E/
Smit J, Kreutzer S, Moeller C, Carlberg M (2016) Industry 4.0. Policy department a: economic and scientific policy. European Parliament, Brussels
State Council People's Republic of China (2015) 'Made in China 2025' plan issued. May 19. http://english.www.gov.cn/policies/latest_releases/2015/05/19/content_281475110703534.htm
Vipond T (2023) Profit Margin. Corporate Finance Institute. https://corporatefinanceinstitute.com/resources/accounting/profit-margin/
Wikipedia (2023) Boeing. https://en.wikipedia.org/wiki/Boeing
Wübbeke J, Meissner M, Zenglein MJ, Ives J, Conrad B (2016) Made in China 2025: The making of a high-tech superpower and consequences for industrial countries. MERICS Papers on China 2, December. https://merics.org/sites/default/files/2020-04/Made%20in%20China%202025.pdf
Zenglein MJ, Holzmann A (2019) Evolving Made in China 2025: China's industrial policy in the quest for global tech leadership. MERICS July 2. https://merics.org/en/report/evolving-made-china-2025

Foreignness in EU Investment Screening Law

Jochem de Kok

Contents

Abstract Concerns regarding foreign direct investments (FDI) from China have played a central role in the adoption and development of the EU framework for FDI screening. The official discourse regarding these concerns initially focussed on economic interests but shifted to security following the introduction of the FDI Screening Regulation. Because the precise security threats posed by FDI were largely unspecified, there is a lack of meaningful indications in the law and the legislative history regarding the definition of security and public policy, as well as the broader objectives of the EU FDI Screening Regulation. Since its adoption, the official discourse on FDI screening has emphasised the importance of European strategic autonomy and economic security, which are used as a wide umbrella term for various industrial political interests. While the Russian invasion of Ukraine has shifted the attention to Russia, the impact of this shift is likely to be limited given the small number of Russian investments in the EU. At the same time, the EU has pursued cooperation with the United States on FDI screening, starting already during

This article is written on personal title. The views expressed in this article are those of the author and do not represent the position of any organization that the author is affiliated to.

J. de Kok (✉)
Allen & Overy LLP, Amsterdam, The Netherlands

University of Amsterdam, Amsterdam, The Netherlands
e-mail: Jochem.deKok@AllenOvery.com

J. H. Pohl et al. (eds.), *National Security and Investment Controls*,
Springer Studies in Law & Geoeconomics (2024) 3: 59–102,
https://doi.org/10.1007/17280_2024_30, Published online: 19 March 2024

the parliamentary debate and formalised by the conclusion of the EU-US Trade and Technology Council. Close cooperation with the United States is, however, hard to reconcile with the purported general objective of European strategic autonomy and the principle of non-discrimination, and risks dragging the EU into the increasingly hostile US-China rivalry.

1 Introduction

The distinction between foreign and non-foreign investors and the perception of the foreigner as a potential security threat is inherent in the legal framework for FDI screening as laid down by Regulation 2019/452, establishing a European framework for the screening of FDI in the EU (the FDI Screening Regulation).[1] Foreignness is thus a central tenet of EU foreign direct investment (FDI) screening law. The FDI Screening Regulation applies equally to different foreign investors, but in practice investments from certain jurisdictions are more likely to raise potential security or public order threat.[2] Concerns regarding Chinese investments have notably been at the forefront of the development of the EU framework for FDI screening and since the Russian invasion of Ukraine, the European Commission (Commission) has raised specific concerns with regard to Russian and Belarussian investments. At the same time, the EU and the United States have intensified transatlantic

[1]Regulation (EU) 2019/452 of the European Parliament and of the Council of 19 March 2019 establishing a framework for the screening of foreign direct investments into the Union (OJ L 79I/1).

[2]The EU FDI Screening Regulation uses the terms security and public order. The author will use these terms in this article. Instead of security, the term "public security" is sometimes used (e.g. in Article 65(1) TFEU) or "national security" (e.g. in Article 4(2) TEU). There does not appear to be any material difference or distinction between "security" and "public security". Notably, this distinction is not present in the German versions of the EU FDI Screening Regulation and Article 65(1) TFEU, which both refer to "security" (*Sicherheit).* There is a (minor) difference between "security" and "national security" (e.g. in Article 4(2) TEU), as the concept of "security" could be argued to include both "national security" and the "security of the Union". In practice, the potential distinction between "national security" and the "security of the Union" would be of limited relevance given that no interpretation of the term "security of the Union" can be imagined that would not wholly or partly overlap with the national security of one or more Member States, and vice versa. In other words, the security of the Union inevitably concerns the national security of one or more Member States, and the national security of a Member State inevitably concerns the security of the Union. Whilst the English version appears to make a distinction between "public order" (EU FDI Screening Regulation) and "public policy" (Article 65(1) TFEU), no such difference exists in the French and German versions, which both refer to public order (*l'ordre public* and *öffentlichen Ordnung*). The concept of "security of the Union" is included in Global Strategy for the EU's Foreign and Security Policy, see EEAS (2016). The distinction in between "national security" and "security of the Union" is also briefly discussed in de Kok (2019). For a comparative overview see OECD (2009).

cooperation on investment screening under the Trade and Technology Council (TCC). This raises the question to what extent EU law and official discourse on FDI screening explicitly or implicitly distinguishes between the nationality of foreign investors, and what type of particular security and public order threats are identified in respect of investments from specific jurisdictions.

Existing literature on the EU FDI Screening Regulation gives only a limited answer to these questions. Concerns regarding Chinese investments are typically placed in the context of geopolitical developments, notably the growing US-China conflict and the increase in Chinese outward investments. Chinese investments tend to be viewed as a particular challenge due to broader concerns regarding China's centrally guided economic system, single party political system, human rights, different conception of world order, different geopolitical interests, and growing Chinese geopolitical ambitions, whereby Chinese investments may be seen as a tool of economic statecraft in service of Chinese objectives.[3] Chinese investments carried out in the context of strategic policies such as the Go Out policy, Made in China 2025 or the Belt and Road Initiative are often cited examples of economic statecraft.[4]

The literature refers to a mix of security, economic and political threats emanating from Chinese investments.[5] Concerns regarding technology and innovation are a common theme, with various academics pointing to the possibility that Chinese investments could result in unreciprocated transfers of technologies and related economic activities to China,[6] and the resulting loss of the European technological edge or competitive advantage.[7] Some academics focus on ensuring a level playing field by addressing the lack of reciprocal market access, sometimes leaving open whether these concerns constitute purely economic or "economic security" concerns.[8] Whilst others point to the potential threat to European unity, notably involving risk that dependency on Chinese investments could be used to leverage those host Member States to act in line with China's ideas on political issues against broader EU consensus, such as the One-China policy or human rights.[9] These concerns relating to a "divide and conquer" strategy behind Chinese investments is

[3] See Zhang (2014); Meunier (2014a); Meunier and Nicolaidis (2019); Hooijmaaijers (2019); van Zon (2023). See, more generally Maher (2016).

[4] The Made in China 2025 strategy sets out ambitious goals for developing ten key industries for which Chinese central and local governments have announced support in the form of significant funding, subsidies and other types of support. See de Kok (2019); Meunier and Nicolaidis (2019); Hooijmaaijers (2019); Chan and Meunier (2022); van Zon (2023). See also, more generally, Reilly (2017); Christiansen and Maher (2017); Pacheco Pardo (2018); Santander and Vlassis (2021).

[5] A similar argument is made in Hindelang and Moberg (2020).

[6] In this respect, see in particular, Meunier (2014a); Chan and Meunier (2022).

[7] Christiansen and Maher (2017), pp. 124–125; Hooijmaaijers (2019); Sattorova (2023).

[8] In this respect, see in particular, Schill (2019); Hooijmaaijers (2019). See also (Meunier and Nicolaidis (2019); Hindelang and Moberg 2020) From a US perspective, see also Roberts et al. (2019).

[9] See, for instance, Meunier (2014b); Meunier and Nicolaidis (2019); Hindelang and Moberg (2020), p. 1433; Riela and Zámborský (2021), p. 68.

notably raised in the context of Chinese investments in critical infrastructures in Southern and Eastern Europe.[10] Concerns over Chinese industrial or political espionage or sabotage tend to be given less prevalent attention.

With respect to the potential threats posed by Chinese investments, literature often refers to other academic literature or think tank reports.[11] However, a comprehensive analysis of which concerns are expressed in official discourse is largely missing.[12] The FDI Screening Regulation itself does not offer a lot of guidance in terms of what particular security and public order concerns are identified in respect of investments from specific jurisdictions, or what specific type of threats screenings should address. Given the overall lack of meaningful indications in the FDI Screening Regulation, an analysis of the official discourse is important. This chapter illustrates that the extensive body of official EU policy documents, preparatory documents and speeches by Commissioners give insight into the objectives pursued under the FDI Screening Regulation, especially with respect to Chinese investments.

This chapter aims to contribute to existing scholarship by providing a detailed analysis of the EU law and official discourse on the treatment of investments from specific jurisdictions under the FDI Screening Regulation, with a notable focus on the objectives of the screening of Chinese, Russian and US investments. Where relevant, the chapter will contextualise these developments in the broader economic or political context. Given the lack of definitions and objectives stated in the EU FDI Screening Regulation itself, an in-depth review of the discourse regarding the FDI Screening Regulation is important to provide a better understanding of *official* EU policy under the FDI Screening Regulation, as opposed to the myriad concerns considered in academic literature and by think tanks. This chapter also challenges the common presumption that the FDI Screening Regulation necessarily aims to address "security" challenges. The development of the official EU discourse rather shows that economic objectives have been securitised, blurring the boundaries between the economic and security objectives. Over time, the objective pursued under the EU FDI Screening Regulation have also shifted towards broad considerations such as the protection of European strategic autonomy. This chapter also questions the intensification of cooperation with the United States from the perspective of consistency in terms of the quest for strategic autonomy and posits that official discourse risks resulting in a discriminatory application of investment screening rules.

This chapter is predominantly based on a legal historic research methodology (the history being a recent one), concluding with a normative assessment. The author has reviewed all identifiable public official EU level documents and speeches relating to

---

[10] In particular, Chinese investments in Greece (notably the investment in and expansion of the port of Piraeus), Hungary (notably. the construction of the Budapest-Belgrade rail link) and Croatia (notably construction of the Pelješac Bridge). For an illustrative example, see Reilly (2017).

[11] See, for instance, Casarini (2015); Garcia-Herrero and Xu (2017); Seaman et al. (2017); Godement and Vasselier (2017); Hanemann and Huotari (2018); Bickenbach and Liu (2018).

[12] With the exception of the published bachelor thesis of Talisha Schilder who focusses on the securitisation of these concerns, see Schilder (2022). See also Rogelja and Tsimonis (2020) and Sattorova (2023), who do discuss the discourse with a relatively high level of detail.

the EU FDI Screening Regulation for guidance on its objectives or screenings of investments from specific jurisdictions between 2008 and June 2023. Relevant sources notably include preparatory documents relating to the adoption of EU FDI Screening Regulation,[13] official EU documents such as Commission Communications and Staff Working Documents, and speeches by Commissioners relating to FDI screening. The concluding section offers a normative assessment of the official European discourse and the developments surrounding the screening of FDI under the EU FDI Screening Regulation. This normative assessment is based on the internal consistency and coherence of the law and discourse.

The chapter is structured as follows. The article will first provide doctrinal analysis of the regulation of foreignness under the EU FDI Screening Regulation. The following sections will provide an overview of the official debates and statements in response to growing Chinese investments preceding the proposal for the EU FDI Screening Regulation, with notable concerned calls for additional restrictions on the basis of economic considerations. The article will show that these economic concerns were securitised following the announcement of the proposed EU FDI Screening Regulation. After the adoption of the FDI Screening Regulation, the attention has shifted from undefined security concerns to strategic autonomy, notably from China, as the EU has simultaneously intensified the transatlantic cooperation in the area of investment screening. The article concludes with a normative assessment, with a call for the development of the regulatory framework for FDI screening to ensure a non-discriminatory application of the FDI screening rules so that only transactions that can reasonably pose a threat to security or public order are made subject to a filing obligation and are assessed on the basis of clearly defined substantive criteria.

2 Foreignness Under the FDI Screening Regulation

Investment screening law makes a distinction between foreign and non-foreign investors. The scope of application of the EU FDI Screening Regulation is specifically limited to "*foreign direct investments*", i.e. investments by "*foreign investors*" that aim to establish or maintain "*lasting and direct links*" between the foreign investor and the target company in order to carry on an economic activity, including

[13]Preparatory documents are "*Documents used to prepare EU legislation, produced during the various stages of the legislative and budgetary process.*" Main document types are Commission legislative proposals, Council common positions, European Parliament legislative and budgetary resolutions and initiatives, European Economic and Social Committee opinions, Committee of the Regions opinions. The author has also viewed the publicly available presentation of the proposal for the EU FDI Screening Regulation before the European Parliament's Committee on International trade. See EUR-Lex (2022).

investments which "*enable effective participation in the management or control of a company carrying out economic activity.*"[14]

A "foreign investor" under EU law means a natural person or undertaking from a third country.[15] The EU FDI Screening Regulation may also apply to indirect investments by foreign investors via EU companies, such as holding or bidding companies.[16] According to Article 54 and case law of the Court of Justice, the status of being an EU company (i.e. the nationality of a company) is based on the location of the corporate seat and the legal order where the company is incorporated, and not on the nationality of the shareholders.[17] Thus, a company that is incorporated in the EU, but is solely owned by foreign shareholders, has the status of being an EU company. With the aim of preventing circumvention, the EU FDI Screening Regulation also applies to investments carried out via EU entities that are ultimately owned or controlled by a natural person or company from a third country.[18] The Commission encourages the Member States to assess whether a "*scheme of circumvention*" is set up with the objective result of avoiding the application of the FDI Screening Regulation, for instance by setting up a European holding company for the purpose of the proposed transaction.[19] Given that it is standard practice in international M&A transactions to set up new holding companies for the purposes of a proposed transaction, qualifying such a structure as a "*scheme of circumvention*" is somewhat disingenuous and feeds into the image of the security or public order threat posed by insidiously scheming foreigners.

The EU FDI Screening Mechanism does not bind Member States to the European definition of "foreign". Member States may thus also subject intra-EU investments to screenings. Under the different screening mechanisms of the Member States,

---

[14]EU FDI Screening Regulation, art. 2(1).

[15]EU FDI Screening Regulation, art. 2(2).

[16]See for further detail Case C-106/22 *Xella Magyarország Építőanyagipari Kft. v Innovációs és Technológiai Miniszter* ECLI:EU:C:2023:568. Various amendments to the EU FDI Screening Regulation have been proposed under the revised Regulation on the screening of foreign investments, which was published on 24 January 2024.

[17]TFEU, art. 54 and Case C-80/12 *Felixstowe Dock and Railway Company Ltd and others v HM Revenue & Customs* ECLI:EU:C:2014:200. See also response to question 12 in Commission (2021a).

[18]FDI Screening Regulation, art. 3(6), provides that: "*Member States which have a screening mechanism in place shall maintain, amend or adopt measures necessary to identify and prevent circumvention of the screening mechanisms and screening decisions.*" Recital 10 provides that the anti-circumvention measures by the Member States "*should cover investments from within the Union by means of artificial arrangements that do not reflect economic reality and circumvent the screening mechanisms and screening decisions, where the investor is ultimately owned or controlled by a natural person or an undertaking of a third country.*" In the abovementioned 'frequently asked questions' document, the Commission notes that "*Investments by EU entities may nevertheless come within the scope of the Regulation when they fall under the anti-circumvention clause.*"

[19]Commission (2021a). In this respect, the "*objective capability of the arrangements to avoid the rules*" in case of a "*lack of economic activity of the investor company*" is sufficient to create a presumption that the arrangement is artificial.

"foreign investor" can mean non-national,[20] non-EEA,[21] or non-OECD,[22] or a combination of those. For instance, in Germany a foreign investor in the defence sector is any non-German investor, while foreign investors in investments in critical infrastructures are non-EU investors.[23] In Denmark, the mandatory filing regime for investments in certain particularly sensitive sectors and activities applies to all non-Danish investors, whilst the additional call-in regime for investments any other sector or activity applies to only to investors from outside the EU/EFTA.[24] Some Member States, such as the Netherlands, have attempted to avoid a distinction on the basis of foreignness by expanding the scope of application of screening regulations to all investors, including nationals.[25] However, the nationality of the foreign investor remains relevant under the Dutch regime, as the screening should for instance take into account whether the investor is established in a country that has offensive programmes aimed at acquiring sensitive technologies in order to obtain a technological or strategic position of power, or aimed at affecting the integrity, security, safety or availability of critical processes.[26] The distinction between nationals and the foreigner is thus inherent in investment screening law.

The EU FDI Screening Regulation in particular addresses concerns with respect to state-owned, -controlled or -funded foreign investors, or investors that are seen as pursuing foreign state policies. Notably, the Member States and the Commission may take into account "*whether the foreign investor is directly or indirectly controlled by the government, including state bodies or armed forces, of a third country, including through ownership structure or significant funding*."[27] As will be discussed in further detail below, the reference to "ownership structure" or "significant funding" is a reference to the concerns regarding Chinese investments. Similarly, recital 13 of the FDI Screening Regulation furthermore provides that the "*context and circumstances of the foreign investment*" should be taken into account, including whether the investor is "*pursuing State-led outward projects or programmes*." The reference to "*State-led outward projects or programmes*" was included in response to concerns regarding the Made in China 2025 strategy and the Belt and Road Initiative. The EU FDI Screening Regulation thus contains only two

[20]This is the case, for instance, in France. See Monetary and Financial Code (*Code monétaire et financier*), art R. 151-1. In Hungary, the temporary regime has extended the scope of the FDI regime to all foreigners as well. Tóth (2022).

[21]This is the case, for instance, in Austria. Weiss and Schulz (2022).

[22]This is the case, for instance, in Poland. Pietrasik and Michalski (2022).

[23]Cotta et al. (2022).

[24]Fabricius (2022).

[25]For a detailed discussion on the framework of investment screening in the Netherlands, see de Kok (2021).

[26]Furthermore, the screening should consider whether there is a sufficient and transparent separation of civil and military research and development programmes in the host country, see the Dutch Act on the security screening of investments, mergers and acquisitions (*Wet veiligheidstoets investeringen, fusies en overnames*), art. 19–21.

[27]EU FDI Screening Regulation, art. 4(2)(a).

implicit references to Chinese investors, despite investments from China playing a central role in the adoption process.

3 Rise of Chinese Investments

The first discussions relating to a European security review mechanism concerned the regulation of investments by Middle Eastern sovereign wealth funds (SWFs) in 2008. At the time, there were increasing concerns that a growing number of investments by SWFs in the EU could interfere with the normal functioning of market economies. Whilst various suggestions had emerged that the EU should adopt an investment screening mechanism, the Commission rejected such suggestions, noting that they would "*run the risk of sending a misleading signal – that the EU is stepping back from its commitment to an open investment regime. They would also be difficult to reconcile with EU law and international obligations.*"[28] The Commission instead proposed to promote a cooperative effort at the international level to establish a set of principles to ensure the transparency, predictability and accountability of SWF investments,[29] noting that Member States already had the ability to review investments on the basis of national security and public policy. The Council affirmed the Commission's approach to SWFs, but noted that "*if international negotiations were not to develop satisfactorily, further action should be considered at the EU level.*"[30]

The discussions on the need for greater scrutiny over foreign investments reignited following the emergence of China as a major source of investment in the early 2010s. One of the first instances of such calls arising on the official level was the letter by Commissioners Antonio Tajani and Michel Barnier to President Barroso, calling for the creation of a European high-level board with powers to reject non-EU investments in February 2011, modelled on CFIUS.[31] The Commissioners also considered that the review should extend beyond mere security considerations to include interventions "*on behalf of European industrial*

[28]Commission (2008).

[29]In this respect, see for instance Sovereign Wealth Funds: Generally Accepted Principles and Practices "Santiago Principles." International Working Group on Sovereign Wealth Funds. For a critical note see Bismuth (2017).

[30]Council (2008). Similarly, the OECD welcomed the constructive contribution that SWFs make to the economic development of the home and host countries, and have been reliable long-term, commercially-driven investors and a force for global financial stability. The OECD recognised that legitimate national security concerns could arise where SWF investments were motivated by political rather than commercial objectives. However, the OECD countries called upon recipient countries not to erect protectionist barriers to foreign investments, should not discriminate among investors in like circumstances, and should safeguard national security concerns in a transparent, predictable, proportional and accountable manner. Council at Ministerial Level (2008).

[31]Commission (2011).

competitiveness".[32] In that respect Vice-President Antonio Tajani noted that he is "*highly favourable to non-EU investments in Europe, but I do not want to mask attempts to close down businesses after having stolen all of their 'know-how'*".[33] One year later, the European Parliament followed suit, requesting the Commission and Member States "*to set up a body entrusted with the ex ante evaluation of foreign strategic investment, along the lines of the Committee on Foreign Investment in the United States (CFIUS), in order to obtain a clear picture of businesses operating and investing in the territory of the EU, and to report to the parliament on a regular basis*".[34]

The (failed) acquisition of the Dutch company Draka, a market leader in cable systems for the energy and telecoms sectors, by China-based Xinmao appears to have been the direct cause of the abovementioned call by Tajani and Barnier, and the European Parliament. The bid by the unknown Chinese company prompted various media outlets to run stories on its founder and CEO, Mr Du Kerong, casting doubt in particular over his military background and the apparent close connections between Xinmao and the Chinese military.[35] Antonio Tajani raised alarm about the Chinese investments being a "*a camouflage to bring know-how to China*" and that Europe should "*support our know-how*".[36] In response to questions by the Dutch Parliament, the former Dutch Minister of Economic Affairs, Maxime Verhagen, however, strongly defended a policy of non-intervention as foreign investments bring in knowledge, skills and technology and result in a dynamic economy.[37] Whilst investments could result in a transfer of know-how to foreign countries, the former Minister considered that the objective to obtain technologies and research capacities is a legitimate objective in international M&A, not just for Chinese enterprises.[38] Furthermore, the transaction was to be funded by China Minsheng Bank, a privately owned bank that is listed on the Hong Kong stock exchange, and according to the Minister, there were no reason to suspect that the transaction was based on more than just commercial reasons. In the end, Xinmao withdrew its offer. Whilst the stated reason that it was unable to raise sufficient funds to finance the deal, the backlash in the media may played an important part in this decision.[39] It is perhaps no coincidence that the FDI Screening Regulation was (many years later) adopted under Antonio Tajani's presidency of the European Parliament.

---

[32] Ibid.

[33] Ibid.

[34] European Parliament (2012).

[35] Peverelli and Song (2012).

[36] Chee (2010). Italy's former Minister of Industry, Paolo Romani, made a similar call for Draka to remain in European hands.

[37] Tweede Kamer (2010a, b).

[38] Ibid.

[39] This is, at least, argued by Peverelli and Song (2012), p. 5. Prysmian, the ultimate purchaser of Draka, argued that Xinmao did not have the funding, that no bank would have been willing to fund the EUR 1 billion bid, plus additional refinancing of EUR 500 to 600 million of debt. Mesters (2011).

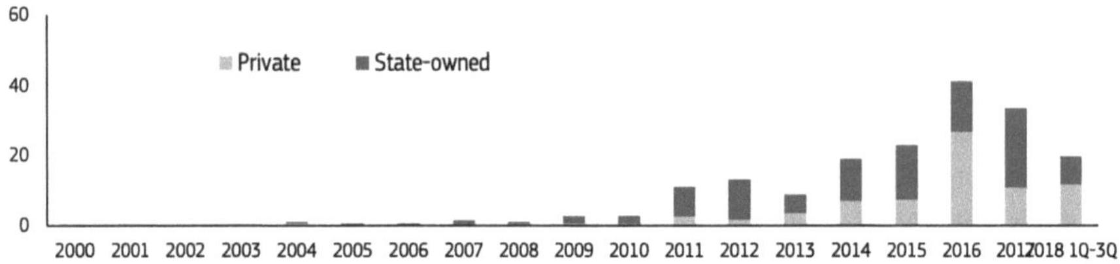

Fig. 1 Chinese FDI Transactions in the EU by Type, 2000–2018 Q3, in million US [Commission (2019a). Based on Rhodium Group data]

Concerns regarding Chinese investments intensified following the sharp increase in investments following the European monetary and financial crisis, with a sharp particularly sharp increase in Southern Europe. Over the course of the crisis, the share of Chinese FDI in southern Member States increased from 8% of total Chinese FDI in the EU in 2009–2011 to 33% in 2012–2014.[40] These Chinese investments were often made in various privatised state-owned companies in South European energy and transportation sectors.[41] These privatisations were among the main objectives of reform programmes, many of which were under the guise of the Troika of the Commission, the ECB and the IMF.[42] These privatisations were predominantly required to raise liquidity, but also partly justified by the alleged benefits of private ownership. The ironic effect of 'privatisation', however, was a transfer of public ownership from European Member States to Chinese state-owned enterprises (Fig. 1).[43]

In Greece, famous examples of a transfer of privatised companies to Chinese state-owned companies were the privatisation of the Athens port Piraeus to COSCO and the acquisition of a 24% interest in Greece national electricity distributor ADMIE by State Grid Corporation of China (SGCC) in 2016. In Portugal, 45% of the total privatised assets were purchased by Chinese investors, including the purchase of a 21% interest in the electricity producer Energias de Portugal by Three Gorges Corporation and an acquisition of a 25% interest in the gas and electricity transmission company, REN by SGCC.[44] These investments made Portugal the largest recipient of Chinese investments following the UK, Germany and France in the period between 2000 and 2014. In Italy, privatisations in the context privatisation programme to reduce national debt also resulted in investments in the

[40]Namely, in Portugal, Italy, Greece, Spain, Cyprus as well as Ireland. Baker & McKenzie et al. (2015); Corre (2018).

[41]Baker & McKenzie et al. (2015); Vila and Peters (2016).

[42]Papadopoulos (2015), p. 14; Papadopoulos (2018).

[43]This is referred to as the "*privatisation paradox*" by Vila and Peters (2016), p. 20.

[44]REN holds the concession for Portugal's two main energy infrastructure networks, the National Electricity Transmission Grid (RNT) and the National Natural Gas Transportation Grid (RNTGN). Baker & McKenzie et al. (2015); Chan and Meunier (2022).

	2007	2008	2009	2010	2011	2012	2013	2014	2015	2016	2017	*Total (2007-2017)*
EFTA	7	10	8	16	10	9	5	4	12	8	10	*99*
China, HK and Macao	0	3	0	1	6	5	5	8	6	17	9	*60*
GCC	1	1	1	1	6	7	16	17	17	7	6	*80*
Russian Federation	4	4	9	10	12	10	17	8	9	7	3	*93*
Dev. Asia	0	2	2	1	1	2	1	1	0	1	3	*14*
RoW	2	1	1	0	1	2	3	1	3	6	2	*22*
Central and South America	0	0	0	0	1	0	1	1	3	3	1	*10*
USA and CAN	1	0	1	1	0	0	0	0	1	0	0	*4*
India	0	0	1	0	0	0	0	1	0	1	0	*3*
Total	*15*	*21*	*23*	*30*	*37*	*35*	*48*	*41*	*51*	*50*	*34*	*385*

Source: EC-JRC Foreign Ownership Database

Fig. 2 M&A in the EU by public authorities, states and governments (typically via SOEs or SWFs) [Commission (2019a), p. 57]

energy sector, such as the acquisition of a 35% interest in CDP Reti by SGCC also,[45] and the acquisition of a 40% interest in Italy's power engineering company Ansaldo Energia by partially state-owned Shanghai Electric.[46] Concerns were raised as to the potential industrial policy objectives of the Chinese investments, notably under the Belt and Road Initiative that launched in 2013. The data on number of M&A transactions by foreign governments (usually via SOEs) in the period of 2007–2017 shows a clear increase in Chinese governmental controlled investments following the crisis, as well as from the Gulf Cooperation Countries (GCC) (Fig. 2).[47]

The Commission initially defended these investments. According to former Commissioner Karel De Gucht, Chinese investments were important because southern European Member States "*need[ed] investors to buy what they [were] selling.*"[48] In his speech on *Chinese Investments in Europe*, De Gucht stressed that foreign investments benefit the economy in many ways and warned that "*we cannot accept – in Europe or elsewhere – that national security concerns are used as a false pretence to justify the protection of vested economic interests.*"[49] According to the Commissioner, Member States already had sufficient mechanisms in place to screen

[45]CDP Reti owns approximately 30% of the Italian energy companies SNAM (Natural gas infrastructure company) and TERNA (Electricity transmission systems operator).

[46]Baker & McKenzie et al. (2015); Chan and Meunier (2022).

[47]In this report, published on the same day as the announcement of the proposal for the EU FDI Screening Regulation, the Commission notes that "*All Chinese acquisitions could be considered linked to the Chinese government since (1) investments are usually authorised by the government and targeted to specific sectors (e.g. those covering the China 2025 strategy), (2) investments generally involve loans given by Chinese banks (most of them directly controlled by the government). The same argument could be applied for Russian federation and for Gulf countries.*" Commission (2019a).

[48]De Gucht (2012).

[49]Ibid.

investments on the basis of national security, warning that concerns were often aimed at the protection of "*vested economic interests*" and that the national security exception should not be used by Member States to protect such interests. Instead, these mechanisms must be applied narrowly and transparently. Whilst Karel De Gucht considered that "*a more strategic overview of this at the European level could be useful [. . .] a full European screening of new investments is neither desirable nor feasible in my view.*"[50]

Former Commissioner Malmström responded in a similar fashion to questions by then MEP Marielle de Sarnez on whether the Commission envisaged establishing an investment assessment body following a "*dramatic increase in Chinese direct investment in Europe between 2010 and 2012*".[51] Former Commissioner Malmström stressed that whilst the increase seems impressive, Chinese investments represented less than 1% of the total inbound FDI and that Member States already have mechanisms to screen investments. The Commissioner considered that the EU is a major beneficiary of the open world economic system and is committed to ensuring that markets remain open.

The consideration that Chinese investments represented merely 1.1% of all non-EU M&A in the EU was, however, an incomplete reflection of the nature of these investments. At that time, the relatively modest number of Chinese M&A represented 5.3% of the value of inbound FDI and involved controlling investments in various key European companies in the area of critical infrastructure and technology. By the year 2016, approximately 9.5% of non-EU controlled EU companies were controlled by investors from China, Hong Kong and Macao, representing 28.000 companies with a value of EUR 160 billion, amounting to 3.0% of the total asset value of non-EU controlled EU companies (Fig. 3).[52]

The increase of "state-led, strategic direct investments by non-EU investors in European key enabling technology companies, as well as issues around the reciprocity of investment conditions" led the ministers of economy of Germany, France and Italy to send two joint letters to the Commission.[53] The Ministers considered that there was a lack of a level playing field and threat to the "fair market-based environment", as European companies were acquired as part of strategic industrial policies—often with support of state subsidies—whilst other countries put up hurdles for European investors.[54] Germany, France and Italy therefore called for "additional protection based on economic criteria, taking into account and with reference to the Commission's expertise."[55] These Member States considered that

[50]Ibid. De Gucht concluded by noting that an EU-China investment agreement could address this debate, and could reinforce legal certainty and transparency about the way foreign investments may be screened.

[51]European Parliament (2015).

[52]Commission (2019a), p. 11.

[53]Germany, Italy and France (2017a); Germany, Italy and France (2017b).

[54]Germany, Italy and France (2017a).

[55]Ibid.

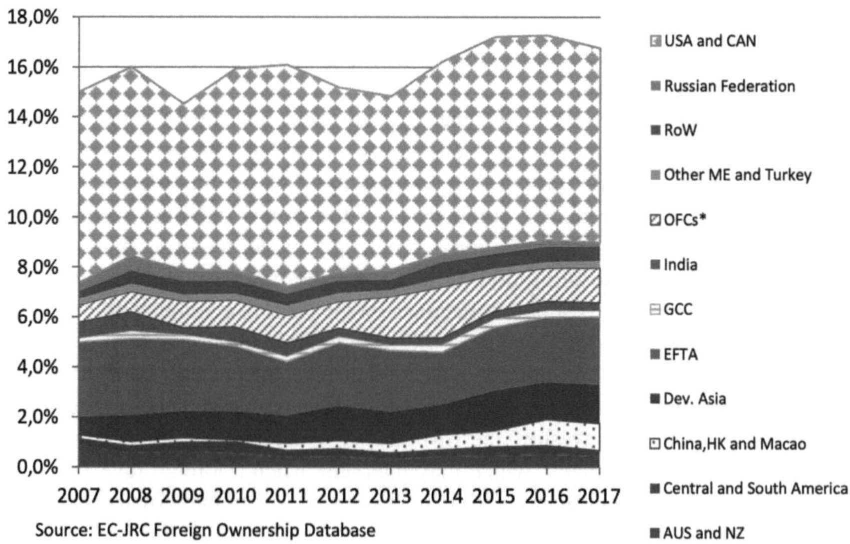

Fig. 3 Non-EU share of the number of M&A deals by origin (2007–2017) [Commission (2019a), p. 15]

an intervention is justified where the investment "does not comply with market rules (e.g. through investment instructions; through state-funded takeovers based on political programmes; through the requirement for state approval of investments)" or where an investment is subsidised and "results in a market disturbance".[56]

This call, which was clearly directed at Chinese investments,[57] followed a series of high-profile acquisitions of technology companies by Chinese investors, especially in Germany, such as the acquisition of the robotics manufacturer Kuka by Midea, a Chinese listed company, and semiconductor equipment supplier Aixtron by a consortium of Chinese investors.[58] Former Commissioner Günther Oettinger had urged European companies to make a counter offer for the strategically important company Kuka.[59] However, even though the sale of Kuka resulted in strong public concerns, the German government ultimately approved the transaction as it saw no grounds for intervention on the basis of national security.[60] In the United States, on the other hand, President Barack Obama required that Kuka divest its US subsidiary engaged in defence-related activities after a review by CFIUS. In the same year, after the United States had provided the German government with "*previously unknown security-related information*" the German authorities withdrew their earlier

[56] Ibid.

[57] See, similarly, Casarini (2022), p. 96; Sattorova (2023), p.704; Hoffmeister (2023), p.678.

[58] For case studies see Popławski (2017); Stanzel (2017); Hooijmaaijers (2019).

[59] Knop and Mihm (2016).

[60] Reuters Staff (2016a).

clearance for the proposed takeover of Aixtron, which had been blocked as well by the US President.[61] The Chinese investors subsequently withdrew their bid, and the transaction was abandoned.[62]

The European Parliament joined the discussion on investment screening and adopted a Proposal for a Union Act on "*the Screening of Foreign Investment in Strategic Sectors*".[63] This Proposal supported the call by the Member States, recognising the Member States' competence in the area of national security and public order and calling for additional protection based on economic criteria, reciprocity and foreign subsidisation. In particular, the European Parliament called for (i) the expansion of investment screenings on the basis of economic criteria with reference to the Commission's expertise, (ii) the adoption of a principle of reciprocity in EU investment policy, under which foreign investments may be restricted if similar investment opportunities are not offered to European companies in the home country of the potential investor, and (iii) the establishment of a "European Committee on Foreign Investment" which may intervene when a foreign investment in strategic sectors does not comply with market rules or is facilitated by foreign state subsidies.

Shortly after, the Commission announced in the *Reflection Paper on Harnessing Globalisation* that additional analysis and appropriate action had to be undertaken to address concerns "*about foreign investors, notably state-owned enterprises, taking over European companies with key technologies for strategic reasons.*"[64] Reflecting concerns regarding reciprocity, it considered that the EU "*should act to restore a level playing field*".[65]

4 Securitisation of Chinese Investments under the Proposal

In 2017, the proposal for the EU FDI Screening Regulation redirected concerns regarding Chinese investments from economic considerations and reciprocity to the security threats posed by these investments to the EU and its Member States. Thus, rather than tackle the issue through additional protection on "*economic criteria*", as had been proposed by Germany, France and Italy and the European Parliament, the Commission decided to tackle concerns over Chinese investments as a security threat. The Commission's proposal for an FDI screening regime based on security

[61] Reuters Staff (2016b); Obama (2016).

[62] Sheahan (2016).

[63] European Parliament (2017). See also Grieger (2019).

[64] Commission (2017a). See also European Political Strategy Centre (EPSC) (2016). As cited in (Valero (2017).

[65] The Reflection Paper on Harnessing Globalisation was welcomed by the European Council, which confirmed the need to fully respect Member States' competences. The topic of reciprocity also featured in a speech by the former Trade Commissioner Celia Malmström. Malmström (2017); European Council (2017).

and public policy considerations constituted a significant shift in the discourse on Chinese investments in the EU and a "securitization" of what had previously been viewed as a technical or political issue.[66]

Barry Buzan, Ole Wæver and Jaap de Wilde describe securitization as a process which takes an issue beyond the established rules by framing it as either a special kind of politics or above politics.[67] Through securitization, "*the issue is presented as an existential threat, requiring emergency measures and justifying actions outside the normal bounds of political procedure*".[68] A key insight from securitization theory is that securitization does not necessarily reflect an objective reality, but reflects a social process whereby speech acts transform normal politics into a security concern.[69] The transformation of the concerns regarding Chinese or other foreign investments into an existential threat to Europe's security is an example of such securitization.[70]

In the context of the legislative process, the Commission and European Parliament were careful in avoiding referring to China by name. References to China were often implicit, but taken as a whole it is evident from preparatory documents and speeches that the EU FDI Screening Regulation in particular aimed to address concerns relating to investments from China, especially by state-owned enterprises.[71] The precise security concerns relating to these Chinese investments were, however, never specified in any detail. Illustrative of this is the announcement of the proposed EU FDI Screening Regulation by former President Jean-Claude Juncker during the 2017 State of the Union, where he stated:

> Let me say once and for all: we are not naïve free traders. Europe must always defend its strategic interests. This is why today we are proposing a new EU framework for investment screening. If a foreign, state-owned, company wants to purchase a European harbour, part of our energy infrastructure or a defence technology firm, this should only happen in transparency, with scrutiny and debate. It is a political responsibility to know what is going on in our own backyard so that we can protect our collective security if needed.[72]

The references to investments harbours and energy infrastructure are a clear reference to the significant number of Chinese investments in Southern Europe, including in the Athens port of Piraeus and various energy infrastructure companies. Juncker's speech depicts investments by (Chinese) state-owned companies in European infrastructure as having been carried out without transparency, scrutiny or without

[66]See, similarly, Sattorova (2022), p. 5.

[67]Buzan et al. (1998), p. 23.

[68]Buzan et al. (1998), p. 24. See, similarly, Vidigal and Schill (2021).

[69]Buzan et al. (1998); Lai (2021).

[70]See also Schilder (2022).

[71]Preparatory documents are "*Documents used to prepare EU legislation, produced during the various stages of the legislative and budgetary process.*" Main document types are Commission legislative proposals, Council common positions, European Parliament legislative and budgetary resolutions and initiatives, European Economic and Social Committee opinions, Committee of the Regions opinions. See EUR-Lex.

[72]Juncker (2017).

debate, involving insidious aims that we must not be "naïve" about. As mentioned above, however, sale of the port of Piraeus and energy infrastructure companies in Southern Europe to Chinese SOEs occurred due to privatisations effectively imposed by the Troika. These investments thus occurred under the Commission's watch. The implication that "we" did not know what went on in "*our own backyard*" is therefore both incorrect and illustrates a paternalistic way of viewing countries like Greece, Portugal and Italy as the EU's backyard, implying a lack of agency and transparency by "the Southerners".[73] The speech also mentions "defence technology firms", even though concerns—at least based on public information—predominantly related to acquisitions of industrial and technology companies by private Chinese enterprises such as Draka (cables), Kuka (robotics), Aixtron (semiconductors) and Leifeld (engineering), which develop important technologies but are in themselves not defence companies. By emphasizing the "defence" related activities of these companies, the speech provided for a justification to shift the discourse from the abovementioned calls by Member States for screening based on additional economic criteria, to a discourse based on security and public order concerns. Juncker furthermore does not give any insights about the ways these investments threaten security and his reference to "collective security" is also noteworthy, given that this term was absent from the proposed or the adopted EU FDI Screening Regulation.

Similarly, the Explanatory Memorandum to the Commission's legislative proposal for the FDI Screening Regulation provided that "*Recently, a series of takeovers of European companies involved foreign investors with strong ties to their home governments which strategy focus on the purchase of European companies that develop technologies or maintain infrastructures that are essential to perform critical functions in society and the economy.*"[74] With respect to the risks that such investments pose, the Explanatory Memorandum only referred to the general concept that "*such investment could be detrimental to security and public order of the Union or its Member States.*" The Explanatory Memorandum considered that the combination of increasing number of strategic investments by foreign investors with strong ties with foreign governments, and the potential security impact of such investments, has "*triggered concerns of European citizens, companies and Member States.*"[75] The Explanatory Memorandum, however, failed to specify the precise nature of these concerns and how they relate to security or public order.

The Commission Staff Working Document accompanying the proposal for the EU FDI Screening Regulation, and the Communication on *Welcoming Foreign Direct Investment while Protecting Essential Interests* similarly paid particular attention to state-owned or controlled investments, without specifying what threat to security or public policy emanates from such investments. The Commission considered that conditions or a prohibition may in particular be required "*where foreign investors – especially but not only when they are state owned or controlled,*

[73] See in similar vein, Schilder (2022).

[74] Commission (2017b).

[75] Ibid.

including through financing or other means of direction – may seek to acquire control of or influence in European undertakings whose activities have repercussions on critical technologies, infrastructure, inputs or sensitive information."[76] In such cases, the Commission considered that these transactions are not only to the detriment of the "*EU's technological edge but also its security and public order.*"[77] The Staff Working Document furthermore makes a distinction between threats to security or public order and "*concerns regarding industrial policy*".[78] However, the Commission does not clarify the differences between the norm of avoiding security "*repercussions on critical technologies*" and avoiding repercussions on the "*EU's technological edge*", nor to what extent "*industrial policy*" may play a role in determining potential security threats. The Commission additionally recognised that most screening mechanisms go beyond the defence sector and are not "*limited to the protection of essential interest of national security, especially production of or trade in arms, munitions, military equipment, war material, etc.*".[79] The FDI Screening Regulation itself broadly provides that Commission and Member States may, in determining whether the FDI is likely to affect security or public order, consider potential effects of the investment on critical technologies, "*including artificial intelligence, robotics, semiconductors, cybersecurity, aerospace, defence, energy storage, quantum and nuclear technologies as well as nanotechnologies and biotechnologies*".[80] The consequence is a lack of meaningful indications in either the law or the legislative history that allow for a delineation between security and public policy interests and economic interests, and to what extent state-ownership or control gives rise to a threat to security or the public order.

The references to China became more explicit in the hearing on the proposal by the European Parliament's Committee on International Trade. In introducing the bill, the Chairman of the Committee on International Trade, Bernd Lange, noted that "*everybody is aware about the fact that in the last year we had a lot of foreign direct investment in the EU, in particular from one big Asian country. I think about three hundred companies were bought by companies and state-owned companies from this country and this was the reason for a stronger discussion about investment screening inside the European Union.*"[81] The former Commissioner Malmström was invited to explain the proposal before the Committee.[82] The Commissioner started her speech by referring to a Chinese proverb and linking this proverb to the need to protect security.[83] Reciting Chinese proverbs is not the usual way for a

---

[76] Commission (2017c). See similarly, Commission (2017d).

[77] Commission (2017c); Commission (2017d).

[78] Commission (2017c), p. 6.

[79] Commission (2019a).

[80] FDI Screening Regulation, art. 4(1)(b).

[81] Committee on International Trade (2018).

[82] Ibid.

[83] Ibid. "*There is a Chinese proverb saying that the best time to plant a tree was twenty years ago, but the second-best time is now. So, public order and security is not about being right one day. It is about being right all the time from day one.*"

Commissioner to introduce legislative proposals before the European Parliament, and can be seen as a clear way to prime the listeners to the central concern being China. In sketching out the context, the Commissioner referred to the rise of state-controlled or supported investments in strategic companies, while major barriers to investments exist in those jurisdictions. These countries pursue their own interests, and "*these interests are sometimes compatible with ours, but not always*."[84] In clear reference to China, the Commissioner warned that "*new powerful players are emerging, not always having the same standards, not always having the same rules, not always playing fair, and some openly use investments to access technologies, infrastructure and information*."[85] She warned that for one Member State to hand energy infrastructure over to a foreign investor without considering the impact on its neighbours or the Union as a whole can be dangerous.[86] The Commissioner concluded with an implicit reference to COSCO's investments in Piraeus by concluding: "*As I started with a Chinese proverb, I will end with a Greek one, saying that: "a society grows great when old men plant trees whose shade they know they shall never sit in". In this case, things are more urgent than it might suggest in the proverb*."[87]

In the same meeting the former Chairman of CFIUS, Aimen Mir, was present to share reflections on the proposal on behalf of CFIUS.[88] The presence of a senior US governmental official was notable given that the proposal was (ostensibly) neutral in nature. Given that at the time of the proposal, 46% of the M&A transactions originated from the United States and Canada, as opposed to 6.5% from China, Hong Kong and Macao, the FDI Screening Regulation would subject a relatively large number of US-originated transactions to additional scrutiny.[89] The reflections of Aimen Mir on behalf of the US government, however, stressed a common interest, underscoring the new challenges brought on by the increasing number of state-directed investments aimed at achieving "*government objectives*", particularly in advanced technologies, manufacturing and infrastructure. Aimen Mir stressed that the security of US allies reinforces the security of the United States, because the "*loss of advanced capabilities in Europe may have a direct consequence not just for European security, but also for US security*."[90] Thus, rather than seeing FDI screening in Europe as a potential risk to US investments, the US representative expressed the hope that this new regime would in fact "*reinforce the deep and open economic relationship, as well as the strong security relationship that we have with you*".[91]

---

[84] Ibid.

[85] Ibid.

[86] Ibid, at 14:37:30.

[87] Ibid.

[88] Ibid, at 14:45:10.

[89] Commission (2017d), pp. 11–12.

[90] Committee on International Trade (2018), at 14:53:36.

[91] Ibid, at 14:54:10.

The European Economic and Social Committee (EESC) was also explicit regarding the focus on China. The EESC specifically refers to the *Made in China 2025* strategy, noting that Chinese investments in the EU "*increased tenfold!*", and warning that additional Chinese takeovers in these strategic sectors "*are to be expected*".[92] The EESC did not specify the concerns with respect to Chinese investments, other than that these are increasingly focused on strategically selected sectors, by companies that are larger than average and increasingly by state companies or investors with close ties to governments.[93] The EESC considered that there are FDI concerns "*with regard to more countries than just China*", pointing out that Russia's investments in the energy sector are raising concerns as well due to potential dependencies in this strategic sector.[94] The EESC considered the calls for instruments to protect security, industrial policy and reciprocity, noting that the Commission decided to limit the proposal to security and public order "*so as to reach a minimum level of agreement between the Member States.*"[95] However, the EESC warned that "*The definition of 'security' and 'public order' alone are not clear enough to avoid problems and differing interpretations*".[96]

To the contrary, the European Parliament's Committee on International Trade considered the lack of definition of security and public order as positive. According to the report on the proposal, prepared by rapporteur MEP Franck Proust, it was difficult to define the key concepts under the FDI Screening Regulation in a way that left leeway for a flexible adaption to different situations.[97] Therefore, the Committee considered it unwise to define concepts such as security and public order, sensitive and/or strategic or the link between the foreign investment and security and public order by means of precise definitions, "*because this would mean that the mechanism would no longer be viable on a case-by-case basis and be subject to too many constraints.*"[98] With respect to state investments, the Committee on International Trade considered that not only state control is relevant, but that the decision-making should also take into account "*the context and the conditions under which the investment is taking or has taken place, including the level of openness of the sector in the country of origin of the foreign investment.*"[99] The FDI Screening Regulation was adopted on 19 March 2019, 14 months after the introduction of the proposal, and just a single reading by the European Parliament and Council.

In the same month as the adoption of the FDI Screening Regulation, the Commission issued its *EU-China – A strategic outlook*, in which China was qualified as a key global actor and leading technological power. In different policy areas, the

[92] European Economic and Social Committee (2017), para 2.2.

[93] Ibid, para. 2.11.

[94] Ibid, para. 2.31.

[95] Ibid, para 2.7.

[96] Ibid, para 2.7.

[97] European Parliament (2018), p. 49.

[98] Ibid.

[99] Ibid, p. 50.

Commission considered that China should be qualified as "*[1] a cooperation partner with whom the EU has closely aligned objectives, [2] a negotiating partner with whom the EU needs to find a balance of interests, [3] an economic competitor in the pursuit of technological leadership, and [4] a systemic rival promoting alternative models of governance.*"[100] With respect to technological leadership, the Commission warned of "*China's increasing military capabilities coupled with its comprehensive vision and ambition to have the technologically most advanced armed forces by 2050 present security issues for the EU, already in the short to mid-term perspective.*"[101] The *EU-China strategic outlook* specifically called for the detection and raised awareness of security risks posed by Chinese investments in critical assets, technologies and infrastructure, and the swift, full and effective implementation of the EU FDI Screening Regulation.[102]

5 The Quest for Strategic Autonomy

Following the adoption of the FDI Screening Regulation, the discourse on the objective of investment screening started to shift towards the achievement of European strategic autonomy, or open strategic autonomy, and economic security. For instance, Vice-President Valdis Dombrovskis stated that "*If we want to achieve an open strategic autonomy, having an efficient EU-wide investment screening cooperation is essential. We are now well equipped for that.*"[103] Particular attention was given to the importance of "*mastery and ownership of key technologies*".[104]

The discussions on European strategic autonomy notably developed after calls for European autonomy in security and defence during the presidency of Donald Trump.[105] Already early into his presidency, the European External Action Service (EEAS) identified that "*[a] sustainable, innovative and competitive European defence industry is essential for Europe's strategic autonomy and for a credible [Common Security and Defence Policy].*"[106] The concept of strategic autonomy has since developed far beyond the scope of defence.

---

[100] Numbering added for clarity. Commission and High Representative (2019), p. 1.

[101] Ibid, p. 4.

[102] Ibid, p. 10.

[103] See, for instance, Commission (2020a); Commission (Undated).

[104] See, for instance, von der Leyen (2019).

[105] Borrell (2020a); Damen (2022). A report by ECFR in 2019 found that the relationship with the US played the most important role in the European debate on strategic autonomy. Franke and Varma (2019). See also Helwig (2022). The EU's focus on strategic autonomy was therefore welcomed by President Xi Jinping and Chinese Europe experts, who tended to characterise the objective as preventing the "*state of total dependence on the United States*", Stec (2021). The concept of strategic autonomy is traced back to the wars in Libya and Syria in 2023 in Hoffmeister (2023), p.668.

[106] EEAS (2016), p. 47.

The concept of Strategic Autonomy notably plays a central role in the Commission's *New Industrial Strategy for Europe*, which was published in March 2020. Strategic autonomy was defined in the *New Industrial Strategy* as being "*about reducing dependence on others for things we need the most: critical materials and technologies, food, infrastructure, security and other strategic areas. They also provide Europe's industry with an opportunity to develop its own markets, products and services which boost competitiveness.*"[107] Under the *New Industrial Strategy*, various policy objectives were subsumed under the objective of "*industrial and strategic autonomy*", including Europe's digital transformation, security and future technological sovereignty, the development of key enabling technologies, the defence and space sectors, the transition of European industry to climate-neutrality, recycling and use of secondary raw materials, sourcing of raw materials, and access to medical products and pharmaceuticals.[108]

Since adoption of the *New Industrial Strategy*, the concept of "strategic autonomy" started to feature in various Commission initiatives and speeches, such as "*Europe's moment: Repair and Prepare for the Next Generation*"[109] and the "*Trade Policy Review – An Open, Sustainable and Assertive Trade Policy.*"[110] In May 2021, the Commission updated the *New Industrial Strategy* by issuing an additional report on *Strategic dependencies and capacities*, which provides a detailed analysis of the EU's possible strategic dependencies and measures to reduce these dependencies.[111] In this update, the Commission also made the link with the importance of "*the ability of the EU to remain at the edge of innovation and transformation towards an increasingly green and digital economy and society*" as important for the "*functioning of the EU economy and the welfare of its citizens*" and notably relates it to critical inputs needed to support the digital and green transition and key enabling technologies.[112] The concept of strategic autonomy is thus used as a wide umbrella term for various industrial political interests with direct or indirect connections to security, including being "*at the edge of innovation*", the green and digital transformations, and welfare of European citizens.

Under the *New Industrial Strategy*, the FDI Screening Regulation plays a pivotal role, with the Commission announcing that it will "*make proposals to further strengthen this tool.*"[113] The relationship between the *New Industrial Strategy* and

---

[107] Commission (2020b), p. 13.

[108] Ibid, pp. 13–14.

[109] Commission (2020c).

[110] Commission (2021b). See also speeches by former Commissioner Hogan and Vice-President Dombrovskis. Hogan (2020a); Dombrovskis (2020).

[111] Strategic dependencies are defined as "*dependencies that are considered of critical importance to the EU and its Member States' strategic interests such as security, safety, health and the green and digital transformation.*" (Commission 2021c).

[112] Commission (2021c), p. 10.

[113] Commission (2020b), p. 13.

the FDI Screening Regulation was also made by Vice-President Valdis Dombrovskis in response to questions by MEPs Silvio Berlusconi and Antonio Tajani (also known for the abovementioned Barnier-Tajani proposal) on "*Chinese capital penetrating Italy's and Europe's economic fabric*."[114] After pointing out the importance that all Member States should adopt investment screening mechanisms, Vice-President Valdis Dombrovskis points to the objective of the *New Industrial Strategy* "*to help EU industry lead the green and digital transformations and driving global competitiveness and open strategic autonomy*."[115]

The calls for strategic autonomy were amplified as lockdowns were implemented across the continent in response to Covid-19.[116] Following the outbreak of the global pandemic, the Commission issued a Guidance to the Member States on the application of the FDI Screening Regulation in the context of the Covid-19 emergency.[117] The Covid-19 crisis triggered two main concerns. Firstly, the concern that healthcare capacities and related industries would be purchased by foreign investors, hampering the EU's capacity to cover the health needs of its citizens. Secondly, the Commission was concerned that the "*volatility and undervaluation of European stock market*" would undermine the EU's broader strategic capacities, due to a sell-off of critical infrastructure or technologies.[118] The Guidance provides that the EU rules "*provide a framework to the protection of legitimate policy objectives*." The call to take measures to protect strategic assets and technologies that could "*threaten public policy objectives*" was welcomed by the European Council, which noted that "*[t]his will contribute to the EU's strategic autonomy, during the crisis and afterwards*."[119] The Guidance essentially called on the Member States to adopt a broad interpretation of security and public order when reviewing investments in the healthcare sector, taking into account broader strategic capabilities, volatility and undervaluation of stock markets, strategic autonomy and "*legitimate policy objectives*" in general.

In the update to the *New Industrial Strategy*, the Commission identified that of the 137 products on which the EU is highly dependent on foreign sources, Chinese imports represent 52% in terms of value of imports.[120] In the area of technologies, the Commission identified that the EU is lagging behind both China and the United States in a number of technological areas, in particular in AI, big data, robotics, and semiconductors.[121] The *New Industrial Strategy* also warns that the EU's R&D efforts in the digital ecosystem lag behind those in the United States and China,

[114] European Parliament (2020).

[115] See, for instance, European Parliament (2021a).

[116] See also Riela and Zámborský (2021).

[117] Commission (2020d).

[118] Commission (2020d); Hogan (2020b).

[119] European Council (2020). This reference to strategic autonomy was repeated by Hogan (2020b).

[120] Commission (2021c).

[121] The EU, however, is leading in the area of advanced manufacturing technologies, the internet of things and IT for mobility. Commission (2021c), p. 32.

providing indications for potential (future) dependencies. The link between strategic autonomy and China was also made in the *New EU-China Strategy* by the European Parliament, which designates the "*Fostering of open strategic autonomy, including in trade and investment relations*" as one of the six pillars of the strategy.[122]

In addition to strategic autonomy, de-risking and economic security are key terms in official discourse relating to investment screening. The concept of de-risking played a central role in President Von der Leyen's speech on EU-China relations of March 2023.[123] In an apparent response on increasing discourse on the decoupling of China and the US (or the West in general), the President underlined that it is neither viable nor in the EU's interest to decouple from China. Rather, the EU should focus on de-risking. The President considered that most trade remained "un-risky", but that there are some areas where trade and investment pose risks to "*our economic and national security, particularly in the context of China's explicit fusion of its military and commercial sectors.*"[124] In her speech, the President stressed that this is true in particular for sensitive technologies, dual use goods or investments which come with forced technology or knowledge transfers. The President considered FDI screening mechanisms, as well as a new instrument for outbound investment screening as key tools in the context of this "economic de-risking strategy".[125] Another pillar of this strategy, as will be discussed in further detail bellow, is alignment with other partners, noting that "*On issues that concern our economic security, we have much in common with our partners around the world. This is especially true of our G7 and G20 partners and those in the region and beyond who are often more integrated with China and more advanced in their thinking on de-risking*".[126]

The FDI screening, and a proposed new instrument for outward investment screening, were also considered as a key tool in the EU's first Economic Security Strategy.[127] The Economic Security Strategy, amongst others, defines four (non-exhaustive) types of categories of risks to economic security, namely risks related to: (1) resilience of supply chains; (2) physical and cyber security of critical infrastructure; (3) technology security and technology leakage; and (4) weaponization of economic dependencies or economic coercion.[128] Examples of such risks in the third category notably include: risk to the "*EU's technological advancements, technological competitiveness, and access to leading-edge technology*", referring that "*in some cases*" technology leakage risks strengthening the military or

[122] European Parliament (2021b), art. 1(b)(5) and 41.

[123] von der Leyen (2023).

[124] von der Leyen (2023).

[125] Other tools in the toolbox are measures on 5G, the Foreign Subsidies Regulation and a new instrument to deter economic coercion. In addition, other 'pillars' of the economic de-risking strategy are making the economy and industry more competitive and resilient.

[126] von der Leyen (2023).

[127] Commission and High Representative (2023a), p. 2.

[128] Commission and High Representative (2023a), p. 4–5.

intelligence capabilities of those that could use them to undermine peace and security, implying that these type of risks are not necessarily limited to dual use and military technologies.[129] In announcing the new strategy, Executive Vice-President Vestager noted that "*In today's fierce competition for the technologies we need the most, Europe needs to have an active role to shape the course of events. Today's proposal sets out our plan to de-risk – rather than decouple – our economic interdependencies. And to assert our position as a leader in the global technology race.*"[130]

The Economic Security Strategy notably does not specifically refer to China. The absence is notable given the specific reference to other jurisdictions. The strategy notably refers to Russia's war of aggression against Ukraine heightening risks to national security, to the intensive cooperation on economic security with various partners, including the US, India and Japan.[131] In the accompanying speech, however, Executive Vice-President Vestager references the abovementioned EU-China relations speech, referring to the "*technology security and technology leakage*" concerns relating to China. At the same time, according to the High Representative and Vice President Borrell "*It is not about China*", though in the sense that "*we do not want to limit the development or prosperity of other countries, but we must be equipped to protect our economic security and our interests from the actions of some other countries.*"[132]

The focus on the protection of European strategic autonomy and economic security, including interests such as technological advancements, technological competitiveness and technologies leadership as objectives of investment screening raises the question of to what extent the EU can or should be autonomous from the outside world, and to what extent investments or cooperation in technology should be restricted or prohibited in order to protect technological leadership. These policy objectives are not specified, which results in a risk of inconsistent and disproportionate restrictions of investments. The elevation of industrial policy interests, such as strategic autonomy and technological advancements, competitiveness, and leadership, to (economic) security interests is also inconsistent with the Commission Staff Working Document accompanying the Proposal for the EU FDI Screening Regulation, which provided that security interests are separate from "*industrial policy*" and the "*EU's technological edge*".[133]

National decision practice indicates that Chinese investments in technologically sensitive areas have been at the forefront of the attention of investment screening authorities. Most transactions are not made public for confidentiality reasons or

---

[129] Commission and High Representative (2023a), p. 4–5.

[130] Commission and High Representative (2023b).

[131] Commission and High Representative (2023a), p. 1 and p. 12.

[132] Commission and High Representative (2023b).

[133] As noted above, the Commission explicitly referred to the importance of "*the ability of the EU to remain at the edge of innovation and transformation towards an increasingly green and digital economy and society*" Commission (2021c), p. 10.

because the Member States are eager to project openness to foreign investments.[134] Insofar as it is known, all publicly reported blocking decisions issued by the German and Italian governments related to Chinese investments in technologically sensitive sectors,[135] including in the automotive,[136] drone,[137] machinery,[138] robotics,[139] satellite and radio communication,[140] seeds,[141] and semiconductor sectors.[142]

In contrast, restrictions of US investments are exceedingly rare, at least based on public information. The United States is the largest foreign investor in the EU, with US investors accounting for 40% of the investments notified to the Commission under the EU FDI Screening Regulation in 2021.[143] Nevertheless, other than the French decision of December 2020 and May 2023 to block the proposed acquisitions of Photonis by US-based Teledyne and of Segault by US-based Flowserve, the author is not aware of any other recent publicly known cases of prohibitions of US transactions.[144] Photonis is active in the area of optronic technologies and supplier of night vision goggles to the French army and lasers used for nuclear weapon test simulations. According to the press release, the decision was "*motivated by the strong desire of the French government to protect and guarantee the French economic and industrial defence sovereignty.*"[145] Segault is active in the area of

[134] See also Kratz et al. (2021); Kratz et al. (2022).

[135] Kratz et al. (2021, 2022).

[136] The Italian and French governments opposed the proposed acquisition of Iveco by FAW Group. The German government opposed the proposed acquisition of Schmiedetechnik Plettenberg, Werkzeugtechnik Plettenberg, VVP Vermögensverwaltung Plettenberg by Zhejiang Shanghuan Transmission Machinery.

[137] The Italian government issued an *ex post* blocking decision of the acquisition of the Italian drone company Alpi Aviation by CRRC.

[138] The German government opposed the acquisition of Leifeld by Yantai.

[139] The Italian government blocked a technology transfer agreement between Italian based ROBOX and Effort Intelligent Equipment.

[140] The German government opposed to the proposed acquisition of satellite communication radar and radio technology ISMT by China Aerospace Science and Industry Corporation. The Ministry of Economic Affairs and Energy said that the transaction would endanger Germany's technological sovereignty.

[141] The Italian government blocked the proposed acquisition of the global seed producer Verisem by Syngenta (owned by the SOE ChemChina).

[142] The Italian government blocked the proposed acquisition of the Italian semiconductor company LPE by Shenzhen Investment Holdings, and blocked the proposed creation of a joint venture between Applied Materials and Zhejiang Jinsheng Mechenical relating to an Italian screen printing business. The German government reportedly blocked the proposed acquisition of PPM Pure Metals by Chinese Vital Material, blocked the proposed acquisition of Elmos Semiconductor by Silex Microsystems (owned by Chinese SAI MicroElectronics), and blocked the acquisition of ERS Electronic by an unknown Chinese company.

[143] Commission (2022a), p. 18.

[144] The French (pre-emptive) opposition to rumors of an attempted acquisition of Danone by Pepsi in 2005 is another, somewhat dated, example. See also Zhang (2014), p. 410.

[145] Ministère Des Armées (2020).

valves in the nuclear and petrochemical fields, including those used in the nuclear boiler rooms on board of all French nuclear submarines and the Charles de Gaulle aircraft carrier.[146] The decisions signals that US investors are not necessarily entirely in the clear either.[147]

The significant drop in Chinese investments in the EU since the adoption of the EU FDI Screening Regulation, especially investments by Chinese state-owned enterprises, can likely be at least partially contributed to the intensified scrutiny of Chinese investments. From October 2020 to 2021, the first year of operation of the EU FDI Screening Regulation, Chinese investments represented 8% of the notifications. At this time, Chinese investments had already dropped by 63% following the outbreak of the Covid-19 pandemic. The Commission notes that the drop in Chinese investments already started prior to the lockdown in Wuhan, which indicates that the fall in investments following the global pandemic cannot be solely attributed the strict Covid-19 policies in China.[148] Chinese investments continued to fall, and amounted just 4% of notified transactions under the cooperation mechanism in the second year of the Regulation's operation.[149] According to the Commission, Chinese investments failed to take off due to strict capital controls and the concentration of investment activities in core industry sectors.[150] The drop in investments lead Rhodium Group and MERICS to conclude that the "*era of massive Chinese investment in Europe seems over for now.*"[151]

6 Transatlantic Cooperation and the Russian Invasion

As Chinese investments have been placed under scrutiny, the EU simultaneously reached out to the United States to intensify cooperation in the area of trade and technology. In 2020, shortly after adoption of the EU FDI Screening Regulation and still during the Trump Presidency, former Commissioner for Trade Phil Hogan travelled to Washington to stress the EU's keenness to "*intensify our cooperation on technology, covering areas such as semiconductors, artificial intelligence, additive manufacturing and quantum technology. This cooperation will be massively important for our economies and our security.*"[152] According to the Commissioner, the EU had followed the United States' example with the introduction of the FDI Screening Regulation. Stressing the importance of "*our trusted transatlantic trading*

[146] Sénat (2023); Bezat (2023).

[147] Bernard (2020).

[148] Commission (2021d), p. 5.

[149] Commission (2021d); Commission (2022a).

[150] Commission (2022a), p. 4.

[151] Kratz et al. (2022), p. 16.

[152] Hogan (2020c). Similarly, Phil Hogan noted in another speech that "*few challenges [are] more complex than China.*" Hogan (2020d).

and investment space", the Commissioner called for "*discussions on a possible agreement to "whitelist" each other when it comes to investment and export controls*" and even noted that "*[n]o other market is as free and open for US businesses as the EU. Where else are you as welcome?*"[153] On the other hand, the Commissioner warned of "*global struggle for technological supremacy*", "*[t]he rise of China*" and the distortion of markets and investment flows by China.[154] Similarly, President Ursula von der Leyen announced in her 2020 State of the Union address (also still during the Trump presidency) that the EU was ready to build a new transatlantic agenda on trade, technology and taxation.[155] Later that year, just one month after the election of President Joe Biden, the Commission and the High Representative put forward a proposal for a new transatlantic agenda, including the creation of a new EU-US Trade and Technology Council (TCC).[156]

In June 2021, President Ursula von der Leyen and President Joe Biden launched the TCC, thereby consolidating EU-US cooperation in investment screening.[157] The main goals of the TCC involve the deepening of bilateral trade and investment, cooperation on key policies on technologies, digital issues and supply chains, support of collaborative research, cooperation on the development of compatible and international standards, cooperation on regulatory policy, and the promotion of innovation and leadership by EU and US firms.[158] Unsurprisingly, one of the working groups established under the TCC is tasked with investment screening, including exchanging information on investment trends impacting security, on best practices with respect to areas such as risk analysis and systems for risks-mitigation measures, and with a focus on sensitive technologies and related sensitive data.[159] In the Pittsburg Joint Inaugural Statement, the EU and United States refer to "*common challenges*" in addressing risks related to foreign investments, which should be mitigated through investment screening mechanisms.[160] At the same time, the Joint Inaugural Statement takes note of the four trillion euros/dollars in investments linking both sides of the Atlantic, which illustrates the "*strength of the transatlantic partnership*".[161] The statement also provides that "*investment screening regimes should be guided by the principles of non-discrimination, transparency, predictability, proportionality, and accountability, as set forth in relevant OECD guidelines.*"[162] The Commission's Economic Security Strategy and the European Parliament's *New EU-China Strategy* confirms the special position of the United

[153] Hogan (2020c).

[154] Hogan (2020c).

[155] von der Leyen (2020).

[156] Commission (2020e).

[157] Commission (2021e).

[158] Commission (2021e).

[159] Commission (2021e); Commission (2021f).

[160] Commission (2021f).

[161] Ibid.

[162] Ibid.

States with respect to strategic autonomy, noting that the EU should foster its strategic autonomy and capacity "*working together with the US and other like-minded partners*".[163]

Following Russia's military aggression against Ukraine, attention shifted to Russian investments as a specific threat, with the Commission adopting a specific Guidance calling on Member States to systematically use their screening mechanisms to assess and prevent the threats related to Russian and Belarussian investments on grounds of security and public order, to ensure compliance with EU sanctions and to prevent money laundering.[164] The Commission considered that in "*current circumstances, there is a significantly heightened risk that FDI by Russian and Belarusian investors may pose a threat to security and public order.*"[165] While the Commission is not very precise, it considered that the governments of Russia and Belarus have a "*strong incentive to interfere with critical activities in the EU*", in particular via investors that are associated with, controlled by, or subject to influence by these two governments.[166] In the Commission's work plan for 2023, the Commission notes that Russia's war of aggression against Ukraine has highlighted the "*need to develop a strong set of strategic trade and investment to strengthen our economic security, while also working to diversify value chains.*"[167] In addition to strengthening strategic export controls, the Commission will examine whether additional tools are necessary in respect of "*outbound strategic investment controls.*"[168] The overall impact on inbound investments into the EU is likely to be limited, given that Russian investments in 2021 accounted for less than 1.5% of the cases notified to the Commission under the EU FDI Screening Regulation cooperation mechanism.[169]

The invasion gave a push to transatlantic cooperation, with EU and US leaders meeting in Paris to strongly condemn Russia and reiterate the central role of the TCC for the renewed transatlantic partnership and the importance of investment screening.[170] In the Joint Declaration, the EU and the United States declared each other as "*trustworthy and reliable trade, technology, and investment partners as well as security partners*" stressing "*shared interests and values*". The Joint Declaration contains particularly strong wording against not only Russia, but "*autocratic countries*" in general, and broadens concerns regarding technologies beyond security to a

[163] Quote from European Parliament (2021b), par. 62. See also Commission and High Representative (2023a), p.12.

[164] Commission (2022b).

[165] Ibid, p. 2.

[166] Ibid, p. 2.

[167] Commission (2022d), p. 7.

[168] Ibid, p. 8.

[169] Commission (2022a).

[170] Commission (2022c).

wide range of interests, such as protecting the transatlantic joint technology leadership, democratic values, and human rights.[171] In particular, the Joint Statement provides that:

> We are acutely aware that trade in technologies can be pivotal to the ability of autocratic countries to implement authoritarian policies, perpetrate human rights violations and abuses, engage in other forms of repression, and undermine the security of other nations. We share a desire for cooperation through coordinated actions using our export control and investment screening tools in defense of our security. We are committed to deeply enhancing our cooperation and to supporting information exchange on dual-use technologies and export controls. The work of the TTC has already proven foundational in developing common approaches in response to Russia's aggression against Ukraine, including by facilitating an unprecedented level of cooperation on export controls.[172]

The Paris Joint Statement is the outcome of a gradual shift in discourse surrounding the risks relating to FDI following the adoption of the EU FDI Screening Regulation. Within a short period of time, official European discourse on the objectives of investment screening has shifted from the securitisation of investments by Chinese SOEs towards the protection of strategic autonomy, and with the adoption of the TCC, the EU has entered into a close alliance with the United States.

7 Reflections and Conclusion

Concerns regarding China have played a central role in the adoption and development of the framework for FDI screening in the EU. The precise concerns have shifted over time. Initially, concerns regarding Chinese investments, notably by Chinese SOEs, were predominantly discussed in economic terms. Common concerns related to the lack of reciprocal market access of European businesses in China, market disturbances due to subsidisations or non-compliance with market rules, and the concern that Chinese investors would transfer the know-how to China and close-down of European businesses.

Following the introduction of the EU FDI Screening Regulation, the official discourse regarding Chinese investments shifted from economic concerns to the (economic) security threat posed by China. The precise security threat posed by Chinese investments was, however, left largely unspecified. One prominent concern related to the links between Chinese investments and the Chinese state. However,

---

[171] TCC (2022), paras. 5–17.

[172] Similarly, in the press release Executive Vice-President Margarethe Vestager noted: "*Russia's war of aggression against Ukraine has further underlined the key importance of our cooperation with the US on economic and technology issues. This cooperation goes beyond our reaction to the war. Together with our transatlantic partners, we can create a positive vision for our economies and for a democratic governance of the internet based on the dignity and integrity of the individual. When we act together, we can set the standards of tomorrow's economy. We are joining forces and when two such determined partners take the lead, we can enable the tides to turn.*" TCC (2022), par.15; Commission (2022c).

even though government ownership or control over an investment warrants additional scrutiny, the specific security threats arising from investments by Chinese SOEs are left unspecified. For instance, former Commissioner Malmström warned of (Chinese) state-owned enterprises "*openly*" using investments to acquire "*technologies, infrastructure and information*". However, the acquisition of technologies, infrastructure and/or information is an inherent feature of FDI that is not specific to Chinese investments, nor does an acquisition of technology, infrastructure or information necessarily result in a threat to security. The securitisation of the discourse on Chinese investments transformed industrial political questions relating to unequal market access and reciprocity and the importance of ownership or exclusivity over innovative companies into the far more pressing and worrying issue of Chinese investments posing an existential threat to Europe's security. The absence of a definition of security and public order was even explicitly viewed as a positive legislative choice in the report of the Committee on International Trade of the European Parliament, as vague criteria ensure that investment screenings would not be subject to too many constraints. Consequently, there is a lack of meaningful indications in either the law or the legislative history of the aims and objectives of the EU FDI Screening Regulation and the threats it seeks to prevent.

Following the adoption of the FDI Screening Regulation, the discourse on the objective of investment screening started to shift towards the achievement of European strategic autonomy, notably from China. Under the *New Industrial Strategy* and *Economic Security Strategy*, investment screening plays a pivotal role in ensuring strategic autonomy and economic security. In the area of key technologies, investment screening, amongst others, aims at ensuring that the EU has the critical inputs and key technologies necessary to be "*at the edge of innovation and transformation towards an increasingly green and digital economy and society*" which are important for the "*functioning of the EU economy and the welfare of its citizens*".[173] Furthermore, in the Economic Security Strategy, interests such as the EU's technological advancement, technological competitiveness, access to leading-edge technology and availability of the inputs linked to the green transition have been designated as economic security interests.[174] The concept of strategic autonomy and economic security are thus used as wide umbrella terms for various industrial political interests. Investment screening should be seen in the context of the broader, multifaceted "strategic autonomy" and "economic security" agenda.[175]

The shift from security to "strategic autonomy" and "economic security" is difficult to reconcile with the view of the Commission at the time of the proposal that security considerations are separate from "*industrial policy*" and the "*EU's technological edge*", and the Commission's earlier warnings against an overexpansive reading of security. The shift of official discourse implies that industrial policy considerations and the protection of the EU's technological edge,

[173] Commission (2021c), p. 10.

[174] Commission (2021c), p. 10.

[175] See also Helwig and Sinkkonen (2022), p. 19.

competitiveness and advancements will likely start to play a central role in security screenings. The subsumption of industrial political objectives as security considerations was perhaps a foreseeable expansion of the scope of the traditional concept of security to economic security objectives.[176] However, a broad use of the term strategic autonomy "*risks unmooring the EU from its collaborative and compromise-oriented essence because it depicts the world outside the EU as a swamp where danger lurks behind every tree.*"[177] This risk disproportionately affects investments by non-Western investors.

It is clear from the discourse and publicly known practice that the FDI Screening Regulation has notably affected Chinese investments in sensitive sectors. The Russia's military aggression against Ukraine resulted in specific attention to Russia, with the Commission adopting a specific Guidance calling on Member States to systematically use their screening mechanisms to assess and prevent the threats related to Russian and Belarussian investments. However, given that Russian investments accounted for less than 1.5% of the cases notified to the Commission under the EU FDI Screening Regulation cooperation mechanism, and in light of the wide range of sanctions in place, Russian investments will likely continue to play a relatively minor role in the area of investment screening.[178] At the same time, the 'wake-up' call of undesirable dependency on Russian oil and gas may trigger additional scrutiny of investments in critical infrastructures in general. China's response to the Russian invasion of Ukraine, which is ambivalent at best and may be interpreted as *de facto* (lukewarm) support of Russia, could also increase skepticism towards Chinese ownership over critical European companies.[179] The decision to maintain the "no-limits friendship" between Russia and China following Russia's invasion of Ukraine was specifically considered in President Von der Leyen's EU-China relations speech, noting that "*How China continues to interact with Putin's war will be a determining factor for EU-China relations going forward.*"[180]

As Chinese and Russian investments have been put under the spotlight, the EU has at the same time pursued cooperation with the United States on investment screening. During the parliamentary debate, the Chairman of CFIUS was invited to speak at the presentation of the EU FDI Screening Regulation by former Commissioner Cecilia Malmström, and US intelligence reportedly played an important role in the assessment of Chinese investments in Kuka and Aixtron. Even though the EU FDI Screening Regulation would bring a vast number of US investments under scrutiny, CFIUS considered that the adoption of the EU FDI Screening Regulation

[176] See de Kok (2019), p. 43. For a warning or critique against the expansion of 'security' to include 'economic security' considerations see also Nicolas (2014), p. 120; Editorial Comments (2018), p. 8; Snell (2019), p. 138; Bickenbach and Liu (2018), p. 18, Nettesheim (2020).

[177] van Veen and Langenberg (2022).

[178] Commission (2022a), p. 18.

[179] See in similar terms Kratz et al. (2022), p. 17.

[180] von der Leyen (2023).

would "*reinforce the deep and open economic relationship, as well as the strong security relationship that we have with you*".[181] Following the adoption of the EU FDI Screening Regulation, the EU and the United States intensified cooperation on trade and technology. Under the TCC, the EU and the United States cooperate on various key policies relating to technologies, digital issues and supply chains, support of collaborative research, international standards, regulatory policy and innovation and leadership by EU and US firms. In the recent Paris Joint Declaration, the EU and the United States declared each other to be "*trustworthy and reliable trade, technology, and investment partners as well as security partners*" stressing "*shared interests and values*".

The close cooperation with the United States on investment screening is hard to reconcile with the FDI Screening Regulation's purported objective of European strategic autonomy and economic security (which include interests such as the EU's technological competitiveness and advancement, or measures targeting the EU, its Member States and EU businesses through measures affecting trade or investments). The debate on European strategic autonomy after all developed following the presidency of Donald Trump, which illustrated that the United States may not always be a reliable security or trade partner. The privileged status of US investments in the context of the TCC, whereby US investments are *de facto* whitelisted, is also hard to reconcile with the principle of non-discrimination enshrined in Article 3(2) of the FDI Screening Regulation.[182] Evidently, the context of Chinese and Russian FDI differs from US investments in many ways and security cooperation with the United States in the context of NATO is clearly a relevant factor. After all, investments originating from a security ally are less likely to result in a threat to security or public policy. However, US investments may equally give rise to or exacerbate undesirable strategic dependencies that may result in a threat to security, at least as apparently perceived by the Commission.[183] For instance, the Commission's warning of increased risks of acquisitions of essential healthcare capacities and related (research) industries in its Covid-19 Guidance followed within days after reports that the Trump administration attempted to move the German coronavirus vaccine developer, CureVac, to the United States in order to get exclusive access to the vaccine.[184] Similarly, in *New Industrial Strategy*, the Commission identified various existing and growing strategic dependencies on American technologies. In this respect it is relevant that various US technological companies at

[181] Committee on International Trade (2018), at 14:54:10.

[182] This provision provides that "*Rules and procedures related to screening mechanisms, including relevant timeframes, shall be transparent and not discriminate between third countries.*" The principle of non-discrimination is also referred to in recital 15.

[183] See also Nettesheim (2020), p. 16. Martin Nettesheim argues: "*For the sake of a coherent argument, concerns about the abandonment of high technology and fears of "falling behind" would also have to be expressed to investors from other Western countries in these sectors.*"

[184] Commission (2020d), p. 1. This report also instantly prompted the Commission to offer up to EUR 80 million in financial support to CureVac. Commission (2020f); Reuters Staff (2020).

the edge of innovation enjoy significant government funding provided in the context of US industrial policy, a relevant factor under investment screening regulations.[185] In particular, the White House has authorised around USD 250 billion in funding for advanced technology research under the US Innovation and Competition Act, aiming to make American "*supply chains stronger and reinvigorate the innovation engine of our economy to outcompete China and the rest of the world for decades to come*."[186] Furthermore, around USD 370 billion in investments is made available under the Inflation Reduction Act to make sure that the United States "*remains the global leader in clean energy technology, manufacturing and innovation.*"[187] A non-discriminatory application of the EU FDI Screening Regulation (assuming a broad interpretation of security and public order) should therefore equally entail a development towards greater European "strategic autonomy" or "economic security" vis-à-vis the United States.[188]

The intensification of transatlantic cooperation on investment screening risks dragging the EU into the increasingly hostile US-China rivalry. Spurred on by concerns that China is "*the only country with both the intent to reshape the international order and, increasingly, the economic, diplomatic, military and technological power to do so*", China has been designated by the Biden administration as "*the most serious long-term challenge to the international order.*"[189] The recent break by President Biden of the principle of strategic ambiguity, vowing that the United States would intervene militarily to defend Taiwan, which President Xi has vowed to "reunite" with China, even points to the no longer purely hypothetical possibility of this great power rivalry spilling over into military conflict.[190] The alignment between the United States and EU on FDI screening forms part of one the three pillars of the Biden's administration on China, summed up as "*invest, align, compete*".[191] For instance, in an interview with CNBC just prior to the Pittsburg inaugural meeting of the TCC, US Secretary of Commerce Gina Raimondo said "*If we really want to slow down China's rate of innovation, we need to work with Europe.*"[192] The way in which the TCC forms part of a broader US coalition on China is illustrated in a recent speech setting out the US administration's approach to China by US Secretary of State Blinken. In this speech, Blinken listed the US-EU

[185] For instance, under the EU FDI Screening Regulation, art. 4(2)(a), significant funding may point to direct or indirect government control, and recital 23 provides that information about subsidies granted is relevant information for the assessment.

[186] The White House (2022). Similarly, see The White House (2020), which provides that the United States also has the objective "*to ensure that the United States continues to lead in innovation and setting standards.*"

[187] The White House (2023).

[188] Commission (2021c), p. 10.

[189] Blinken (2022). See also Sinkkonen and Martin (2022).

[190] Garcia and Tian (2021); Boak et al. (2022); G7 Foreign Ministers (2022); Spokesperson of the Chinese Mission to the EU (2022).

[191] Blinken (2022).

[192] Macia and Tausche (2021).

TCC together with the security, economic and technology alliance with South Korea and Japan, the launch of the Indo-Pacific Economic Framework for Prosperity,[193] the alliance with the Quad countries (Australia, Japan, India the United States), the US partnership with ASEAN, and the security partnership between Australia, the UK and the United States known as AUKUS.[194] The EU must be vigilant that the TCC does not become a tool for US foreign policy vis-à-vis China.[195] In line with EU policy, Chinese investments should not just be viewed only through the lens of systematic competition, but also in the context of China as "*a cooperation partner with whom the EU has closely aligned objectives*" and "*a negotiating partner with whom the EU needs to find a balance of interests*".[196] In the EU-China relations speech, President Von der Leyen for instance specifically considered climate change and nature protection as important "islands of opportunity" on which the EU and China can work together productively "in the global system of the future".[197]

The recent TCC Paris Joint Statement is exemplary of the way in which discourse on investments is shifting away from a traditional confines of the security or public order exceptions. The Paris Joint Statement places the transatlantic cooperation in trade and technology in a broader context of protecting the transatlantic joint technological leadership, democratic values, and human rights, placing these values in contrast to the authoritarian policies, human right violations and abuses and other forms of repression by "*autocratic countries*". This focus on democratic values, human rights, repression and authoritarianism moves the discourse beyond security threats, strategic autonomy or technological leadership, and places investment screening in a broader actual or perceived conflict between democracies and autocracies at large. These broader considerations are, however, far removed from the question whether a specific investment poses a threat to security or public order of a Member State concerned. The incorporation of democratic values and human rights into investment screening policy furthermore does not necessarily imply a privileged position for the United States either. Democracy is clearly under pressure in the United States, where attempts by former President Trump to overturn the election results culminated in the storming of the Capital Building on the 6 January 2021. Without prejudice to the human rights record in China, the United States equally does not have a blank slate with respect to human rights violations and abuses and other forms of repression. UN working groups and rapporteurs have expressed a wide variety of concerns with respect to the human rights situation in the United States. Such concerns pertain to, amongst others, mass surveillance, racial disparities in the criminal justice system, excessive use of force by law enforcement officials,

---

193 The current Member States are Australia, Brunei, Fiji, India, Indonesia, Japan, South Korea, Malaysia, New Zealand, the Philippines, Singapore, Thailand, the United States and Vietnam. According to Blinken, the Economic Framework "*renews American economic leadership*".

194 Blinken (2022).

195 See more generally, Casarini (2022).

196 Commission and High Representative (2019).

197 von der Leyen (2023)

gun violence, condition of detention, the death penalty, treatment of immigrants, accountability for past human rights violations, targeted killings using drones, torture, detainment at Guantánamo Bay, prevalence of domestic violence, rights to sexual and reproductive health, LGBT rights, homelessness, voting rights and rights of indigenous peoples.[198] While the laws, regulations and policies of the home country of the investor are not irrelevant (for instance those relating to the protection of data privacy), these broad considerations are far removed from the core question of whether a certain (specific) foreign investments may pose a threat to security or public order.

The so-called "China threat" discourse from across the Atlantic, which appears to increasingly inform the EU framework for FDI screening, gives rise to the risk of disproportionate restrictions or prohibitions of Chinese investments for reasons other than genuine security and public order concerns. This risk is exacerbated by the lack of clear assessment criteria and a framework of assessment to determine which Chinese investments are beneficial, and which are not. More fundamentally, the trend towards securitisation pushes the EU ever closer towards competition, rivalry and conflict with China and hampers possible cooperation on common interests.[199] The China threat discourse may result in cooperation with Chinese partners being shunned by European governments, businesses, and universities, to avoid (deal) uncertainty and conflicts with governments and regulators, even if there is a mutual benefit and aligned objectives. The wholesale securitisation of European-Chinese relations moreover increasingly risks depicting politicians, employees, scholars, students, and citizens involved in European-Chinese economic or scientific cooperation as agents of a hostile social and economic order.[200]

At the official level, the case for a European approach—one that involves greater neutrality vis-à-vis China and the United States—has been most clearly made by Josep Borrell, High Representative of the Union for Foreign Affairs and Security Policy. His stress on the importance of the EU doing things "*in its own way*" was nicknamed as the "Sinatra Doctrine":[201] "*If the EU does not want to remain entrenched in the dispute between the US and China, it must look at the world from its own point of view and act to defend its values and interests, which do not always coincide with those of the US.*"[202] Josep Borrell warned against falling into "*the trap of seeing things in black and white*". Whilst strengthening the EU's

[198] For an overview, see, for instance, United Nations Human Rights Committee (2014); Office of the United Nations High Commissioner for Human Rights (2020); United Nations Office of the High Commissioner for Human Rights (2022).

[199] As also identified as a common interest in Commission and High Representative (2019).

[200] See also Rogelja and Tsimonis (2020).

[201] This led some commentators calling the approach the "*Sinatra doctrine*", which Josep Borrell did not mind "*as long as it makes it easier to get my message across. I could have said that Europe must increase its strategic autonomy or its sovereignty, but this would probably not have aroused as much interest.*" Borrell (2020b) This article was also published on the website of the EEAS. Borrell (2020c).

[202] Borrell (2020b), p. 7. For similar calls, see Bermann (2021).

strategic sovereignty, by protecting technologies which are key in ensuring autonomy and promoting European values and interests, he highlighted the importance of continued cooperation with China to address global challenges, such as climate change, (at the time) combatting the coronavirus, regional conflicts and development in Africa.[203] In a possible attempt to desecuritise the discourse, Borrell points to the importance of "*ensuring that European companies have reciprocal access to its markets and innovation and research programmes. It is vital that we ensure a balance in our economic relationship and dispense with some of the naivety of the past.*"[204] In addition, "*China subsidises its state-owned enterprises and has the largest series of trade and investment barriers*".[205] Independence from these "*two competitors/rivals*" does not equate equal distance from them: "*Our lengthy common history and shared values with the US mean that we are closer to Washington than we are to Beijing.*"[206] However, the High Representative cautions that the EU must avoid arriving at the point where "*we Europeans have to choose between being a Chinese colony or an American colony.*"[207]

In order to provide greater transparency and predictability in the application of the EU FDI Screening Regulation and national screening regimes, to ensure a non-discriminatory application, a broader reflection on the precise objectives of FDI screening is required. Clarity on the objective of the FDI screening regime helps to ensure that transactions are assessed on the basis of clearly defined substantive criteria. In this respect, additional public guidance would notably contribute to more transparent, accountable, non-discriminatory and fact-based screenings of investments on the basis of foreseeable criteria, resulting in decisions that are more amenable to judicial review, including a clearer interpretation of the concept such as strategic autonomy and economic security. Such guidance also helps to ensure that investment screening decisions are constrained by law, helps to avoid arbitrary exercises of executive powers and contributes to the development of a European conception of the security and public order exceptions under the Treaties and the EU FDI Screening Regulation. A clearer set of objectives also helps to shift the focus from open-ended security-based to more predictable economic screening criteria. The EU framework for investment screening should notably be developed so that it specifies the different types of risks or threats that are the object of protection under FDI screening, the criteria that may be used to assess such possible threats, the threshold for intervention, and the possibility of addressing such risks with mitigating measures.

---

[203] Borrell (2020b), p. 7.

[204] Ibid.

[205] Borrell (2020b), p. 8. Citing Commission (2019b), p. 7.

[206] Borrell (2020b), p. 7.

[207] Borrell (2020b), p. 9. Citing Letta (2019).

References

Baker & McKenzie, CICC, Rhodium Group (2015) Reaching New Heights: An Update on Chinese investment into Europe. https://www.bakermckenzie.com/-/media/files/insight/publications/2016/03/reaching-new-heights/ar_emea_reachingnewheights_mar16.pdf?la=en

Bermann S (2021) European strategic autonomy and the US–China rivalry: can the EU "Prefer not to Choose"? Instituto Affari Internazionali 21

Bernard J (2020) The French Government rejects an American industrial conglomerate's acquisition of a national optronic technologies firm (Photonis/Teledyne). In: Concurrences e-Competitions

Bickenbach F, Liu W-H (2018) Chinese direct investment in Europe – challenges for EU FDI policy. CESifo Forum 19(4):15–22

Bismuth R (2017) The "Santiago Principles" for sovereign wealth funds: the shortcomings and the futility of self-regulation. Eur Bus Law Rev 28(1):69–88

Blinken A (2022) Administration's approach to the People's Republic of China (Speech by the Secretary of State Antony J. Blinken at the George Washington University). https://www.state.gov/the-administrations-approach-to-the-peoples-republic-of-china/

Boak J, Madhani A, Miller Z (2022) Biden: US would intervene with military to defend Taiwan. Associated Press. https://apnews.com/article/russia-ukraine-biden-taiwan-china-4fb0ad0567ed5bbe46c01dd758e6c62b

Borrell J (2020a) Why European strategic autonomy matters. EEAS. https://www.eeas.europa.eu/eeas/why-european-strategic-autonomy-matters_en

Borrell J (2020b) The Sinatra Doctrine. how the EU should deal with the US–China competition. Instituto Affari Internazionali 20

Borrell J (2020c) The Sinatra Doctrine. How the EU Should Deal with the US–China Competition. EEAS. https://www.eeas.europa.eu/eeas/sinatra-doctrine-how-eu-should-deal-us%E2%80%93china-competition_en

Buzan B, Wæver O, de Wilde J (1998) Security: a new framework for analysis. Lynne Rienner Publishers

Casarini N (2015) Is Europe to benefit from China's belt and road initiative? Istituto Affari Internazionali 15(40)

Casarini N (2022) A European strategic "third way?" The European Union between the traditional transatlantic alliance and the pull of the Chinese market. China Int Strat Rev 4(1):91–107. https://doi.org/10.1007/s42533-022-00095-1

Chan ZT, Meunier S (2022) Behind the screen: understanding national support for a foreign investment screening mechanism in the European Union. Rev Int Organ 17(3):513–541. https://doi.org/10.1007/s11558-021-09436-y

Chee FY (2010) INTERVIEW - EU industry chief worried about Xinmao's Draka bid. Reuters

Christiansen T, Maher R (2017) The rise of China—challenges and opportunities for the European Union. Asia Eur J 15(2):121–131. https://doi.org/10.1007/s10308-017-0469-2

Commission (2008) A common European approach to Sovereign Wealth Funds (Communication) (COM(2008) 115 final)

Commission (2011) Cabinet Newsletter n. 33, 11 February 2011

Commission (2017a) Reflection Paper on Harnessing Globalisation (COM(2017) 240)

Commission (2017b) Proposal for a Regulation of the European Parliament and of the Council establishing a framework for screening of foreign direct investments into the European Union (COM/2017/0487 final - 2017/0224 (COD))

Commission (2017c) Commission Staff Working Document accompanying the Proposal for a Regulation of the European Parliament and of the Council establishing a framework for screening of foreign direct investments into the European Union (SWD(2021) 99 final)

Commission (2017d) Welcoming Foreign Direct Investment while Protecting Essential Interests (Communication) (COM(2017) 494 final)

Commission (2019a) Foreign Direct Investment in the EU, following up on the Commission Communication "Welcoming Foreign Direct Investment while Protecting Essential Interests" of 13 September 2017 (Staff Working Document) (SWD(2019) 108 final)
Commission (2019b) Report on Trade and Investment Barriers 1 January 2019-31 December 2019 (COM(2020) 236 final)
Commission (2020a) EU foreign investment screening mechanism becomes fully operational (Press Release). https://ec.europa.eu/commission/presscorner/detail/en/ip_20_1867. Accessed 2 Aug 2022
Commission (2020b) A New Industrial Strategy for Europe (Communication) (COM(2020) 102 final)
Commission (2020c) Europe's moment: Repair and Prepare for the Next Generation (Communication) (COM(2020) 456 final)
Commission (2020d) Guidance to the Member States concerning foreign direct investment and free movement of capital from third countries, and the protection of Europe's strategic assets, ahead of the application of Regulation (EU) 2019/452 (FDI Screening Regulation) (Communication) (OJ C 991/1)
Commission (2020e) EU-US: A new transatlantic agenda for global change. https://ec.europa.eu/commission/presscorner/detail/en/IP_20_2279
Commission (2020f) Coronavirus: Commission offers financing to innovative vaccines company CureVac. https://ec.europa.eu/commission/presscorner/detail/en/IP_20_474
Commission (2021a) Frequently asked questions on Regulation (EU) 2019/452 establishing a framework for the screening of foreign direct investments into the Union. https://trade.ec.europa.eu/doclib/docs/2019/june/tradoc_157945.pdf
Commission (2021b) Trade Policy review - An Open, Sustainable and Assertive Trade Policy (Communication) (COM(2021) 66 final)
Commission (2021c) Strategic dependencies and capacities updating the 2020 New Industrial Strategy: Building a stronger Single Market for Europe's recovery (SWD(2021) 352 final)
Commission (2021d) First Annual Report on the screening of foreign direct investments into the Union (COM(2021) 714 final)
Commission (2021e) EU-US launch Trade and Technology Council to lead values-based global digital transformation (Press Release). https://ec.europa.eu/commission/presscorner/detail/en/IP_21_2990
Commission (2021f) EU-US Trade and Technology Council Inaugural Joint Statement. https://ec.europa.eu/commission/presscorner/detail/en/STATEMENT_21_4951
Commission (2022a) Second Annual Report on the screening of foreign direct investments into the Union (COM(2022) 433 final)
Commission (2022b) Guidance to the Member States concerning foreign direct investment from Russia and Belarus in view of the military aggression against Ukraine and the restrictive measures laid down in recent Council Regulations on sanctions (OJ C 151 I/1)
Commission (2022c) EU-US Trade and Technology Council: strengthening our renewed partnership in turbulent times (Press Release). https://ec.europa.eu/commission/presscorner/detail/en/IP_22_3034
Commission (2022d) Commission work programme 2023: A Union standing firm and united (COM(2022) 548 final)
Commission (Undated) Foreign Direct Investment EU Screening Framework https://trade.ec.europa.eu/doclib/docs/2019/february/tradoc_157683.pdf
Commission and High Representative (2019) EU-China – A strategic outlook (Joint Communication) (JOIN(2019) 5 final)
Commission and High Representative (2023a) European economic security strategy (Joint Communication).
Commission and High Representative (2023b) Press remarks on economic security strategy by Executive Vice-Presidents Vestager and Dombrovskis and High Representative/Vice-President

Borrell on economic security strategy. In: European Commission - European Commission. https://ec.europa.eu/commission/presscorner/detail/en/speech_23_3388. Accessed 30 Jun 2023.
Committee on International Trade (2018) Hearing on the screening of foreign investment in the EU. https://multimedia.europarl.europa.eu/en/webstreaming/committee-on-international-trade_20180123-1430-COMMITTEE-INTA
Corre PL (2018) On Chinese Investment and Influence in Europe (Testimony before the US House of Representatives Foreign Affairs Committee). https://carnegieendowment.org/2018/05/23/on-chinese-investment-and-influence-in-europe-pub-76467
Cotta P, Huebner PA, von Wistinghausen C (2022) Foreign Direct Investment Regime Germany 2022. ICLG. https://iclg.com/practice-areas/foreign-direct-investment-regimes-laws-and-regulations/germany
Council (2008) 2857th Council meeting Economic and Financial Affairs (Press Release). https://ec.europa.eu/commission/presscorner/detail/en/PRES_08_61
Council at Ministerial Level (2008) OECD Declaration on Sovereign Wealth Funds and Recipient Country Policies (C/MIN(2008)8/FINAL)
Damen M (2022) EU strategic autonomy 2013–2023: from concept to capacity. European Parliamentary Research Service (PE.733.589)
De Gucht K (2012) EU-China Investment: A Partnership of Equals speech at Bruegel Debate: China Invests in Europe Patterns Impacts and Policy Issues, Brussels. https://ec.europa.eu/commission/presscorner/detail/en/SPEECH_12_421
de Kok J (2019) Towards a European framework for foreign investment reviews. Eur Law Rev 44(1):24–49
de Kok J (2021) Investment screening in the Netherlands. Legal Iss Econ Integr 48(1):43–66
Dombrovskis V (2020) European Parliament Plenary: Opening statement by Executive Vice-President Dombrovskis on the EU Trade Policy Review. https://ec.europa.eu/commission/commissioners/2019-2024/dombrovskis/announcements/european-parliament-plenary-opening-statement-evp-dombrovskis-eu-trade-policy-review_en
Editorial Comments (2018) Playing by the rules – free and fair trade. Common Mark Law Rev 55(2):373–386
EEAS (2016) Shared vision, common action: a stronger Europe: a global strategy for the European Union's foreign and security policy. Publications Office of the European Union, Luxemburg
EUR-Lex Preparatory Documents. https://eur-lex.europa.eu/collection/eu-law/pre-acts.html. Accessed 14 July 2022
European Council (2017) European Council meeting (22 and 23 June 2017) – Conclusions (EUCO 8/17)
European Council (2020) Joint statement https://www.consilium.europa.eu/media/43076/26-vc-euco-statement-en.pdf. Accessed 13 January 2023
European Economic and Social Committee (2017) Opinion of the European Economic and Social Committee on the 'Proposal for a Regulation of the European Parliament and of the Council establishing a framework for screening of foreign direct investments into the European Union' (OJ C 262/94)
European Parliament (2012) Report on EU and China: Unbalanced Trade? (A7-0141/2012)
European Parliament (2015) Answer given by Ms Malmström on behalf of the Commission. In: No E-009974/14 | E-009974/2014(ASW). https://www.europarl.europa.eu/doceo/document/E-8-2014-009974-ASW_EN.html
European Parliament (2017) Proposal for a Union Act on the Screening of Foreign Investment in Strategic Sectors (B[8-0000/2017])
European Parliament (2018) Report on the proposal for a regulation of the European Parliament and of the Council establishing a framework for screening of foreign direct investments into the European Union by the Committee on International Trade. Rapporteur: Franck Proust (COM (2017)0487 – C8-0309/2017 – 2017/0224(COD))

European Parliament (2020) Parliamentary question by Silvio Berlusconi (PPE) and Antonio Tajani (PPE) on Chinese capital penetrating Italy's and Europe's economic fabric. In: E-006143/2020. https://www.europarl.europa.eu/doceo/document/E-9-2020-006143_EN.html.
European Parliament (2021a) Answer given by Executive Vice-President Dombrovskis on behalf of the European Commission. In: E-006143/20 | E-006143/2020(ASW). https://www.europarl.europa.eu/doceo/document/E-9-2020-006143-ASW_EN.html.
European Parliament (2021b) Resolution on a new EU-China strategy (2021/2037(INI))
European Political Strategy Centre (EPSC) (2016) Engaging China at a Time of Transition Capitalising on a New Era of Chinese Global Investment and Foreign Policy Initiatives. EPSC Strategic Notes 16
Fabricius J (2022) Foreign Direct Investment Regime Denmark 2022. ICLG. https://iclg.com/practice-areas/foreign-direct-investment-regimes-laws-and-regulations/denmark
Franke U, Varma T (2019) Independence Play: Europe's Pursuit of Strategic Autonomy. European Council on Foreign Relations. https://ecfr.eu/special/independence_play_europes_pursuit_of_strategic_autonomy/
G7 Foreign Ministers (2022) Statement on Preserving Peace and Stability Across the Taiwan Strait. EEAS Website. https://www.eeas.europa.eu/eeas/g7-foreign-ministers%E2%80%99-statement-preserving-peace-and-stability-across-taiwan-strait_en
Garcia C, Tian YL (2021) China's Xi vows "reunification" with Taiwan. Reuters https://www.reuters.com/world/china/chinas-xi-says-reunification-with-taiwan-must-will-be-realised-2021-10-09/
Garcia-Herrero A, Xu J (2017) How to Handle State-Owned Enterprises in EU-China Investment Talks. SSRN Electronic Journal. https://doi.org/10.2139/ssrn.3160514
Germany, Italy and France (2017a) Proposals for ensuring an improved level playing field in trade and investment. https://www.bmwk.de/Redaktion/DE/Downloads/E/eckpunktepapier-proposals-for-ensuring-an-improved-level-playing-field-in-trade-and-investment.pdf?__blob=publicationFile&v=4
Germany, Italy and France (2017b) European investment policy: A common approach to investment control. https://www.politico.eu/wp-content/uploads/2017/08/170728_Investment-screening_non-paper.pdf. Accessed 29 July 2022
Godement F, Vasselier A (2017) China at the gates: a new power audit of EU-China relations. European Council on Foreign Relations, London
Grieger G (2019) EU framework for FDI screening. European Parliamentary Research Service (PE 614.667)
Hanemann T, Huotari M (2018) EU-China FDI: working towards reciprocity in investment relations. Mercator Institute for China Studies and Rhodium Group 3
Helwig N (2022) The Ambiguity of the EU's global role: a social explanation of the term 'Strategic Autonomy.' Eur Foreign Aff Rev 27:21–38. https://doi.org/10.54648/EERR2022010
Helwig N, Sinkkonen V (2022) Strategic autonomy and the EU as a global actor: the evolution, debate and theory of a contested term. Eur Foreign Aff Rev 27:1–20. https://doi.org/10.54648/EERR2022009
Hindelang S, Moberg A (2020) The art of casting political dissent in law: the EU'S framework for the screening of foreign direct investment. Common Mark Law Rev 57(5):1427–1460. https://doi.org/10.54648/COLA2020743
Hoffmeister F (2023) Strategic autonomy in the European Union's external relations law. Common Mark Law Rev 60(3):667–700
Hogan P (2020a) Speech by Commissioner Phil Hogan at Launch of Public Consultation for EU Trade Policy Review - Hosted by EUI Florence. https://ec.europa.eu/commission/commissioners/2019-2024/hogan/announcements/speech-commissioner-phil-hogan-launch-public-consultation-eu-trade-policy-review-hosted-eui-florence_en
Hogan P (2020b) Introductory statement by Commissioner Phil Hogan at Informal meeting of EU Trade Ministers. https://ec.europa.eu/commission/commissioners/2019-2024/hogan/

announcements/introductory-statement-commissioner-phil-hogan-informal-meeting-eu-trade-ministers_en
Hogan P (2020c) "Refreshing Transatlantic Relations": Keynote Address by Commissioner Phil Hogan at Centre for Strategic and International Studies (CSIS), Washington DC. https://ec.europa.eu/commission/commissioners/2019-2024/hogan/announcements/refreshing-transatlantic-relations-keynote-address-commissioner-phil-hogan-centre-strategic-and_en
Hogan P (2020d) Keynote address by Commissioner Phil Hogan at the Centre for European Reform. https://ec.europa.eu/commission/commissioners/2019-2024/hogan/announcements/keynote-address-commissioner-phil-hogan-centre-european-reform_en
Hooijmaaijers B (2019) Blackening skies for Chinese investment in the EU? J Chinese Polit Sci 24(3):451–470. https://doi.org/10.1007/s11366-019-09611-4
Juncker J-C (2017) State of the Union Address 2017. https://ec.europa.eu/commission/presscorner/detail/en/SPEECH_17_3165
Knop C, Mihm A (2016) Maschinenbau: Oettinger gegen Chinesen beim Roboterhersteller Kuka. Frankfurter Allgemeine. https://www.faz.net/aktuell/wirtschaft/unternehmen/guenther-oettinger-gegen-kauf-von-kuka-durch-chinesen-14260546.html
Kratz A, Zenglein M, Sebastian G (2021) Chinese FDI in Europe: 2020 Update. Rhodium Group and MERICS
Kratz A, Zenglein M, Sebastian G, Witzke M (2022) Chinese FDI in Europe: 2021 Update. Rhodium Group and MERICS
Lai K (2021) National security and FDI policy ambiguity: a commentary. J Int Bus Policy 4(4): 496–505
Letta E (2019) Our second identity, protected by a united Europe. TEDxVicenza. https://www.ted.com/talks/enrico_letta_technological_humanism_our_second_identity_protected_in_europe
Macia A, Tausche K (2021) U.S. needs to work with Europe to slow China's innovation rate, Raimondo says. CNBC. https://www.cnbc.com/2021/09/28/us-needs-to-work-with-europe-to-slow-chinas-innovation-rate-raimondo-says.html
Maher R (2016) The elusive EU–China strategic partnership. Int Aff 92(4):959–976. https://doi.org/10.1111/1468-2346.12659
Malmström C (2017) Building bridges: strengthening EU-China trade and investment relations (Speech at China's reform agenda: what's next for European companies)
Mesters B (2011) Bod Xinmao was niet netjes. NRC. https://www.nrc.nl/nieuws/2011/01/27/bod-xinmao-was-niet-netjes-11991829-a1219219
Meunier S (2014a) A Faustian bargain or just a good bargain? Chinese foreign direct investment and politics in Europe. Asia Eur J 12(1–2):143–158. https://doi.org/10.1007/s10308-014-0382-x
Meunier S (2014b) Divide and conquer? China and the cacophony of foreign investment rules in the EU. J Eur Public Policy 21(7):996–1016. https://doi.org/10.1080/13501763.2014.912145
Meunier S, Nicolaidis K (2019) The geopoliticization of European trade and investment policy. J Common Mark Stud 57(S1):103–113. https://doi.org/10.1111/jcms.12932
Ministère Des Armées (2020) Communiqués Souveraineté des entreprises statégiques: Florence Parly annonce que L'tat travaille à une solution alternative de reprise de Photonis https://www.concurrences.com/IMG/pdf/communique_s_souverainete_des_entreprises_strate_giques___florence_parly_annonce_que_l_e_tat_travaille_a_une_solution_alternative_de_reprise_de_photonis-2.pdf?65820/d2dacb6ae0ad0bce005e3a19bd98d9c582e313a62084e73dfe315d00c7a98aac
Nettesheim M (2020) Screening for what threat: preserving "Public Order and Security", securing reciprocity in international trade, or supporting certain social, environmental, or industrial policies? In: Hindelang S, Moberg A (eds) YSEC yearbook of socio-economic constitutions 2020. Springer International Publishing, pp 481–504
Nicolas F (2014) China's direct investment in the European Union: challenges and policy responses. China Econ J 7(1):103–125. https://doi.org/10.1080/17538963.2013.874070

Obama B (2016) Presidential order regarding the proposed acquisition of a controlling interest in Aixtron SE by Grand Chip Investment GMBH
OECD (2009) Security-related Terms in International Investment Law
Office of the United Nations High Commissioner for Human Rights (2020) Compilation on the United States of America (Report)
Pacheco Pardo R (2018) Europe's financial security and Chinese economic statecraft: the case of the Belt and Road Initiative. Asia Eur J 16(3):237–250. https://doi.org/10.1007/s10308-018-0511-z
Papadopoulos T (2015) Privatized companies, golden shares and property ownership in the Euro Crisis Era: a discussion after Commission v. Greece. Eur Company Financ Law Rev 12(1):1–18. https://doi.org/10.1515/ecfr-2015-0001
Papadopoulos T (2018) Privatizations of state-owned enterprises in Greece after the third economic adjustment programme. Eur Comp Law 15(6):205–212. https://doi.org/10.54648/EUCL2018030
Peverelli P, Song J (2012) Chinese entrepreneurship: a social capital approach. Springer, Berlin Heidelberg
Pietrasik J, Michalski J (2022) Foreign Direct Investment Regimes Poland 2022. ICLG. https://iclg.com/practice-areas/foreign-direct-investment-regimes-laws-and-regulations/poland
Popławski K (2017) Capital does have nationality: Germany's fears of Chinese investments. OSW Centre for Eastern Studies
Reilly J (2017) Leveraging Diversity: Europe's China Policy. EUI Working Paper
Reuters Staff (2016a) German ministry to clear takeover of Kuka by China's Midea. Reuters. https://www.reuters.com/article/uk-kuka-midea-group-ministry-idUKKCN10S0PB
Reuters Staff (2016b) Germany withdrew approval of Aixtron deal on new "security-related information." Reuters. https://www.reuters.com/article/aixtron-ma-fujian-ministry-idUSB4N19L00M
Reuters Staff (2020) Germany tries to stop US from luring away firm seeking coronavirus vaccine. Reuters. https://www.reuters.com/article/health-coronavirus-germany-usa-idUSL8N2B8075
Riela S, Zámborský P (2021) Screening of foreign acquisitions and trade in critical goods. Asia-Pac J EU Stud 18(3):55–83
Roberts A, Choer Moraes H, Ferguson V (2019) Toward a geoeconomic order in international trade and investment. J Int Econ Law 22(4):655–676. https://doi.org/10.1093/jiel/jgz036
Rogelja I, Tsimonis K (2020) Narrating the China threat: securitising Chinese economic presence in Europe. Chinese J Int Polit 13(1):103–133. https://doi.org/10.1093/cjip/poz019
Santander S, Vlassis A (2021) The EU in search of autonomy in the era of Chinese expansionism and COVID-19 pandemic. Global Policy 12(1):149–156. https://doi.org/10.1111/1758-5899.12899
Sattorova M (2022) EU investment law at a crossroads: open strategic autonomy in timers of heightened security concerns. Common Mark Law Rev 60(3):701–732
Schilder T (2022) Securitisation, China and FDI: The EU's Foreign Direct Investment Screening Regulation. E-International Relations. https://www.e-ir.info/2022/03/15/securitisation-china-and-fdi-the-eus-foreign-direct-investment-screening-regulation/
Schill SW (2019) The European Union's foreign direct investment screening paradox: tightening inward investment control to further external investment liberalization. Legal Issues Econ Integr 46(2):105–128
Seaman J, Huotari M, Otero-Iglesias M (2017) Chinese investment in Europe: a country-level approach. French Institute of International Relations, Elcano Royal Institute, Mercator Institute for China Studies
Sheahan M (2016) China's Fujian drops Aixtron bid after Obama blocks deal. Reuters. https://www.reuters.com/article/us-aixtron-m-a-fujian-idUSKBN13X16H
Sinkkonen V, Martin G (2022) Past as prologue? The United States and European Strategic Autonomy in the Biden Era. Eur Foreign Aff Rev 27:99–120. https://doi.org/10.54648/EERR2022013

Snell J (2019) EU Foreign Direct Investment Screening Europe qui protège? Eur Law Rev 44:137–138

Spokesperson of the Chinese Mission to the EU (2022) A Question Concerning the Remarks on Taiwan by the EU High Representative. Mission of the People's Republic of China to the European Union. http://eu.china-mission.gov.cn/eng/fyrjh/202208/t20220807_10736503.htm

Stanzel A (2017) Germany's turnabout on Chinese takeovers – European Council on foreign relations. ECFR. https://ecfr.eu/article/commentary_germanys_turnabout_on_chinese_takeovers_7251/

Stec G (2021) "Correct choice" on strategic autonomy: What China wants from the EU | Merics. MERICS. https://merics.org/en/merics-briefs/correct-choice-strategic-autonomy-what-china-wants-eu

TCC (2022) EU-U.S. Joint Statement of the Trade and Technology Council Paris-Saclay, France. https://circabc.europa.eu/ui/group/09242a36-a438-40fd-a7af-fe32e36cbd0e/library/14bf0332-62ee-411b-8c74-bea38cd79efb/details

The White House (2020) U.S. Strategic Approach to the People's Republic of China. https://trumpwhitehouse.archives.gov/wp-content/uploads/2020/05/U.S.-Strategic-Approach-to-The-Peoples-Republic-of-China-Report-5.24v1.pdf

The White House (2022) Statement by President Biden on the America COMPETES Act of 2022. https://www.whitehouse.gov/briefing-room/statements-releases/2022/01/25/statement-by-president-biden-on-the-america-competes-act-of-2022/

The White House (2023) Building a Clean Energy Economy: A Guidebook to the Inflation Reduction Act's Investments in Clean Energy and Climate Action. Version 2 <https://www.whitehouse.gov/wp-content/uploads/2022/12/Inflation-Reduction-Act-Guidebook.pdf>

Tóth J (2022) Foreign Direct Investment Regimes Hungary 2022. ICLG. https://iclg.com/practice-areas/foreign-direct-investment-regimes-laws-and-regulations/hungary

Tweede Kamer (2010a) Response to questions by Gesthuizen on potential Chinese state aid regarding the sale of Draka *(Antwoord vragen Gesthuizen over eventuele Chinese staatssteun bij de verkoop van Draka)* (Vergaderjaar 2010-2011, nr.943). https://zoek.officielebekendmakingen.nl/ah-tk-20102011-943.html

Tweede Kamer (2010b) Response to Questions by Verburg regarding Draka *(Antwoord vragen Verburg over Draka)* (Vergaderjaar 2010-2011, nr.942). https://zoek.officielebekendmakingen.nl/ah-tk-20102011-942.html#ID-2010Z18595-d28e82

United Nations Human Rights Committee (2014) Concluding observations on the fourth periodic report on the United States of America (CCPR/C/USA/CO/4)

Valero J (2017) Commission says proposal to block Chinese takeovers is "worth discussing." Euractiv. https://www.euractiv.com/section/trade-society/news/commission-says-proposal-to-block-chinese-takeovers-is-worth-discussing/

van Veen E, Langenberg R (2022) Phoenix or Icarus? European strategic autonomy in light of Ukraine. Clingendael CRU Policy Brief

van Zon W (2023) The application of regulation 452/2019 in response to Chinese Foreign Direct Investment. Legal Iss Econ Integr 50(2):129–164

Vidigal G, Schill SW (2021) International economic law and the securitization of policy objectives: risks of a Schmittean exception. Legal Iss Econ Integr 48(2):109–118

Vila ST, Peters M (2016) The privatising industry in Europe. Transnational Institute Issue Brief

von der Leyen U (2019) Speech in the European Parliament Plenary Session. https://ec.europa.eu/info/sites/default/files/president-elect-speech-original_en.pdf

von der Leyen U (2020) State of the Union Address by President von der Leyen at the European Parliament Plenary. https://ec.europa.eu/commission/presscorner/detail/en/SPEECH_20_1655

Weiss V Schulz S (2022) Foreign Direct Investment Regimes Austria 2022. ICLG. https://iclg.com/practice-areas/foreign-direct-investment-regimes-laws-and-regulations/austria

Zhang AH (2014) Foreign direct investment from China: sense and sensibility. Northwestern J Int Law Bus 34(3):395–453. https://doi.org/10.2139/ssrn.2307617

The Coin of the Realm: Foreign Investment Screening & Trust in International Relations

Manu Misra

Contents

Abstract Investment screening mechanisms ("ISMs") have been in a state of flux, both in practice and design, with a notable recent increase in new regulatory frameworks and significant amendments to existing screening systems that can be observed globally. Trust, or the lack of it, has been at the heart of the recent cluster of state activity related to ISMs. Accepting foreign investment proposals, especially in critical sectors and/or involving state-controlled entities, naturally increases the host state's potential vulnerability and thus requires a higher level of trust toward both the investor and its governing home state. ISMs are therefore a manifestation of mistrust in their legislative form and a test of trust in their individual decisions. Despite being elusive empirically, as a distinct concept in international relations ("IR") theory, trust is multidimensional in its abstract form and defies being easily captured within a singular definition. Nonetheless, taking this contribution poses two key questions. First, within the prominent schools of thought that provide alternative explanations of the concept in IR theory, how can we define trust and identify its role in foreign

M. Misra (✉)
Rio de Janeiro, Brazil
e-mail: manu.misra@bocconialumni.it

J. H. Pohl et al. (eds.), *National Security and Investment Controls*,
Springer Studies in Law & Geoeconomics (2024) 3: 103–128,
https://doi.org/10.1007/17280_2024_27, Published online: 24 February 2024

investment policy for the purpose of ISMs? Second, what are the appropriate legal tools that may be adopted to either build trust itself or at least to help mitigate the security threats that inward foreign investment may entail thus allowing for investment flows to safely continue despite the general presence of mistrust?

1 Introduction

> Trust is the coin of the realm. When trust was in the room, whatever room that was—the family room, the schoolroom, the coach's room, the office room, the government room, or the military room—good things happened. When trust was not in the room, good things did not happen. Everything else is details.[1]

Against the backdrop of the COVID-19 pandemic, two specific observations from 2020 are now vividly discernible. First, it is well established that ISMs have witnessed a significant global increase. One could not only witness a proliferation of new regulatory frameworks but also some significant amendments to existing screening systems. Regulatory approaches pertaining to the screening and review of foreign investments is an issue that states have increasingly been coming to terms with, while several are reconsidering their incumbent stance toward who they partner with and what constitutes their security interests.

Although the state of flux observed in the application and design of ISMs had in fact started even a few years prior to the pandemic, the latter introduced fresh concerns relating to inward foreign investment and reaffirmed the need for scrutinising the same on security grounds.[2] This acceleration of a pre-existent shift has dramatically changed the global landscape of foreign investment policies. The UNCTAD notes that in 2020, the ratio of restrictive investment policy measures based on security grounds was the highest in almost two decades.[3]

A second observation pertaining to the COVID-19 pandemic relates to the importance of trust and, at the same time, its lack. Often regarded as the bedrock of all relationships, whether interpersonal, social, commercial or political, trust is a fundamental element of sustaining positive outcomes in every sphere of human interaction and even more so during a global pandemic. However, an immense shortfall of multiple kinds of trust is observable, whether trust towards national governments by their citizens or trust towards the media by its viewership. On that front, the context of international relations has been no exception. The current Secretary-General of the United Nations and at least two of his last predecessors

---

[1] Shultz (2020a, b).

[2] Especially, but not exclusively, in terms of erratic or heavily dented corporate valuations and protecting assets connected to the health sector.

[3] UNCTAD (2021).

have on multiple occasions highlighted a global trust deficit and how "trust within and among nations is on the decline."[4]

Alarmingly, within the last year, the level of mistrust rose to a historical high, especially but not exclusively concerning the bilateral relations between one of the geopolitically most dominant nations of the twenty-first century, the People's Republic of China ("China") and specific other states or regions.[5] This includes not only, as one might expect, the United States[6] but also Canada,[7] the United Kingdom,[8] several parts of Europe,[9] Australia,[10] India[11] and several states within Southeast and East Asia.[12]

This contribution argues that the above two observations from 2020, seen against the backdrop of the COVID-19 pandemic, i.e., the dramatic rise in the expansion and usage of ISMs and the heightened international mistrust (especially but not exclusively toward China), are not coincidental and that while the latter certainly may not exhaustively explain the former, it has nonetheless been important, if not decisive, toward the nature and degree that the former has empirically taken and will continue to take the latter into account in the future. While both observations have generally predated 2020 and a recent global rise in geo-economic activity, i.e., the usage of international economic instruments for geostrategic ends, already contributed to a perception of foreign inward capital as a security threat, the specific conditions that the pandemic has induced (including exposure of existent vulnerabilities, human casualties, economic losses, uncertainty and time pressure[13]) have acted as a catalyst for this reaction and significantly increased the perceived need for ISMs.

It also argues more generally that ISMs and trust in IR are interrelated in both theory and practice. In that sense, ISMs in their legislative form may be seen as a legal 'symptom' or manifestation of mistrust in international relations and a test of trust in their individual decisions, the two being policy acts where ISMs and trust overlap.[14]

As an important caveat, trust is not the only potential factor driving the emergence and use of ISMs. There are indeed several motivations that states may have individually or simultaneously, which may lead them to adopt such mechanisms. Some of these potential motivations may be based on the perception of a genuine security threat, while others may be characterised as 'illiberal' or disingenuous motivations

[4]UN (2020).

[5]Younis (2021); Silver et al. (2020).

[6]Silver (2022).

[7]Korzinski (2023).

[8]Gaston (2020).

[9]Turcsányi (2021).

[10]Lowy Institute (2022).

[11]India Today (2020).

[12]ISEAS (2021).

[13]Farrell and Newman (2020).

[14]Misra (2023a, b).

(such as protectionism, economic nationalism and xenophobia) aimed at introducing ISMs to abuse the concept of national security.[15]

However, trust is a distinct, although fluid, concept with different forms, each of which contains its own explanatory value that may overlap and operate simultaneously with others. In other words, not trusting a state's involvement in a proposed foreign investment (and as a result to either block or condition it) does not necessarily imply being solely protectionist, nationalist or prejudiced against a group or community as a whole, as is sometimes blanketly assumed.

Second, it is also acknowledged that the level of trust a state places in a foreign state may at times not be sufficiently (or at all) relevant to ultimately have any effect on actual investment policy or ISM practice. Instead, it is entirely plausible that, for some states, especially developing countries, economic or geopolitical realities may not allow investment screening policy to be practiced with intergovernmental trust as an underlying basis. Following one's trust is therefore, a privilege for some and a luxury beyond reach for others.

Last, this theoretical link between trust and FDI flows has been confirmed empirically in the recent past. Although not directly concerning the context of investment screening, a 2019 cross-country study examined the effect of social trust on economic exchange between China and its major trading partners over the period 2005–2013 and concluded that "social trust significantly increases bilateral trade and foreign direct investment (FDI) between China and its partners."[16]

1.1 ISM Legislations as a Symptom of Mistrust

Accepting foreign investment proposals, especially in critical sectors and involving state-controlled entities, naturally creates more potential vulnerabilities of the host state[17] and thus requires compensation by a greater level of trust toward both the investor and its governing home state. Once the investment is legally established, it is not just that capital is flowing into the host state but, depending on the nature of the deal, the foreign investor typically also receives rights, control and access in return, legally and practically.

The unrestricted admission of foreign state-controlled capital is therefore tantamount to exercising a "discretion granting policy,"[18] defined as "policies that grant other states discretion over outcomes previously controlled by the first."[19] The

[15] A further, relatively exceptional form of motivation behind the introduction or usage of ISMs may be 'weaponization' where ISMs can be used as weapons themselves, as opposed to being used as shields. See Carrai (2020); Danzman (2021).

[16] Wang et al. (2019).

[17] Moran (2009, 2013).

[18] Hoffman (2002), p. 385.

[19] Ibid.

discretion granted in the context of ISMs is the discretion that the foreign investor over its newly-acquired assets located in its host jurisdiction enjoys once the investment is legally established. Such discretion would then allow the foreign investor to produce an outcome that would otherwise have been 'controlled' by the government of the host state, had only domestic entities been allowed as investors. The authorisation of FDI and the affording of control and access to foreign investors may therefore be a position of vulnerability for the host state, especially if the asset in question may be 'strategic' or related to critical infrastructure or data.

The existence of such a discretion granting policy, in conjunction with the host state's demonstrable subjective belief in the trustworthiness of the foreign state has been suggested as a possible standard for empirically identifying 'trusting relationships.'[20]

Based on such an understanding, the bilateral relationship between the United Kingdom and China, for example, may thus be classified as a trusting relationship until 2020,within the context of security threats resulting from foreign investment. On the one hand, the UK government allowed a Chinese state-controlled entity (in this case, the China General Nuclear Power Group or "CGN") to invest in a nuclear project known as Hinkley Point[21] (and thus legally have access and one-third control of it), and on the other hand, it announced the beginning of a 'golden era' of UK-China relations as a "global comprehensive strategic partnership for the twenty-first century"[22] since "no economy in the world is as open to Chinese investment as the UK".[23] Furthermore, the ey Point investment would only be a "first step in a grand plan for CGN to roll out a string of nuclear plants in the UK."[24]

Nonetheless, in theory, states need to prepare for the worst case, i.e., cases where it lost or never had any trust toward another state. Thus, states introduce ISMs or strengthen existing ones, allowing themselves to react in an adequate manner. While intended at blocking particular threats, the ISMs also show a state's general mistrust towards foreign states in a legislative form.

1.2 ISM Decisions as a Test of Trust

Once an ISM is in place or further strengthened, depending on its substantive criteria and institutional design, a multitude of factors (whether either legal, economic, political) pertaining to the proposed transaction (for example, the sector or assets

[20] Ibid.

[21] Gracie (2015). Interestingly, it was reported that "Chinese government and business leaders talk approvingly about the UK's openness to Chinese investment, even in areas of critical infrastructure" which the Chinese Ambassador to the UK 'conceded might be "unthinkable" in other countries.'

[22] FCO (2015).

[23] Wintour (2020a).

[24] Watt (2017).

involved, the amount or proportion of equity purchased, the transacting entities or the home state of the foreign investor) would typically be considered by a screening authority.

However, the amount of weight ISM decision-makers apply to each of such factors, and whether they consider a factor to be a pro or a con, is ultimately a subjective estimate that is heavily dependent on the nationality of the foreign investor. Therefore, inevitably, ISM decisions are an exercise of self-judgement and executive political discretion, which is a reflection or a test of existent trust, not just toward the foreign investor but also its home state.[25]

2 Trust in IR Theory: A Multi-Lens Approach

Trust should therefore be a topic of greater interest in research related to ISMs (and policy practice). However, what *is* trust in the theory of international relations and how can it be defined or understood for the purpose of ISMs? Additionally, what circumstances and dynamics have contributed to the dramatic shift in the global landscape of foreign investment regulations and the historic trust deficit facing Chinese state-controlled investors today in certain parts of the world?

As a distinct concept in international relations theory, trust is multidimensional and 'slippery' in its abstract form and defies being easily captured in a single definition. This makes it an analytical challenge, both in the theoretical sense and in its application to empirical contexts to solve explanatory puzzles. This contribution adopts a multi-lens approach wherein trust in IR theory is considered under three diverging or competing typologies that provide alternative explanations of trust in IR theory, namely, rationality, sociology and psychology.[26] The selected typologies are not meant to be exhaustive. However, each follow general, themes that facilitate the unpacking of the concept of trust to a considerable extent.

2.1 *IR Trust & Rational Choice: Trust as a Function of Reciprocity*

Under a rational choice prism for understanding trust, the trustor would exist under conditions of uncertainty and incomplete information concerning the intentions of the trustee, and perceive the concept of trust on a predominantly calculative basis. The degree of trust applied would essentially be derived from a cost–benefit analysis,

[25] In that there is no precise 'technical' or 'objective' standard that is generally applicable for all foreign investment proposals in the practice of ISMs, which are inherently a legalised extension of foreign policy, rather than a politicised area of economic law.

[26] Broadly following a manner suggested by Ruzicka and Keating (2015).

where it would be rational to place trust on the opposing party if the predicted gains of cooperating with a state are higher than expected losses. Trust is thus "a rational prediction about the nature or characteristics of the other state."[27]

A specific notion of trust derived from rational choice, which fits the context at hand most appropriately, revolves around the concept of reciprocity, which plays an important role not only in the study of international relations but also as a central principle of international law, including international economic law. Reciprocity can explain how, despite the absence of an overarching coercive authority, self-interest may drive parties to seek cooperation.[28] Trust under such an approach is characterised by a calculated acceptance of a position of vulnerability based on the existence of means to carry out retaliation in the event a security threat from foreign investment materialises, with the possibility of such retaliation thus having a deterrent effect.[29] In the absence of such reciprocity, the potential for threat remains unilateral, thus leading to a state of mistrust toward the other state and the arrangement. Reciprocity is therefore a prerequisite for building trust and, when present, an indicator of existent trust.

For example, an empirical study that conducted survey experiments in the United States and China to examine how reciprocity influences opposition to foreign acquisitions of domestic companies found that "reciprocity is an important determinant of public opinion on the regulation of foreign investments."[30]

Another study conducted interviews with high-level EU and country officials involved in the negotiation process for the EU-wide investment screening mechanism found that "countries with higher technological levels were more supportive of FDI screening due to concerns over unreciprocated technological transfer."[31]

Further examples of the issue of reciprocity and trust in the context of foreign investment relations with China, where such reciprocity (particularly in strategically important sectors) has been relatively rare,[32] can be observed in diplomatic exchanges and public statements of state officials from the EU. For example, the European Parliament Committee on Economic and Monetary Affairs suggested an amendment to the text of the European Commission's proposed EU-wide ISM, suggesting that "when screening foreign direct investment, Member States and the

[27] Ibid, 14.

[28] Keohane (1986).

[29] Reciprocity in international economic relations brings other advantages to states as well, including for example greater volume of interactions, better dispute resolutions mechanisms and the development of common or more compatible technical standards.

[30] Chilton et al. (2017). Importantly, while reciprocity was found to clearly matter, the authors left open the question of *why* reciprocity might affect public opinion, suggesting that either "individuals care about reciprocity because they believe that it will induce co-operative behaviour from other countries, or they because believe fairness norms are important."

[31] Chan and Meunier (2021).

[32] To be clear, the policy measure through which this reciprocity has been denied in China has primarily been administrative measures that manage a negative list of market access for foreign investment, which are then further subject to potential security review under the PRC's ISM.

Commission should also consider whether similar possibilities for investment exist for European investors in the third countries concerned, thus respecting the principle of reciprocity."[33]

The suggestion is that the steady increase in incoming Chinese state-controlled investment in critical sectors of European economies on the one hand and the lack of reciprocity or "great asymmetry"[34] in investment market access in China for European firms on the other, reinforced the perceived vulnerability of European policymakers and created a sense of rational mistrust, which eventually led to the creation of the EU-wide ISM. In fact, EU officials and European member state officials repeatedly framed the proposal on investment screening presented by the EU Commission in September 2017 as a tool to *level the playing field* with China.

As noted above, while it is clear that IR trust may be theorised as a function of investment reciprocity in the rational choice framework and that reciprocity (or a 'level playing field') has been an important policy concern for the EU in its relations with China, determining whether such concerns were in fact, empirically and accurately related to mistrust, would require greater empirical investigation.[35] As acknowledged in Chilton et al. (2020), the insistence on reciprocity may be driven by the realisation of other concepts, such as fairness.

2.2 IR Trust & Sociology: Trust as a Product of Identity

A sociological or constructivist approach to trust in IR theory perceives trust as a social phenomenon and is dissatisfied with rational approaches since they fail to "fully capture the reasons that may prevent or encourage state actors to engage in cooperative behaviour."[36] Instead, it adopts a line of reasoning that emphasises the role of identity in the formation of trust, with shared norms and values being the key. The more similar states are in terms of their social identity, the greater sense of security they create in their perception of an international arrangement, and the more likely they are to be able to establish and develop a trusting relation. Identity may thus shape state behaviour "beyond the cognitive calculation of risks in a given situation."[37]

[33] Committee on International Trade (2018).

[34] Brunsden and Fleming (2020).

[35] Official public statements and press notes leave open a fair amount of ambiguity on the issue. For example, during the June 2020 EU-China Summit, the President of the European Commission, Ursula von der Leyen, stated that "Progress implies cooperation by both sides, implies reciprocity, and implies trust." This could either imply that with greater reciprocity, greater trust may be built, or it could imply that reciprocity and trust are entirely separate concepts. See European Commission (2020b).

[36] Weinhardt (2015).

[37] Ibid.

If one were to accept such a conception of trust and apply it within the context of ISMs (and the trust required to offset the vulnerability resulting from allowing foreign state-controlled entities to invest in a host state's critical sectors), then it would follow that authorities in applying ISMs would have to either block or condition investment proposals from states in which the degree of commonality in social identities is low, since such states may not be considered sufficiently trustworthy.[38]

In addition, in 2017, the European Parliament Committee on International Trade proposed a regulation to be added to the EU ISM:

> In determining whether a foreign investment might affect security or public order, Member States and the Commission might also have regard to the context and the circumstances under which the investment is or was made including whether, inter alia, the investment might lead to a monopolistic structure, and whether the market in the foreign investor's country of origin is open, restricted or closed, whether there is reciprocity and a level playing field and whether there is a risk of breach of international human rights instruments or core ILO standards.[39]

In a similar vein, it was also suggested that for the purpose of determining whether a foreign direct investment is likely to affect security or public order, it should not only be considered whether the investor is controlled by the government of a third country, including through significant funding, as the EU Commission proposed but also "especially if that government does not fully respect international human rights law, international humanitarian law and is not complying with relevant international arms control norms such as the Arms Trade Treaty (ATT), whether opaque ownership structures are used where the ultimate owner is not clear, or if common market rules are contravened."[40]

This demonstrates a view in which it is considered plausible that a foreign investment might affect security or public order if there is a risk of breach of international labour law standards or that the home state of the investor did not sufficiently respect international human rights law and international humanitarian law. If trust plays a role in ISM policymaking and trust may be a product of social identity, then it could be argued that such a human rights-based view toward foreign investment and national security could, in part, be a symptom of mistrust. However, just as with the rational trust-based understanding of ISMs, a sense of fairness or morality (as a notion independent of trust) may be an underlying reasoning.

In the case of the UK, a similar tone was evident when the law effectively banning Chinese firm Huawei Technologies from accessing its future critical network infrastructure referred to the 'ethical risks' of accepting Chinese investment.[41] Such

---

[38] For example, what may constitute as an appropriate use of economic means (such as foreign investment) for strategic ends may vary across social norms and values and as a result negatively affect the trustworthiness of a foreign investor and its home state.

[39] Committee on International Trade (2018).

[40] Ibid.

[41] Reuters (2020a).

events, especially when seen in light of the national parliaments of certain liberal democratic states declaring the PRC government as having "committed genocide",[42] may either indicate existent mistrust or the creation of greater mistrust in a sociological model, which in turn may have implications for ISM design and practice.

Another way in which concepts related to values and identity have been observed to be gradually entering ISM policy and hence form an indicator or symptom of mistrust are on questions of regime-type and domestic political system. The US Secretary of State Anthony Blinken stated in September 2020 that "the US must work with allies to set similar policies on investment restrictions, technical standards and export controls" to ensure an "ecosystem that protects and promotes liberal democratic values."[43]

For the EU, the general principles guiding EU external relations state that "the Union's action on the international scene shall be guided by the principles which have inspired its own creation, development and enlargement, and which it seeks to advance in the wider world: democracy, the rule of law",[44] among others. The EU-wide ISM falls under the EU Common Commercial Policy,[45] which is meant to be "conducted in the context of the principles and objectives of the Unions external action."[46]

Such observations of reference to values and norms in ISM policy and other areas of international economic policy are in line with a broader shift in foreign policy objectives based on an 'ideological challenge against liberal democracy' and 'shared values', envisioning an 'alliance of democracies' to defend a 'rules-based international order'. These observations give the impression that even if for narrative-building, IR trust based on social identity is not only theoretically plausible but also empirically demonstrable, either in the form of mistrust toward a foreign state for holding a completely different set of values as the host state (or worse, challenging the values themselves[47]) or in the form of growing trust between states of similar values.

---

[42] Reuters (2021).

[43] Whalen (2020).

[44] Article 21(1) TEU.

[45] The EU investment screening regulation also includes an indicative list of factors that member states and the European Commission may consider when assessing whether a foreign direct investment is likely to affect security or public order, one of which is "freedom and pluralism of the media." See Article 4(1) EU Regulation 2019/452.

[46] Article 207(1) TFEU.

[47] Chang (2020).

2.3 IR Trust & Psychology: Trust as Emotion

Psychological approaches in IR[48] understand trust on a non-calculative, emotive basis and not as an outcome of a specific structural or social context.[49] As a result, different states may arrive at different positions of trust, even under the same set of conditions. Trust here is a form of an innate, preconceived intuition or belief that precedes conscious decision making,[50] in which situational factors (such as labels, images, historical narratives and events) may hold significant explanatory value, as they might strongly shape such pre-existing beliefs, which then trigger a propensity to trust or mistrust the intention or motive of another state, which ultimately then guides policy choices.[51] Psychological factors may thus be an important 'prefigurative' piece of the puzzle in explaining state behaviour, which may not always be based on rational or sociological considerations, including in international economic relations."[52]

Two such psychological concepts on which trust between states is commonly understood relate to credibility and goodwill. Trusting a state's credibility essentially means being confident that it shall live up to its word and fulfil the promises or commitments it makes.[53] On the other hand, to perceive a state as being inherently well-intentioned (or at the very least, not ill-intentioned), i.e., having goodwill is considered another form of trust where even if a state is perceived as likely to not keep its promises or fulfil its obligations, it is not thought to be seeking to exploit other states for its own benefit or worse, harming other states as an end to itself.[54] Both concepts stem from human psychology studies and play a distinct role in understanding IR trust.[55] The most problematic situation arises, of course, when a state mistrust toward another is based simultaneously on *both* the perception of a lack of credibility and a perception of bad faith.

In addition to the two relatively common understandings of psychological trust mentioned above, two additional relatively specific and serious forms of psychological trust (or rather, mistrust) are discussed below and suggested as being directly relevant to the context at hand.

---

[48] See generally, Goldgeier and Tetlock (2001).

[49] Mercer (2005); Rathbun (2009).

[50] Pettit (1995).

[51] Dunn and Schweitzer (2005).

[52] van Aaken and Kurtz (2019).

[53] Larson (1997), p. 714. This is also in line with the opinion in Shultz (2020a, b). Schultz opines that "trust as an idea implies a belief that what a nation or a public official commits to do will, in fact, be done."

[54] Larson (1997), p. 714.

[55] Important to note however, that "trust based on the belief that the other is well-intentioned toward us is less fragile than credibility." Larson (1997), p. 715. In other words, it is easier to overcome conflicting situations arising purely from issues of non-compliance with obligations, if the intentions behind such non-compliance are nonetheless perceived as positive, reasonable or at the very least, not malicious."

2.3.1 Mistrust from 'Bias'

The first form refers to a sense of bias or prejudice in assuming an image of inherent bad faith on the part of another state that denies even the possibility that a state might have genuine bona fide intentions.[56] Relying primarily on hyperbole and ideological rhetoric, such "distrust is deeply embedded in antagonistic domestic structures and ideologies"[57] and typically entails a deliberately contrived element of artificiality in its assessment of another state's motives and is often promoted by domestic political leaders to legitimize their internal rule.[58]

By presenting an image of a constant 'enemy' that is inherently untrustworthy, the motives of the foreign state are suspect, not so much on their own merits but more in order to portray domestic political leaders as "striving to achieve societal values, as portrayed in an ideology,"[59] which may ultimately help secure their own political legitimacy.[60] This exaggerated and inherently negative image is then exploited to rationalize specific partisan domestic policies or exercises of power by such leaders, potentially leading to what has been argued as a "missed opportunity"[61] where decisions that would otherwise have led to mutually beneficial results are unduly rejected.

In considering the interaction of psychological trust in IR theory with ISMs, a potential for a 'missed opportunity' may be theorised here, in which an ISM is used to block foreign investment by a Chinese firm, not based on any legitimately inferred security threats, wherein a clear and plausible vulnerability is established, but rather simply due to its Chinese origin. Such 'abusive' use of ISMs would be the result of psychologically biased mistrust generated by disingenuously propagating an exaggerated negative perception of China, for domestic political purposes and as such, unrelated to the host state's security concerns. In short, a 'lose–lose' situation from an economic perspective.

Along similar lines of determining the operation of a psychological bias against Chinese foreign investment in the general public, a 2019 study that conducted a survey experiment analysing the relation between threat perceptions and FDI preferences in the United States, concluded that "respondents are indeed less likely to support Chinese FDI when primed with information that highlights the security and economic threats posed by China than when they receive no such priming."[62]

---

[56] Holsti (1967).

[57] Larson (1997).

[58] Ibid.

[59] Ibid.

[60] Scholarly opinions from China, when commenting on the source of mistrust between the US and China often fall directly in line with such an understanding of IR trust. See for example, Peng (2021).

[61] Larson (1997).

[62] Zeng and Li (2019). Another study considered the role of the English-language media and discursive strategies in shaping negative judgement among readership on the legitimacy of Chinese foreign investments. See Wang (2020).

While such an abuse of ISMs is indeed plausible (and reprehensible), determining where and to what extent the blocking or conditioning of Chinese foreign investment has been empirically based on mistrust derived primarily from such domestic political exploitation of negative psychological biases would require individual case-study analyses. Nonetheless, there are numerous examples in the public sphere where such psychological bias-centred mistrust against Chinese foreign investment has been pointed out.[63]

2.3.2 Mistrust from 'Betrayal'

The second form of psychological mistrust relevant here pertains to the specific notion of 'betrayal' in the IR theory of trust.[64] Unlike a negative bias based on hyperbole or political rhetoric, betrayal derives from a prior lived experience that deeply violates a profound normative belief in the general trustworthiness of a state. A betrayal is thus an emotionally and morally charged concept, the experience of which importantly provokes a fundamental re-evaluation of the nature of the relationship itself.

Scholars have pointed out the importance of distinguishing between betrayal and mere disappointment that arises in response to "a specific let-down following a rational and conscious process of decision-making" or when a calculated rational choice-based reliance or a 'strategic bet' fails to materialise.[65] While disappointment can be caused by both animate and inanimate entities and invokes a relatively nonchalant response, betrayal is caused by serious breaches of trust in human relationships, and the harm suffered is qualitatively more profound and existential in nature.[66]

The year 2020 saw at least two events that have been characterised in popular discourse and in public statements made by state officials as 'betrayals' by the Chinese state and have had a profound impact on trust on a psychological level, one of which is discussed below.[67]

In May 2020, the Hong Kong National Security Law was introduced through a vote by the Chinese National People's Congress,[68] which also passed a resolution by the Chinese National People's Congress Standing Committee to enable the

---

[63] See for example AFR (2019); Oliveira (2017).

[64] Michel (2012).

[65] Ibid, 881.

[66] Larson (1997), p. 714. The author describes the distinction as "when the other party violates our trust, we are morally outraged, not just disappointed."

[67] The first example pertains to the May 2020 China–India skirmishes in the Galwan Valley. See ENS (2020); Bhattacharyya (2020); Manoj (2020); Kumar (2020); Sinha (2021). The second example pertains to the promulgation of the Hong Kong National Security Law, also in May 2020. See AFP (2022); Michael (2020); Reuters (2020c); Kammerer (2020).

[68] Xinhua (2020).

disqualification of 'pro-democracy' members of the Hong Kong legislature.[69] The law granted sweeping powers to the Chinese central government resulting in no effective opposition[70] in Hong Kong.

These measures by the Chinese state have been perceived as the end of the 'one country-two systems' model and were officially described as "a clear breach of the legally binding Sino-British Joint Declaration."[71]The Joint Declaration was a treaty signed conjointly in 1984 by then UK Prime Minister Margaret Thatcher and Chinese Premier Zhao Ziyang. It guaranteed Hong Kong a high degree of autonomy and protected the civil liberties of its residents for a period of 50 years beginning 1997, both of which were denied as a result of the measures taken by the Chinese state in 2020, 27 years earlier than it had promised to not do so.

The UK Prime Minister described these measures as "a grave and deeply disturbing step"[72] by China that would "erode trust in its willingness to keep its word and live up to its promises."[73] In addition, the UK Foreign Secretary stated that "China, through this national security legislation, is not living up to its promises"[74] and that "it is a matter of trust, and lots of countries around the world are asking this question - does China live up to its international obligations? Because if they cannot be trusted to keep their word on Hong Kong, why would they be trusted to live up to their wider international responsibilities?"[75]

Furthermore, later in 2020, a wide-scale study surveying public opinion on China conducted among 13 countries between September and October 2020 concluded that perceptions of China worsened most significantly in the UK and that only Russia and North Korea were seen more negatively than China by British respondents.[76]

Given that under IR theory, these events are considered to be due to psychological mistrust, a 'fundamental re-evaluation' of the UK-China relationship should be expected to take place. Such a re-evaluation has indeed been described as the end of the UK-China 'golden era'[77] and has been marked in particular by a hard turnaround on the UK's stance at the time on allowing Huawei equipment to be utilised in the UK's 5G networks.

While US sanctions on Huawei did have a significant impact on the viability of Huawei as a supplier for 5G networks and forced the UK into rethinking its

---

[69] Ho (2020).

[70] Wong (2020).

[71] FCDO (2020).

[72] Wintour (2020b).

[73] Ibid.

[74] Griffiths (2020).

[75] Ibid. Outside of the UK and China, references to Hong Kong and resultant distrust towards the Chinese state have been observed as well. See for example, Reuters (2020b).

[76] Summers (2020).

[77] Ford and Hughes (2020). Instead, today the official UK government slogan on economic relations with China now reads, "See the Potential. Know the Challenge." See HM Government (2021).

previously accommodating position towards the firm,[78] the impact of the mistrust developed in the UK by China's actions towards Hong Kong contributed to the formation of a bipartisan domestic political consensus that had, prior to the events in Hong Kong, been one-sided and led by mostly Conservative MPs. This earlier political pressure from conservative backbenchers of the UK House of Commons had in fact proven to be insufficient and had been successfully defeated in favour of Huawei's continued participation.[79]

It was the aftermath of the Hong Kong 'betrayal' that fostered greater mistrust and rallied greater support to successfully push through what had otherwise been a failed cause that may well had been primarily by 'anti-China' biases.[80] The Huawei ban also then triggered an attempt by the UK Prime Minister at the time to form a '5G Club of Democracies' which hints at a social identity-based trust being subsequently relied upon.[81] It is worth also noting that the notion of trust also generally plays, or at least *should* play, a key role in selecting equipment suppliers for critical 5G infrastructure[82] and that even in January 2020, survey data revealed that only 10% of people in the UK trusted Huawei as a brand.[83]

With respect to ISM design and practice, while the bill that led to the 2021 National Security and Investment Act had already been in the pipeline prior to 2020 (with discussions on the reform of the UK ISM beginning as far back as 2017–18[84]), the experience of a perceived betrayal, particularly from a state with which the UK was in a 'trusting relationship' brought into question not just UK foreign policy but also the adequacy of existent ISM rules.[85] It reinforced the need to strengthen the UK government's ability to scrutinise and intervene in transactions that it considered as raising national security concerns. This is reflected in the official rationale for the bill offered in November 2020 which refers to concerns about the effectiveness of the current regime to deal with new threats.[86]

Subsequently, the heightened mistrust and the fundamental re-evaluation of the UK China relationship manifested in the U-turn that the UK ISM practice took towards Chinese investments in critical sectors such as semiconductors[87] and nuclear energy.[88]

Most recently, the lack of trust in the UK-China relationship has persisted, indeed cemented, across successive UK governments led by the Conservative Party. The

---

[78] Leoni (2022).

[79] Smith (2020).

[80] Corera (2020).

[81] Sherman (2020).

[82] Lysne (2018).

[83] Feldman and Rowe (2020).

[84] DBEIS (2018).

[85] Eaton (2020).

[86] UK Parliament (2021).

[87] MacLellan (2022).

[88] Reed (2022).

current UK Prime Minister has declared the golden-era of UK-China relations to be over[89] and stated that instead, China poses "the biggest state-based threat"[90] to the UK's economic security. This is reflected in the most recent reforms to public procurement rules proposed by the UK government[91] and policy measures banning Chinese-made surveillance systems from government sites in the UK, which includes stripping out substantial amounts of existing equipment from government properties.[92]

3 Chinese Investments & (De Facto) State Control as a Challenge for ISMs

The distinction between private firms and state-controlled enterprises has always been considered significant to ISM practice, the latter naturally requiring greater scrutiny and a higher level of trust given its foreign state involvement. To that end, the notion of 'ultimate beneficial ownership' of the investing foreign entity is often explicitly provided for in ISM designs as a factor to be considered in screening decisions.

On that front, Chinese investment poses as an additional, potentially unique, challenge.[93] The year 2020 saw a surge in official calls from within the Chinese state for state bodies to increase "ideological work and influence in the private sector"[94] and to 'guide' private enterprises to "improve their corporate governance structure and explore the establishment of a modern enterprise system with Chinese characteristics."[95] More specifically, such guidance is said to involve "control over the human resources decisions of the enterprise and allowing it to carry out company audits, including monitoring internal behaviour."[96]

Such a "blending of state and commercial, or social, interests in China,"[97] which manifests itself in "two signature ways: (1) expansion of party-state authority in firms through changes in corporate governance and state-led financial instruments; and (2) enforcement of political fealty among various economic actors"[98] marks a qualitative change in the political role of the Chinese state in private firms within its domestic economy. Indeed, it is based on its links to the Chinese party-state that

89 Mason (2022).

90 Elgot (2022).

91 Smout (2023).

92 Yang and Fisher (2023).

93 Chen and Rithmire (2020).

94 Livingston (2020).

95 Ibid.

96 Ibid.

97 Pearson et al. (2022), p. 167.

98 Pearson et al. (2022), p. 136.

several states have sought to ban TikTok, the social media platform owned by the Beijing-based internet technology firm ByteDance.

The question that remains then is, if and when Chinese firms approach ISMs in order to acquire security clearances to make foreign investments in critical sectors, while claiming to be completely privately-owned and controlled, how should ISM authorities interpret the abovementioned qualitative change visible in China? At what point may such 'blending' of party, state and private interests begin to be considered *de facto* state-control?

There are no easy, clear-cut answers here but regardless of how states and their ISMs deal with this question in practice, the more the lines between party, state and private sector appear blurred in the Chinese economy, the more important the concept of trust is rendered for ISMs. On that note, attention should also be paid to the extent to which the form of governance under Chinese President and General Secretary of the Chinese Communist Party, Xi Jinping, may be classified as a form of 'bossism' given how empirical data suggests that such personalist, party-based regimes have historically been less trustable in terms of their international commitments.[99]

4 ISMs, Trust & the Role of Law

On one hand, excessive trust by states may lead to a lax usage of ISMs or to them not introducing one at all, thereby unwittingly exposing themselves to national security risks. On the other, excessive mistrust too would be undesirable as it may lead to the unnecessary blocking of foreign investments, which would result in states unduly forgoing potential economic and development gains.[100] It is desirable then that trust is either rebuilt where it is found to be insufficient or at the very least that trust is rendered inessential by curtailing the security vulnerabilities which require it.

Law can play a potential role towards achieving both outcomes. In terms of building trust between states, traditionally, non-aggression pacts, peace treaties and neutrality pacts have served such a purpose, to varying degrees of success. They were particularly popular in the early twentieth century and later during the Cold War.[101] Examples of such agreements include the Camp David Accords 1978 and the subsequent Egypt-Israel Peace Treaty of 1979. These were landmark instances of international law being used to build trust between Egypt, Israel and the United States. Further examples include the Intermediate-Range Nuclear Forces Treaty (INF) Treaty of 1987 between the United States and the Soviet Union, along with the Soviet–Japanese Neutrality Pact of 1941.

[99] Chyzh (2013).

[100] Or what Larson (1997) referred to as 'missed opportunities.'

[101] Sinkkonen (2018).

However, in addition to helping build trust, they themselves required some amount of pre-existent trust, in order for parties to consider them viable options. When such pre-existent trust may not exist, or where international law is not seen as sufficiently effective by itself, then domestic legal instruments and reforms are also of potential use. For example, the 2013 Global Surveillance Disclosures or the 'Snowden Revelations' which saw the leakage of massive evidence proving illegal and global surveillance of both domestic and foreign nationals by the United States, marked a major damage to trust towards both the US government and US technology companies with operations abroad.[102] This was particularly evident in the EU where it was perceived as a major betrayal of trust.[103]

Following this event, the US "reformed several laws to introduce new safeguards. . .including the Judicial Redress Act of 2015 that allows designated countries to challenge and seek redress in the case of mishandling personal information by espionage."[104]

These reforms "thwarted the threat from several countries that may otherwise have shut down online platforms like Google and Facebook and blocked cross-border data flows for US multinationals"[105] and were seen in the EU as "a historic achievement"[106] towards restoring trust and on the US side. On the US side, they were presented as evidence of "America's commitment to rebuilding trust between allies"[107] and a demonstration of its "willingness to act in good faith."[108]

It remains to be seen whether the Chinese government would also be willing to pass domestic legal reforms aimed at rebuilding trust with states that have been actively screening Chinese investments. As a proposition it seems unlikely to materialise given the policy direction abovementioned domestic reforms in China have taken and also the position that Chinese scholars and officials have expressed wherein, the problem of the trust deficit towards China is predominantly one of undue bias or prejudice on the part of other states and hence, not one for the Chinese government to resolve. It is also unclear what type of domestic reforms could fulfil such a purpose, if at all.

In such a scenario, to rebuild trust using bilaterally negotiated international legal instruments instead of domestic legal reforms remains a more plausible course of action, one which indeed was attempted in the form of the EU-China Comprehensive Agreement on Investment ("CAI").

The CAI was hailed as "the most ambitious agreement that China has ever concluded with a third country"[109] and sought to alleviate what the EU considered

---

[102] Naughton (2013); Rauscher (2015).

[103] Pollak (2014); Knigge (2013); Ashford (2013).

[104] Lee-Makiyama (2019).

[105] Ibid.

[106] European Commission (2016).

[107] Krotoski (2016).

[108] Ibid.

[109] European Commission (2020a).

to be "little progress"[110] on economic promises made by China. As an international agreement purported to provide greater market access to EU investors in China and to set greater labour standards for the Chinese government, its realisation may have been a positive step towards alleviating both rational trust based on reciprocity and sociological trust based on identity and values.

However, the minimum trust required for an international agreement of its kind to gain political approval and be ratified by the European Parliament had been psychologically dissipated when an escalated exchange of sanctions, took place between the EU and China, making it a "political impossibility of the parliament voting through an economic pact with a country actively attacking its members."[111] This illustrates how precarious trust-building in IR can be and the complexity of how various forms of IR trust may interact within the same context.

So, when trust-building measures may not be feasible, the only remaining role for law is to provide the means to render trust inessential by curtailing the security vulnerabilities which require it to begin with. Such means are available in the form of *ad hoc* risk mitigation agreements concluded between the host state and a foreign investor. Risk mitigation agreements recognise the operational afterlife of potential security threats arising from foreign investments and apply certain post-establishment conditionalities that mitigate such threats, thereby allowing for investment flows to safely continue, despite the general presence of mistrust.

While older, more rudimentary ISMs tended to restrict themselves to either accepting or rejecting a proposed investment, most new-generation ISMs that have either been introduced or reformed in recent years, especially in the EU, explicitly provide for the possibility of conditionalities to be applied via such risk mitigation agreements. In fact, out of the cases formally screened by EU member states in 2021, 23% "involved an approval with conditions or mitigating measures."[112] Examples of post-establishment conditions pertain to the selection of business locations, hiring of personnel, access to specific intellectual properties, auditing of security protocols and data localisation requirements. The UK ISM in 2022, for example, applied five such conditions to a transaction in the aerospace industry, a critical sector under the NSIA, where the foreign investor was a Chinese state-owned entity.[113]

To be clear, mitigation agreements are no panacea and certainly not without weaknesses. For one, they could be prone to abuse and perceived by foreign investors as unreasonable or unfair in and of themselves, prompting them to withdraw or abandon their investment proposal entirely. Providing appropriate justifications and setting precise limitations to their purpose or scope of application would therefore be of particular importance to maintain a sense of fairness and proportionality. Secondly, they would require sufficient bargaining power for the host state to successfully negotiate and conclude such agreements with the foreign investor

[110] Lau (2021).

[111] Brunsden and Yang (2021). See also Wong (2021).

[112] European Commission (2022).

[113] UK Cabinet Office (2022).

during the pre-establishment stage and once concluded, would then require sufficient administrative capacity to effectively monitor and enforce the terms of the agreement. Thirdly, even with their successful application, they might yet leave open the problem of foreign investment in critical assets being used as "leverage to pursue political aims."[114]

5 Conclusion

This contribution presents an interdisciplinary study of foreign investment policy, arguing that investment screening, by its very nature, is deeply linked with the concept of trust in IR, both as a manifestation of mistrust in its legislative form and as a test of trust in its individual decisions. It also proposes a starting point for a framework of IR trust, in light of which the empirical practice and design of ISMs may be potentially examined.

The contribution also highlights two empirical observations that peaked in 2020, one related to the dramatic rise in ISMs and another related to the increased international mistrust (particularly, although not exclusively, toward the Chinese state), suggesting that the two observations are not coincidental but rather that the former can, to a large extent, explain the latter.

Delving into the various forms and dimensions of trust allows us to realise that psychological mistrust derived from politically induced biases and prejudices against the Chinese state, while real and reprehensible, is not the whole story, or at least not anymore. There are different motivations or types of mistrust, both in theory and in practice, that are not necessarily due to exaggeration or rhetoric but to observed behaviour and lived experiences. While these forms of mistrust, are unfortunate and ideally resolved, they are not a wrong in themselves but instead arise from reasonable concepts such as rationality, social values or simply a human instinct for survival.

The growth of such further forms of mistrust was an unintended but predictable consequence of the COVID-19 pandemic, which coincided with the change in tone in the foreign relations of the Chinese state in 2020. Not only did states suddenly become increasingly aware of their dependence on China for their critical supply chains, but they also observed on several occasions during the same period the Chinese state's willingness to exploit such dependencies.

Such willingness, which is certainly not unique to the Chinese state, inevitably has negative consequences on trust in IR, especially when based on perceptions of credibility and goodwill. The notion that economic or technological interdependence with China could be a serious vulnerability or a security threat, rather than a beneficial or benign cooperative opportunity, has become entrenched beyond partisan circles of bias and prejudice. It is these forms or sources of mistrust that may

[114] Marsh (2022).

have accelerated or solidified the shift toward the now dramatically changed global landscape of foreign investment policies.

This two-sided perception of foreign investment, where it can be perceived simultaneously as both a valuable resource to promote economic development and as a potentially serious vulnerability (exemplified by terms such as 'predatory' and 'unwanted'), regardless of its country of origin, appears to be irreversible in at least the short to medium-term. It is also likely to be the hallmark of a post-pandemic period of foreign investment policies, especially investment screening. It is suggested that the crucial concept for dealing with this precarious scenario, is bound to be trust.

Moving forward, policymaking may consider emphasising more on issues pertaining to trust. This could be either in terms of building trust (or protecting existent trust) or, as this contribution intended to show, in terms of how investment flows can flow safely, despite the general presence of mistrust. A heightened perception of threat from foreign investment does not and indeed should not necessarily require complete prohibition. Therefore, instead of rushing to bring down the sledgehammer, states should retain focus on the potential development gains from inward foreign investment and first explore whether a scalpel could be used instead.

References

AFP (2022) A promise kept or betrayal? Hong Kong 25 years on from handover. In: France 24. https://www.france24.com/en/live-news/20220628-a-promise-kept-or-betrayal-hong-kong-25-years-on-from-handover

AFR (2019) Milking Sinophobia is the real security threat. In: Australian Financial Review. https://www.afr.com/policy/foreign-affairs/milking-sinophobia-is-the-real-security-threat-20191202-p53g58

Ashford W (2013) EU calls on US to rebuild trust in post-Snowden era: computer weekly. In: ComputerWeekly.com. https://www.computerweekly.com/news/2240210101/EU-calls-on-US-to-rebuild-trust-in-post-Snowden-era

Bhattacharyya U (2020) Chinese buildup in Galwan betrays trust, it's time for India to up the Ante. In: Outlook India. https://www.outlookindia.com/website/story/opinion-opinion-chinese-buildup-in-galwan-betrays-trust-its-time-for-india-to-up-the-ante/355411

Brunsden J, Fleming S (2020) Eu warns China that investment talks are entering "critical stage". In: Financial Times. https://www.ft.com/content/a5197502-6106-48e9-bb81-e4d87925d619

Brunsden J, Yang Y (2021) Sanctions row threatens EU-China investment deal. In: Financial Times. https://www.ft.com/content/6b236a71-512e-4561-a73c-b1d69b7f486b

Carrai MA (2020) The rise of screening mechanisms in the global north: weaponizing the law against China's weaponized investments? Chin J Comp Law 8:351–383. https://doi.org/10.1093/cjcl/cxaa026

Chan ZT, Meunier S (2021) Behind the screen: understanding national support for a foreign investment screening mechanism in the European Union. Rev Int Organ 17:513–541. https://doi.org/10.1007/s11558-021-09436-y

Chang Y-Y (2020) The post-pandemic world: between constitutionalized and authoritarian orders – China's narrative-power play in the pandemic era. J Chin Polit Sci 26:27–65. https://doi.org/10.1007/s11366-020-09695-3

Chen H, Rithmire M (2020) The rise of the investor state: State Capital in the Chinese economy. Stud Comp Int Dev 55:257–277. https://doi.org/10.1007/s12116-020-09308-3
Chilton AS, Milner HV, Tingley D (2017) Reciprocity and public opposition to foreign direct investment. Br J Polit Sci 50:129–153. https://doi.org/10.1017/s0007123417000552
Chyzh O (2013) Can you trust a dictator: a strategic model of authoritarian regimes' signing and compliance with international treaties. Confl Manag Peace Sci 31:3–27. https://doi.org/10.1177/0738894213501132
Committee on International Trade (2018) Report on the Proposal for a Regulation of the European Parliament and of the Council Establishing a Framework for Screening of Foreign Direct Investments into the European Union: A8-0198/2018: European Parliament. In: Report - A8-0198/2018. https://www.europarl.europa.eu/doceo/document/A-8-2018-0198_EN.html#title5
Corera G (2020) Huawei: ministers signal switch in policy over 5G policy. In: BBC News. https://www.bbc.com/news/technology-53239789
Danzman SB (2021) Investment screening in the shadow of weaponized interdependence. In: Drezner D, Farrell H, Newman A (eds) The uses and abuses of weaponized interdependence. Brookings Institution Press, Washington DC
DBEIS (2018) National security and investment: proposed legislative reforms. In: GOV.UK. https://www.gov.uk/government/consultations/national-security-and-investment-proposed-reforms
Dunn JR, Schweitzer ME (2005) Feeling and believing: the influence of emotion on trust. J Pers Soc Psychol 88:736–748. https://doi.org/10.1037/0022-3514.88.5.736
Eaton G (2020) China's ownership of UK assets exposes Britain's broken model. In: New Statesman. https://www.newstatesman.com/politics/uk-politics/2020/07/china-s-ownership-uk-assets-exposes-britain-s-broken-model
Elgot J (2022) Rishi Sunak calls China "systemic challenge", in sign of softer UK stance. In: The Guardian. https://www.theguardian.com/politics/2022/nov/15/uk-china-rishi-sunak-g20-summit-bali
ENS (2020) China betrayed us, repeated 1962: Uttarakhand CM. In: The Indian Express. https://indianexpress.com/article/india/china-betrayed-us-repeated-1962-uttarakhand-cm-trivendra-singh-rawat-6464036/
European Commission (2016) Statement by Commissioner Věra Jourová on the Signature of the Judicial Redress Act by President Obama. In: Press Corner. https://ec.europa.eu/commission/presscorner/detail/en/STATEMENT_16_401
European Commission (2020a) Key elements of the EU-China comprehensive agreement on investment. In: Press Corner. https://ec.europa.eu/commission/presscorner/detail/en/IP_20_2542
European Commission (2020b) Von der Leyen following EU-China summit: we must make progress, one that implies reciprocity and trust. In: European Commission Press Corner. https://ec.europa.eu/commission/presscorner/detail/en/ac_20_1170
European Commission (2022) Second annual report on the screening of foreign direct investments into the union. In: Register of Commission documents. https://ec.europa.eu/transparency/documents-register/detail?ref=COM%282022%29433&lang=en
Farrell H, Newman A (2020) Will the coronavirus end globalization as we know it? In: Foreign Affairs. https://www.foreignaffairs.com/world/will-coronavirus-end-globalization-we-know-it
FCDO (2020) Foreign secretary declares breach of Sino-British Joint Declaration. In: GOV.UK. https://www.gov.uk/government/news/foreign-secretary-declares-breach-of-sino-british-joint-declaration
FCO (2015) UK-China Joint Statement 2015. In: GOV.UK. https://www.gov.uk/government/news/uk-china-joint-statement-2015
Feldman R, Rowe O (2020) Just one in Ten Brits Trust Huawei. In: YouGov UK. https://yougov.co.uk/topics/technology/articles-reports/2020/01/06/just-one-ten-brits-trust-huawei

Ford J, Hughes L (2020) UK-China relations: from "golden era" to the deep freeze. In: Financial Times. https://www.ft.com/content/804175d0-8b47-4427-9853-2aded76f48e4
Gaston S (2020) A UK-China engagement strategy. In: British Foreign Policy Group. https://bfpg.co.uk/2020/05/intro-uk-china-strategy/
Goldgeier JM, Tetlock PE (2001) Psychology and international relations theory. Annu Rev Polit Sci 4:67–92. https://doi.org/10.1146/annurev.polisci.4.1.67
Gracie C (2015) China and "the Osborne Doctrine". In: BBC News. https://www.bbc.com/news/world-asia-china-34539507
Griffiths J (2020) UK foreign secretary warns China "can't be trusted" as London passes Magnitsky-style sanctions law. In: CNN. https://edition.cnn.com/2020/07/06/uk/uk-magnitsky-raab-hong-kong-china-intl-hnk/index.html
HM Government (2021) Digital & Tech China. In: Digital and Tech China. https://digitalandtechchina.campaign.gov.uk/
Ho K (2020) Hong Kong gov't ousts four democratically-elected lawmakers from legislature. In: Hong Kong Free Press. https://hongkongfp.com/2020/11/11/breaking-hong-kong-govt-ousts-four-democratically-elected-lawmakers-from-legislature/
Hoffman AM (2002) A conceptualization of trust in international relations. Eur J Int Relat 8:375–401. https://doi.org/10.1177/1354066102008003003
Holsti OR (1967) Cognitive dynamics and images of the enemy. J Int Aff 21:16–39
India Today (2020) Mood of the nation poll: 64% say India cannot trust China. In: India Today. https://www.indiatoday.in/mood-of-the-nation/story/motn-can-india-trust-china-ladakh-lac-standoff-1708888-2020-08-07
ISEAS (2021) The State of Southeast Asia: 2021 Survey Report. In: ISEAS - Yusof Ishak Institute. https://www.iseas.edu.sg/frontpage-featured/the-state-of-southeast-asia-2021-survey-report
Kammerer P (2020) National security law is a bitter betrayal of Hong Kong's promise. In: South China Morning Post. https://www.scmp.com/comment/opinion/article/3086820/national-security-law-bitter-betrayal-hong-kongs-promise-and
Keohane RO (1986) Reciprocity in international relations. Int Organ 40:1–27. https://doi.org/10.1017/s0020818300004458
Knigge M (2013) Strained ties. In: dw.com. https://www.dw.com/en/nsa-surveillance-eroded-transatlantic-trust/a-17311216
Korzinski D (2023) Canadian opinions of China reach new low. In: Angus Reid Institute. https://angusreid.org/covid19-china/
Krotoski ML (2016) The Judicial Redress Act of 2015 becomes law. In: The National Law Review. https://www.natlawreview.com/article/judicial-redress-act-2015-becomes-law
Kumar P (2020) Galwan Clash: PM Modi says deaths not in vain, India warns China of impact on ties, proof of Chinese betrayal. In: India Today. https://www.indiatoday.in/india/story/galwan-clash-pm-modi-says-deaths-not-in-vain-india-warns-china-of-impact-on-ties-proof-of-chinese-betrayal-1690131-2020-06-17
Larson DW (1997) Trust and missed opportunities in international relations. Polit Psychol 18:701–734. https://doi.org/10.1111/0162-895x.00075
Lau S (2021) EU slams China's "authoritarian shift" and broken economic promises. In: Politico. https://www.politico.eu/article/eu-china-biden-economy-climate-europe/
Lee-Makiyama H (2019) Geopolitics & technology – the core of the 5G problem. In: RSIS. https://www.rsis.edu.sg/rsis-publication/rsis/geopolitics-technology-the-core-of-the-5g-problem/
Leoni Z (2022) The end of the "golden era"? The conundrum of Britain's China policy amidst Sino-American relations. J Curr Chin Aff 51:313–326. https://doi.org/10.1177/18681026221090315
Livingston S (2020) The Chinese Communist Party targets the private sector. In: CSIS. https://www.csis.org/analysis/chinese-communist-party-targets-private-sector
Lowy Institute (2022) Trust in global powers. In: Lowy Institute Poll. https://poll.lowyinstitute.org/charts/trust-in-global-powers/

Lysne O (2018) The Huawei and Snowden questions: can electronic equipment from untrusted vendors be verified? Can an untrusted vendor build trust into electronic equipment? Springer Nature
MacLellan K (2022) UK orders national security assessment of sale of microchip factory to China's Nexperia. In: Reuters. https://www.reuters.com/world/uk/uk-carry-out-national-security-assessment-sale-microchip-factory-chinas-nexperia-2022-05-25/
Manoj GC (2020) A K Antony Interview: "Galwan Valley was Never a Point of Dispute. It is a Betrayal by China". In: The Indian Express. https://indianexpress.com/article/india/india-china-border-dipute-a-k-antony-on-ladakh-indian-army-6474828/
Marsh S (2022) German Spy Chief: "Russia is the Storm, China is Climate Change". In: Reuters. https://www.reuters.com/world/german-spy-chief-russia-is-storm-china-is-climate-change-2022-10-17
Mason C (2022) Rishi Sunak: golden era of UK-China relations is over. In: BBC News. https://www.bbc.com/news/uk-politics-63787877
Mercer J (2005) Rationality and psychology in international politics. Int Organ 59:77–106. https://doi.org/10.1017/s0020818305050058
Michael C (2020) Chris Patten: China's security laws a betrayal of Hong Kong People. In: The Guardian. https://www.theguardian.com/world/2020/may/23/chris-patten-chinas-security-laws-a-betrayal-of-hong-kong-people
Michel T (2012) Time to get emotional: phronetic reflections on the concept of trust in international relations. Eur J Int Relat 19:869–890. https://doi.org/10.1177/1354066111428972
Misra M (2023a) Foreign Investment in Critical National Infrastructure (CNI) by State-Controlled Entities (SCEs) and Investment Screening Mechanisms (ISMs). In: Delimatsis P, Dimitropoulos P, Gourgourinis A (eds) State capitalism and international investment law. Bloomsbury Publishing
Misra M (2023b) Thinking Past Naivete: investment screening by the EU as a problem of (mis)trust in IR. Eur Foreign Aff Rev 28: forthcoming
Moran TH (2009) Three threats: an analytical framework for the CFIUS process. Peterson Institute for International Economics, Washington DC
Moran TH (2013) Foreign acquisitions and national security: what are genuine threats? What are implausible worries? World Sci Stud Int Econ:371–393. https://doi.org/10.1142/9789814390842_0011
Naughton J (2013) After Edward Snowden's revelations, why trust US cloud providers? In: The Guardian. https://www.theguardian.com/technology/2013/sep/15/edward-snowden-nsa-cloud-computing
Oliveira G d LT (2017) Chinese land grabs in Brazil? Sinophobia and foreign investments in Brazilian soybean agribusiness. Globalizations 15:114–133. https://doi.org/10.1080/14747731.2017.1377374
Pearson MM, Rithmire M, Tsai KS (2022) China's party-state capitalism and international backlash: from interdependence to insecurity. Int Secur 47:135–176. https://doi.org/10.1162/isec_a_00447
Peng W (2021) How to rebuild strategic mutual trust between China and the U.S. In: CGTN Opinion. https://news.cgtn.com/news/2021-02-25/How-to-rebuild-strategic-mutual-trust-between-China-and-the-U-S%2D%2DY9fSsuRgVW/index.html
Pettit P (1995) The cunning of trust. Philos Public Aff 24:202–225. https://doi.org/10.1111/j.1088-4963.1995.tb00029.x
Pollak S (2014) Trust between EU and US "profoundly shaken" by NSA revelations. In: The Irish Times. https://www.irishtimes.com/news/world/europe/trust-between-eu-and-us-profoundly-shaken-by-nsa-revelations-1.1721152
Rathbun BC (2009) It takes all types: social psychology, trust, and the international relations paradigm in our minds. Int Theory 1:345–380. https://doi.org/10.1017/s1752971909990121
Rauscher KF (2015) How to restore trust in American technology. In: Scientific American. https://www.scientificamerican.com/article/how-to-restore-trust-in-american-technology/

Reed S (2022) U.K. backs giant nuclear plant, squeezing out China. In: The New York Times. https://www.nytimes.com/2022/11/29/business/uk-nuclear-plant-china.html
Reuters (2020a) Britain warns tech firms over risks of China expansion. In: Reuters. https://www.reuters.com/article/us-britain-china-investment-idUSKBN284179
Reuters (2020b) EU says Hong Kong decision damages trust with China - Borrell. In: Reuters. https://www.reuters.com/article/hongkong-protests-eu-idUKL8N2DB2KY
Reuters (2020c) U.S. Vice President Pence: China's Hong Kong Law is a "Betrayal" - CNBC interview. In: Reuters. https://www.reuters.com/article/us-usa-china-hongkong-pence-idUSKBN2432CM
Reuters (2021) Dutch parliament becomes second in a week to accuse China of genocide in Xinjiang. In: CNN. https://edition.cnn.com/2021/02/25/europe/netherlands-china-xinjiang-genocide-intl-hnk/index.html
Ruzicka J, Keating VC (2015) Going global: trust research and international relations. J Trust Res 5: 8–26. https://doi.org/10.1080/21515581.2015.1009082
Sherman J (2020) The UK is forging a 5G Club of democracies to avoid reliance on Huawei. In: Atlantic Council. https://www.atlanticcouncil.org/blogs/new-atlanticist/the-uk-is-forging-a-5g-club-of-democracies-to-avoid-reliance-on-huawei/
Shultz GP (2020a) Life and learning after one hundred years. In: Hoover Institution Press Essays. Available via https://www.hoover.org/research/trust-coin-realm
Shultz GP (2020b) On trust. In: The Foreign Service Journal. https://afsa.org/on-trust
Silver L (2022) Some Americans' views of China turned more negative after 2020, but others became more positive. In: Pew Research Center. https://www.pewresearch.org/short-reads/2022/09/28/some-americans-views-of-china-turned-more-negative-after-2020-but-others-became-more-positive/
Silver L, Devlin K, Huang C (2020) Unfavorable views of China reach historic highs in many countries. In: Pew Research Center Global Attitudes Project. https://www.pewresearch.org/global/2020/10/06/unfavorable-views-of-china-reach-historic-highs-in-many-countries/
Sinha S (2021) India-China ties "profoundly disturbed" by first act of bloodshed in 45 years: Jaishankar. In: Hindustan Times. https://www.hindustantimes.com/india-news/indiachina-ties-profoundly-disturbed-by-first-act-of-bloodshed-in-45-years-jaishankar-101610440666374.html
Sinkkonen V (2018) Understanding the trust-distrust nexus between the United States and Egypt. In: Trust in international relations: rationalist, constructivist, and psychological approaches, 1st edn. Routledge, Taylor & Francis Group, London, pp 9–36
Smith N (2020) Huawei: government wins vote after backbench rebellion. In: BBC News. https://www.bbc.com/news/uk-politics-51806704
Smout A (2023) Britain proposes tougher procurement laws to protect national security. In: Reuters. https://www.reuters.com/world/uk/britain-proposes-tougher-procurement-laws-protect-national-security-2023-06-06/
Summers T (2020) British public opinion on China in the age of Covid-19. In: CEIAS. https://ceias.eu/wp-content/uploads/2020/12/UK-poll-report.pdf
Turcsányi R, Šimalčík M, Kironska K et al (2021) Survey: Europeans' views of China in the age of Covid-19. In: CEIAS. https://ceias.eu/survey-europeans-views-of-china-in-the-age-of-covid-19/
UK Cabinet Office (2022) Acquisition of Ligeance Aerospace Technology Co. Ltd by Sichuan Development Holding Co. Ltd: Notice of Final Order. In: GOV.UK. https://www.gov.uk/government/publications/acquisition-of-ligeance-aerospace-technology-co-ltd-by-sichuan-development-holding-co-ltd-notice-of-final-order
UK Parliament (2021) National Security and Investment Bill 2019-21. In: https://www.parliament.uk. https://commonslibrary.parliament.uk/research-briefings/cbp-8784/
UN (2020) Secretary-General Highlights 'Trust Deficit' amid Rising Global Turbulence, in Remarks to Security Council Debate on 'Upholding United Nations Charter'. United Nations. https://press.un.org/en/2020/sgsm19934.doc.htm

UNCTAD (2021) Investment Policy Monitor 24. UNCTAD Division on Investment and Enterprise. https://unctad.org/system/files/official-document/diaepcbinf2021d2_en.pdf
van Aaken A, Kurtz J (2019) Beyond rational choice: international trade law and the behavioral political economy of protectionism. J Int Econ Law 22:601–628. https://doi.org/10.1093/jiel/jgz034
Wang Y (2020) The legitimacy of Chinese outward investment in English news — a cognitive approach to discursive legitimation. Theory Pract Lang Stud 10:557–568. https://doi.org/10.17507/tpls.1005.09
Wang C, Li Z, Zhong T (2019) Social trust, rule of law, and economic exchange: evidence from China and its major trading partners. Emerg Mark Finance Trade 55:3134–3150. https://doi.org/10.1080/1540496x.2019.1572505
Watt H (2017) Hinkley Point: the "dreadful deal" behind the world's most expensive power plant. In: The Guardian. https://www.theguardian.com/news/2017/dec/21/hinkley-point-c-dreadful-deal-behind-worlds-most-expensive-power-plant
Weinhardt C (2015) Relational trust in international cooperation: the case of north–south trade negotiations. J Trust Res 5:27–54. https://doi.org/10.1080/21515581.2015.1007460
Whalen J (2020) Biden likely to remain tough on Chinese Tech like Huawei, but with more help from allies. In: The Washington Post. https://www.washingtonpost.com/technology/2020/11/16/biden-huawei-trump-china/
Wintour P (2020a) UK and China: how the love affair faded. In: The Guardian. https://www.theguardian.com/world/2020/dec/18/uk-and-china-how-the-love-affair-faded
Wintour P (2020b) China is breaking Hong Kong Treaty with UK, says Boris Johnson. In: The Guardian. https://www.theguardian.com/politics/2020/jul/01/china-is-breaking-hong-kong-treaty-with-uk-says-boris-johnson
Wong R (2020) All Hong Kong democrats to quit after Gov't Ousts 4 lawmakers, leaving legislature with no effective opposition. In: Hong Kong Free Press. https://hongkongfp.com/2020/11/11/breaking-all-hong-kong-democrats-quit-after-govt-ousts-4-lawmakers-leaving-legislature-with-no-effective-opposition/
Wong C (2021) EU envoy urges China to bridge "trust deficit" to revive investment deal. In: South China Morning Post. https://www.scmp.com/news/china/diplomacy/article/3139783/eu-envoy-urges-china-bridge-trust-deficit-revive-investment
Xinhua (2020) China adopts decision to make Hong Kong national security laws. In: Xinhua. http://www.xinhuanet.com/english/2020-05/28/c_139095012.htm
Yang Y, Fisher L (2023) UK to strip Chinese surveillance cameras from sensitive government sites. In: Financial Times. https://www.ft.com/content/740516c0-96f3-4a5e-aae8-25a63b914428
Younis M (2021) China, Russia images in U.S. hit historic lows. In: Gallup.com. https://news.gallup.com/poll/331082/china-russia-images-hit-historic-lows.aspx
Zeng K, Li X (2019) Geopolitics, nationalism, and foreign direct investment: perceptions of the China threat and American public attitudes toward Chinese FDI. Chin J Int Polit 12:495–518. https://doi.org/10.1093/cjip/poz016

The International Legal Framework for Foreign Investment Control

Pascale Accaoui Lorfing

Contents

Abstract The provision on security interest (SI) inserted in an international investment agreement (IIA) allows the State to take regulatory measures without compensating the foreign investor whose rights are affected, provided that the specific conditions inserted in the provision or the general principles of customary international law are met. Art. XXI of the general agreement on tariffs and trade signed in 1994. (the GATT, 1994) which provides for such a SI in the context of international trade, serves as model for such SI provisions in IIAs. The way it is drafted has been

P. Accaoui Lorfing (✉)
CREDIMI (University of Burgundi), Dijon, France

Affiliate Professor ESCP Business School - Paris, Affiliate Researcher CREDIMI University of Burgundy, Dijon, France

J. H. Pohl et al. (eds.), *National Security and Investment Controls*,
Springer Studies in Law & Geoeconomics (2024) 3: 129–146,
https://doi.org/10.1007/17280_2024_26, Published online: 22 February 2024

interpreted along lines that are of great interest, as they open the way to a possible approach that could be adopted by arbitral tribunals assessing the same type of provision. Indeed, we are witnessing the insertion of SI and its equivalents into IIAs. Far from being homogeneous, the variety of their formulations is reflected in the complexity of their interpretation. The approach of the arbitral tribunal remains to be determined after the rejection of Art. 25 ILC and the limited scope of the nexus requirement where it is admitted. A harmonised approach to interpretation can be ensured by guidelines for the interpretation of these clauses and an institutional structure such as a multilateral investment court for their implementation.

1 Introduction

International investment agreements (IIAs) have been signed by the home and host States to promote and protect foreign investors when investing in the host State. Their objective was and remains the protection of the home State foreign investor from regulatory measures that may impact the rights of the foreign investor. Specific provisions have been devoted to this protection (expropriation (direct and indirect), fair and equitable treatment, and national treatment). The right of the State to regulate has been addressed through the investor's standard of protection within the treaty (UNCTAD Reform Package 2018), taking into account not necessarily the nature of the regulatory measure but the impact of that measure on the investor.[1] The adequate formulation of IIAs is therefore not the recognition of the State's right to regulate, but the compensation of the foreign investor to the host State's regulatory power.[2]

The landscape of the IIAs is changing. We have witnessed recently, provisions on exception, whether general (GE) or related to security concerns (essential security interest (ESI) or equivalent) being increasingly included in IIAs (UNCTAD IIA Note July 2020, Issue 1). The new treaties recalibrate the IIAs, with an agreement by the parties allowing the State to regulate without compensating the foreign investor, even if the investor's rights are affected by the regulatory measure. This recognition illustrates a rebalancing of these IIAs, as they take into account the characteristics of the sovereign State, which may be required to adopt regulatory measures under specific conditions without incurring liability to the foreign investor.

GE and ESI, also called non-precluded measures (NPM) (Henckels 2020), are very common in new model IIAs (UNCTAD 2018) after having appeared in some

[1]See the sole effect doctrine or the impact of the measure as illustrated by the case law: Starrett Housing Corp. v. Iran, 4 Iran-US Cl. Trib. Rep. 154 (1983)), Burlington Resources Inc. v. Republic of Ecuador, para. 398; Pope & Talbot, para. 96–98; LG&E v. Argentina, para200; Enron Corporation & Ponderosa Assets L.P. v. Argentine Republic, para. 245.

[2]For the evolution of such an approach see Accaoui Lorfing and Burghetto (2018)

old treaties (Burke-White and von Staden 2010; Pathirana and McLaughlin 2020). These escape provisions (Viñuales 2020) are far from homogeneous, and the variety of their wording is reflected in the complexity of their interpretation. A possible harmonisation could be brought about by a more homogeneous approach to these provisions.

The chapter will analyse the usefulness of exploring the caselaw on the interpretation of WTO Article XXI of the general agreement on tariffs and trade signed in 1994. (GATT, 1994) on Security Exception (2) for the understanding and the interpretation of the non-precluded State measures in international investment agreements (IIAs) (3) and offer a proposal on an institutional structure for a better interpretation and harmonisation of such provisions (4).

2 WTO Article XXI of the GATT (1994) on Security Exception

The provision on security exception (SE) that appears first and paved the way to the possible insertion of such a provision in an international agreement is Article XXI of the GATT (1994). We will analyse the drafting of the provision (Sect. 2.1) and its interpretation (Sect. 2.2).

2.1 Drafting of Article XXI of the GATT (1994) on SE

Art. XXI of the GATT 1994 on SE states the following:

> Nothing in this Agreement shall be construed
>
> (a) to require any contracting party to furnish any information the disclosure of which it considers contrary to its essential security interests; or
>
> (b) to prevent any contracting party from taking any action which it considers necessary for the protection of its essential security interests
>
> (i) relating to fissionable materials or the materials from which they are derived;
>
> (ii) relating to the traffic in arms, ammunition and implements of war and to such traffic in other goods and materials as is carried on directly or indirectly for the purpose of supplying a military establishment;
>
> (iii) taken in time of war or other emergency in international relations; or
>
> (c) to prevent any contracting party from taking any action in pursuance of its obligations under the United Nations Charter for the maintenance of international peace and security.

The article shows, for the State, the importance of its essential security interest. The provision recalls that the State cannot be obliged to provide information (a) nor be prevented from taking measures related to its essential security interest. The provision also provides for a list of areas that the State considers to be of its essential security interest (b (i), (ii) and (iii), and c). The self-judging character of such provision (Schill and Briese 2009) derived from the terms "which it considers" raises awareness of the meaning of the provision to be clarified, in order to specify what falls within the reserved domain of the State, in respect of which it may adopt measures without incurring liability for the effects of such measures.

2.2 *The Interpretation of Art. XXI of the GATT (1994) on SE*

Art. XXI of the GATT (1994) on security exception (SE) was first *invoked* in 1985. In US—Trade measures affecting Nicaragua after an executive order issue by the USA prohibiting all trade with Nicaragua and transactions relating to air and see transportation between Nicaragua and the USA, with effect on 7 May 1985 (Report of the Panel in *Russia – Measures Concerning Traffic in Transition,* 2019 (Panel Report)). The Panel could not examine or judge the validity of the US invocation of Article XXI, as this issue was precluded by the strict terms of reference of the Panel. The terms of reference clearly recall that

> (. . .) The Panel cannot examine or judge the validity of or motivation for the invocation of Article XXI(b)(iii) by the United States, (. . .) (Panel Report)

The first decision to deal with art. XXI of the GATT (1994) is *Russia – Measures Concerning Traffic in Transition* (2019).[3] The case concerned various measures imposed by Russia on Ukraine regarding transit by road and rail through the territory of Russia and the publication and administration of those measures (Panel Report, para. 2.1). Russia invoked the Panel's lack of jurisdiction to review Russia's invocation of Art. XXI(b)(ii) as such provision is self-judging and that the Panel should only take act of the invocation of such provision by Russia without analysing the substance of the claims by Ukraine (Panel Report, Para. 7.4)

The Panel composed of prominent judges raises the issue of the self-judging character of the provision by the interpretation of the terms "which it considers".

According to the Panel, Article XXI of the GATT (1994) on SE can be interpreted in different ways because of the terms "which is considered" (para. 7.6.3)

Art. XXI could

> qualify only the word "necessary", i.e., the necessity of the measure for the protection of "its essential security interests", or to qualify also the determination of these "essential security interests", or finally and maximally, to qualify the determination of the matters described in the three subparagraphs of Article XXI(b) as well (Para. 7.63)

[3] See *Russia – Measures Concerning Traffic in Transition* (2019); Report of the Panel, World Trade Organization, WT/DS512/R, 5 April 2019, (19-2105), https://www.wto.org/english/tratop_e/dispu_e/512r_e.pdf. The Panel was composed as follows: Professor Georges Abi-Saab (Chairperson), Professor Ichiro Araki and Dr. Mohammad Saeed, (Members).

However, the ordinary meaning of Art. XXI should be found in its context and in light of the object and purpose of the GATT and WTO Agreement. From that perspective, the Panel considers

> (. . .) that the adjectival clause "which it considers" in the chapeau of Article XXI(b) does not qualify the determination of the circumstances in subparagraph (iii). Rather, for action to fall within the scope of Article XXI(b), it must objectively be found to meet the requirements in one of the enumerated subparagraphs of that provision. (Para. 7.82)

More importantly, the Panel went to analyse the negotiating history to confirm the Panel's approach as

> (. . .) requiring that the evaluation of whether the invoking Member has satisfied the requirements of the enumerated subparagraphs of Article XXI(b) be made objectively rather than by the invoking Member itself. In other words, there is no basis for treating the invocation of Article XXI(b)(iii) of the GATT 1994 as an incantation that shields a challenged measure from all scrutiny. (Para. 7.100)

The Panel's interpretation of the SE is to objectively determine the meeting of the requirements enumerated in the provision. Indeed, the Panel concludes

> (. . .) that the adjectival clause "which it considers" in the chapeau of Article XXI(b) does not extend to the determination of the circumstances in each subparagraph. Rather, for action to fall within the scope of Article XXI(b), it must objectively be found to meet the requirements in one of the enumerated subparagraphs of that provision. (Para. 7.101)

The conclusion of the Panel is that its interpretation of Art. XXI (b),

> (. . .) as vesting in panels the power to review whether the requirements of the enumerated subparagraphs are met, rather than leaving it to the unfettered discretion of the invoking Member, that Article XXI(b)(iii) of the GATT 1994 is not totally "self-judging" in the manner asserted by Russia. (Para. 7.102).

From that perspective, the Panel has jurisdiction to review the invocation by Russia of Art. XXI(b)(iii). Its role is to determine whether the requirements stated in the provisions are fulfilled (para. 7.104).

The interpretation of Art. XXI of the GATT 1994 is important. First, this provision has its equivalent in the new IIAs. Second, this interpretation could facilitate the interpretation of identical provisions in IIAs.

3 Interpreting Non-Precluded Measures (NPM) in International Investment Agreements (IIAs)

Prior to the early 2000s, IIA signatories did not insert any provision that considered States' regulatory measures without compensation. In an evolutionary approach, the limits to what was considered indirect expropriation (Accaoui Lorfing and Burghetto 2018) have paved the way for such State measures that, taken in specific areas, may not be considered expropriatory. The NPM provisions that mirror Art. XXI of the

GATT (1994) are characterised by the variety of their wording (Sect. 3.1) and the non-uniformity of their interpretation by arbitral tribunals (Sect. 3.2).

3.1 Variety of Drafting

IIAs have two sorts of provisions that reflect Art. XXI of the GATT (1994): a general exception and security exception (SE). Both have in common to recall the State's regulatory measures without compensation, even if their scope may be limited by the way these provisions are drafted (Mantilla Blanco and Pehl 2020, 31 fd). Some provisions are widely drafted (Sect. 3.1.1), some are drafted with additional details (Sect. 3.1.2), and others are restrictively worded (Sect. 3.1.3).

3.1.1 **Provision** Widely **Drafted**

Article 18 on Essential Security of the 2012 US Model BIT that states the following

> Nothing in this Treaty shall be construed:
>
> 1. to require a Party to furnish or allow access to any information the disclosure of which it determines to be contrary to its essential security interests; or
> 2. to preclude a Party from applying measures that it considers necessary for the fulfillment of its obligations with respect to the maintenance or restoration of international peace or security, or the protection of its own essential security interests.

The wording of this provision makes it possible to measure the freedom of the State to adopt measures that it considers to be in its own essential interests and that prevent it from compensating the foreign investor whose rights have been affected by the regulatory measure it has adopted. The conditions and therefore limits for the State to adopt such a measure are first, the measure should be related to the protection of the essential security interests of the State, and second, the State considers it necessary to adopt this measure to protect its essential security interests. The question remains is to determin what the State considers to be its national security interest. Such a broadly drafted provision gives the State the freedom to determine what constitutes its essential ESI. Its perception may change over time, making the scope of this clause very broad.

3.1.2 Provision Drafted with Additional Details in Footnotes

A provision on SE may be included in the IIA, completed by footnotes as illustrated by Article 30 on SE in the 2019 BIT between Singapore and Myanmar.[4] This widely drafted provision on SE is as follows:

> Nothing in this Agreement shall be construed to (. . .)
>
> b) preclude a Party from applying measures that it considers necessary for the fulfilment of its obligations with respect to the maintenance or restoration of international peace or security, or the protection of its own essential security interests.

The footnote to this provision recalls that

> For greater certainty, nothing in this Agreement shall prevent a party from taking any action which it considers necessary for the protection of critical public infrastructure, such as the communications, power, water and transportation infrastructure, including but not limited to imposing restrictions on operators of such infrastructure and preventing deliberate attempts intended to disable or degrade such infrastructure.

The explanation given in the footnote may restrict the freedom of the State to determine what it considers necessary for the protection of its national interest. The footnote mentions the protection of critical public infrastructure followed by examples such as communications and power. The footnote also mentions what public infrastructure includes but is not limited to. Is it to be understood that freedom must concern what is equivalent to such public infrastructure? Should the non-limitation to the above list concern more than what is mentioned (restrictions on operators . . .)? By providing such an explanation in the footnote, the parties clarify their intention and at the same time allow for the possibility to expand the scope of the provision.

3.1.3 Provision Restrictively Drafted: "Related to + List"

A provision that is restrictively drafted provides the connection between the measure and the necessity of such a measure within the list provided for by the provision. Article 13 on 'Essential Security Interests' of the 2017 Agreement between Ethiopia and Qatar states that

> The Contracting Party may take actions that it deems necessary for the protection of its essential security interests related to;

[4] See Agreement between the Government of the Republic of Singapore and the Government of The Republic of the Union of Myanmar on the Promotion and Protection of Investments, signed 24 September 2019, but not yet in force, https://investmentpolicy.unctad.org/international-investment-agreements/countries/190/singapore.

(a) criminal or penal offences related to the operational activities investment; or
(b) traffic in arms, ammunition and implements of war and transactions in other goods, materials, services and technology undertaken directly or indirectly for the purpose of supplying a military or other security establishment;
(c) taken in time of war or other emergency in international relations; or
(d) in pursuance of its obligations under the United Nations Charter for the maintenance of international peace and security.
(e) relating to the implementation of national policies or international agreements respecting the non-proliferation of nuclear weapons or other nuclear explosive devices;

2. Any action taken by a Contracting Party should be equitable, non-discriminatory, and in good faith taking into account the objectives of this Agreement.[5]

It can be concluded that measures taken by the State which it considers necessary for the protection of what it regards as its essential security interests must also be linked to what the provision lists. In this sense, any measure taken outside the enumerated list must be considered as falling outside the scope of the provision, thus making the State responsible for the impact of such a measure on the investor's rights. In addition, the provision recalls that regulatory measures must be equitable, non-discriminatory and taken in good faith with regard to the objectives of the agreement. The scope of the regulatory measure is limited by these requirements. In this sense, even if the regulatory measure is taken within the list contained in the provision, that regulatory measure may not fall within the scope of the provision and therefore be protected if such a measure does not also meet the conditions of being taken in good faith, fair and non-discriminatory, which the competent court will assess.

The difference between this provision and the ones mentioned above is notable. The more precise the provision is about the intention of the parties, the less room it leaves for interpretation of their intention.

3.2 *Interpretation of NPM by Arbitral Tribunals*

Since the ESI provision is designed to take into account the State measure taken for what the State may consider to be its essential security interest, the generally primary condition recalled by the provision is the requirement of a nexus between the State measure and the need to take it for essential security reasons (Sect. 3.2.1) before concluding the State will not compensate the foreign investor (Sect. 3.2.2).

[5] See Agreement between The Government of the Federal Democratic Republic of Ethiopia and the Government of the State of Qatar for the Promotion and Reciprocal Protection of Investments, signed 14 November 2017, but not yet entered into force, https://investmentpolicy.unctad.org/international-investment-agreements/treaty-files/5982/download.

3.2.1 Nexus Requirement Approaches

The nexus requirement is the link between the regulatory measure and the necessity for the State to do so (Burke and von Staden 2008, p. 331 fd). Arbitral tribunals have relied on Article 25 of the Responsibility of States for Internationally Wrongful Acts of 2001[6] (ILC) first (Sect. 3.2.1.1) and then on the determination of the meaning of the will of the parties taking into consideration the way the provision is drafted (Sect. 3.2.1.2).

3.2.1.1 Nexus Requirement Under Art. 25 ILC

In assessing the necessity requirement, arbitral tribunals have relied on Article 25 ILC as customary international law. The first paragraph of this provision states the following:

> 1. Necessity may not be invoked by a State as a ground for precluding the wrongfulness of an act not in conformity with an international obligation of that State unless the act:
>   (a) is the only way for the State to safeguard an essential interest against a grave and imminent peril; and
>   (b) does not seriously impair an essential interest of the State or States towards which the obligation exists or of the international community as a whole.
> 2. In any case, necessity may not be invoked by a State as a ground for precluding wrongfulness if:
>   (a) the international obligation in question excludes the possibility of invoking necessity; or
>   (b) the State has contributed to the situation of necessity.

The state of necessity is defined as

> (. . .) a ground recognized by customary international law for precluding the wrongfulness of an act not in conformity with an international obligation. (. . .) such ground for precluding wrongfulness can only be accepted on an exceptional basis (. . .) (*Gabcíkovo-Nagymaros Project* case, para 51 – 52)

In the commentary to Art. 25 ILC, it is stated that

> the term "necessity" (état de nécessité) is used to denote those exceptional cases where the only way a State can safeguard an essential interest threatened by a grave and imminent peril is, for the time being, not to perform some other international obligation of lesser weight or urgency. Under conditions narrowly defined in article 25, such a plea is recognized as a circumstance precluding wrongfulness (Commentary of Art. 25 ILC, para 1))

The exceptional character of the necessity is also recalled in the explanations under Art. 25 (al. 2) in the sense that

---

[6] See Responsibility of States for Internationally Wrongful Acts, adopted by the International Law Commission in 2001, https://legal.un.org/ilc/texts/instruments/english/draft_articles/9_6_2001.pdf; https://legal.un.org/ilc/texts/instruments/english/commentaries/9_6_2001.pdf.

> it arises where there is an irreconcilable conflict between an essential interest on the one hand and an obligation of the State invoking necessity on the other. These special features mean that necessity will only rarely be available to excuse non-performance of an obligation and that it is subject to strict limitations to safeguard against possible abuse. (*idem, para 2)*)

The restrictive approach requires strictly defined conditions to be cumulatively satisfied to be assessed not only by the State (*Gabcíkovo-Nagymaros Project* case, para 51–52).[7] To that end, two conditions must be fulfilled. First,

> (...) necessity may only be invoked to safeguard an essential interest from a grave and imminent peril (...) the peril has to be objectively established and not merely apprehended as possible. In addition to being grave the peril has to be imminent ((*ibidem*, para 15),

and

> the course of action taken must be the "only way" available to safeguard interest (*Ibid.* para 15)

Second,

> the conduct in question must not seriously impair an essential interest of the other State or States *(Ibid.* para 17).

In case law the term "necessary" has been analysed in light of the state of necessity of Article 25 ILC (UNCTAD 2009, p. 8).

In CMS v. Argentina, it has been held that

> (...) while there were elements of necessity partially present here and there (....) the requirements of necessity under customary international law have not been fully met so as to preclude the wrongfulness of the acts (CMS v. Argentina, 2005 para 331).

The same approach has been followed in Enron v. Argentina, where the arbitral tribunal concluded that

> (...) in light of the various elements that have been examined... the requirements of the state of necessity under customary international law have not been fully met in this case (Enron v. Argentina 2007 para 313).

Even if there may be a similarity in terms of necessity, this approach has evolved. The provision on ESI and Art. 25 ILC are to be distinguished, as they are substantially different and therefore subject to different requirements with different content (Sornarajah, 2015, p. 309 fd). This has been the position of the CMS *ad hoc* Committee, which affirmed that

> Art. XI (ESI provision of the US-Argentina BIT) is a threshold requirement: if it applies, the substantive obligations under the Treaty do not apply. By contrast, Art. 25 (of the ILC Articles on State Responsibility) is an excuse which is only relevant once it has been decided

[7]See ICJ, Case Concerning the Gabcikovo-Nagymaros Project (Hungary/Slovakia), Judgment of 25 September 1997, *Gabcikovo-Nagymaros Project (Hungary/Slovakia), Judgment, I.C.J. Reports 1997, p. 7*; https://www.icj-cij.org/public/files/case-related/92/092-19970925-JUD-01-00-EN.pdf.

> that there has otherwise been a breach of those substantive obligations[8] (CMS v. Argentina, 2007Annulment, para 129)

This approach has been confirmed in a recent case, where an arbitral tribunal interpreting Article 12 of the German – India BIT recalls that

> Article 12 must be distinguished from the customary international law defense of state of necessity, which is codified in Article 25 of the ILC Articles. As explained by the *CMS ad hoc committee,* the essential security interest clause and the state of necessity defense are "substantively different"; they are subject to different requirements and have "a different operation and content".
>
> Thus, as further remarked by the *ad hoc* Committee in *Sempra v. Argentina*, "Article 25 cannot (...) be assumed to 'define necessity and the conditions for its operation' for the purpose of interpreting Article XI" of the US-Argentina BIT. (Deutsch Telekom v. India, PCA 2017, para 228)

3.2.1.2 Nexus Requirement Under the Terms of the Provision

The nexus requirement in the ESI provision may be of a higher or a lower threshold depending on the terms chosen by parties (UNCTAD, Reform Accelerator 2020, p. 26).

Where the arbitral tribunal analyses the provision on ESI, the tribunal pays careful attention to the way the ESI provision is drafted to determine the conditions under which the treaty provision may be applied (DT v. India, Interim Award, 2017, para 230). The meaning of the terms is to be understood according to what parties said. Having the term "essential" added to the "security interest" makes the condition more demanding, as stated by an arbitral tribunal:

> (...) the natural meaning of the treaty terms requires the presence of interests concerned with *security* (as opposed to other public or societal interests) that are *essential*, i.e., that go to the core (the essence) of state security ((DT v. India, Interim Award, 2017, para 236).

The meaning of the terms will depend on the provision. An interesting example is the one opposing India to two different foreign investors who alleged their rights being impacted by the Indian annulment of the agreement for the lease of electronic spectrum on two satellites concluded with Deutsch Telekom (DT) and the same kind of contract concluded with another foreign investor CC/Devas.

With regard to one investor, Art. 11(3) in the Mauritius-India BIT was drafted as follows:

> The provisions of this Agreement shall not in any way limit the right of either Contracting Party to apply prohibitions or restrictions of any kind or take any other action which is directed to the protection of its essential security interests, or to the protection of public health or the prevention of diseases in pests or animals or plants (CC Devas v. India, PCA 2016, highlighted by the author).

---

[8]See *CMS Gas Transmission Company v. Argentine Republic, Decision of the Ad hoc Committee on the Application for Annulment of the Argentine Republic*, 25 September 2007, para 129.

As concerns the other investor, Article 12 of the German – India BIT was drafted as follows:

> Nothing in this Agreement shall prevent either Contracting Party from applying prohibitions or restrictions to the extent necessary for the protection of its essential security interests, or for the prevention of diseases and pests in animals or plants. (DT v. India, PCA 2017, highlighted by the author)

The nuance between these two provisions, in one case "to the extent necessary" and in another case "directed to", led the arbitral tribunal to two different conclusions (Kabra 2019) as the tribunal recalls:

> (. . .) while these terms provide the State with considerable freedom as to the action it can take, it is important to note that such action must be directed not to any security interest but only to "essential security interests." Measures that would not actually be directed to the protection of the essential security interests would not qualify (CC Devas v. India, PCA 2016, para 235)

The other tribunal states the following:

> The phrase "to the extent necessary" implies a more stringent nexus between the measure at issue and the interests pursued (. . .) the Tribunal finds that India has not established the presence of such nexus in the circumstances of this case, Deutsche Telekom AG v. The Republic of India (PCA 2017), para 288).

The interpretation of an ESI provision requires assessing the necessity of such a measure to safeguard the ESI of the State. To do so, the tribunal

> (. . .) will determine whether the measure was principally targeted to protect the essential security interests at stake and was objectively required in order to achieve that protection (. . .) (DT v. India, 2017, para 239)

One can conclude that the nexus requirement is assessed in consideration of the measure taken and the conditions stated for in the provision, in other words, depending on the way the provision is drafted. In the case of an exhaustive list, the measure should be in connection with the list, and if the provision states the following term of "included but not limited to", then the arbitral tribunal will have more latitude in interpreting the nexus requirement.

3.2.2 Non-Compensation of the Foreign Investor

The other issue is whether the foreign investor whose rights have been impacted will be compensated as a result of such security-related measures taken under an ESI provision, as this provision is, in essence, envisaged for that purpose. In that sense, the very existence of the provision is aimed at avoiding the State paying compensation to foreign investors, provided that the conditions of the ESI provision are met. It has been recalled that if the provision on ESI applies, the substantive obligations that aimed at protecting the foreign investor do not apply (CMS v. Argentina, Annulment, para 129).

Case law has evolved to consider

> Article XI is a threshold requirement: if it applies, the substantive obligations under the Treaty do not apply. (CMS v. Argentina, Decision on Annulment, 2007, para 129)

A year later, it was said that

> if Art. XI is applicable because the measure at issue was necessary in order to safeguard essential security interest, then the treaty is inapplicable to such measure. (Continental v. Argentina, 2008, para 236)

Recently, an arbitral tribunal concluded that

> (. . .) if a State properly invokes a national security exception under an investment treaty, it cannot be liable for compensation of damages going forward. (CC/Devas v. India (2016), para 293)

To consider the inclusion of an ESI provision in the treaty as an agreement of the parties to exclude compensation to the foreign investor if the conditions set out in the provision are fulfilled implies excluding the obligation of the parties to specify this also in the clause. A recent arbitral award said the opposite. It has been stated that

> Given that the FTA is equally supportive of investment protection, had it been the intention of the Contracting Parties that a measure could be taken pursuant to (ESI Provision) without any liability for compensation, the Article would have been drafted in similar terms (. . .) namely, making explicit that the taking of such measure would not give rise to any right to seek compensation (. . .) (Eco Oro v. Colombia, 2021, para 829).

The position of the arbitral tribunal in the Eco Oro case is a denial of the specificity of the ESI provision, while the previous case law highlighted the very essence of an ESI provision, i.e., the non-compensation of the foreign investor where the security-related measure is taken according to the conditions set for in the provision. The arbitral tribunal's inconsistency when considering an ESI has raised the awareness of scholars (Dissenting Opinion Ph. Sands in Eco Oro, 2021) The interpretation of an ESI requires a more harmonized approach in case law which clearly indicates the methodological approach and the non-compensation that resulted from such provision. Perhaps the harmonisation of the interpretation of investment treaty provisions can be achieved by an institutional structure.

4 Harmonisation of Interpretation by an Institutional Structure: Proposal

Harmonization of the interpretation of treaty standards may take different steps (Eisenhut 2010, p. 457 fd). One of those is the recognition of a public law context with investment arbitration and the development of public law standards of review that protect regulatory measures (Burke-White and von Staden 2010). Another step in the need for a comprehensive understanding would be through an institutional structure that can help provide a better assessment of treaty provisions such as the ESI provision, especially in the context of such treaties designed for the protection of foreign investors. Rebalancing the understanding of these agreements can be achieved through interpretive guidelines (Sect. 4.1) and the proposal of a specific structure such as a multilateral investment court (Sect. 4.2).

4.1 Interpretative Guidelines

The first step is to examine the content of the treaty to understand what the parties have provided for in terms of the allocation of risks between the parties and the agreed solution. Considering the existence of the treaty provision itself, attention must also be paid to the examination of all the treaty provisions to assess their articulation with a view to evaluating the obligations of the parties, particularly in the context of the provision on ESI.

The competent court should also consider legal instruments and principles in the interpretation of the will of the parties. The Vienna Convention of the Law of the Treaties (VCLT) provides guidelines in Art. 31 on general rule of interpretation and 32 on supplementary means of interpretation. Art. 31 recalls the interpretation of the treaty in accordance with the ordinary meaning of the terms in their context and in light of the object and the purpose of the treaty. As a supplementary means of interpretation, Art. 32 recalls for the preparatory work of the treaty, the circumstances of its conclusion. This approach has been the one the arbitral tribunals have taken to determine the intention of the parties and to assess their obligations and the way they have been implemented.

In addition, the competent court may also apply as a matter of general principles of law. The principle of good faith will help to determine if the parties acted in a way that is in accordance with the treaty, assessment based on a case-by case analysis. The principle of proportionality will help to determine the proportionality of the measure in light of its purpose as agreed on in the treaty. Finally, the principle of non-discrimination will also play an important role in assessing the liability of the State vis-à-vis the foreign investor, as the regulatory measure not only targets the foreign investor but also applies to all investors in the same situation.

4.2 Institutional Structure for Their Implementation in the Multilateral Investment Court (MIC)

Arbitration as a method of dispute settlement faces criticism resulting from the interpretation of treaty provisions supposedly favouring the foreign investor, accentuated by recent developments regarding the ESI provision. In this context, recent studies also show a broad category of concern that led to envisaging reforms of investment dispute settlement (UNCTAD IIA Issues March 2019, Issue 1). A MIC may be a possible option at the international level with certain specificities to avoid the criticism of arbitration.

The need to amend the system is at the heart of the most important international institutions (UNCITRAL Report, 6 November 2018). UNCITRAL is dedicating a working group III to this topic, providing an interesting approach and ideas on what should be considered and how to achieve these goals. These discussions illustrate innovations in ISDS and dispute resolution procedures. Recent meetings show the need to agree on a code of conduct.

ICSID is following the trend by proposing amendments to its rules dedicated to this new approach to arbitration (ICSID Rules and Regulations Amendment 2022). At the European level, the Multilateral Investment Court in on study and we see some proposals and prospects on the reform (EU Briefing, January 2020). State support for this approach is reflected in recent international investment agreements.[9]

Such fora have advantages at various levels. First, with regard to the selection of adjudicators, which requires independence and impartiality, limitation of multiple roles, integrity and competence, among other obligations[10] (UNCITRAL Working Group III, Code of Conduct). Second is the skills required for the selection of adjudicators, being a jurist and having expertise in the field (public international law, international investment law, etc.).[11] In addition, their availability over a long period avoids other activities at the same time. Third, an MIC will help adjudicators from different continents to become aware of the need to consider different approaches to the same issue, thus helping to provide a solution that will be understood and therefore accepted by the arbitration community. Fourth, the existence of a permanent tribunal will make it possible to harmonise solutions on specific issues that may have been interpreted differently by arbitral tribunals. In this sense, the MIC will avoid the fragmentation of decisions, as witnessed by some case law where the same facts have led to different solutions.[12] Finally, an appellate mechanism can help to provide a second level of analysis of the award, within limits such as possible error of law or manifest errors in the assessment of the facts.

5 Conclusion

IIAs were envisaged for the promotion and protection of the foreign private investor. The provisions included in the IIAs provide protection to the investor from State action that may infringe on investor rights. This is the case with the provisions on FET, national treatment, and expropriation. These provisions provide for

[9] See CETA – Canada, (2016), signed but not yet in force; https://investmentpolicy.unctad.org/international-investment-agreements/treaty-files/5380/download.

[10] See UNCITRAL Working Group III on Possible reform of investor-State dispute settlement (ISDS), Commentary to the Code of Conduct, https://uncitral.un.org/sites/uncitral.un.org/files/media-documents/uncitral/en/220825_initial_draft_commentary_to_coc_upload_version.pdf.

[11] See CETA – Canada, Art. 8.27 on Constitution of the tribunal, https://investmentpolicy.unctad.org/international-investment-agreements/treaty-files/5380/download.

[12] See for instance the Argentina cases.

compensation to the investor for any infringement of its rights resulting from State action. IIAs signed in the last decade have included provisions recognising the exercise of regulatory power by the State in areas of public interest that affect investors' rights. The State's right to regulate thus determined does not entail investor compensation if such measures have been adopted in accordance with the conditions set out in the IIAs and principles such as good faith and proportionality and non-discrimination.

This type of exception, also known as the non-precluded measures clause, was drafted taking into account the security exception of Art. XXI of the WTO Agreement, even though the latter concerns trade contracts. Their insertion and interpretation in IIAs have shown a variety of drafts and interpretations that have evolved on various grounds without necessarily reflecting a harmonised approach to the understanding of these provisions and their interpretation. The need to develop comprehensive interpretive guidelines within an institutional structure such as a multilateral investment tribunal may be the best option to achieve the objective of this provision: to consider the State's right to regulate under certain conditions without compensation to the foreign investor, even if those regulatory measures impact the foreign investor's rights.

Case Law

Eco Oro Minerals Corp. v. Republic of Colombia, ICSID Case N° ARB/16/41, Decision on Jurisdiction, Liability and Directions on Quantum, 9 September 2021, https://www.italaw.com/cases/6320

Russia – Measures Concerning Traffic in Transition (2019); Report of the Panel, World Trade Organization, WT/DS512/R, 5 April 2019, (19-2105), https://www.wto.org/english/tratop_e/dispu_e/512r_e.pdf

Deutsche Telekom AG v India, UNCITRAL, PCA Case No 2014-10, Interim Award 13 December 2017, Final Award 27 May 2020, https://www.italaw.com/cases/2275

CC/Devas (Mauritius) Ltd, Devas Employees Mauritius Private Limited and Telecom Devas Mauritius Limited v India, UNCITRAL, PCA Case No 2013-09, Award on Jurisdiction and Merits 25 July 2016; Dissenting opinion of David R. Haig, https://www.italaw.com/cases/1962

Burlington Resources Inc. v. Republic of Ecuador, ICSID Case No. ARB/08/5, Decision on Liability 14 December 2012, https://www.italaw.com/cases/181

Continental Casualty Co. v. The Argentina Republic, ICSID Case No ARB/03/9, Award 5 September 2008, https://www.italaw.com/cases/329

National Grid plc v. The Argentina Republic, UNCITRAL, award 3 November 2008. https://www.italaw.com/cases/732

Enron Corporation & Ponderosa Assets L.P. v. Argentine Republic, ICSID Case No. ARB/01/3, Award 22 May 2007, https://www.italaw.com/cases/401

CMS Gas Transmission Co. v. The Republic of Argentina, ICSID Case No. ARB/01/8, Award 12 May 2005, Decision on Annulment 25 September 2007, https://www.italaw.com/cases/288

LG&E Energy Corp., LGE&E Capital Corp., and LG&E International, Inc. v. Argentina Republic, ICSID Case No. ARB/02/1, Decision on Liability 3 October 2006, https://www.italaw.com/cases/621

CMS Gas Transmission Company v. The Argentine Republic, ICSID Case n° ARB/01/8, 12 May 2005, https://www.italaw.com/sites/default/files/case-documents/ita0184.pdf

Pope & Talbot Inc. v. The Government of Canada, UNCITRAL (NAFTA), Interim Award 26 June 2000, https://www.italaw.com/cases/863

UNITED STATES - TRADE MEASURES AFFECTING NICARAGUA, Report by the Panel (L/6053), 13 October 1986, https://www.wto.org/english/tratop_e/dispu_e/gatt_e/85embarg.pdf

Gabcíkovo-Nagymaros Project (Hungary/Slovakia) ICJ, Judgment of 25 September 1997, https://www.icj-cij.org/en/case/92

References

Accaoui Lorfing P, Burghetto M-B (2018) The evolution & current status of the concept of indirect expropriation in investment treaties and arbitration. Indian J Arbitr Law 6(2):98–123

Bartels L, Paddeu F (eds) (2020) Exceptions in international law. Oxford University Press

Blanco SM, Pehl A (2020) National security exception in international trade and investment agreements. Justiciability and standards of review. Springer

Burke-White WW, von Staden A (2008) Investment protection in extraordinary times: the interpretation and application of non-precluded measures provisions in bilateral investment treaties. Faculty Scholarship at Penn Law. 146. https://scholarship.law.upenn.edu/faculty_scholarship/146

Burke-White W, von Staden A (2010) Private litigation in a public law sphere: the standard of review in investors-state arbitrations. Yale J Int Law 35(2):283–346

Eisenhut D (2010) Sovereignty, national security and international treaty law, archive des Völkerrechts, Band 48 Heft 4, Dezember, pp 432–466

European Parliament,. Briefing Multilateral Investment Court Overview of the reform proposals and prospects https://www.europarl.europa.eu/RegData/etudes/BRIE/2020/646147/EPRS_BRI(2020)646147_EN.pdf

Henckels C (2020) Scope limitation or affirmative defence? The purpose and role of investment treaty exceptions clauses. In: Bartels L, Paddeu F (eds) Exceptions in international law. Oxford University Press, pp 360–371

ICSID Rules and Regulations Amendment, 2022, https://icsid.worldbank.org/resources/rules-amendments

Jorge E (2020) Viñuales, seven ways of escaping a rue: of exceptions and their avatars in international law. In: Bartels L, Paddeu F (eds) Exceptions in international law. Oxford University Press, pp 65–87

Kabra R (2019) Return of the inconsistent application of the 'Essential Security Interest' clause in investment treaty arbitration: CC/Devas v India and Deutsche Telekom v India. ICSID Rev 34(3):723–753

Dilini Pathirana & Mark McLaughlin, Non-precluded measures clauses: regime, trends, and practice, Julien Chaisse, Leïla Choukroune, Sufian Jusoh (ed), Handbook of international investment law and policy, 2020, Springer 2020,
Sornarajah M (2015) Resistance and change in the international law on foreign investment. Cambridge University Press, Cambridge
UNCTAD, based on UNCITRAL, Possible reform of investor-State dispute settlement (ISDS), Note by the Secretariat, A/CN.9/WG.III/WP.149, 5 September 2018
UNCTAD, International Investment Agreements. Reform Accelerator, 2020, https://unctad.org/system/files/official-document/diaepcbinf2020d8_en.pdf
UNCTAD, IIA Issues Note, The Changing IIA Landscape: New Treaties and Recent Policy Developments, July 2020, Issue 1
UNCTAD IIA Issues, Reforming Investment Dispute Settlement: A Stocktaking, March 2019, Issue 1, https://investmentpolicy.unctad.org/publications/1194/reforming-investment-dispute-settlement-a-stocktaking
UNCITRAL, Report of the Working Group III (Investor-State Dispute Settlement Reform) on the work of its thirty-sixth session (Vienna, 29 October – 2 November 2018), A/CN.9/964, 6 November 2018
UNCITRAL Working Group III on Possible reform of investor-State dispute settlement (ISDS), Commentary to the Code of Conduct, https://uncitral.un.org/sites/uncitral.un.org/files/media-documents/uncitral/en/220825_initial_draft_commentary_to_coc_upload_version.pdf
UNCTAD's Reform Package for the International Investment Regime, 2018. https://investmentpolicy.unctad.org/uploaded-files/document/UNCTAD_Reform_Package_2018.pdf
UNCTAD, The Protection of National Security in IIAs, Series on International Investment Policies for Development, 2009. https://unctad.org/system/files/official-document/diaeia20085_en.pdf
Schill S, Briese R (2009) If the States Considers: Self-Judging Clauses in International Dispute Settlement, Max Planck Yearbook of United Nations Law 13 pp 61–140

Regulating Sovereign-Driven Investments in International Trade and Investment Agreements: The Role of Investment Screening Mechanisms

Georgios Dimitropoulos

Contents

Abstract The cross-border economic activity of sovereign investors has been increasing over the last decades. This proved vital in an international economy wrecked by financial, economic, health and other crises. The chapter highlights the two main design principles governing sovereign-driven investments in international trade and investment agreements: first, ownership-neutrality that is conditioned on the commercially-driven nature of a sovereign investment; second, the sovereign power of the host state to regulate market access of foreign (sovereign) investors. The open-ended nature of these principles has allowed for a major—and ongoing—change in the structure of the contemporary international economic law regime. The change has been spearheaded by the introduction of Investment Screening Mechanisms. Investment Screening Mechanisms move the focus from international to domestic law. They may also be bringing about a re-interpretation of the permissibility of foreign sovereign investments in international trade and investment agreements.

G. Dimitropoulos (✉)
Hamad Bin Khalifa University (HBKU) College of Law, Doha, Qatar
e-mail: gdimitropoulos@hbku.edu.qa

J. H. Pohl et al. (eds.), *National Security and Investment Controls*,
Springer Studies in Law & Geoeconomics (2024) 3: 147–164,
https://doi.org/10.1007/17280_2024_22, Published online: 1 March 2024

1 Introduction

International economic law (IEL) is not designed to regulate cross-border activities of sovereign investors.[1] IEL is rather the body of law that has developed to protect cross-border trade and investment arising out of private activity. Still, the cross-border economic activity of sovereign investors has been increasing. This raises the question of protection and the overall status of sovereign-driven investments in international economic law.[2] There are three possible responses to this question: IEL disallows sovereign-driven investments. Second, IEL protects sovereign-driven investments. Third, IEL is indifferent towards sovereign-driven investments.

Sovereign-driven overseas investments are investments undertaken by agencies owned and/or controlled by the home state. Most often than not, these investments are conducted by State-Owned Enterprises (SOEs);[3] overseas investments may be made by Sovereign Wealth Funds (SWFs), or other SOEs, such as construction and energy production companies. SWFs are investment funds established and/or owned by a government to invest and hold its foreign assets—usually for long-term purposes.[4] SWFs are not a new phenomenon. The Kuwait Investment Authority (KIA) was established in 1953; the Abu Dhabi Investment Authority (ADIA) in 1976; Singapore's Temasek Holdings in 1974; Government Investment Corporation (GIC) of Singapore in 1981. Sovereign investments have been increasing in the last decades. Two thirds of SWFs were established during the beginning of the 2000s.[5] They are more common in natural resource-rich countries with large balance of payment surpluses. Other emerging and commodity-based emerging economies have been establishing and operating SWFs as well.[6]

Sovereign investment turns the government into an active investor. This proved vital in an international economy which has been wrecked by financial, economic, health and other crises over the last decades. Given their goals, SWFs have focused on investments that the private sector was not looking at when budgets were tight and there was no liquidity. SWFs have long-term financial return policies and distant investment horizons. SWFs have contributed to providing market liquidity when the private sector would not.[7]

Still, the cross-border activity of sovereign investors raises concerns in recipient countries. The typical cash-flow direction is reversed compared to that of private

[1] See also Sornarajah (2011), pp. 278–279.

[2] See generally Burgstaller (2011); Chaisse et al. (2011); Sauvant et al. (2012); Lippincott (2013); Poulsen (2013); Dekastros (2016); Kratsas and Truby (2015); Hsu (2017); Chaisse (2018); Borlini (2020). Sornarajah claims that sovereign investors must not be treated any different from multinational corporations in international economic law; see Sornarajah, note 1 above, at 273.

[3] See, for example, Chaisse (2016).

[4] See Rozanov (2005); Wang (2016); Epstein and Rose (2009); Bassan (2015).

[5] Lipsky (2008).

[6] See Al-Hassan et al. (2018).

[7] See generally Peterson Institute for International Economics.

investment. Sovereign investors in the South and East would typically invest in a market in the North and West.[8] Recipient country governments fear the lack of transparency and public accountability of sovereign investors; they also fear that decisions on sovereign investments may be based on non-commercial motives, such as geopolitical and geoeconomic objectives.

Two principles govern the law of sovereign-driven foreign investment in the post-WWII international economic order:[9] Ownership-neutrality and the power to regulate market access. Ownership-neutrality highlights that the ownership of the capital or investment vehicle is not important. It is irrelevant—for investment protection purposes—who owns the money.[10] This is qualified though: Sovereign investments are only protected in international law so long as they are driven by commercial considerations.[11]

IEL has been largely developed to spearhead cross-border economic activity. Still, it operates within the traditional framework of international law that is shaped by the principle of sovereignty. This is reflected in the sovereign power of states to regulate access to their domestic market. International economic agreements do not typically include rules on market access—and as such pre-entry protection of foreign investments.[12] Domestic law and institutions decide whether a foreign investment and investor may be admitted in any domestic market in the first place.[13]

---

[8] Sornarajah, note 1 above, at 268 ('Another issue is how the developed world itself would respond. It could respond by changing the rules to protect its interests, by advocating the very rules that the developing states had advanced in the past by seeking refuge in sovereignty-centred, protectionist norms that it has hitherto resisted. The emergence of new and competing trends would provide interesting contexts in which change in international law could be studied').

[9] The term 'principle' – here and throughout the chapter – is not used in the technical sense of the 'general principles of law recognized by civilized nations' under Article 38(1)(c) of the Statute of the International Court of Justice. It is rather used in a broader sense to describe design rules that permeate international economic agreements.

[10] There has been an effort to move in (international) trade law beyond 'ownership-neutrality' and towards 'competitive neutrality'; see OECD Recommendation of the Council on Competitive Neutrality, OECD/LEGAL/0462 (31/05/2021). Professor Robert Howse has explained the politics behind this move, as well as the importance of sticking to the principle of ownership-neutrality; see Howse (2023), p. 76 ('While ownership neutrality of this kind is arguably a matter of good economic governance (preventing the organisation of assets in ownership structures that undermine policy objectives and circumvent regulatory obligations), it is not this kind of neutrality that the trade policy community is concerned about when they seek to introduce 'competitive neutrality' into the trade legal order. Rather, what is supposed is that state enterprises are often not subject to the same anti-trust norms under domestic law than private enterprises, and this allows them to compete unfairly in international trade. This seems simply a reformulation of the critique that WTO law is hobbled in its capacity to ensure competitive global markets for lack of an anti-trust code'); see also Borlini (2020), note 2 above, at 321; Borlini and Silingardi (2023).

[11] See Sect. 2 below.

[12] See Sect. 3.1. below.

[13] The chapter discusses developments in IEL. Similar principles largely govern the EU internal market as well; on ownership-neutrality, see Article 345 of the Treaty on the Functioning of the European Union (TFEU). With regard to market access for investors, see Article 63 TFEU covering

A change in international law is currently being spearheaded by domestic law. The push to protect national security interests from risks deriving from foreign investors[14] has led—among others—to a 'domestication' process in international economic law.[15] Many countries around the world have historically had in place, or have recently introduced, investment screening mechanisms (ISMs) to control inward investment.[16] The principles that govern sovereign-driven investments in international trade and investment agreements have allowed for a major change in the structure of the contemporary international economic regime.[17] This has been brought about by the introduction of ISMs.

The chapter discusses the principles that govern sovereign-driven investments in different areas of IEL. It is structured as follows: Section 2 discusses ownership neutrality. Section 3 discusses the sovereign power of states to regulate market access. Section 4 elaborates on how changes in national law impact IEL. The open-ended nature of international trade and investment agreements has allowed for domestic law to jump-start a process of reforming international law. New ISMs bring about changes in the overall structure of the international investment regime, and the way it deals with sovereign investments.

2 Ownership-Neutrality

International (economic) law does not traditionally distinguish between investors on the basis of ownership. It rather focuses on the function of economic activity. Sovereign investors are expected to operate on a commercial basis. This part of the chapter discusses the principle of ownership-neutrality in international law drawing on examples from international trade and investment, hard and soft law.

The Preamble of the Convention on the Settlement of Investment Disputes Between States and Nationals of Other States (ICSID) states in its first sentence that the Contracting Parties '[c]onsider the need for international cooperation for economic development, and the role of private international investment therein'. International Investment Agreements (IIAs) do not typically distinguish between investors based on ownership. Most IIAs are ownership-neutral in that they only make generic references to 'investors'. One of the few multilateral IIAs, the Energy Charter Treaty, for example, defines an investor for the purposes of the treaty as

---

free movement of capital of both intra-EU and extra-EU investments, as well as the broad powers to derogate regarding movement of capital to or from third countries under Articles 64-66 TFEU.

[14] See generally DeSouza and Reisman (2012).

[15] See Dimitropoulos (2020b); Chaisse and Dimitropoulos (2021); Chaisse and Dimitropoulos (2023); Dimitropoulos (2023).

[16] See generally Dimitropoulos (2020a).

[17] On the impact of investment treaties on ISMs see Hillebrand Pohl (2020); see also Dekastros (2023).

(i) a natural person having the citizenship or nationality of or who is permanently residing in [the] Contracting Party in accordance with its applicable law;
(ii) a company or other organisation organised in accordance with the law applicable in [the] Contracting Party[18]

No references are made in this treaty to the private or public nature of the company – or, more generally, of the legal person.

Some Bilateral Investment Treaties (BITs) make explicit mention of sovereign investors, or even the 'contracting party', or the 'government of a contracting party'.[19] This is mostly done with the intention of leaving no doubt as to whether sovereign investors are covered under the definition of an investor. The BITs of the Gulf states—such as Kuwait, Qatar, UAE and Saudi Arabia—are the most vocal on this point.[20] The Association of South-East Asian Nations (ASEAN) Comprehensive Investment Agreement also covers sovereign investments.[21] At least three BITs specify that sovereign investors are not covered. Panamanian SOEs are not covered under the definition of a 'company' for the purposes of the BITs with Germany, Switzerland and the UK.[22] These BITs impose an asymmetric obligation on the sovereign investors of Panama.

The wording of international treaties raised early on the question of the exact scope of application of the principle of ownership-neutrality. Aron Broches, first Secretary-General of ICSID and one of the principal drafters of the ICSID Convention, famously stated that

> [I]n today's world the classical distinction between private and public investment, based on the source of the capital, is no longer meaningful, if not outdated. There are many companies which combine capital from private and governmental sources and corporations all of whose shares are owned by the government, but who are practically indistinguishable from the completely privately owned enterprise both in their legal characteristics and in their activities. It would seem, therefore, that for purposes of the Convention a mixed economy company or government-owned corporation should not be disqualified as a 'national of another Contracting State' unless it is acting as an agent for the government or is discharging an essentially governmental function.[23]

This has been later defined as the 'Broches Test',[24] and has largely shaped the interpretation of ICSID, as well as all provisions of IEL that refer to sovereign investors.

[18]Article 1(7) Energy Charter Treaty.

[19]See generally Shima (2015).

[20]See, for example, Saudi Arabia-India BIT (2006) (terminated); Kuwait-Germany BIT (1994); UAE-Germany BIT (1997).

[21]See Articles 4(d) and (e) of the ASEAN Comprehensive Investment Agreement, 26 February 2009.

[22]Germany-Panama BIT (1983); Panama-Switzerland BIT (1983); Panama-United Kingdom BIT (1983).

[23]Broches (1972), pp. 354–355.

[24]Schreuer et al. (2009), p. 161.

At the same time, sovereign investors are only protected under IIAs to the extent that they operate on a commercial basis. This is explicitly stated in the Multilateral Investment Guarantee Agency Convention (MIGA Convention) of 1988 that defines 'eligible investors':

> (a) Any natural person and any juridical person may be eligible to receive the Agency's guarantee provided that: . . . (iii) such juridical person, whether or not it is privately owned, operates on a commercial basis.[25]

The definition of the operation of an investor as governmental or commercial has also been shaped by the Broches test in the case law of investment tribunals. Tribunals have been repeatedly called upon to interpret the broad notion of 'investor' in BITs and other IIAs, and as such the extent to which an investor operates in a governmental or commercial capacity. The Tribunal in *CSOB v The Slovak Republic*, for example, said that

> It cannot be denied that for much of its existence, CSOB acted on behalf of the State in facilitating or executing the international banking transactions and foreign commercial operations the State wished to support and that the State's control of CSOB required it to do the State's bidding in that regard. But in determining whether CSOB, in discharging these functions, exercised governmental functions, the focus must be on the nature of these activities and not their purpose. While it cannot be doubted that in performing the above-mentioned activities, CSOB was promoting the governmental policies or purposes of the State, the activities themselves were essentially commercial rather than governmental in nature.[26]

The same interpretation has been followed by tribunals in other disputes too.[27]

This more functional approach to the interpretation of sovereign—and in juxtaposition, commercial—activity is also followed in international trade law. Article I (3)(b) of the General Agreement on Trade in Services (GATS) defines services for the purposes of the agreement as 'includ[ing] any service in any sector except services supplied in the exercise of governmental authority'; 'services supplied in the exercise of governmental authority', according to Article I:3(c) GATS, means 'any service which is supplied neither on a commercial basis, nor in competition with one or more service suppliers'.[28]

Other agreements of the WTO framework follow similar approaches. The Agreement on Subsidies and Countervailing Measures (ASCM) includes the notion of a

---

[25] Article 13(a)(iii) MIGA Convention.

[26] *Ceskoslovenska Obchodni Banka (CSOB), AS v. The Slovak Republic (ICSID Case No ARB/97/4)*, Decision of the Tribunal on Objections to Jurisdiction, 24 May 1999, at para 20.

[27] See *Telenor Mobile Communications A.S. v. The Republic of Hungary*, ICSID Case No. ARB/04/15, Award, 13 September 2006; *Rumeli Telekom A.S. and Telsim Mobil Telekomunikasyon Hizmetleri A.S. v. Republic of Kazakhstan* (ICSID Case No. ARB/05/16), Award, 29 July 2008; *CDC Group PLC v Republic of Seychelles*, ICSID Case No. ARB/02/14, Award, 17 December 2013; *Beijing Urban Construction Group Co. Ltd. V. Republic of Yemen* (ICSID Case No ARB/14/30), Decision on Jurisdiction, 31 May 2017, at 31–44.

[28] See generally Krajewski (2003).

'public body'.[29] 'A public body within the meaning of Article 1.1. (a)(1) of the SCM Agreement', according to the WTO Appellate Body, 'must be an entity that possesses, exercises or is vested with government authority'.[30]

The same ideas pertain to the regulation of foreign activity of sovereign investors in soft law. On the host country side, the OECD Declaration on Sovereign Wealth Funds and Recipient Country Policies highlights the obligation for SWFs to operate on a commercially-driven basis and be motivated by commercial objectives.[31] The same idea is expressed on the home country side in the 24 Santiago Principles adopted by the major SWFs to guide their activities.[32]

Before moving on to the discussion of the power to regulate market access, it is worth revisiting the question posed at the beginning of the chapter regarding the way IEL treats sovereign-driven investments: International economic agreements are generally indifferent as to the ownership of the capital. Absent more specific provisions, sovereign-driven investments are protected so long as they are commercial in nature.

3 Sovereign Power to Regulate Market Access

For all the efforts of post-war IEL to accommodate cross-border economic activity, the fundamental rule, principle and premise of an international order based on sovereignty persists. States have the sovereign power to regulate access to their national markets. States do exercise this power.[33] This principle applies to varying degrees in the different areas of international law. This section of the chapter focuses on the application of the principle in cross-border investment activity, and as it applies to sovereign-driven investments.

[29] Article 1.1. (a)(1) ASCM.

[30] AB, *United States – Definitive Anti-Dumping and Countervailing Duties on Certain Products From China*, WT/DS379/AB/R (11 March 2011), para 290.

[31] OECD Declaration on Sovereign Wealth Funds and Recipient Country Policies Adopted, C/MIN (2008)8/FINAL (05/06/2008).

[32] International Working Group on Sovereign Wealth Funds (2008), esp. Principles 14 and 19 with 19.1. At the same time, Principle 13 allows SWFs to consider ethical standards in their investment decisions.

[33] This power is exercised in different ways; see Sornarajah (2011), p. 274.

3.1 Pre-Admission

States have the sovereign power under IEL to regulate the entry and establishment of foreign investors within their borders.[34] This is reflected in various international trade and investment treaties.

The ICSID Convention does not include any rules on pre-entry protection of foreign investors. States may grant foreign investors admission or establishment rights in their markets using IIAs. Only a limited number of IIAs grant market access rights—or any other pre-entry protections—to prospective investors. Such 'pre-entry IIAs' grant a right of establishment, which is often limited in scope.[35] The limitation is imposed either by subjecting this right to a 'national law' clause,[36] or by framing the equivalent obligations of the state in a 'soft' or 'best endeavour' way.[37] Traditional European BITs do not generally provide market access rights. Market entry and establishment rights are more common in investment treaties of counties such as the US, Canada, Japan and South Korea.[38] A commonly cited example is the US Model BIT of 2012:

> Each Party shall accord to investors of the other Party treatment no less favorable than that it accords, in like circumstances, to its own investors with respect to the *establishment*, acquisition, expansion, management, conduct, operation, and sale or other disposition of investments in its territory.[39]

The General Agreement on Tariffs and Trade (GATT) generally recognises market access rights for foreign products. At the same time, broad-based exceptions are also introduced to protect public morals, health, life, the environment, etc.[40] In addition, state monopolies are allowed under Article XVII GATT on State Trading Enterprises (STEs). Monopolies are then made subject to the trade disciplines. Article VIII GATS also allows state monopolies under the condition that member countries must ensure that monopolies and exclusive service suppliers do not abuse their position.

The GATS applies to sovereign investment in services.[41] Market access in the GATS is subject to stricter regulation in comparison to market access for products under the GATT. The provision on commercial presence in the GATS aims at

---

[34] See UNCTAD (2019), p. 92.

[35] See generally on the differentiation between 'post-entry' and 'pre-entry' investment treaties UNCTAD (1999), p. 8.

[36] See on the scope of the limitation F*raport A.G. Frankfurt Airport ServicesWorldwide v. Republic of the Philippines*, Award of 16 August 2007, ICSID Case No. ARB/03/25; *Desert Line Projects LLC v. Republic of Yemen*, Award of 6 February 2008, ICSID Case No. ARB/05/17.

[37] See, for example, Article 2(1) of the Germany Model BIT (2008); Article 2(1) of the UK Model BIT (2008).

[38] Sornarajah (2011), p. 281.

[39] Article 3(1) of the US Model BIT (2012) (emphasis added).

[40] See Sect. 3.2. below.

[41] Chaisse (2015).

liberalizing services market to foreign investment.[42] At the same time, Article XX GATS requires each member to maintain a schedule of the specific commitments it undertakes. A WTO member can include specific limitations or conditions to market access and national treatment in its schedule of specific commitments. The schedules are annexed to the GATS and form an integral part of the agreement.

Contrary to the GATT, national treatment is not automatically accorded across the board. The GATS adopts in Articles XVI and XVII an opt-in or positive list approach for market access and national treatment.[43] Article XVII of the GATS requires national treatment only regarding services and service suppliers that are included in the schedule. Market access is only granted to the extent that a member has undertaken market access commitments for a specific sector or sub-sector of services by using the four modes of supply laid out in Article I:2 of the GATS. In addition, Article II:2 GATS allows members to list exemptions from MFN in a separate annex. This article adopts an opt-out or negative list approach for obligations to grant MFN status to like services and service suppliers.[44]

Overall, only by reference to a country's schedule, as well as its MFN exemption list (where applicable), can it be determined which service sectors—and under what conditions—the basic principles of the GATS apply to in a member country.

Some countries have explicitly excluded foreign government ownership from the scope of their commitments under the GATS for some sectors. This means that these countries have retained the right to disallow sovereign investments in these sectors.[45] The commitment of the United States in the insurance sector, for example, provides that US or foreign government-owned or government-controlled insurance companies are not authorized to conduct business in a large number of states.[46] In basic telecommunications services, no license may be granted to or held by a foreign government or representatives thereof.[47] Broad-based limitations are introduced in the audiovisual services sector and the sub-sector of radio and television transmission services. Sovereign investments are generally excluded:

---

[42] Article I(2)(c) GATS.

[43] Article XVI:1 GATS reads as follows: 'With respect to market access through the modes of supply identified in Article I, each Member shall accord services and service suppliers of any other Member treatment no less favourable *than that provided for under the terms, limitations and conditions agreed and specified in its Schedule*' (emphasis added). Article XVII(1) reads as follows: '*In the sectors inscribed in its Schedule, and subject to any conditions and qualifications set out therein*, each Member shall accord to services and service suppliers of any other Member, in respect of all measures affecting the supply of services, treatment no less favourable than that it accords to its own like services and service suppliers' (emphasis added).

[44] Article II:2 GATS reads as follows: 'A Member may maintain a measure inconsistent with paragraph 1 provided that such a measure is listed in, and meets the conditions of, the Annex on Article II Exemptions'.

[45] See generally Mattoo and Subramanian (2008).

[46] U.S. Schedule of Specific Commitments, GATS/SC/90, Page 55.

[47] U.S. Schedule of Specific Commitments, GATS/EL/90/Suppl.2 Page A-1.

> Radio and television licences may not be held by: a foreign government; a corporation chartered under the law of a foreign country or which has a non-US citizen as an officer or director or more than 20 per cent of the capital stock of which is owned or voted by non-US citizens; a corporation chartered under the laws of the United States that is directly or indirectly controlled by a corporation more than 25 per cent of whose capital stock is owned by non-US citizens or a foreign government or a corporation of which any officer or more than 25 per cent of the directors are non-US citizens.[48]

The principle of a broad-based sovereign right to regulate foreign investment was also established in early GATT case law. A GATT panel recognised already in 1984 that states retain under the GATT their sovereign power to accept or reject FDI. 'The General Agreement' the panel said, 'does not prevent Canada from exercising its sovereign right to regulate foreign direct investments' under the Foreign Investment Review Act.[49]

3.2 Post-Admission

Even after admission, there are certain measures—expressions of sovereign power—that may be justified under international law. All WTO agreements include general exceptions, such as Article XX GATT, for the protection of life, health and the environment. Other provisions include exceptions for the protection of 'essential security interests',[50] or 'national security'.[51] Such provisions were rarely invoked during the GATT years. This has changed more recently. There are three main sets of cases that have raised the issue of national security before the WTO dispute settlement system. First, disputes that arose between Russia and Ukraine in 2014;[52] second, disputes revolving around the severance of diplomatic relations between Qatar and four countries of the Middle East North Africa (MENA) Region in 2017;[53] third, the 'trade war' cases, which are the result of the reassessment of US

---

[48] U.S. Schedule of Specific Commitments, GATS/SC/90 Page 48.

[49] *Canada - Administration of the Foreign Investment Review Act*, Report of the Panel adopted on 7 February 1984 (L/5504 - 30S/140) para 5.1.

[50] See Article XXI GATT 1994, Article XIVbis GATS, Article 73 TRIPS Agreement, Article 10.8.3 TBT Agreement and Article III:1 of the Revised Agreement on Government Procurement.

[51] See Articles 2.2, 2.10, 5.4 and 5.7 TBT Agreement, and Article III:1 of the Revised Agreement on Government Procurement. See generally Akande and Williams (2003); Alford (2011); Schill and Briese (2009), pp. 97–110; Emmerson (2008); Heath (2019); Heath (2020); Pinchis-Paulsen (2020); Lacerda Prazeres (2020); Trujillo (2020).

[52] *Russia – Measures Concerning Traffic in Transit*, WT/DS512/R (5 April 2019); see generally Crivelli and Pinchis-Paulsen (2021).

[53] See, for example, *Saudi Arabia – Measures concerning the Protection of Intellectual Property Rights*, WT/DS567/R (16 June 2020) (the panel report remains unadopted and the appeal filed by Saudi Arabia has been suspended based on the Al-Ula Declaration signed on 5 January 2021; see *Saudi Arabia – IPRs*, Communication from the Kingdom of Saudi Arabia, WT/DS567/9 (7 January 2021)).

trade policy during the Trump Administration.[54] There is no definitive answer on these questions under the GATS. Article XIV bis, the security exceptions clause of the GATS, has never been invoked.[55]

Respondent states in investor-state dispute settlement have resorted to security exceptions to justify the adoption of domestic measures – in deviation from investment treaty standards such as national treatment, most favoured nation, and fair and equitable treatment.[56] Security considerations are assessed in international investment law under two heads. First, investment tribunals have granted the application of the necessity defense of customary international law[57]—such as in the cases arising out of the Argentinian economic and financial crisis.[58] BITs and other IIAs have traditionally not included national security exceptions—in contrast to international trade agreements.[59] More recent BITs and other IIAS have started including 'essential security' exceptions that resemble those of the WTO.[60] Investment tribunals generally recognize that states should be treated with some deference in their assessment of national security measures.[61]

---

[54] See generally van Aaken et al. (2019); see also Claussen (2020); Claussen (2021).

[55] See generally Cottier and Delimatsis (2008).

[56] See, for example, *Bear Creek Mining Corporation v Peru*, ICSID Case No ARB/14/21, Award (30 November 2017) paras 122, 149, 202, 341, 473.

[57] See, for example, *Sempra Energy International v Argentina*, ICSID Case No ARB/02/16, Award (18 September 2007) para 344; but see *Sempra Energy International v Argentina*, ICSID Case No ARB/02/16, Decision on Annulment (10 June 2010) paras 159, 168, 177, 200, 223. The necessity defense is codified under Article 25 of the 2001 *Articles on State Responsibility* of the International Law Commission. Article 25 *Responsibility of States for Internationally Wrongful Acts*, GA Res 56/83, UN GAOR, 56th sess, 85th plen mtg, Supp No 49, UN Doc A/RES/56/83 (28 January 2002, adopted 12 December 2001) annex.

[58] See, for example, Kurtz (2010).

[59] See generally Knight and Voon (2020).

[60] The case law suggests that national security clauses are not self-judging except when they are expressly stated to be such in the relevant treaty. See generally UNCTAD, 'The Protection of National Security in IIAs, UNCTAD Series on International Investment Policies for Development, UNCTAD/DIAE/IA/2008/5, United Nations, New York/Geneva 2009' 72.

Most cases on essential security exceptions have arisen in response to the measures adopted by the government of Argentina under Article XI of the Argentina-US BIT during the economic crisis of 2002; see Treaty between United States of America and the Argentine Republic Concerning the Reciprocal Encouragement and Protection of Investment (signed 14 November 1991, entered into force 20 October 1994); see the following cases: *CMS Gas Transmission Co v Argentina*, ICSID Case No ARB/01/8, Award (25 April 2005) paras 370, 373; *Enron Corporation v Argentina*, ICSID Case No ARB/01/3, Award (22 May 2007) paras 331, 332; *El Paso Energy International Co v Argentina*, ICSID Case No ARB/03/15, Award (27 October 2011) paras 561, 589, 610. See also, for example, Article 11(3) of the Mauritius–India BIT (Agreement between the Republic of Mauritius and the Republic of India for the Promotion and Protection of Investments (signed 4 September 1998, entered into force 20 June 2000).

[61] *Deutsche Telekom AG v Republic of India*, PCA Case No 2014–10, Interim Award (13 December 2017) (*Deutsche Telekom v India*) para 235. Tribunals have also debated whether domestic measures in response to an economic crisis are covered under the protection of essential security

International trade and investment agreements generally allow domestic measures for the protection of various national interests even after an investment has taken place. Post-admission measures for the protection of national security are expected to be increasingly used vis-à-vis sovereign investors.[62] '[Their] very nature [. . .]', according to Sornarajah, 'as funds linked to foreign states, sometimes perceived to be potentially hostile, makes them easy targets of the national security preclusion.'[63]

Before moving on to more recent developments and as a matter of interim conclusion, IEL is generally protective of sovereign-driven investments, unless they are explicitely excluded from the scope of an IIA. Outright bans on sovereign investments are few and far between.

4 Moving Beyond Ownership Neutrality? The Impact of ISMs

Two main principles govern the activity of sovereign investors in international law: Ownership-neutrality that is conditioned on the premise of commercially-driven investments; at the same time, the host state has the sovereign power to regulate market access of foreign investors. These two principles that govern sovereign-driven investments in international trade and investment agreements have allowed for a major change in the structure of the contemporary international economic law regime. This has been brought about by the introduction of ISMs – as will be discussed below.

As explained above, the ICSID Convention, BITs as well as other international agreements do not typically include rules on market access—and as such pre-entry protection of foreign investments. Domestic law and institutions decide whether a foreign investment and investor may be admitted in the domestic market in the first place. Many countries around the world have historically had in place, or have recently introduced, ISMs to control inward investment. The most common ground for the establishment, continuation, proliferation and/or expansion of ISMs is national security.[64]

The legal frameworks of different legal orders provide various interpretations of national security; the general tendency is to keep the grounds of review broad—thus allowing considerable discretion to national agencies performing the screening assessment. National security is generally not restricted to national defense or foreign affairs.[65] Contemporary investment screening laws have started to also

interests; see *CC/Devas (Mauritius) Ltd v Republic of India*, PCA Case No 2013–09, Award on Jurisdiction and Merits (25 July 2016).

[62] See generally Delimatsis and Hrynkiv (2023).

[63] Sornarajah (2011), p. 287.

[64] See Dimitropoulos (2020a).

[65] Grieger (2017), p. 9.

cover 'geoeconomic' considerations in the foreign investment screening assessment.[66]

This new direction has one main addressee: sovereign-driven investors. Investment screening laws establish direct links between national security threats and the involvement of sovereign investors in an investment. The link becomes a triangular relationship in the case of investment in two main sectors: 'critical technologies', and 'critical infrastructure'—broadly defined to cover both physical and digital infrastructure.[67] The reform of longstanding as well as recent introduction of ISMs—especially in the US and Europe—can be attributed to the rise of sovereign investors in the international economy.[68]

Article 4 of the EU FDI Screening Regulation,[69] for example, reads as follows:

> 1. In determining whether a foreign direct investment is likely to affect security or public order, Member States and the Commission may consider its potential effects on, inter alia:
>
>   (a) critical infrastructure, whether physical or virtual, including energy, transport, water, health, communications, media, data processing or storage, aerospace, defence, electoral or financial infrastructure, and sensitive facilities, as well as land and real estate crucial for the use of such infrastructure;
>   (b) critical technologies and dual use items [...], including artificial intelligence, robotics, semiconductors, cybersecurity, aerospace, defence, energy storage, quantum and nuclear technologies as well as nanotechnologies and biotechnologies;
>
> [...]

The second paragraph of the same article highlights the triangular link between national security—critical infrastructure/technologies—investments by sovereign investors:

> 2. In determining whether a foreign direct investment is likely to affect security or public order, Member States and the Commission may also take into account, in particular:
>
>   (a) whether the foreign investor is directly or indirectly controlled by the government, including state bodies or armed forces, of a third country, including through ownership structure or significant funding;
>
> [...]

Screening practice in European Union member states confirms that an important number of investments or attempts to invest are in the areas of critical infrastructure and critical technology, as well as possibly involve government ownership or control of—or influence over—the foreign investor.[70]

---

[66] On the transition to an international 'geoeconomic order' see Roberts et al. (2019).

[67] See also Dimitropoulos (2020a); Misra (2023), p. 143.

[68] See European Commission (2022), pp. 7–10; see also Georgaki (2023), p. 123.

[69] Regulation (EU) 2019/452 of the European Parliament and of the Council of 19 March 2019 establishing a framework for the screening of foreign direct investments into the Union.

[70] European Commission (2022), p. 19.

The Committee on Foreign Investment in the United States (CFIUS) is established and operates under Section 721 of the Defense Production Act of 1950. Section 721(f) includes factors that are to be considered for the purposes of making the national security assessment. The eighth criterion is 'whether the covered transaction is a foreign government-controlled transaction, as determined under subsection (b)(1)(B)'. Section 721(a)(4) defines a foreign government-controlled transaction as

> any covered transaction that could result in the control of any person engaged in interstate commerce in the United States by a foreign government or an entity controlled by or acting on behalf of a foreign government.

Section 1702(c)(2) of the Foreign Investment Risk Review Modernization Act (FIRRMA) of 2018 that amended Section 721 of the Defense Production Act added that CFIUS may consider 'the cumulative control of, or pattern of recent transactions involving, any one type of critical infrastructure, energy asset, critical material, or critical technology by a foreign government or foreign person' in considering national security risks.[71]

These provisions are markedly different from the criteria of 'operation on a commercial basis' or the 'commercial nature of activities' previously identified as the relevant considerations for the permissibility of sovereign investment under international law.[72] Their preferred criterion is organizational. Their focus is on the nature of the body, not the nature of the activity.

ISMs—as well as the broader 'domestication tendency'—may be fundamentally changing the nature of the law of foreign investment which developed in the post-WWII world. First, they shift the focus from international to domestic law. Second, they may be leading the way towards a re-interpretation of the permissibility of foreign sovereign investors and sovereign investments in international law too.

5 Conclusion

The chapter highlighted the two main principles governing the activity of sovereign investors in international trade and investment agreements: first, ownership-neutrality that is conditioned on the commercially-driven nature of an investment; second, the sovereign power of the host state to regulate market access of foreign investors. The open-ended nature of these principles has allowed for a major ongoing change in the structure of the contemporary international economic law regime. This has been spearheaded by the introduction of ISMs. ISMs move the focus from international to domestic law. They may also be bringing about a

[71] These provisions have been further strengthened by a series of CFIUS regulations and guidance; see, for example, Executive Order 11,858 and Executive Order 14,083.

[72] See Sect. 2 above.

re-interpretation of the permissibility of foreign sovereign investors and investments in international trade and investment agreements.

References

Akande D, Williams S (2003) International adjudication on national security issues: what role for the WTO? Virginia J Int Law 43:365–404
Alford RP (2011) The self-judging WTO security exception. Utah Law Rev 2011:697–759
Al-Hassan A, Brake S, Papaioannou MG, Skancke M (2018) Commodity-based Sovereign Wealth Funds: Managing Financial Flows in the Context of the Sovereign Balance Sheet, Working Paper No. 2018/026 (9 February 2018)
Bassan F (ed) (2015) Research handbook on sovereign wealth funds and international investment law. Edward Elgar, Cheltenham
Borlini L (2020) When the leviathan goes to the market: a critical evaluation of the rules governing state-owned enterprises in trade agreements. LJIL 33:313–334
Borlini L, Silingardi S (2023) The foundations of international economic order in the age of state capitalism. In: Delimatsis P, Dimitropoulos G, Gourgourinis A (eds) State capitalism and international investment law. Hart, London, pp 17–41
Broches A (1972) The convention on the settlement of investment disputes between states and nationals of other states. Recueil des Cours. Collected Courses Hague Acad Int Law 136:331–410
Burgstaller M (2011) Sovereign wealth funds and international investment law. In: Brown C, Miles K (eds) Evolution in investment treaty law and arbitration. CUP, Cambridge, pp 163–186
Chaisse J (2015) Assessing the relevance of multilateral trade law to sovereign investments: sovereign wealth funds as 'Investors' under the general agreement on trade in services. Int Rev Law 2015.swf.9, https://doi.org/10.5339/irl.2015.swf.9
Chaisse J (2016) Untangling the triangle: issues for state-controlled entities in trade, investment and competition law. In: Chaisse J, Lin TS (eds) International economic law and governance: essays in honour of Mitsuo Matsushita. OUP, Oxford, pp 233–257
Chaisse J (2018) State capitalism on the ascent: stress, shock, and adaptation of the international law on foreign investment. Minn J Int Law 27:342–419
Chaisse J, Dimitropoulos G (2021) SEZs in international economic law: towards unilateral economic law. JIEL 24:229–257
Chaisse J, Dimitropoulos G (2023) Domestic investment laws and international economic law in the liberal international order. WTR 22:1–17
Chaisse J, Chakraborty D, Mukherjee J (2011) Emerging sovereign wealth funds in the making: assessing the economic feasibility and regulatory strategies. JWT 45:837–875
Claussen K (2020) Trade's security exceptionalism. Stanford Law Rev 72:1097–1164
Claussen K (2021) Trade administration. Virginia Law Rev 107:845–917
Cottier T, Delimatsis P (2008) Article XIV bis GATS: security exceptions. In: Wolfrum R, Stoll P-T, Feinäugle C (eds) 6 Max Planck commentaries on World Trade Law, WTO – trade in services. Martinus Nijhoff Publishers, Leiden/Boston, pp 329–348
Crivelli P, Pinchis-Paulsen M (2021) Separating the political from the economic: the Russia–Traffic in Transit Panel Report. WTR 20:582–605
Dekastros M (2016) Sovereign Wealth Funds in International Economic Law. EUI PhD Thesis (Florence 2016), https://cadmus.eui.eu/handle/1814/42004?show=full. Accessed 30 Nov 2022
Dekastros M (2023) Sovereign wealth funds and foreign investment screening under international investment law. In: Delimatsis P, Dimitropoulos G, Gourgourinis A (eds) State capitalism and international investment law. Hart, London, pp 99–121

Delimatsis P, Hrynkiv O (2023) Sovereign investors and national security exceptions in WTO and investment law. In: Delimatsis P, Dimitropoulos G, Gourgourinis A (eds) State capitalism and international investment law. Hart, London, pp 213–244
DeSouza P, Reisman WM (2012) Sovereign wealth funds and national security. In: Sauvant KP, Sachs LE, Schmit Jongbloed WPF (eds) Sovereign investment: concerns and policy reactions. OUP, Oxford, p 283
Dimitropoulos G (2020a) National security: the role of investment screening mechanisms. In: Chaisse J, Choukroune L, Jusoh S (eds) Handbook of international investment law and policy. Springer, Singapore, p 507
Dimitropoulos G (2020b) National sovereignty and international investment law: sovereignty reassertion and prospects of reform. JWIT 21:71–103
Dimitropoulos G (2023) The right to hospitality in international economic law: domestic investment laws and the right to invest. WTR 22:90–108
Emmerson A (2008) Conceptualizing security exceptions: legal doctrine or political excuse? JIEL 11:135–154
Epstein RA, Rose AM (2009) The regulation of sovereign wealth funds: the virtues of going slow. Univ Chicago Law Rev 76:111–134
European Commission (2022) Report from the Commission to the European Parliament and the Council, Second Annual Report on the Screening of Foreign Direct Investments into the Union, COM(2022) 433 final (Brussels 1 September 2022)
Georgaki K (2023) The screening of cross-border investments by state-owned enterprises under EU law. In: Delimatsis P, Dimitropoulos G, Gourgourinis A (eds) State capitalism and international investment law. Hart, London, pp 123–141
Grieger G (2017), Foreign Direct Investment Screening: A Debate in Light of China-EU FDI Flows, European Parliamentary Research Service (Briefing May 2017), Members' Research Service PE 603.941
Heath JB (2019) National security and economic globalization: toward collision or reconciliation? Fordham Int Law J 42:1431–1449
Heath JB (2020) The new national security challenge to the economic order. Yale Law J 129:1020–1098
Hillebrand Pohl J (2020) The impact of investment treaty commitments on the design and operation of EU investment screening mechanisms. In: Hindelang S, Moberg A (eds) YSEC yearbook of socio-economic constitutions. Springer, Cham, pp 725–768
Howse R (2023) Disciplining state capitalism under international economic law: non-discrimination vs. competitive neutrality. In: Delimatsis P, Dimitropoulos G, Gourgourinis A (eds) State capitalism and international investment law. Hart, London, pp 67–80
Hsu L (2017) The role and future of sovereign wealth funds: a trade and investment perspective. Wake Forest Law Rev 52:837–856
International Working Group on Sovereign Wealth Funds (2008) Generally Accepted Principles and Practices for Sovereign Wealth Funds (GAPP) of 2008 (Santiago Principles)
Knight L, Voon T (2020) The evolution of national security at the interface between domestic and international investment law and policy: the role of China. JWIT 21:104–139
Krajewski M (2003) Public services and trade liberalization: mapping the legal framework. JIEL 6: 341–367
Kratsas G, Truby J (2015) Regulating sovereign wealth funds to avoid investment protectionism. J Financ Regul 1:95–134
Kurtz J (2010) Adjudging the exceptional at international investment law: security, public order and financial crisis. Int Comp Law Q 59:325–371
Lippincott M (2013) Depoliticizing sovereign wealth funds through international arbitration. Chicago J Int Law 13:649–683
Lipsky J (2008) Sovereign Wealth Funds: Their Role and Significance -- A Speech by John Lipsky, First Deputy Managing Director, International Monetary Fund (3 September 2008), https://www.imf.org/en/News/Articles/2015/09/28/04/53/sp090308

Mattoo A, Subramanian A (2008), Currency undervaluation and sovereign wealth funds: a new role for the World Trade Organisation, Peterson Institute for International Economics, Working Paper No. 8
Misra M (2023) Foreign Investment in Critical National Infrastructure (CNI) by State-Controlled Entities (SCEs) and Investment Screening Mechanisms (ISMs). In: Delimatsis P, Dimitropoulos G, Gourgourinis A (eds) State capitalism and international investment law. Hart, London, pp 143–157
OECD Declaration on Sovereign Wealth Funds and Recipient Country Policies Adopted, C/MIN (2008)8/FINAL (05/06/2008)
OECD Recommendation of the Council on Competitive Neutrality, OECD/LEGAL/0462 (31/05/2021)
Peterson Institute for International Economics, Sovereign Wealth Funds and the Global Economy, https://piie.com/publications/chapters_preview/4983/01iie4983.pdf
Pinchis-Paulsen M (2020) Trade multilateralism and U.S. national security: the making of the GATT security exceptions. Mich J Int Law 41:109–193
Poulsen LNS (2013) Investment treaties and the globalisation of state capitalism: opportunities and constraints for Host States, in Roberto Echandi and Pierre Sauvé (eds) Prospects in international investment law and policy: World Trade Forum. CUP
Prazeres TL (2020) Trade and national security: rising risks for the WTO. WTR 19:137–148
Roberts A, Moraes HC, Ferguson V (2019) Toward a geoeconomic order in international trade and investment. JIEL 22:655–676
Rozanov A (2005) Who holds the wealth of nations? Central Bank J 15:1
Sauvant KP, Sachs LE, Wouter PF, Jongbloed S (2012) Sovereign investment: concerns and policy reactions get access arrow. OUP
Schill S, Briese R (2009), "If the State Considers": self-judging clauses in international dispute settlement. In: von Bogdandy A, Wolfrum R (eds) Max Planck Yearbook of United Nations Law 13:61
Schreuer C, Malintoppi L, Reinisch A, Sinclair A (2009) The ICSID convention: a commentary, 2nd edn. p 161
Shima Y (2015) The policy landscape for international investment by government-controlled investors: a fact finding survey. OECD Working Papers on International Investment, 2015/01, OECD Publishing https://doi.org/10.1787/5js7svp0jkns-en
Sornarajah M (2011) Sovereign Wealth Funds and the Existing Structure of the Regulation of Investments. Asian Journal of International Law 1:267–288
Trujillo E (2020) An introduction to trade and national security: new concepts of national security in a time of economic uncertainty. Duke J Comp Int Law 30:211–222
UNCTAD (1999) Most-Favoured Nation Treatment. Series on Issues in International Investment Agreements, UNCTAD/ITE/IIT/10(Vol.III), Geneva
UNCTAD (2009) The Protection of National Security in IIAs, UNCTAD Series on International Investment Policies for Development, UNCTAD/DIAE/IA/2008/5. United Nations, New York/Geneva
UNCTAD (2019) World investment report 2019: special economic zones. UNCTAD, Geneva
van Aaken A, Bown CP, Lang A (2019) Introduction to the special issue on trade wars. JIEL 22: 529–533
Wang J (2016) State capitalism and sovereign wealth funds: finding a 'Soft' location in international economic law. In: Lim CM (ed) Alternative visions of the international law on foreign investment: essays in Honour of Muthucumaraswamy Sornarajah. CUP, Cambridge, pp 405–427

Definition of Foreign Investors and Protected Investments: A Comparative Analysis

Yarik Kryvoi

Contents

Abstract This chapter first identifies problems arising out of definitions of "foreign investor" and "foreign investment" in domestic legislation. The chapter then analyses bilateral and multilateral investment treaties, awards of investment tribunals, and recommendations of international organizations and experts concerning the definition of "foreign investor" and "protected investments". It shows that the criteria defining "investment", "investor", "investment activity" and "investment dispute" differ in domestic laws and international investment agreements. In the absence of detailed definitions, investor-State tribunals have wide discretion when interpreting these terms.

The chapter then focuses on controversial issues arising out of definitions of foreign investments and investors or the lack of such definitions. More specifically, it

Y. Kryvoi (✉)
British Institute of International and Comparative Law, London, UK
e-mail: y.kryvoi@biicl.org

J. H. Pohl et al. (eds.), *National Security and Investment Controls*,
Springer Studies in Law & Geoeconomics (2024) 3: 165–186,
https://doi.org/10.1007/17280_2024_25, Published online: 23 February 2024

discusses the relationship between a state's sovereign right to regulate the activity of foreign investors, on the one hand, and the protection of their legitimate expectations, on the other. Many international treaties lack specific provisions to clarify the limits of a state's ability to regulate in this context, including in the area of taxation and other areas of public law.

The chapter also examines how international law and international tribunals approach corporate features of individual companies and corporate groups, as well as approaches to defining the concept of "investor" based on location, incorporation and control. Before concluding, the final section presents an overview of recent reforms in various jurisdictions, as well as specific policy options related to the definition of "investment", "investor", and related terms.

1 Introduction

This chapter identifies shortcomings concerning the definitions of "foreign investor" and "foreign investment" found in the legislation of some states. It then proceeds to develop specific recommendations for improvement of these definitions. More specifically, the chapter analyses bilateral and multilateral investment treaties, the legislation of different countries, awards of investment tribunals, and recommendations of international organizations and experts concerning the definition of "foreign investor" and "protected investments".

This analysis aims to benefit primarily policymakers who consider amending and supplementing existing domestic laws or treaties to clarify these definitions, which should finally contribute to the development of a uniform judicial practice. It can also serve as a source for comparative analysis when formulating definitions of foreign investments and foreign control for other purposes, such as foreign investment screening.

While literature concerning the definition of "foreign investor", "foreign investment", or "investment activity" exists,[1] this chapter focuses on the most recent approaches of states to this topic—both internationally and domestically. While the analysis acknowledges and presents the international perspective, it aims to benefit, first and foremost, policymakers. As such, an additional novelty element is that the chapter will compare the international/domestic interface and explain why a one-size fits all cannot be used by every state.

The chapter begins by reviewing the key criteria which define the terms "investment", "investor", "investment activity" and "investment dispute". These criteria differ based on the international investment agreements that contain them. In any

[1] *See, generally*, Mortenson (2010), p. 257; Potestà (2012), pp. 341, 343–344 and 346, Grabowski (2014), p. 287; Ashiya (2016), p. 263; Nakajima (2016), p. 472; Simon Foote and Jeffs (2021), p. 18.

case, in the absence of detailed definitions, arbitral tribunals have wide discretion when interpreting these terms. Subsequently, the chapter addresses the most common criteria used for defining these terms and the ways states adapt to avoid overly broad interpretations.

The next section then discusses the relationship between a state's sovereign right to regulate the activity of foreign investors, on the one hand, and the protection of their legitimate expectations, on the other. Many international treaties lack specific provisions to clarify the limits of a state's ability to regulate in this context, including in the area of taxation and other areas of public law.[2] The chapter also examines how international law and international tribunals approach corporate features of individual companies and corporate groups, as well as approaches to defining the concept of "investor" based on location, incorporation and control.

Before concluding, the final section presents an overview of recent reforms in various jurisdictions, as well as specific guidance on the definition of "investment", "investor", and related terms.

2 Criteria to Define Foreign Investors and Investments

2.1 Criteria in International Investment Treaties

The definition of key concepts such as "investor", "investment", "investment activity" and "investment disputes" has significant legal implications. This influences, among others, the scope of persons who can sue host States under a treaty or who can rely on special dispute resolution procedures in accordance with domestic law.[3]

Indirect corporate ownership structures (for example, using subsidiaries) significantly expand the scope of protection offered by international investment agreements.[4] According to the United Nations Commission on Trade and Development (UNCTAD), claimants owned, or controlled, by companies from third countries initiated about a third of the investor-state proceedings started between 2010 and 2015.[5] More than a quarter of these applicants were mailbox companies with no significant economic activity in the host country.

In this context, regulators in host States face three specific challenges: claims brought by mailbox companies[6]; claims brought by foreign entities which are

[2]This is the case with investment treaties signed before the 2010s, which were heavily focused on investor protection and not so much on state responses and justifications to (potential) investment claims. *See*, generally, Levashova (2019).

[3]See, e.g., Ren and Shan (2022), pp. 357, 364 and 369.

[4]*See e.g.*, Poulton et al. (2020).

[5]United Nations Conference on Trade and Development. World Investment Report 2016: Investor Nationality: Policy Challenges. UN, 2016, https://unctad.org/en/PublicationsLibrary/wir2016_en.pdf (WIR 2016).

[6]Baumgartner (2016), p. 14.

controlled by another entity from the host State[7]; and claims brought by entities that own the investment and are specifically set up in anticipation of a claim ("urgent restructuring").[8]

The drafters of the ICSID Convention envisioned the consent of the parties to a dispute as the primary factor used to determine ICSID jurisdiction, and not the definition of terms such as "investment". One of the drafters mentioned that "the requirement that the dispute must have arisen out of an 'investment' may be merged into the requirement of consent to jurisdiction."[9] In other words, the state parties to the Convention must determine for themselves what is considered an "investment". If the issue of subject matter jurisdiction is not raised, the dispute before the tribunal is considered to be an investment.[10]

The report of the ICSID Executive Directors clarifies this issue:

> No attempt was made to define the term "investment" given the essential requirement of consent by the parties, and the mechanism through which Contracting States can make known in advance, if they so desire, the classes of disputes which they would or would not consider submitting to the Centre (Article 25(4)).[11]

Definitions and criteria used to define terms such as "investor", "investment" and "investment activity" under international law depend on the wording of each treaty and vary according to each tribunal's interpretation of the relevant treaty provision.[12] In practice, these concepts are interrelated, and often none of the three is defined in treaties. On the other hand, the definition of one concept, such as "investment", may contain the criteria used to define the term "investor".

The ICSID Convention, for instance, does not define the concept of foreign investment.[13] It is important to note that in cases of conflict between definitions under international law (for example, the jurisdiction of a tribunal over disputes arising out of foreign investment) and national law, the definition under international law shall prevail.[14] Thus, changes in domestic law are unlikely to have a significant impact if treaties contain different criteria, and international treaties and national law should be harmonized in terms of the definition of these terms.

International investment agreements (IIAs) use the following three approaches to define the term "investor".[15] First, the incorporation approach remains the prevailing

---

[7] Alexandrov (2005), pp. 19, 37.

[8] Baumgartner (2016), p. 202.

[9] Broches (1996), pp. 263, 268.

[10] See, Kryvoi (2016), pp. 139–141.

[11] Article 25(4), International Centre for Settlement of Investment Disputes. ICSID convention, regulations and rules. International Centre for Settlement of Investment Disputes, 2003, https://icsid.worldbank.org/en/Documents/resources/ICSID_Conv%20Reg%20Rules_EN_2003.pdf.

[12] Ren and Shan (2022), pp. 357, 359–360.

[13] Grabowski (2014), pp. 287, 289.

[14] Hepburn (2017), p. 104.

[15] ILA (2011).

approach, according to which the company must be legally incorporated in the jurisdiction of the contracting party.[16]

Second, the control-based approach does not matter where the company is established. What matters is whether that company is controlled, directly or indirectly, by citizens of a foreign state.[17] The treaties typically do not define what control means, while others provide for specific criteria, discussed in more detail below.

It should be noted that the control-based approach does not involve ascertaining the nationality of the controlling person in order to determine the ultimate owner. Most investment treaties of the 1990s provide for this option.[18] In practice, this means that as long as the state uses a relatively broad definition of "investment", an investor from any third country can structure its investment in such a way as to benefit from the protection offered by the treaty. This allows investors to choose an international investment protection agreement that has the most favourable terms.

However, treaties may require effective investment control, without defining the terms. Definition of foreign investments and investors has a direct impact on procedural rights, such access to investor-state arbitration. Some treaties address the problem of possible "urgent restructuring" by denying access to dispute resolution mechanisms if the claimant investor was restructured at a time when a dispute could have arisen, was foreseeable in the near future, or if the dispute had already arisen.[19]

Third, according to the location-based approach - the various subsidiaries must have a significant level of interaction with the foreign investor's parent company, which is more important than ascertaining actual ownership and control.[20] The key question here is whether the investor has an effective place of management or

---

[16] *See, for example*, Article 1(d) of the Agreement between the Government of the United Kingdom of Great Britain and Northern Ireland and the Government of the Republic of Sierra Leone for the Promotion and Protection of Investments (in force 20 November 2001) ("[c]ompanies" means: (i) in respect of the United Kingdom: corporations, firms and associations incorporated or constituted under the law in force in any part of the United Kingdom or in any territory to which this Agreement is extended in accordance with the provisions of Article 12; (ii) in respect of the Republic of Sierra Leone.")

[17] *See, for example*, Article 1(b)(iii) of the Agreement on Promotion and Protection of Investments between the Government of the Kingdom of Bahrain and the Government of the Kingdom of the Netherlands (in force 01 December 2009) ("the term "nationals" shall comprise with regard to either Contracting Party: (iii) legal persons not constituted under the law of that Contracting Party but controlled, directly or indirectly, by natural persons as defined in (i) or by legal persons as defined in (ii).")

[18] For instance, *see* Article 1(b)(iii) of the Agreement on encouragement and reciprocal protection of investments between Georgia and the Kingdom of the Netherlands (in force 01 April 1999). *See, also*, Article 8.1 of the 2016 Comprehensive Economic and Trade Agreement between Canada and the European Union and its Member States (CETA).

[19] *Strabag and others v. Poland*, ICSID Case No. ADHOC/15/1, Partial Award on Jurisdiction of 4 March 2020, § 7.25.

[20] *See, for example*, Article 10.12(2) of the Peru-United States Trade Promotion Agreement (in force 01 February 2009).

principal place of business in the State of the investor's alleged nationality.[21] Certain treaties, especially new-generations ones, contain the presumption that the investor conducts a substantial business activity in the state of the declared nationality,[22] which in practice is combined with the incorporation or location approach.

International investment law, including the ICSID Convention,[23] does not contain a generally accepted definition of "investment disputes". In international arbitration much depends on the consent of the parties. Unlike many other arbitration institutions, ICSID can only resolve legal disputes (arising directly in connection with investments) between a Contracting State (or a constituent part of a State or its agency) and a national or legal person of another Contracting State. The parties to the dispute agree in writing to submit that dispute to ICSID. Within these limits, ICSID arbitrators determine whether they have jurisdiction over a particular dispute.

The definition of "foreign investor" plays an important role in determining the jurisdiction of investment tribunals and who has the right to bring claims against states. In this context, the issue of indirect investment ownership has become particularly relevant.[24] Such ownership structures have the potential to expand the jurisdiction established by IIAs. As mentioned above, one third of all investor claims against foreign governments were filed by investors whose ultimate owner (parent company) was based in a country that was not a party to the applicable treaty in the dispute. More than a quarter of such claimants were "letterbox companies" without any significant transactions in the home state.[25]

The scope of an IIA can be greatly expanded through the use of "letter box companies". These are foreign entities ultimately controlled by a host state entity.[26] In such cases, claims are filed by legal entities deliberately created in anticipation of those claims ("urgent restructuring"). One way to counteract this is through "denial of benefit clauses", which deny treaty protection to companies that are effectively controlled by nationals of a third state.[27] A large-scale study by UNCTAD shows that 58% of treaties concluded between 2012 and 2014 included "denial of benefits clauses", compared to 7% of treaties signed between 1962 and 2011.[28] New-generation treaties explicitly exclude portfolio investments,[29] or sovereign debt obligations.[30]

[21] WIR 2016, *supra* note 6.

[22] OECD (2008), p. 24.

[23] Schill et al. (2022), p. 120.

[24] Olmedo (2020), pp. 301, 315–316.

[25] WIR 2016, *supra* note 6.

[26] *Adamakopoulos and others v. Cyprus*, ICSID Case No. ARB/15/49, Decision on Jurisdiction, § 331.

[27] Poulton et al. (2020).

[28] WIR 2016, *supra* note 6.

[29] Karas and Brocková (2021), pp. 127, 132.

[30] Fyrigou-Koulouri (2017), pp. 355, 361.

Some recent IIAs require significant commercial activity in the host country in order to have recourse to investor-state arbitration. This approach is becoming more frequent: while only 16% of bilateral investment treaties (BITs) of the 1990s required significant commercial activity in their definition of "investor", this proportion rose to 30% in a sample of recent BITs. In addition, 55% of recent BITs include "denial of benefits clauses", compared to only 5% of older generation BITs.[31]

To determine the meaning of the term "effective control", it is useful to consider existing international investment agreements. Some IIAs, by listing a non-exhaustive list of factors to be considered by tribunals, clarify what is meant by effective control. Such factors include ownership of more than 50% of the capital of the company or participation in the share capital, the right to vote, which gives a decisive position in the management bodies of the company, and the right to choose or exercise significant influence over the choice of the management boards of the company.[32] Other factors include contractual or other obligations of shareholders to appoint board members in a particular way, or rights to veto certain corporate decisions or provide multiple-voting rights.[33]

When determining effective control, legal factors (the right to vote, the right to choose members of the company's governing bodies) are relevant, but not necessarily sufficient, for the tribunal to establish the existence of control—which will, in any case, depend on all the circumstances of the case.[34]

So far, only a few IIAs have clarified the meaning of essential commercial activities. For example, the China-Hong Kong agreement, CEPA (2003), China-Macau (2004), and some agreements include additional criteria in the "rules of origin" for trade in services section. These criteria include:

(1) activity of the organization (nature and scope of activities, number and type of clients and contracts, sales volume, turnover, tax returns, payment of income tax in accordance with local law, years of establishment or requirement to carry out similar activities at home, as in the host country);
(2) employees of the organization (number of employees, proportion of employees with permanent residence in, or citizenship of, the country of origin);
(3) signs pointing towards the physical presence of the entity in the state (ownership or rental of premises, costs of maintaining the physical location, telephone and fax numbers offered to customers and others to contact the company).[35]

The Netherlands in its 2019 Model BIT provides an indicative list of factors relevant for establishing a significant commercial activity. These include:

---

[31] WIR 2016, *supra* note 6.

[32] *Ibid.*

[33] *Ibid.*

[34] Vastardis (2020), pp. 140 and 144–161.

[35] WIR 2016, *supra* note 6.

(i) the registered office and/or management of a company established in a Contracting Party;
(ii) the company's headquarters and/or management are located in that Contracting Party;
(iii) the number of employees and their qualifications in that Contracting Party;
(iv) the turnover occurring in that Contracting Party; as well as
(v) the establishment of an office, production facility and/or research laboratory in that Contracting Party.[36]

This model, like the Indian Model BIT, also allows certain activities, such as passive shareholding, to be expressly excluded from the definition of a substantial commercial activity.[37]

2.2 Criteria Used by Arbitration Tribunals

In the absence of generally accepted definitions, tribunals have considerable discretion in interpreting the relevant treaties and other instruments providing for arbitration between host states and investors. The best-known definition of foreign investment in an international context is the Salini test, which provides for: (1) the contribution of money or assets; (2) a certain duration of that investment; (3) an element of risk; and (4) contribution to the economic development of the host state.[38]

One explanation for the popularity of this test is that it is based on the preamble of the ICSID Convention, which mentions the contribution to the economic development of the host state. However, some tribunals argue that the contribution to the host State's economy, while a desired investment outcome, is difficult to measure in practice.[39]

Arbitral tribunals have also touched upon what is meant by effective control. Some found that controlling interest usually implies control, but this is not absolutely necessary.[40] The tribunals have also examined the issue of effective control in cases where establishing the question of foreign ownership of an investment did not lead to

[36] German Model Treaty 2008, https://investmentpolicy.unctad.org/international-investment-agreements/treaty-files/2865/download.

[37] Model Text for the Indian Bilateral Investment Treaty, https://investmentpolicy.unctad.org/international-investment-agreements/treaty-files/3560/download.

[38] *Salini Costruttori S.p.A. and Italstrade S.p.A. v. Kingdom of Morocco [I]*, ICSID Case No. ARB/00/4, https://www.italaw.com/cases/958.

[39] *L.E.S.I.-DIPENTA v. Algeria*, Award of 10 January 2005, ICSID Case No. ARB/03/08, para 13. *See*, *also*, Mukherjee and Chakrabarti (2021), pp. 429, 445.

[40] *Aucoven v. Venezuela*, Decision on Jurisdiction of 27 September 2001, paras 106–107.

a clear answer.[41] In deciding whether there is effective oversight, the tribunals have taken into account various factors, including:

- Ability to effectively make and implement key business decisions of the entity (e.g., initiate investment operations, authorize expenses, approve budget and dividend payments, make branding and marketing strategy decisions, receive reports on the activities of a controlled entity);
- Participation in the day-to-day management of the organization (e.g. holding meetings on behalf of the company, receiving relevant correspondence); formal confirmation of participation in the minutes of meetings of the governing bodies that make decisions;
- Access to know-how (e.g., technologies, consumables, and machinery; choosing suppliers); access to capital (e.g., start-up costs).

Arbitration tribunals have used the following *criteria* to establish substantial commercial activity[42:]

- The place where the board of directors meets and the existence of minutes of that board[43];
- Permanent physical presence[44];
- Availability of permanent staff[45];
- Active ownership of shares in subsidiaries.[46]

A recent empirical study, led by the author of this chapter, shows that when tribunals find that an investor has had a significant activity in the respondent State, investors have generally been successful in obtaining a favourable ruling on jurisdiction.[47] However, in the absence of real economic activity in the respondent state, the tribunals almost always (in 93% of cases) agree with the states' jurisdictional objections.[48]

---

[41] *Pac Rim Cayman LLC v. El Salvador*, Decision on the Respondent's Jurisdictional Objections, para 4.72.

[42] For a more detailed analysis of awards rendered by investment treaty arbitral tribunals, *see*: Kryvoi (2020), pp. 191–206.

[43] *Pac Rim Cayman LLC v. El Salvador*, Decision on the Respondent's Jurisdictional Objections, para 4.72.

[44] *Ibid*, para 4.72. *See, also, Limited Liability Company AMTO v. Ukraine*, SCC Case No. 080/2005, Final Award of 26 March 2008, para 69.

[45] *Limited Liability Company AMTO v. Ukraine*, SCC Case No. 080/2005, Final Award of 26 March 2008, para 69.

[46] *Pac Rim Cayman LLC v. El Salvador*, Decision on the Respondent's Jurisdictional Objections, para 4.72.

[47] Poulton et al. (2020).

[48] *Ibid.*

2.3 Criteria Found in Domestic Legislation

IIAs usually do not contain detailed provisions on the admission of foreign investors. Such provisions are often found in national legislation. As such, the former is generally complementary to, and usually does not conflict with, the latter.

Definitions in international law (if any) will take precedence over national law in the event of a conflict,[49] but domestic law can be seen as state practice that may influence the interpretation of treaties by a tribunal. Therefore, it is important to strive to achieve coherence between the approaches of domestic and international law.

In one study, UNCTAD examined 111 investment laws in 109 countries and found that governments are redefining terms such as "investor" and "investment".[50] They are doing this in order to address issues of citizenship, ownership and control. The majority of laws (87 out of 111) require that investors enjoying treaty protection be directly incorporated or registered in another state party to an international investment protection treaty.[51] The legislation of some states specifies that foreign investors must have an effective place of management in a foreign state. It should be noted that none of the laws reviewed by UNCTAD explicitly excluded "letter box companies" that do not conduct real economic activity.[52]

Different states take different approaches to whether they should establish a separate legal regime for foreign investors or treat them as domestic investors. For example, Qatar treats non-Qatari investors differently than Qatari investors. Investors who are not citizens of Qatar are generally prohibited from investing in banks and insurance companies, commercial agencies and any other areas for which the decision of the Council of Ministers has been issued.[53]

Some host States lack detailed definitions. For example, in the United Arab Emirates, a foreign investor is simply defined as "a natural or legal person who does not have the citizenship of the state and invests in the state in accordance with the provisions of this Law".[54]

In Uzbekistan, the relatively recently adopted Law on Investments and Investment Activities contains the following definitions:

---

[49] Article 27 of the Vienna Convention on the Law of Treaties (1969); see also Article 3 of the ILC Articles on State Responsibility, *supra* note 84 ("The characterization of an act of a State as internationally wrongful is governed by international law. Such characterization is not affected by the characterization of the same act as lawful by internal law.")

[50] WIR 2016, *supra* note 6.

[51] On the notions of seat and registered office of a company, which is considered to be an investor, as jurisdictional issues for investment arbitrations, see Papadopoulos (2022), pp. 131–141.

[52] *Ibid.*

[53] Law no. (1) of 2019 On Regulating Non-Qatari Capital Investment in the Economic Activity, https://investmentpolicy.unctad.org/investment-laws/laws/314/qatar-law-no-1-of-2019.

[54] New Foreign Direct Investment Law for the UAE, 23 September 2018, https://investmentpolicy.unctad.org/investment-policy-monitor/measures/3311/united-arab-emirates-new-foreign-direct-investment-law-for-the-uae.

> direct foreign investments – investments established pursuant to the investor's own expenses or through funds borrowed by that foreign investor who takes on the risk, without state guarantees;
>
> foreign investments - tangible and intangible benefits and rights to them, including intellectual property rights, as well as reinvestment by a foreign investor in objects of the social sphere, entrepreneurial, scientific and other activities;
>
> foreign investors - foreign states, administrative or territorial bodies of foreign states, international organizations established in accordance with conventions or other agreements between states or being subjects of public international law, legal entities, other partnerships, organizations or associations created and operating in accordance with legislation of foreign states, citizens of a foreign state and stateless persons permanently residing outside the Republic of Uzbekistan;
>
> enterprises with foreign investments in the territory of the Republic of Uzbekistan - enterprises in which foreign investments make up at least fifteen percent of the shares or the authorized fund (authorized capital).[55]

In other words, the legislation of Uzbekistan combines the place of registration and the element of control when determining foreign investors.

The Code of Civil Procedure of the Republic of Kazakhstan empowers specialized courts with jurisdiction over civil cases and defines such foreign investors as:

(1) a foreign legal entity (its branch, representative office) carrying out entrepreneurial activities in the territory of the Republic of Kazakhstan;
(2) a legal entity established with foreign participation in the manner prescribed by the legislation of the Republic of Kazakhstan, fifty or more percent of voting shares (stakes in the authorized capital) of which belong to a foreign investor;
(3) investors that have concluded a contract concluded with the state for the implementation of investments.[56]

3 Controversial Issues Related to Defining Foreign Investors and Investments

3.1 Investment Disputes Referring to Public Law Issues and the State's Right to Regulate

The right to regulate is commonly referred to as one of the general exceptions, that is, treaty provisions that allow derogation from certain state obligations.[57] This right can become relevant in several ways in international treaties, such as in the preamble

[55]Law of the Republic of Uzbekistan 'On Investments and Investment activity' (2019), https://investmentpolicy.unctad.org/investment-laws/laws/328/uzbekistan-the-law-on-investments-and-investment-activity.

[56]Article 27 of the Code of Civil Procedure of the Republic of Kazakhstan.

[57]*See, generally*, Kim (2018), p. 289.

of the treaty ("[r]eaffirming the right of Parties to regulate investments in their territory in accordance with their law and policy objective")[58] or as part of the fair and equitable treatment (FET) principle analysis. Although the principle itself does not usually contain any reference to such a right. Investment tribunals show respect for the regulatory powers of states by setting a high threshold before allowing indirect or "regulatory" expropriation. Only in a few cases was indirect expropriation established.[59]

Examples of arbitral tribunals intervening in the regulatory activities of a host state include the Philip Morris-Australia tobacco regulatory dispute, after which Australia undertook to exclude investor-state dispute settlement mechanisms in its investment agreements.[60] Other issues arose in the context of regulatory problems in the nuclear energy sector in Germany[61] or in the renewable energy sectors in Bulgaria and Spain, which raised concerns that foreign corporations could now interfere in the regulatory affairs of the host state.

In practice, states' concern about tribunals interfering with their sovereign right to regulate has led to more restrictive IIA provisions establishing the jurisdiction of international tribunals and greater use of national courts to resolve disputes between investors and states.

3.2 *Tax Disputes as a Special Type of Regulatory Disputes*

Usually, international treaties are silent about what constitutes taxation, and this is determined by the arbitration tribunal. The definition of such disputes is important not only for establishing the jurisdiction of the tribunal,[62] but also for deciding whether aggregate taxes can be qualified as confiscation of property.[63]

The protection of international investment and tax regulation are closely interrelated and are usually based on bilateral agreements.[64] For various political and

[58] *Bilateral Investment Treaty between the Government of the Kyrgyz Republic and the Government of the Republic of India* (signed 14 June 2019, not yet in force). *See, also*, Kim (2018), pp. 289, 323–326.

[59] Yannaca-Small (2010), pp. 445–477.

[60] *Philip Morris Asia Limited v. The Commonwealth of Australia*, UNCITRAL, PCA Case No. 2012–12, Award on Jurisdiction and Admissibility of 17 December 2015, https://www.italaw.com/cases/851.

[61] *Vattenfall AB and others v. Federal Republic of Germany*, ICSID Case No. ARB/12/12, available at https://www.italaw.com/cases/1654, accessed 6 November 2022.

[62] *Hydro Energy 1 and Hydroxana v. Spain*, ICSID Case No. ARB/15/42, Decision on Jurisdiction, Liability and Directions on Quantum of 9 March 2020, § 514.

[63] Buriak and Petsche (2017), p. 29.

[64] United Nations Conferences on Trade and Development. World investment report 2015: Reforming international investment governance. 2015, https://unctad.org/en/PublicationsLibrary/wir2015_en.pdf.

economic reasons, states are reluctant to allow tax cases to be heard by arbitration tribunals. This is usually limited to cases where the host state takes extreme measures, such as disguising expropriation as a tax measure, in which case disputes fall under the jurisdiction of investor-state tribunals.[65]

For example, the US$50 billion requested in *Yukos v. the Russian Federation* (the largest investor-state arbitration) primarily concerned a criminal investigation into alleged tax evasion, fraud and embezzlement by Yukos, then the largest Russian oil company. In this case, the tribunal ruled that Russia's main goal was not to collect taxes, but to bankrupt the investor and expropriate his valuable assets.[66]

Some investment protection instruments limit the application of treaty obligations to indirect taxes only, while direct taxation issues fall under double taxation treaties.[67] Most investment treaties also provide that the contracting parties are not under an obligation to extend national treatment (NT) or most favoured nation treatment (MFN) on the basis of treaties concluded with third countries, wholly or mainly in matters of taxation or any domestic legislation relating wholly or mainly to taxation.[68]

Although most IIA provisions are silent on the application of the fair and equitable treatment (FET) principle to tax matters, some treaties explicitly provide for it. In some agreements, language regarding taxation safeguards the power of the contracting parties to legislate and governs the freedom to transfer funds.[69]

When the question arises as to whether a tax stabilization guarantee falls under tax exemptions in an international treaty, this issue will be decided on the basis of an analysis of the specific language of the tax exemption treaty, umbrella clauses and the facts of the case.[70] If the tax dispute as a result of such an analysis is not covered by the relevant treaty, then the investor will need to seek help from the national courts or convince his state to raise the issue using the dispute resolution procedures provided for in double taxation treaties.

Particular difficulties arise in connection with agreements concluded between an investor and a state-owned enterprise, or investment agreements in which states undertake not to set tax rates in a certain sector.[71] The tribunals in such cases try to strike a balance between the host State's right to regulate and the legitimate expectations of investors.[72]

---

[65] Walde and Kolo (2007), p. 424.

[66] See *Yukos Universal Limited (Isle of Man) v The Russian Federation*, PCA, UNCITRAL, Award (18 July 2014).

[67] Rolland (2020), pp. 74–77.

[68] Walde, *supra note* 66.

[69] *Ibid*, at 437.

[70] Rolland (2020), pp. 48, 68–69.

[71] Marian (2020), p. 67.

[72] Rolland (2020), pp. 48, 68.

3.3 Breach of a Contract with a Foreign Investor as a Violation of International Law

Investors can bring claims arising not only from international treaties, but also from private law instruments, where investment agreements or other contracts concluded with the state provide investors with the right to arbitrate. The subject matter jurisdiction of the investment tribunals in this case is much broader, when the international treaty contains "umbrella clauses" that guarantee that the host state will comply with all obligations towards foreign investors.[73] A typical umbrella clause provides that "each party must comply with any obligations it may have entered into in relation to the investment".[74]

In other words, breaches of contractual obligations may amount to breaches of international law due to umbrella clauses that are often found in traditional IIAs. By virtue of such provisions, the host State is obliged to comply with any obligations in relation to specific investments, such as obligations assumed under a concession agreement or an investment contract. Umbrella clauses have been heavily criticized for over-expanding the tribunals' jurisdiction and creating parallel proceedings at the national and international levels.[75]

The tribunals' approaches to assessing violations of private law contracts as violations of international law remain inconsistent. According to one tribunal:

> the government's prerogative to violate investment contracts appears to be inconsistent ... with contemporary standards of national and international law concerning government responsibility for the performance of a contract.[76]

Other tribunals have explained that fair and equitable treatment (FET) provisions cover breaches of contractual obligations,[77] or that such breaches only occur if public power is used in a discriminatory manner. In *AMTO v. Ukraine*, the tribunal ruled that non-payment of a debt under a commercial contract was not related to the exercise of sovereign power and was not the result of the instructions of the state or its instructions.[78]

---

[73] *See, generally*, Gözlügöl (2020), p. 558.

[74] Article 2.2 of the United States-Argentina BIT of 14 Nov. 1991.

[75] Gözlügöl (2020), pp. 558, 583–586.

[76] *Mondev International Ltd. v. United States of America* (ICSID Case No. ARB(AF)/99/2), Award of 11 Oct. 2002.

[77] See, e.g., in *SGS Société Générale de Surveillance S.A. v. Republic of the Philippines* (ICSID Case No. ARB/02/6) Decision of the Tribunal on Objections to Jurisdiction of 29 Jan. 2004, 8. ICSID Reports 518 (2005); *Noble Ventures, Inc. v. Romania* (ICSID Case No. ARB/01/11) Award of 12 Oct. 2005.

[78] *Limited Liability Company Amto v. Ukraine*, SCC Case No. 080/2005, final Award of 26 March 2008.

No consistency exists in the decisions of investment tribunals as to whether "umbrella clauses" apply to purely commercial contracts.[79] Some tribunals have considered these clauses to automatically qualify breaches of contract as a breach of treaty,[80] while others have rejected this interpretation without explaining the meaning of the umbrella clauses.[81] If the tribunals do not extend their jurisdiction to contract disputes, then these disputes are considered by the national courts.[82]

3.4 Investment Disputes Involving Entities that Are Directly or Indirectly Owned by the State

When faced with the question of whether the actions of entities directly or indirectly owned by the state can be considered acts of the state, investment tribunals refer to the international law on State responsibility.[83] As a rule, if a legal entity has a legal personality independent of the state, its actions will not be identified with the actions of that state. Exceptions arise if there is evidence of direct government control over the entity's decision-making, or if the entity performs certain regulatory functions or otherwise exercises sovereign powers in some areas.[84] In such cases, one can attribute the conduct of such entities to the state, as follows from the analysis below.

The question of the responsibility of states in disputes between them and foreign investors is relevant for two reasons. Firstly, jurisdiction under the ICSID Convention depends on whether there is state conduct. Secondly, in order to establish liability in substance, it is important to demonstrate attribution. It is now generally accepted that state-owned enterprises (SOEs) can have a separate legal personality from the state, but situations arise when it comes to determining the circumstances in which the State should be held responsible for the activities of a SOE.[85]

The International Law Commission (ILC) articles on state responsibility help to understand the obligations of non-state actors, especially when it comes to attributing conduct to the state. In accordance with article 8 of the articles of the ILC:

---

[79] See UNCTAD, Bilateral Investment Treaties 1995–2006: Trends in Investment Rulemaking 74–75 (2007), https://unctad.org/en/Docs/iteiia20065_en.pdf.

[80] See, e.g., *SGS Société Générale de Surveillance S.A. v. Republic of the Philippines* (ICSID Case No. ARB/02/6) Decision of the Tribunal on Objections to Jurisdiction of 29 Jan. 2004, 8 ICSID Reports 518 (2005); *Noble Ventures, Inc. v. Romania* (ICSID Case No. ARB/01/11) Award of 12 Oct. 2005.

[81] See, e.g., *Societe Generale de Surveillance S.A. v. Islamic Republic of Pakistan* (ICSID Case No. ARB/01/13) Decision on Objections to Jurisdiction of 6 Aug. 2003, paras 164–173.

[82] Oliveira (2013), pp. 175, 186.

[83] Feit (2010), p. 142.

[84] *Gustav F W Hamester GmbH & Co KG v. Republic of Ghana*, Award of 18 June 2010, para 189–190.

[85] Cortesi (2017), p. 2.

> The conduct of a person or group of persons shall be considered an act of a State under international law if the person or group of persons is in fact acting on the instructions of, or under the direction or control of, that State in carrying out the conduct.[86]

The issue of identifying the actions of an enterprise with the actions of the state is of great practical importance, mainly for determining whether the state can act as a defendant. However, state-owned enterprises can also act as plaintiffs in investment disputes.[87]

4 Recent Reforms Related to Defining Foreign Investments and Investors

The governments of various states are concerned about the increased role of foreign states in accessing and managing their infrastructure and influencing national security.[88] Some host States charge fees for the foreign investment screening process or criminalize non-compliance with the foreign investment entry regime. The nationality of a foreign investor and whether the investor is controlled by a foreign government may affect whether an investment is subject to additional entry rules. For example, the EU Screening Regulation defines foreign investments and as follows:

1. 'foreign direct investment' means an investment of any kind by a foreign investor aiming to establish or to maintain lasting and direct links between the foreign investor and the entrepreneur to whom or the undertaking to which the capital is made available in order to carry on an economic activity in a Member State, including investments which enable effective participation in the management or control of a company carrying out an economic activity;
2. 'foreign investor' means a natural person of a third country or an undertaking of a third country, intending to make or having made a foreign direct investment[89];

This definition of investment refers to effective participation and control while the foreign investor definition is rather brief and without such references. In practice, the EU Screening Regulation criteria for foreign control (or lack thereof) means the need

[86] Crawford (2002).

[87] Haeri et al. (2021), pp. 21–27.

[88] For instance, *see* Charles McConnell, "Italy uses national security power to block Chinese investment in robot maker", *Global Competition Review* (09 June 2022), available at: https://globalcompetitionreview.com/gcr-fic/article/italy-uses-national-security-power-block-chinese-investment-in-robot-maker, and Dentons, "Chinese Investors Ordered to Divest Interests in Critical Minerals Sector", *Dentons Insights* (25 November 2022), available at: https://www.dentons.com/en/insights/articles/2022/november/25/chinese-investors-ordered-to-divest-interests-in-critical-minerals-sector.

[89] Regulation (EU) 2019/452 of the European Parliament and of the Council of 19 March 2019 establishing a framework for the screening of foreign direct investments into the Union.

to refer to other sources of European Union law (e.g., EU merger control law),[90] and perhaps beyond them.

Some states have recently adopted more restrictive approaches to the treatment of foreign investment in international treaties (for example, through new model BITs) by narrowing both the definition of foreign investment and the range of protections (for example, abandoning the FET standard) or limiting dispute resolution provisions only to determining the amount of compensation due. Some states deliberately avoid the investor-state arbitration system (for example, Brazil) and instead prefer to use dispute resolution mechanisms between states and national courts.

India's Model Bilateral Investment Treaty takes the approach that the investor must be a registered legal entity under the national laws of the host country.[91] The idea is to narrow the definition of covered investments and minimize investor and government dispute resolution requirements for India. The Model BIT limits the possibility of filing claims related to pre-investment activities. It also states that local government measures and tax measures are covered by the BIT.

The 2016 EU-Canada Comprehensive Economic and Trade Agreement (CETA) introduces a restrictive approach to investor rights.[92] For example, it makes the legitimate expectations of investors dependent on specific promises to the investor by the host state (e.g., obligations included in a contract). This agreement also includes an exhaustive list of actions that violate the standard of fair and equitable treatment, which limits its application.

Faced with a growing number of investor disputes, governments around the world have begun reforming the content of IIAs to balance their right to regulate with the need to protect investor rights and streamline the dispute resolution system.[93] Several states (including Venezuela and Bolivia) have chosen to withdraw from the ICSID Convention in order to reduce regulatory scrutiny from international tribunals, and others are making deliberate efforts to terminate their bilateral and multilateral investment treaties.

UNCTAD's review of recent model investment treaties indicates that States are revising their definitions of investment, limiting access to investor-State dispute resolution and adding exceptions to capital repatriation obligations.[94]

Many jurisdictions have adopted specific laws applicable to foreign investment, containing definitions of investments, investors, procedural options for resolving

[90] For example, or the notion of foreign direct investment in the context of EU FDI Screening Regulation- Regulation (EU) 2019/452, see: Otto (2020), pp. 507–587.

[91] Model Text for the Indian Bilateral Investment Treaty, https://dea.gov.in/sites/default/files/ModelBIT_Annex_0.pdf.

[92] The Comprehensive and Economic Trade Agreement (CETA), https://ec.europa.eu/trade/policy/in-focus/ceta/ceta-chapter-by-chapter/index_en.htm.

[93] *See*, e.g., United Nations Conferences on Trade and Development. World investment report 2015: Reforming international investment governance. 2015, https://unctad.org/en/PublicationsLibrary/wir2015_en.pdf.

[94] UNCTAD, Recent Developments in the IIA Regime: Accelerating IIA Reform (August 2021), https://unctad.org/system/files/official-document/diaepcbinf2021d6_en.pdf.

investment disputes, and restrictions on foreign direct investment (FDI). The principles and guarantees established by these special laws can play an important role in disputes between investors and the state.

For example, according to the 2013 Mongolian Law "On Investments", "investment" means "tangible and intangible assets related to joint capital and reflected in the financial statements of economic entities that carry out profit-oriented activities in the territory of Mongolia."[95] The 2013 Belarusian Law "On Foreign Investments" provides that investment disputes can be referred to UNCITRAL or ICSID tribunals at the choice of a foreign investor.[96]

In many developed countries, there is no special legislation aimed at attracting and creating special favourable conditions specifically for foreign investors. In such countries, the regulatory regime for foreign investors is generally the same as that for domestic investors, with the exception of additional restrictions that may be related to national security. Such countries include the United Kingdom, which in 2021 expanded the government's ability to block or amend acquisitions of British assets by foreigners if they raise national security concerns.[97] UK officials acknowledge that the initiative is primarily focused on China, which has ramped up acquisitions of a number of sensitive assets, from energy grids to IT companies. The new regime will reduce the barriers to possible government intervention.

5 Policy Options for Regulators

At this point, it seems that legislators around the world have three main options when it comes to resolving the issue of determining the jurisdiction of tribunals in cases involving foreign investors.

Option 1: No Additional Benefits and Special Dispute Resolution Procedures for Foreign Investors

As mentioned above, in many countries foreign investors enjoy the same rights as domestic investors. However, this approach appears to be suboptimal. Different countries already provide for a special regime for attracting foreign investors to the national economy. Secondly, an approach that does not provide the investor with additional rights, as a rule, is characteristic of capital-exporting states with judicial and legal guarantees for doing business and the rule of law that have developed over many decades. Some states, however, have less experience with creating a

[95] Mongolia's Law "On Investment" (2013), https://investmentpolicy.unctad.org/investment-laws/laws/124/mongolia-investment-law.

[96] The Law of the Republic of Belarus "On Investment" dated 12 July 2013 г. No 53–3, https://kodeksy-by.com/zakon_rb_ob_investitsiyah.htm.

[97] UK National Security and Investment Act 2021, https://www.gov.uk/government/collections/national-security-and-investment-act.

favourable business climate, so providing additional guarantees and rights for foreign investors seems justified.[98]

Option 2: Identifying Foreign Investors According to the Criterion of Formal Incorporation

This approach involves categorization of foreign investors based on the place of incorporation (registration) of a legal entity. For example, foreign legal entities that do not have a branch or representative office in the host state may be included; representative offices of a foreign legal entity registered in the host state; a legal entity established with foreign participation in the host state, in which foreign entities or individuals own 50% or more of voting shares or shares in the authorized.

The advantage of this approach is that it is a relatively simple way to distinguish between foreign and domestic investors based on formal criteria. The disadvantage is the possibility of granting additional rights and privileges to foreign investors by legal entities that are ultimately controlled by host state investors, as well as investors that do not carry out significant activities abroad (for example, the so-called "mailbox companies" already mentioned above or "one-day firms").

Option 3. Identifying Foreign Investors on the Basis of an Integrated Approach, Taking Into Account the Implementation of Real Commercial Activities Abroad and Being Under the Control of a Foreign Investor

The international treaties analysed above, the practice of tribunals and other materials indicate that many states have recently preferred to move away from the formal *criteria* for incorporation and more clearly define the range of protected investments and include additional criteria in the definitions of "investor" or "investment", such as the requirement to engage in substantial commercial activities in the host or foreign country, and to be under the effective control (direct or indirect) of foreign investors.

On the basis of the analysis, above it makes more practical sense for policymakers not to put an emphasis on the formal incorporation of a legal entity or on the percentage of ownership in determining foreign investors. Providing additional benefits and rights makes sense for investors who are actually controlled by foreign investors, and not just registered abroad. This approach will allow avoiding abuses through the creation of companies by host state investors abroad only to receive additional benefits. This approach will also allow foreign investors, regardless of their formal nationality (registered in the host state or abroad), to receive additional protection guarantees, including procedural ones. The disadvantage of this approach is the more complicated process of identifying entities that can be considered as foreign investors in the event of disputes.

---

[98]Dixon and Haslam (2016), pp. 1080, 1083.

6 Conclusion

This chapter gave an overview of different approaches to defining foreign investments and foreign contrail in international investment law, and the difficulty in reaching an all-encompassing definition.

Foreign investors might prefer all-encompassing definitions, permitting a wide range of companies to access domestic investment protection mechanisms and investment dispute settlement schemes. On the other hand, States may look to safeguard their own interests—for instance, limiting access to investor-state arbitration only to certain investors, mainly those who have had substantial business interests in the host state before the dispute arose). In any case, States should also be wary of their own investment climate. More specifically, domestic decision-makers should ask whether a more favourable investment protection framework (including broad definitions of foreign investments and investors) might be necessary to attract foreign investment.

The policy options presented in this chapter offer a toolkit from which they can choose, and mix, a suitable definition, in accordance with their own interests. However, even if states develop a widely accepted definition, adjudication of investment disputes will turn on the interpretation of this definitions, including threshold definitions concerning the foreign nature of investment.

References

Alexandrov S (2005) The "Baby Boom" of treaty-based arbitrations and the jurisdiction of ICSID tribunals: shareholders as "Investors" and Jurisdiction Ratione temporis. Law Pract Int Courts Trib 4:19, 37

Ashiya B (2016) The shift towards an enterprise based definition of investment: the Quagmire of the Salini Test and India's model BIT. Jindal Glob Law Rev 7(2):263

Baumgartner J (2016) Treaty shopping in international investment law. Oxford University Press, p 14

Broches A (1996) The convention on settlement of investment disputes: some observations on jurisdiction. CJTL 5:263, 268

Buriak S, Petsche MA (2017) Tax measures under international investment treaties: current regulation, arbitral practice and perspectives. Central European University, p 29

Cortesi GA (2017) ICSID Jurisdiction with regard to state-owned enterprises – moving toward an approach based on general international law. Law Pract Int Courts Trib 16(1):108–138. https://doi.org/10.1163/15718034-12341344

Crawford J (2002) The international law commission's articles on state responsibility: introduction, text and commentaries. CUP, Cambridge

Dixon J, Haslam PA (2016) Does the quality of investment protection affect FDI flows to developing countries? Evidence from Latin America. World Econ 39(8):1080, 1083

Feit M (2010) Responsibility of the state under international law for the breach of contract committed by a state-owned entity. Berkeley J Int Law 28:142

Fyrigou-Koulouri M (2017) Sovereign debt restructuring: is there a place for international investment arbitration. Manchester J Int Econ Law 14(3):355, 361

Gözlügöl AA (2020) The effects of Umbrella clauses: their relevance in interpretation and practice. J World Invest Trade 21:558

Grabowski A (2014) The definition of investment under the ICSID convention: a defense of Salini. Chicago J Int Law 15(1):287

Haeri H, Kryvoi Y, Gamberini C, Kovacs R (2021) Sovereign wealth funds: transnational regulation and dispute resolution. British Institute of International and Comparative Law and Withers, pp 21–27. Available at: https://www.biicl.org/documents/144_sovereign-wealth-funds-regulation-dispute-resolution-.pdf

Hepburn J (2017) Domestic law in international investment arbitration. Oxford University Press, p 104

ILA, German Branch (2011) The Determination of the Nationality of Investors under Investment Protection Treaties", Beiträge zum Transnationalen Wirtschaftsrecht, No. 106, March, http://telc.jura.uni-halle.de/sites/default/files/BeitraegeTWR/Heft%20106.pdf

Martin Karas and Katarina Brocková (2021) Investment treaties and national sovereignty: latest developments. J Int Trade Law Policy 20(2):127, 132

Kim J (2018) Balancing regulatory interests through an exceptions framework under the right to regulate provision in international investment agreements. George Washington Int Law Rev 50: 289

Kryvoi Y (2016) International centre for settlement of investment disputes (ICSID). Kluwer Law International, pp 139–141

Kryvoi Y (2020) International centre for settlement of investment disputes. Kluwer Law International, pp 191–206

Levashova Y (2019) The right of states to regulate in international investment law: the search for a balance between public interest and fair and equitable treatment. Kluwer Law International

Marian C (2020) The state's power to tax in the investment arbitration of energy disputes: outer limits and the energy charter treaty. Kluwer Law International, p 67.

Mortenson JD (2010) The meaning of "Investment": ICSID's Travaux and the domain of international investment law. Harv Int Law J 51(1):257

Mukherjee S, Chakrabarti NK (2021) Is "Contribution to Host State Development" an essential criterion to define investment under international investment law?: A search through the lens of arbitral awards. Liverpool Law Rev 42:429, 445

Nakajima K (2016) Parallel universes of investment protection? A divergent finding on the definition of investment in the ICSID Arbitration on Greek Sovereign Debts. Law Pract Int Courts Trib 15(3):472

OECD (2008) International investment law: understanding concepts and tracking innovations. OECD, p 24

Oliveira TPJ (2013) The authority of domestic courts in adjudicating international investment disputes: beyond the distinction between treaty and contract claims. J Int Disp Settlement 4(1):175, 186

Olmedo JG (2020) Recalibrating the international investment regime through narrowed jurisdiction. Int Comp Law Q 69:301, 315–316

Otto L (2020) What Is a foreign direct investment?. In: Hindelang S, Moberg A (eds) YSEC Yearbook of Socio-Economic Constitutions, vol 2020. Springer, Cham, pp 507–587

Papadopoulos T (2022) The different legal concepts of 'Seat' and 'Registered Office' in Cyprus company law. Eur Comp Law 19(5):131–141

Potestà M (2012) Republic of Italy v. Republic of Cuba. Am J Int Law 106(2):341, 343–344 and 346

Poulton E, Kryvoi Y, Finkel E, Bednarz J (2020) Empirical study: corporate restructuring and investment treaty protections. BIICL/Baker McKenzie, London

Ren R, Shan SL (2022) How to identify insiders and intruders disguising as investors in the assignment of investments. Int Comp Law Q 71:357, 364 and 369

Rolland SE (2020) The impact of trade and investment treaties on fiscal resources and taxation in developing countries. Chicago J Int Law 21(48):74–77

Schill SW, Schreuer C, Sinclair A (2022) Article 25. In: Schill SW, Malintoppi L, Reinisch A, Schreuer CH, Sinclair A (eds) Schreuer's commentary on the ICSID convention, 3rd edn. Cambridge University Press, p 120

Simon Foote QC, Jeffs S (2021) The investor/investment dichotomy in investment treaty law. Auckland Univ Law Rev 27(2):18

Vastardis AY (2020) The nationality of corporate investors under international investment law. Hart Publishing, pp 140 and 144–161.

Walde T, Kolo A (2007) Investor-state disputes: the interface between treaty-based international investment protection and fiscal sovereignty. Intertax 01:424

Yannaca-Small K (2010) Indirect expropriation and the right to regulate: how to draw the line? In: Yannaca-Small K (ed) Arbitration under international investment agreements: a guide to the key issues. pp 445–477

Investor Obligations Through the Prism of the EU Foreign Investment Screening Framework

Yulia Levashova and Niccolò Zugliani

Contents

Abstract Foreign Direct Investment (FDI) screening instruments adopted in recent years do not directly impose corporate social responsibility (CSR) obligations on foreign investors. This is in contrast with the latest generation of international investment agreements (IIAs), which increasingly incorporate CSR norms into the

While the chapter results from joint research and reflections and its conclusions are shared by the authors, Yulia Levashova has written Sects. 3 and 4, whereas Niccolò Zugliani has written Sects. 1 and 2.

Y. Levashova (✉)
Nyenrode University, Breukelen, The Netherlands
e-mail: j.levashova@nyenrode.nl

N. Zugliani
Bocconi University and University of Milan, Milan, Italy

J. H. Pohl et al. (eds.), *National Security and Investment Controls*,
Springer Studies in Law & Geoeconomics (2024) 3: 187–208,
https://doi.org/10.1007/17280_2024_31, Published online: 22 February 2024

treaty language. CSR obligations seem to exceed the scope of FDI screening mechanisms, that are devised as safeguard mechanisms against the establishment of certain types of FDI in the territory of the State. However, even though FDI screening instruments contain no apparent CSR investor obligations, they may do so indirectly. By focusing on the FDI screening framework of the European Union (EU), this chapter investigates the presence of indirect investor obligations with regard to environmental standards and capital transfer.

1 Introduction

In the ever-changing panorama of international investment law and policy, one of the issues that has emerged prominently over the last decade is the search for a better balance between rights and obligations of States and investors through a progressive "responsabilization" of foreign investors (Boisson de Chazournes 2017, p. 53). The incorporation of corporate social responsibility (CSR) standards requiring businesses to respect social, environmental, and human rights can be found, albeit in a fragmented and often "sectorial" fashion, in domestic legislations, as well as in domestic investment legislations specifically aimed at foreign direct investment (FDI) (Levashova 2018). CSR terminology linked to international standards and detached from the level of development of domestic laws has become increasingly frequent in international investment agreements (IIAs), usually through soft or hortatory language, and more recently in the form of investor obligations in IIAs (De Brabandere and Hazelzet 2018, pp. 221–243).

The wave of domestic FDI screening instruments adopted in recent years, particularly since the start of the COVID-19 pandemic, appears to deviate from the above-mentioned developments, imposing no apparent CSR obligations on foreign investors. Screening instruments, however, may serve as a means for indirect imposition of obligations on foreign investors, rather than simply being a safeguard mechanism to oppose the establishment of FDI in the territory of the State. This can be seen in the foreign investment screening framework established by the European Union (EU), either through IIAs or EU secondary law. For instance, IIAs currently being negotiated by the EU, such as the Comprehensive Agreement on Investment (CAI) with China, or the modernised version of the Energy Charter Treaty (ECT) require that FDI be subject to an environmental impact assessment.[1] As to EU secondary law, the main example is the screening framework introduced by EU

[1] See, e.g., '*EU-China Comprehensive Agreement on Investment*' (CAI) (2020); '*EU-Angola Sustainable Investment Facilitation Agreement*' (SIFA) (2022) https://circabc.europa.eu/ui/group/09242a36-a438-40fd-a7af-fe32e36cbd0e/library/a17ccfe1-ce36-428f-bc7f-76bcb902c36a/details?download=true; '*EU Text Proposal for the Modernisation of the Energy Charter Treaty*' (24 June 2022) https://trade.ec.europa.eu/doclib/docs/2020/may/tradoc_158754.pdf.

Regulation 2019/452,[2] which set up the European policy response to upcoming security challenges, later further exacerbated by the COVID-19 pandemic. The Regulation provides a framework to assess FDI transactions according to 'security' and 'public order' concerns. The concepts of 'security' and 'public order' are not clearly defined in the Regulation, albeit the examples of sectors that are especially vulnerable to security threats are listed in its Article 4(1). However, Member States have regulatory autonomy to fill in the requirements for national screening mechanisms. The latter might well mandate—either directly or indirectly—respect for CSR standards on investors as possible additional grounds for screening of FDI, although this language needs to be reconciled with the commitments made by EU or Member States to liberalise FDI.

This chapter will examine two applications for possible enforcement of investor obligations in the context of the EU foreign investment screening framework. The first application concerns the role of investor environmental obligations, which will be explored from the perspective of various Member States' screening mechanisms and relevant investment agreements concluded or negotiated by the EU. The second application considers several exemptions to capital transfer provisions that may also facilitate the enforcement of investor obligations. Finally, the implications of IIAs' exemptions of public policy and public security grounds that may restrict capital transfer under the EU foreign investment screening regulation will be discussed from the perspective of investor obligation to comply with the national law of the host State.

2 The EU Foreign Investment Screening Framework and Environmental Obligations

Since the EU acquired exclusive competence in the regulation of FDI, it has been at the forefront of the international panorama when it comes to including environmental language in its IIAs or Free Trade Agreements (FTAs) with investment chapters. Environmental concerns have generally found place in EU IIAs and FTAs through treaty preambles,[3] non-regression provisions,[4] or otherwise clauses framed in

[2] *Regulation (EU) No 1215/2012 of the European Parliament and of the Council of 12 December 2012 on jurisdiction and the recognition and enforcement of judgments in civil and commercial matters (recast) of 2012* OJ L351/1 (European Union 2012) (Regulation (EU) 2019/452).

[3] See, e.g., '*Association Agreement between the European Union and the European Atomic Energy Community and their Member States, of the one part, and Georgia, of the other part*' (1 July 2016), preamble: 'Committed to respecting the principles of sustainable development, to protecting the environment and mitigating climate change, to continuous improvement of environmental governance and meeting environmental needs, including crossborder cooperation and implementation of multilateral international agreements'.

[4] See, e.g., '*Association Agreement between the European Union and the European Atomic Energy Community and their Member States, of the one part, and the Republic of Moldova, of the other*

hortatory language,[5] that are relevant for hermeneutic purposes although devoid of mandatory character. However, recent developments in the EU approach to FDI show that environmental concerns are being included—or are likely to be included—in the screening of FDI, which has found its way into the EU framework for investment regulation, both in IIAs and in member State FDI legislations. The next subsections will examine the extent to which environmental obligations are imposed on investors under FDI screening mechanisms. Initially, it will focus on instruments specifically designed for investment screening, namely EU Member States' legislations enacted or aligned with under the framework of EU Regulation 2019/452. It will then analyse whether the EU IIAs or FTAs currently being negotiated mandate investment screening on environmental grounds.

2.1 Investment Screening Under the Framework of EU Regulation 2019/452

In the EU context, the screening of FDI can be found primarily in security legislations adopted under (or already existing and harmonized with) the framework recently established by EU Regulation 2019/452. Under the mechanisms provided for in EU Member States' screening legislations, FDI (or some categories of FDI) can be subject to a mandatory screening by the relevant domestic authority, achieved either by imposing mandatory procedural requirements on investments or by mandating the relevant domestic authority to screen listed categories of FDI.[6]

Designed in this way, screening instruments do not place direct substantive obligations upon foreign investors. Still, the screening requires domestic authorities to evaluate the conformity of the activity under scrutiny with the grounds for review provided by the specific legislation. In this sense, investor's compliance with such conditions can be considered an *indirect* obligation for foreign investors. In this regard, the regulation does not have an environmental focus, as it allows member States to screen inward FDI on the grounds of 'security or public order', while also providing a mechanism for cooperation among Member States.[7] Notwithstanding

part' (1 July 2016), art 371(1): 'The Parties recognise that it is inappropriate to encourage trade or investment by lowering the levels of protection afforded in domestic environmental or labour law.'

[5]See, e.g., '*Enhanced Partnership and Cooperation Agreement between the European Union and its Member States, of the one part, and the Republic of Kazakhstan, of the other part*' (1 March 2020), art 153(1): 'The Parties recognise the right of each Party to establish its own levels of domestic environmental and labour protection, and to adopt or modify its relevant law and policy accordingly, consistently with the internationally recognised standards and agreements referred to in Article 152. The Parties shall aim at high levels of environmental and labour protection.'

[6]As to the first case see, among the many, Malta *ACT No LX of 2020 of 18th December* (18th December), art 11(1); as to the second one, see, e.g., Latvia *National Security Law of 2017* (2017), Section 38(1).

[7]Regulation (EU) 2019/452 (n 3) art 1(1).

this, security or public order are inherently vague terms. The regulation leaves member States ample autonomy to fill in the meaning of security or public order, allowing them to include—either directly or indirectly - environmental concerns.

2.1.1 Domestic Legislations Including Environmental Concerns Within the Scope of FDI Screening

The scope of the FDI screening can be explicitly clarified by national laws. In the exercise of their discretion, States can limit the screening to grounds pertaining to military interests or the functioning of the constitutional structure of the State. This is the case, for instance, of the Danish Investment Screening Act, which defines national security as covering threats to the State's

> international relations, the peaceful coexistence of nations or threats to military interests, as well as actions intended to cause damage to Denmark, including crimes against the [S]tate's independence or crimes against the constitution and the supreme [S]tate authorities.[8]

It then follows suit in the qualification of public order, defined as the '[c]onditions relating to Denmark's ability to maintain an independent, democratic and secure society'.[9] In other cases, the grounds for FDI screening may be explicitly—though not exclusively—framed in terms of national defence, such as in the case of Italy, Portugal, or Finland.[10] Despite the expanding scope of the security concept, as will be seen below, the specific limitation to the military safety of the State narrows the scope of the screening mechanism in a manner that excludes environmental interests connected to the exercise of FDI from the evaluation of domestic authorities.

EU Member States can, at the same time, adopt a different approach and broaden the notions of security or public order in a manner that can accommodate environmental considerations. Among others, this is the case of France, which includes 'activities *relating to measures designed to deal with the illicit use of pathogens or toxic substances* or to prevent the health consequences of such use' among the FDI that are likely to jeopardize the maintenance of public order.[11] Other security legislations further broaden the scope of the screening mechanism to the point where environmental obligations are clearly included. This can be seen, for example, in the case of Poland, in which the relevant screening authority can oppose the

---

[8]Denmark *Act on screening of certain foreign direct investments, etc in Denmark (the Investment Screening Act) of 2021* No 842 (2021), Section 4(1).

[9]Ibid., Section 4(2).

[10]Italy *Decree Law 15 March 2012 of 2012* 21 (2012), art 1(1); Portugal *Decree-Law No 138/2014 of 2014* (2014); Finland, *Act on the Screening of Foreign Corporate Acquisitions of 1342012* 172/2012 (1342012), Section 2(1).

[11]France *Monetary and Financial Code of 2019* (France 2019), art R. 151–3(1)(j) (emphasis added); see also Slovenia *Act determining the intervention measures to mitigate and remedy the consequences of the covid-19 epidemic of 2020* (2020), art 72(3); Hungary *Act LVII of 2018 on Controlling Foreign Investments Violating Hungary's Security Interests of 2018* (2018), art 1.

acquisition of shares or control of a company if, among other things, 'it is justified for the purpose of [...] ensuring freedom and human and civil rights, safety of citizens and *the protection of the environment*.'[12] A similar conclusion can be drawn whenever the domestic authority is given the power to block the investment in the case of violations of human rights, notoriously intertwined with the environment.[13] Austria allows the authorization of FDI whenever 'there is no clear risk that the goods could be used for internal repression, severe human rights violations or severe violations of international humanitarian law',[14] specifying that the term internal repression encompasses, among other things, '*violations of human rights and basic rights*, as established in the applicable human rights instruments'.[15]

Domestic screening legislations can thus identify the grounds of security or public order in a manner that includes environmental interests, either directly, like Poland or France (though in this latter case limited to the specific field of chemicals), or indirectly, through reference to human rights, like Austria. In these cases, opposing the establishment or the operation of the investment on environmental grounds clearly falls within the scope of the screening for public order and security, indirectly placing respect for the relevant environmental obligations as the condition upon foreign investors.

2.1.2 Environmental Obligations within the Meaning of 'Security and Public Order' Under EU Primary Law

Almost half of the screening mechanisms notified by Member States and made publicly available by the EU Commission, however, do not provide an explicit definition of the scope of their FDI screening.[16] In some cases, domestic legislations offer a non-qualified reference to 'grounds of security or public order',[17] or solely

---

[12] Poland, *Act of 24 July 2015 on the Control of Certain Investments of 2020* 2,145 (2020), art 11(2)(a) (emphasis added).

[13] Human Rights Council, 'Report of the Special Rapporteur on the Issue of Human Rights Obligations Relating to the Enjoyment of a Safe, Clean, Healthy and Sustainable Environment' (24 January 2018); UN General Assembly *The human right to a clean, healthy and sustainable environment of 2022* A/RES/76/300 (2022).

[14] Austria *Foreign Trade and Payments Act 2011 of 11.10.2019* (11.10.2019), Chapter II, Section 6 (1) .

[15] ibid. Chapter II, Section 6(3) (emphasis added).

[16] European Commission, 'List of Screening Mechanisms Notified by Member States' (10 May 2022) https://circabc.europa.eu/ui/group/be8b568f-73f3-409c-b4a4-30acfcec5283/library/7e72cdb4-65d4-4eb1-910b-bed119c45d47/details?download=true.

[17] Malta (n 7), art 2(c); Spain *Real Decreto 664/1999, de 23 de abril, sobre inversiones exteriores of 1999* (1999), art 10(1); Romania *Law of Competition n21 of 1996* (1996), art 46(9); Slovakia *ACT of 8 February 2011 on Critical Infrastructure of 2011* (2011), Section 9(b)(1); Czech Republic *Act No 34/2021 Coll on screening of foreign direct investments of 2021* (2021), art 1(a); Finland (n 11), Section 2(1).

mention 'national security' without further content.[18] In other cases, the notion is drafted in terms so broad that it might arguably be indetermined. This is the case of Latvia, which defines national security as reflecting, among other things, 'the prospect of free development of society, welfare and stability'.[19]

Whenever the domestic legislation does not define the grounds of FDI screening, their meaning must be interpreted in the light of EU Regulation 2019/452. The latter resorts to the formula 'likely to affect *security or public order*',[20] which departs from the language used by the Treaty on the Functioning of the EU (TFEU) to describe the grounds by which EU member States may restrict the EU fundamental freedoms. The regulation lists some factors that EU Member States may take into consideration in determining whether a foreign direct investment is likely to affect security or public order.[21] However, given the non-exhaustive nature of the list, it is possible to envisage a narrow reading of the formula 'security or public order' that does not impinge on the fundamental EU freedom of circulation of capitals by adhering to the meaning of Article 65(1)(b) TFEU (Moberg and Hindelang 2020, pp. 1448–1453; Verellen 2021, p. 34).

Article 65(1)(b) TFEU allows Member States to derogate from the free movement of capital based on 'grounds of *public policy* or *public security*',[22] which, according to the case law of the European Court of Justice (ECJ or the Court), are to be interpreted narrowly as 'genuine and sufficiently serious threat to a fundamental interest of society'[23] (Tomkin and Steiblytė 2019, pp. 770–71). Although this does not prevent environmental interests from being incorporated into the notion of security (Nettesheim 2020, pp. 492–93), the ECJ has been reticent to include non-defence interests in its scope. As a matter of example, the Court has not accepted purely economic or administrative reasons as ground to restrict free movement[24] (Zwartkruis and de Jong 2020, p. 457; Velten 2022, p. 115 ff) and has instead required a link with national defence, such as in the case of the freezing of assets of individuals accused of being connected to terrorist groups.[25]

[18] Lithuania *The Law on Protection of Objects Important to Ensuring National Security of the Republic of Lithuania of 2018* No IX-1132 (new edition No XIII-992) (2018), art 2(7); Germany *Foreign Trade and Payments Ordinance of 2013* (2013), Section 4(1)(a). Germany, however, provides a definition of what is encompassed in the notion of national security by indicating the different economic sectors in *Foreign Trade and Payments Ordinance* (Federal Law Gazette (BGBl.) Part I p. 2865) (2013) as last amended by the Ordinance of 25 April 2022 (BAnz AT 02.05.2022 V1), Section 55(a).

[19] Latvia (n 7), art 1(1).

[20] Regulation (EU) 2019/452 (n 3), art 4(1) (emphasis added).

[21] Ibid., art 4.

[22] 'Consolidated Version of the Treaty on the Functioning of the European Union' (1 December 2009), art 65(1)(b) (TFEU) (emphasis added).

[23] Case C-54/99 *Église de Scientology* [2000], para 17; Case C-171/08 *Commission v Portugal* [2010], paras 72–74.

[24] *Église de Scientology* (n 24), para 17.

[25] Case T-306/01 *Ahmed Ali Yusuf* [2005], para 146.

The inclusion of environmental concerns in the notions of 'security or public order' through an interpretation based on EU primary law is certainly difficult to envisage. In the absence of specific indications to this end contained in the member State's legislation, the narrow reading of the exceptions to the EU freedoms offered by the ECJ will hardly justify the rejection of FDI on environmental grounds. This scenario cannot be entirely excluded in the light of the increasing relevance of a safe environment among the interests of society. The same ECJ, in the context of crises, has admitted exceptions to the provision to safeguard, among other things, derogations in the field of energy supply.[26] Still, the inclusion of environmental grounds within the scope of Article 65(1)(b) TFEU will require a change in the approach the ECJ has so far adopted towards the exception.

2.1.3 Environmental Obligations within the Meaning of 'Essential Security Interests' and 'Public Order' Under International Trade Law

Against the reading that links the notion of 'security or public order' to EU primary law, an alternative view points to the Recitals of EU Regulation 2019/452 and links the scope of the restrictive measures to that provided by international economic law. The Regulation initially recalls, at Recital (3), the commitments undertaken in the World Trade Organization (WTO), that allow the enactment of restrictive measures relating to foreign direct investment on the grounds of security or public order.[27] At Recital (35), it then states that

> [t]he implementation of this Regulation by the Union and the Member States should comply with the relevant requirements for the imposition of restrictive measures on grounds of security and public order in the WTO agreements, including, in particular, Article XIV (a) and Article XIV bis of the General Agreement on Trade in Services (GATS).[28]

Resorting to the well-known hermeneutic value of recitals[29] (Baratta 2014, pp. 302–03), these scholars read the specific reference to Article XIV(a) and Article XIV *bis* GATS as requiring an interpretation that harmonizes the meaning of 'security or public order' with that of the GATS (Cremona 2020, pp. 53–54; Velten 2022, pp. 60–61, 81). The concept of security is dealt with at Article XIV *bis* GATS, which allows States to 'tak[e] any action which [they] consider[...] necessary for the protection of [their] *essential security interests*',[30] in line with the long-standing clause of Article XXI of the General Agreement on Tariffs and Trade (GATT) and in parallel to Article 73 of the Agreement on Trade-Related Aspects of Intellectual

[26] Case C-503/99 *Commission v Belgium* [2002].

[27] Regulation (EU) 2019/452 (n 3), Recital (3).

[28] Ibid., Recital (35) (footnotes omitted).

[29] See, among the many, Case C-435/06 *C* [2007] 06, paras 51–52.

[30] 'General Agreement on Trade in Services' (1 January 1995) (GATS), art XIV bis (1) (b) (emphasis added).

Property Rights (TRIPS). So far, the scant case law of WTO dispute-settlement bodies has not departed from interpreting essential security interests as strictly military interests, rejecting broader notions. In the recent case *Russia - Traffic in Transit*, the Panel defined 'essential security interests' as 'those [...] relating to the quintessential functions of the State, namely, the protection of its territory and its population from external threats, and the maintenance of law and public order internally'.[31]

Notwithstanding the WTO Panel's extremely narrow reading, there is no consensus in international law on the meaning and scope of essential security interest. As a matter of example, international investment arbitral tribunals have considered economic interests as falling within the concept of essential security, unlike WTO case law.[32] On the other hand, legal scholarship that has focused on Article XIV *bis* GATS has long read the provision as including non-military security interests in light of the evolution of technology and, more generally, of threats to the State (Delimatsis and Hrynkiv 2022, para 28). The notion of security is deemed to gradually reflect the challenges of the globalized world and include measures against environmental degradation, resource depletion, pollution, or climate change, to mention only a few[33] (Osisanya 2014). Despite a lack of formal recognition by WTO dispute-settlement bodies, the close relations of these spheres with international trade under this approach can provide reasons to justify departure from WTO obligations through the use of the national security exception, whenever environmental threats are considered capable of affecting the essential functions of the State (Boklan and Bahri 2020, p. 124; Buzan et al. 2022, pp. 74 ff).

The concept of public order, on the other hand, is covered by Article XIV (a) GATS and allows for a departure from the substantive GATS obligations when a measure is 'necessary to protect public morals or to maintain *public order*'.[34] The specific reference to subparagraph (a) might lead to immediately rule out the inclusion of environmental considerations under the present article, as discrimination on environmental grounds is usually debated under the specific exception listed at subparagraph (b).[35] Yet, the provision is not completely free of environmental links. It is apparent, according to commentators, that the term 'public morals' encompasses activities that display cruelty, such as animal torture and arguably

---

[31] *Russia—Measures Concerning Traffic in Transit* No. WT/DS512/R (5 April 2019), para 7.130.

[32] See, e.g., *CMS Gas Transmission Company v The Republic of Argentina* No. ICSID Case No ARB/01/8, Award (12 May 2005); *LG&E Energy Corp, LG&E Capital Corp, and LG&E International, Inc.v Argentine Republic* No. ICSID Case No ARB/02/1, Decision on Liability (3 October 2006).

[33] US Office of the Secretary of Defense, 'Report of the Quadrennial Defense Review' (March 2014) 8 https://history.defense.gov/Historical-Sources/Quadrennial-Defense-Review/.

[34] 'GATS' (n 31), art XIV(a) (emphasis added).

[35] Ibid., art XIV(1)(b), allows discrimination for reasons 'necessary to protect human, animal or plant life or health'. Environmental measures can then find relevance under Article XX(1)(g) of the General Agreement on Tariffs and Trade (GATT), though the latter is not replicated in Article XIV GATS.

eco-labelling, chemical testing, and the like (Gonzalez 2006, pp. 976–77). In light of the expansive approach adopted by WTO dispute-settlement bodies towards the exceptions contained in Article XX(1)(b) and (g) GATT, the ample leeway that States enjoy in determining what constitutes public morals is increasingly considered in the sense that Article XIV(a) GATS encompasses measures related to environmental justice and climate change, such as banning imports from countries that continue to subsidize fossil fuels (Marwell 2006, pp. 807–10; Eliason 2016, pp. 735–37; Babu 2018, p. 352). There is thus overlap between the concept of public morals and that of public order, the latter including the notion of public morals and, according to some, being a catch-all term which includes 'all other legitimate objectives identified under Art[icle] XIV' (Delimatsis and Gargne 2022, para 27).

Consequently, environmental reasons could be considered to fall within the concept of public order, provided that they are 'invoked only where a genuine and sufficiently serious threat is posed to one of the fundamental interests of society' to avoid a protectionist use of the exception.[36] Arguably, the scope of the concepts of 'security' and 'public order' in the GATS is broader than that contained in the narrow exceptions to the circulation of capitals in the EU and might allow environmental considerations to enter the scope of member States' screening mechanisms adopted under the regulation. Still, it is important to note that investors will challenge the rejection of FDI on the basis of GATS notion of security and public order in EU and member State courts. The latter, not being bound by the normative power of the WTO regime, could reject the GATS-oriented interpretation in favour of the narrower one based on EU primary law.

2.1.4 Compatibility with EU International Commitments Towards Economic Liberalization

As seen above, even if EU member States' screening legislations do not explicitly include environmental grounds, the evolution of the concepts of public order and of security allows to envisage environmental interests being part of the fundamental interests of society.

Whenever screening relates to inward third country investments, this capacity of EU Member States' legislations to impose indirect obligations and limit FDI might conflict with the EU international commitments towards investment liberalization and entail international responsibility for the State that does not authorize the investment. This is not much the case of investment agreements with third countries that follow the tradition of EU Member States and adopt the so-called admission model, under which protection is offered solely to investment made 'in accordance with the applicable law' of the host State and thus already authorised under the

[36] 'GATS' (n 31), art XIV, footnote 5.

applicable legislation[37] (Joubin-Bret 2008). It is apparent that in this scenario the State is free to reject the establishment of FDI without incurring in international responsibility.

What might reveal troublesome is instead the compatibility of screening legislations with the so-called pre-establishment model, usually adopted by EU FTAs with investment provisions. Under this model, the standard of national treatment and of most-favoured-nation treatment are granted already at the establishment phase of the investment, usually in pair with a negative list of sectors excluded or limited to those reflected in a positive list.[38] This can often be found in the recent EU treaty practice, especially in agreements with major trading partners such as the EU-Canada Trade Agreement (CETA) or the EU-UK Trade and Cooperation Agreement (Dolzer et al. 2022, p. 138). In such cases, the member States' flexibility to screen FDI from IIAs or FTAs partner countries may be significantly limited and may trigger investor-State proceedings before the relevant international adjudicatory body (Velten 2022, pp. 213–15).

Although the issue is closely linked to the alleged violation of the respective IIA or FTA being raised and cannot be dealt with in depth here, it must be noted that EU international instruments concluded in the last decade include GATT-like general and security exceptions, modelled on Articles XX and XXI of the GATT, that can potentially be invoked by EU Member States to justify an investment screening process or decision (Voon and Merriman 2022). In addition, the emphasis on the State's right to regulate might be relevant in determining the legality of the screening under the relevant treaty. The compatibility of the screening decision with the relevant EU IIA or FTA could thus reveal problematic and ultimately fetter the State's capacity to block FDI for environmental reasons included in the notions of security or public order. However, this will depend on the exact wording of the international agreement.

2.2 Environmental Screening Framework in EU IIAs

Since receiving exclusive competence for the regulation of FDI, the EU has notoriously linked its effort for investment liberalization with its attention towards environmental concerns. Environmental clauses have found place in EU IIAs and FTAs with investment chapters ever since the conclusion of the EU-Korea Free Trade

---

[37] 'EU-Singapore Trade and Investment Agreements' (April 2018), art 2(1); European Commission, 'EU-Vietnam Trade and Investment Agreements' (*European Commission News Archive*, 24 September 2018) http://trade.ec.europa.eu/doclib/press/index.cfm?id=1437, arts 2(3) and 2(4).

[38] For examples of IIAs with a positive list, see, e.g., the 'Association Agreement between the European Union and its Member States, of the one part, and Ukraine, of the other part' (2014), art 88; A negative list can be found, among the others, in the 'Trade and Cooperation Agreement between the European Union and the European Atomic Energy Community, of the one part, and the United Kingdom of Great Britain and Northern Ireland, of the other part', art SERVIN.2.7.

Agreement in 2011 as part of the UE's approach to Trade and Sustainable Development, a fundamental tenet of which is the protection of the environment.[39] Environmental issues are generally included through hortatory language (Hoffmeister 2016, pp. 357–376), either in treaty preambles, in non-regression standards, in provisions restating the parties' right to regulate, or more generally in sustainable development chapters, applicable also to investment activities.[40] Despite occasionally being drafted in a seemingly binding language, such as 'the Parties *shall* [. . .] *strive to* increase their respective environmental levels of protection',[41] these provisions are generally drafted in 'soft' language, which is relevant for hermeneutic purposes but has no binding force (Ortino 2012).

In recent years, the increasing interest of the EU in linking investment liberalization with environmental protection can be noted, among other things, in the inclusion in its IIAs and FTAs of clauses that directly address the environmental impact of FDI. These clauses generally do not deviate from the 'soft' approach recalled above and mention environmental impacts among the policy objectives of the treaty. As a matter of example, Article 284(1)(c) of the Armenia-EU CEPA provides that the parties '*may cooperate* in [. . .] the labour and environmental impacts of trade and investment rules, including on the development of labour and environmental regulations and policy'.[42]

However, some instruments mark a departure from this approach and resort to more decisive language in their text when dealing with the environmental screening of FDI. On the one hand, the obligation can only touch upon the parties to the treaty and not necessarily have effects on foreign investors. One example can be seen in the CAI, agreed in principle with China. At Article 5, the agreement provides that 'the Parties [. . .] *agree to co-operate* by exchanging experiences and good practices related to environmental impact assessments in respect of investments which are likely to have significant impact on the environment'.[43]

On the other hand, EU IIAs can impose obligations that directly affect the operation or establishment of the investment with regard to its environmental

[39] European Commission, 'Communication from the Commission to the European Parliament, the Council, the European Economic and Social Committee and the Committee of the Regions' COM (2022) 409 final (22 June 2022). See also European Economic and Social Committee, 'The power of trade partnerships: together for green and just economic growth' REX 561 (24 January 2023).

[40] See, e.g., 'Comprehensive Economic and Trade Agreement (CETA) between Canada and the European Union', art 8.9(1); 'Free Trade Agreement between the European Union and the Republic of Korea' (7 January 2011), arts 1.1(2)(h) and 13.3; 'Comprehensive and Enhanced Partnership Agreement between the European Union and the European Atomic Energy Community and Their Member States, of the One Part and the Republic of Armenia, of the Other Part' (Armenia - EU CEPA), art 284; 'Free Trade Agreement between the EFTA States and Georgia' (9 January 2017), art 235.3.

[41] See. e.g., 'Association Agreement between the European Union and the European Atomic Energy Community and Their Member States, of the One Part, and Ukraine, of the Other Part' (1 January 2016), art 7.2.5 (emphasis added).

[42] 'Armenia - EU CEPA' (n 41), art 284(1)(c) (emphasis added).

[43] 'CAI' (n 2), art 5(b) (emphasis added).

screening. The Sustainable Investment Facilitation Agreement (SIFA) between the EU and Angola provides that

> [t]he Parties *shall promote the uptake by enterprises and investors of corporate social responsibility* or responsible business practices with a view to contributing to sustainable development and responsible investment, [in light of] the importance of *investors implementing due diligence in order to identify and address adverse impacts, such as on the environment* [...] in their operations.[44]

An even more determined approach can finally be found in modernization process of the ECT, in which the EU has so far proposed an amended text which states that '[e]ach Contracting Party *shall ensure in its legislation that an environmental impact assessment is carried out prior to granting authorisation for a project* for the production of energy goods, where the project may have a significant impact on the environment'.[45]

These latter examples arguably imply that the contracting parties are binding themselves to impose on investors an environmental screening of their FDI. This marks a departure from the inclusion of environmental concerns in EU IIAs or FTAs concluded even in recent years, and points towards a greater harmonization between investment liberalization and respect for the environment. As mentioned above, the focus of this harmonization remains on the States, with EU international treaties imposing only indirect environmental obligations on investors. In doing so, the EU confirms its reluctance to impose direct investor obligations, unlike other countries that directly bind investors to carry out an environmental impact assesment of the investment. One of the forerunners in this sense is certainly the 2016 Morocco-Nigeria bilateral investment treaty (BIT), which among the many obligations placed upon foreign investors provides that investors 'shall comply with environmental assessment screening and assessment processes applicable to their proposed investments prior to their establishment, as required by the laws of the host [S]tate [...] or the laws of the home [S]tate [...], whichever is more rigorous in relation to the investment in question'.[46]

[44] 'SIFA' (n 2), art 5.7 (emphasis added).

[45] 'EU Text Proposal for the Modernisation of the Energy Charter Treaty' (n 2), art 19(j)(1) (emphasis added). The EU proposal must then be read in light of the current amended version of the ECT as agreed in principle by the contracting parties, which includes a flexibility mechanism under which investment protection for fossil can be excluded, on the basis of the State's individual energy security and climate goals.

[46] 'Reciprocal Investment Promotion and Protection Agreement between the Government of the Kingdom of Morocco and the Government of the Federal Republic of Nigeria', art 14.

3 Investor's Obligations Through Restrictions on Capital Transfer in the EU and Investment Law

Indirect investor obligations might also appear in express exceptions to capital transfer provisions provided under EU law and in some of the latest IIAs. Under some of these exceptions that may require compliance with the host State's law in the field of taxation or even environment, a non-compliant foreign investor might be prevented from transfering its capital out of the host State. On the one hand, these restrictions are a mechanism by which States can balance their national interests in preserving monetary sovereignty with maintaining an attractive regime for foreign investors to repatriate profits freely. Similar to the objective of the screening mechanism to protect national security and public order, the restrictions on capital transfer aim to secure the stability of the national economic and financial system. On the other hand, some explicit restrictions included in some IIAs (further addressed in sections below) can also be seen as an intention of a State to impose indirect obligations on investors. This is because under some IIAs, the investor is obliged to comply with specific domestic regulations in order to enjoy its right to transfer the gains from her investments. These indirect obligations can be further understood as an investor's duty to diligently consider the State's regulatory framework not only before making an investment but also post-establishment.

3.1 The Transfer of Capital in the EU Framework

Under EU law, free movement of capital has become one of the fundamental freedoms with the adoption of Maastricht Treaty (Ospanova 2022). The free movement of capital between Member States and third countries are guaranteed under Article 63 TFEU. Any restrictions in capital transfer are prohibited.[47] However, there are several exceptions to this rule. According to Article 65 TFEU, Member States are allowed to constrain the outflow of capital in order (i) to prevent infringements of national law (specifically in the field of taxation and prudential supervision of financial services); (ii) to undertake procedures for the declaration of capital movements for administrative or statistical purposes; and (iii) to take measures that are justified on the grounds of public policy or public security.[48] Further, the Council may implement limiting measures in regard to capital transfer for the purpose of preventing terrorism or similar activities that threaten freedom, security and justice.[49] However, the aforementioned restrictions should not be discriminatory towards a third country. The ECJ has provided an interpretation of restrictions under

[47] 'TFEU' (n 23), art 63.

[48] Ibid., art 65.

[49] Ibid., art 75.1.

Article 65 TFEU that Member States may apply vis-à-vis third countries. For example, restrictive measures may be imposed to exercise effective supervision over financial institutions,[50] or to prevent violation of tax regulations.[51]

Capital transfer restrictions are one of the measures used by States to mitigate the devastating consequences in case of an economic meltdown. An example of EU-wide restrictions that prevented capital transfers was the sovereign debt crisis that in particular affected Cyprus and Greece. Greece had no choice but to impose capital controls in 2015 in order to prevent a massive outflow of capital (Samitas and Polyzos 2016). These constraints included limits on the amount of cash that could be withdrawn from banks, a prohibition on early loan repayment, and a cap on transfers to third countries.

3.2 *Capital Transfer Under IIAs*

The free transfer of funds without geographical restrictions is a cornerstone of the legal regime of FDI (Krajewski and Hoffmann 2019, p. 187). Under the concept of monetary sovereignty, States have full authority to regulate their policies concerning the transferability and movement of capital, for example, by imposing restrictions to protect their national interests (Aniodoh 2021). At the same time, by entering into international agreements the State's freedom can be subjected to certain limitations. The Articles of Agreement of the International Monetary Fund (IMF) ratified by 190 member countries is one of the most important international instruments regulating the movement of capital in the context of international transactions.[52] The IMF promotes the removal of barriers to capital controls and the elimination of foreign exchange restrictions impeding the liberalisation of world trade. In a similar vein, the trade regime under the GATT and GATS aims to reduce any restrictions, albeit with several exceptions for States that encounter balance of payment issues. Article XII GATT allows countries to impose quantitative restrictions on imports, which must be proportional to the extent of a balance of payment crisis and conducted transparently.[53]

In this regard, IIAs are essential mechanisms to protect the transfer of funds deriving from foreign investments. Most IIAs, as well as national laws regulating foreign investments, contain provisions that guarantee that a foreign investor can make free use of invested capital, returns on investment, and other payments

---

[50] Case C-439/97 *Sandoz GmbH v. Finanzlandesdirektion für Wien, Niederösterreich und Burgenland* [1999].

[51] Case C-319/02 *Manninen* [2004].

[52] 'Articles of Agreement of the International Monetary Fund' (27 December 1945). The Articles of Agreement have been amended seven times, with the latest amendment adopted on 15 December 2010 (effective 26 January 2016).

[53] 'GATT' (n 36), art XII.

concerning the establishment, operation, or disposal of an investment (Krajewski and Hoffmann 2019, p. 187). These provisions are designed to ensure that the investor is able to transfer funds in a convertible currency without undue delay. The flows to which the free transfer guarantee generally applies include profits, interest, dividends, and other current investment income; funds necessary to finance an investment; payments under a contract; management fees and royalties; loan payments, etc. A majority of BITs and other types of IIAs include a non-exhaustive list of funds that an investor can transfer. A clear framework for money transfers that are outlined in IIAs, and national legislation of a host State is crucial for investors since it indicates the stability and security of the State's FDI regulatory system (Milanesi 2014, p. 289). At the same time, States must retain a specific level of control over transfers to protect their national policies (Dolzer and Schreuer 2008, p. 191). Significant capital outflows during economic or political turmoil may threaten national security or public order. Also, large inflows of capital in a country could result in inflation. Therefore, many IIAs, especially recent ones, have included restrictions on the free transfer of funds to secure the safety and integrity of the financial system, ensure compliance of an investor with tax obligations, etc.[54] Some IIAs provide that the restrictions to transfers can be justified if it is required for the enforcement of the laws of contracting parties (e.g., to prevent fraud on creditors etc.). In a new generation of IIAs, there is a clear trend to incorporate detailed provisions on the transfer of funds that provide a list of conditions under which monetary transfers can occur (Milanesi 2014, p. 289). At the moment of writing, 372 out of 2,584 IIAs have incorporated the specific exceptions to the transfer of funds obligations, e.g., compliance with various domestic laws and regulations.[55]

The specific exceptions are formulated differently across the IIA spectrum. In the EU-Singapoure FTA, the possible capital transfer limitations are formulated restrictively. Under Article 2.7(2), transfers should not 'prevent a Party from applying in an equitable and non-discriminatory manner its law' concerning bankruptcy, compliance with orders or judgments in judicial or administrative proceedings, taxation etc.[56] Further, Article 2.7(3) allows a Party to take temporary safeguard measures to restrict transfers in 'exceptional circumstances of serious difficulties, or threat thereof, for the operation of the economic and monetary policy or exchange rate policy in either Party.' These safeguard measures are limited in time and may not last longer than 6 months.

More explicit exceptions have been formulated in the *Israel – United Arab Emirates BIT* (2020). Article 7 of the the later BIT provides that a Party may 'prevent or delay a transfer' through the equitable, non-discriminatory, and good faith

[54] In 74% of IIAs concluded between 2011–2016, the provisions on the free transfer of funds contain explicit exceptions. UNCTAD, 'World Investment Report 2017' https://unctad.org/system/files/official-document/wir2017_en.pdf.

[55] UNCTAD, Investment Policy Hub, Mapping IIA Content (2023), https://investmentpolicy.unctad.org/international-investment-agreements/iia-mapping.

[56] 'Investment Protection Agreement between the EU and its Member States, of the part, and the Republic of Singapoure, of the other part'.

application of its legislation relating to: (a) the payment of taxes; (b) bankruptcy; (d) criminal or penal offences; (e) financial reporting or record keeping of transfers when necessary to assist law enforcement or financial regulatory authorities; (f) ensuring compliance with an order or judgment in judicial or administrative proceedings; or (g) social security, public retirement, or compulsory savings schemes.[57] According to the exceptions provided in Article 7 of the *Israel – United Arab Emirates BIT*, the foreign investor must comply with tax and fiscal obligations under Israel's national laws to transfer its capital. Further, Article 7 attempts to prevent fraudulent fiscal behaviour of an investor by restricting transfers upon its involvement in socially significant areas like retirement or compulsory saving schemes.

The Africa Arbitration Academy Model Bilateral Investment Treaty for African States (AAA Model BIT) includes an even more explicit set of exceptions to the free transfer of funds. According to Article 8(4) each Contracting Party may prevent the transfer of funds under its laws on 'labour obligations, taxation and environmental protection,' or to ensure 'compliance with the Articles of Agreement and/or request (s) of the International Monetary Fund.'[58] This implies that a host State may prevent the transfer of funds of an investor upon non-compliance with the obligations related to labour or environmental legislation. The reference to the IMF in a list of exceptions can be explained by the fact that African States are among the Member States of the IMF and hence obliged to adhere to the IMF Articles of Agreement.[59]

The trend in new-generation IIAs is to include a detailed list of capital transfer exemptions that include specific obligations regarding compliance with tax, environmental, and labour laws. The latter is consistent with States' efforts to protect their national interests through screening mechanisms and modernization of their IIAs, reflecting the balanced approach between protecting investors' rights and the State's right to regulate. (Levashova 2019).[60] The elaborate capital transfer provisions incorporated into a new generation of IIAs demonstrate States' desire to require investors to comply with their various domestic regulations to transfer profits and gains from foreign investments. This approach differs from older IIAs, which had only a few restrictions on serious offenses related to criminal acts, dealing with securities, etc. The inclusion by States of a more extensive and precise list of exceptions in transfer clauses has two goals: firstly, to achieve a greater balance between the interests of States and investors, and, secondly, to have more control over financial and monetary policies as a matter of national security. This is in accordance with the general shift observed in treaty drafting over the previous

[57] 'Agreement between the Government of the State of Israel and The Government of the United Arab Emirates on Promotion and Protection of Investments' (20 October 2020).

[58] The Africa Arbitration Academy Model BIT (2022), art 8(4).

[59] Ibid., Explanatory Note.

[60] According to the UNCTAD World Investment Report 2022, 'two-thirds of the policy measures less favourable to investment adopted in 2021 concerned the introduction or tightening of national security regulations affecting FDI'. UNCTAD, World Investment Report 2022, https://unctad.org/system/files/official-document/wir2022_en.pdf 58.

decade, reflecting States' intention to safeguard greater regulatory flexibility in all aspects of their IIAs, which intends to limit arbitral tribunal interpretations of treaty provisions.

The case law on capital transfer provisions under IIAs is limited. Investors infrequently invoke transfer clauses (Hildebrandt 2022). In most existing cases, arbitral tribunals have interpreted the transfer clauses in a restrictive manner, rarely finding a violation of this provision under an applicable IIA. Several arbitral decisions in which tribunals denied a violation of the capital transfer provision shed light on the criteria under which States may restrict the transfer of capital. The examples of these cases are discussed in the next section.

3.3 Arbitral Decisions on Restrictions of Capital Transfer

The right of investors to transfer funds inward and outward of a host State has been interpreted by tribunals with caution. Most tribunals have considered the protection of State's monetary sovereignty, even in the absence of detailed clauses providing for a list of exceptions to the capital transfer (Kolo 2010, p. 366).

Tribunals in *Metalpar v Argentina* (2008)[61] and *Continental v. Argentina* (2008)[62] have assessed the State's obligation to transfer the capital of foreign investors in the circumstances of a severe economic crisis that occurred in Argentina in the early 2000s (Nataraj and Sahoo 2003). In a series of investment cases involving Argentina, the economic and financial crisis triggered a range of state emergency measures in the interest of stabilising the economy. The most severe impact of the economic crisis was the devaluation of the Argentinian currency, which generated a wave of investment cases, including the claims for the breach of capital transfer provision.

In *Continental v. Argentina*[63] and *Metalpar v. Argentina*, investors had relied on the promise provided by Argentina's authorities that the original currency convertibility regime adopted before the crisis would be maintained. However, since 2001 Argentina enacted several regulatory measures, including restrictions on transfers out of its country, e.g., '*pesified'* United States (US) dollar deposits, to preserve economic stability. In both cases, tribunals concluded that Argentina had not violated the provision covering transfers. In *Metalpar v Argentina,* a tribunal denied a breach of the capital transfer provision under Article 5(b) of the Argentine-Chile BIT because the investor failed to comply with the national enforcement procedures. To make the transfer, the investor had to request authorization from the Central Bank.[64]

[61] *Metalpar S.A. and Buen Aire S.A. v. The Argentine Republic* (Metalpar v Argentina), ICSID Case No. ARB/03/5, Award (6 June 2008).

[62] *Continental Casualty v. Argentina,* ICSID Case No. ARB/03/9, Award (5 September 2008).

[63] Ibid., para 252.

[64] Metalpar v Argentina (63), para 176.

A tribunal emphasised that investors were aware of the domestic regulations regarding the movement of capital and the failure to comply with the procedure of authorisation cannot constitute a breach of Article 5(b).[65]

In the case *Ryan v. Poland* (2015), the claimant argued that he was prevented from transferring the management fees to the US under Article V of the US Poland BIT, which ensures the free transfer of funds. The claimant argued that he could not make the transfer due to the tax proceedings initiated against an investor. The tribunal disagreed with the investor by finding that from 1994 to 1997, the tax proceedings did not prevent the transfer of funds.[66] However, in the subsequent years, the claimant has not presented proper supporting documentation required by tax authorities in order for management fees to be considered as legitimate deductions for the transfer. Hence, the tribunal concluded that the investor has not demonstrated that Poland, through its tax legislation, has imposed restrictions on the free transfer guaranteed in the US-Poland BIT.[67]

In sum, restrictions on capital transfer under IIAs can sometimes serve as the enforcement mechanism for investor obligations to comply with domestic law and procedure if a host State can demonstrate that these restrictions were imposed through equitable, non-discriminatory, and good faith application of laws and regulations.

4 Conclusion

Over the last decade, the issue of investor obligations emerged as an important topic in international investment law and policy. Departing from the traditional structure of FDI protection and promotion, new generation IIAs have increasingly included CSR provisions that either directly or indirectly impose social, environmental, and human rights obligations on foreign investors, in order to achieve a better balance between FDI protection and promotion and the right of a State to regulate in the public interest. This chapter has examined whether such recent developments characterize also investment screening mechanisms, initially envisioned as a security tool to prevent foreign investors from acquiring strategic companies in sensitive technologies and potentially not designed to impose obligations on foreign investors.

As noted with regard to environmental and capital transfer concerns analysed above, EU IIAs do in fact provide indirect obligations on foreign investors and investments through their screening provisions. In the case of capital transfer, for example, the right of investors to repatriate profits was initially subject to no or a minimal number of exceptions. With the broadening of the notion of security

65 Ibid., para 179.

66 *Vincent J. Ryan, Schooner Capital LLC, and Atlantic Investment Partners LLC v. Republic of Poland* (2015), ICSID Case No. ARB(AF)/11/3, Award (24 November 2015), para 508.

67 Ibid., paras 509–510.

concerns and the course towards protectionism reflected in modern IIAs, the restrictions to capital transfer have become more detailed, going so far as to impose implicit obligations on investors to comply with national law.

At the same time, EU IIAs give host States wide discretion when it comes to the grounds for screening and to the areas in which the screening should be carried out. Although EU Regulation 2019/452 has attempted to harmonize EU Member State's domestic screening laws, the inherent vagueness of its terms has led to a fragmented EU security framework, in which the precise scope of the screening is uncertain and can potentially address CSR concerns. On the one hand, this creeping expansion of the scope of FDI screening could conflict with liberalization commitments contained in other IIAs. On the other hand, this picture is inherently problematic at the EU level, as it brings FDI screening into conflict with the fundamental freedoms of capital movements enshrined in the EU treaties.

In light of the future challenges that are looming in the international panorama, screening mechanisms will play an increasingly more important role in the regulation of FDI. While the global pandemic has intensified the need to protect the national industries, particularly in the healthcare and pharmaceutical fields, new emerging threats, such as climate change and the energy crises, are widening the range of issues impacting national security and public order. Accordingly, investor obligations contained in such instruments will become more and more relevant, possibly limiting the openness of the FDI regulation in an unwarranted fashion. In the EU system, historically open to FDI, this scenario calls for a greater harmonization of national instruments, to provide transparency and certainty of the obligations to which foreign investors are subject. This will help to effectively foster the achievement of an attractive, yet safe, legal framework for FDI.

References

Aniodoh A (2021) Host states' monetary sovereignty within the construct of bilateral investment treaties. J Afr Law 65(1):1–23

Babu R (2018) WTO and the protection of public morals. Asian J WTO Int Health Law Policy 13: 333–354

Baratta R (2014) Complexity of EU law in the domestic implementing process. Theory Pract Legisl 2:293–308

Boisson de Chazournes L (2017) Changes in the balance of rights and obligations: toward investor Responsibilization. Proc ASIL Annual Meeting 111:53–55

Boklan D, Bahri A (2020) The first WTO's ruling on National Security Exception: balancing interests or opening Pandora's box? World Trade Rev 19:123–136

Buzan B, Wæver O, de Wilde J (2022) Security - a new framework for analysis. Lynne Rienner Publishers, Boulder

Cremona M (2020) Regulating FDI in the EU legal framework. In: Bourgeois JHJ (ed) Eu framework for foreign direct investment control. Kluwer Law International, Alphen aan den Rijn, pp 31–55

De Brabandere E, Hazelzet M (2018) Corporate responsibility and human rights: navigating between international, domestic and self-regulation. In: Radi Y (ed) Research handbook on human rights and investment. Edward Elgar Publishing, Cheltenham, pp 221–243

Delimatsis P, Gargne L (2022) Article XIV GATS - general exceptions. In: Stoll P-T, Hestermeyer H (eds) . Brill Academic Publishers, Commentaries on World Trade Law Online
Delimatsis P, Hrynkiv O (2022) Article XIVbis GATS - security exceptions. In: Hestermeyer H (ed) Stoll P-T. Brill Academic Publishers, Commentaries on World Trade Law Online
Dolzer R, Schreuer C (2008) Principles of international investment law. Oxford University Press, Oxford
Dolzer R, Schreuer C, Kriebaum U (2022) Principles of international investment law, 3rd edn. Oxford University Press, Oxford
Eliason A (2016) Public morals and environmental. In: Faure M (ed) Elgar encyclopedia of environmental law. Edward Elgar Publishing, Cheltenham, pp 729–738
Gonzalez MA (2006) Trade and morality: preserving public morals without sacrificing the global economy note. Vanderbilt J Transnatl Law 39:939–972
Hildebrandt J (2022) An Unlikely Couple – The Use of Transfer of Funds Clauses for the Determination of Exchange Rates in Investor State Disputes. https://arbitrationblog.kluwerarbitration.com/2022/01/04/an-unlikely-couple-the-use-of-transfer-of-funds-clauses-for-the-determination-of-exchange-rates-in-investor-state-disputes/
Hoffmeister F (2016) The contribution of EU trade agreements to the development of international investment law. In: Hindelang S, Krajewski M (eds) Shifting paradigms in international investment law: more balanced, less isolated, increasingly diversified. Oxford University Press, Oxford, pp 357–376
Joubin-Bret A (2008) Admission and establishment in the context of investment protection. In: Reinisch A (ed) Standards of investment protection. Oxford University Press, Oxford, pp 9–28
Kolo A (2010) Transfer of funds: the interaction between the IMF articles of agreement and modern investment treaties: a comparative law perspective. In: Schill S (ed) International investment law and comparative public law. Oxford University Press, Oxford, pp 345–374
Krajewski M, Hoffmann RT (eds) (2019) Research handbook on foreign direct investment. Edward Elgar Publishing Limited, Cheltenham
Levashova Y (2018) The accountability and corporate social responsibility of multinational corporations for transgressions in host states through international investment law. Utrecht Law Rev 14(2):40–55
Levashova Y (2019) The right of states to regulate in international investment law: the search for balance between public interest and fair and equitable treatment. Wolters Kluwer, Alphen aan den Rijn
Marwell JC (2006) Trade and morality: the WTO public morals exception after gambling. N Y Univ Law Rev 81:802–842
Milanesi E (2014) European Union restrictions to the free movement of capital v. BITs guarantees. In: Acconci P et al (eds) General interests of host states in international investment law. Cambridge University Press, Cambridge, pp 287–307
Moberg A, Hindelang S (2020) The art of casting political dissent in law: the EU'S framework for the screening of foreign direct investment. Common Mark Law Rev 57:1427–1460
Nataraj G, Sahoo P (2003) Argentina's crisis: causes and consequences. Econ Polit Wkly 38(17): 1641–1644
Nettesheim M (2020) Screening for what threat: preserving "Public Order and Security", securing reciprocity in international trade, or supporting certain social, environmental, or industrial policies? In: Hindelang S, Moberg A (eds) YSEC yearbook of socio-economic constitutions. Springer, pp 481–504
Ortino F (2012) Legal reasoning of international investment tribunals: a typology of egregious failures. J Int Disp Settlement 3(31):31–52
Osisanya S (2014) National Security versus Global Security. https://www.un.org/en/chronicle/article/national-security-versus-global-security
Ospanova G (2022) Integrating Markets in Banking Services. https://doi-org.proxy.library.uu.nl/10.1007/978-3-031-15282-5_4

Samitas A, Polyzos S (2016) Freeing Greece from capital controls: were the restrictions enforced in time? Res Int Bus Financ 37:196–213

Tomkin J, Steiblytė A (2019) Article 65 TFEU. In: Kellerbauer M, Klamert M, Tomkin J (eds) The EU treaties and the charter of fundamental rights: a commentary. Oxford University Press, Oxford, pp 743–774

Velten J (2022) Screening foreign direct investment in the EU: political rationale, legal limitations. Springer International Publishing, Cham

Verellen T (2021) When integration by stealth meets public security: the EU foreign direct investment screening regulation. Legal Issues Econ Integr 48:19–42

Voon T, Merriman D (2022) Incoming: how international investment law constrains foreign investment screening. J World Investment Trade 1:1–40

Zwartkruis W, de Jong B (2020) The EU regulation on screening of foreign direct investment: a game changer? Eur Bus Law Rev 31:447–474

Facilitating and Scrutinizing National Security Measures: Analysis of an Investment Screening Case in the European Union

Bálint Kovács

Contents

Abstract In the current context of global affairs, geopolitical strategies blend into economics, with a slew of new regulatory measures reflecting this trend. Among these are mechanisms for the screening of foreign direct investment. The shift in attitude towards economic relations poses a number of challenges to the rule of law, as national security considerations allow for a wide margin of appreciation from the part of states as to what constitutes a threat. Investment screening facilitates unilateral measures to contain such threats, whether genuine or perceived, which may ultimately frustrate business ventures. The paper aims to explore the consequences of such a unilateral state measure through the prism of a case from Hungary. The case of VIG's acquisition of AEGON Group's subsidiaries shines a light on the effectiveness of the remedies economic actors have against screening decisions, and how such decisions are scrutinized by the EU. The paper argues that the swiftness with which states are able to act is not matched by the effectiveness of the remedies investors are provided with, consequently having the potential to frustrate business plans. This may prompt investors to seek compensation for their losses through international arbitration.

B. Kovács (✉)
Department of Private International Law, Faculty of Law and Political Sciences, University of Szeged, Szeged, Hungary
e-mail: kovacs.balint@szte.hu

J. H. Pohl et al. (eds.), *National Security and Investment Controls*,
Springer Studies in Law & Geoeconomics (2024) 3: 209–230,
https://doi.org/10.1007/17280_2024_24, Published online: 22 February 2024

1 Introductory Remarks

The rise of China in the twenty-first Century and the development of its economy have increasingly been viewed as challenges to the Western development model. Its accession to the World Trade Organization in 2001 benefited both China and Western countries and was hailed at the time as an important step towards the eventual opening up and democratization of China.[1] Growing economic interdependence was considered on the one hand as enabling the opening up of China's economy and nudging it towards the adoption of Western democratic values, on the other hand, it was believed by many to promise peace.[2] While China's ascent was admired worldwide, scrutiny and criticism of its state-led development model have gained traction in recent years, as many of the expectations and optimistic forecasts of systemic change failed to become reality. Indeed, China's development model of *party-state capitalism* proved to be stronger and more stable than many expected. It is not uncommon to read about China's economic gains and its rise in the high-tech sector as a threat to the long-term strategic goals of the US as a world leader. Counter to the optimism manifested at the turn of the millennium, Chinese leaders have used the tools of state capitalism to achieve their goals in terms of economic growth, while also maintaining and strengthening, their autocratic regime. The democratic reform aspired to be brought to China through its rapid economic development and major role in international trade never came due to this economic-political model of state capitalism. This manner of conducting business is viewed with increased suspicion in the West, not least because it might be considered by other states as a new way to compete. Counterintuitively, this actually led to an industrial policy with more government intervention in the economy, also in the West.[3] This occurrence is, however, more worrisome in the case of China, due to its perceived ambitions of using its economic and military power to shape global politics. The European Commission (Commission) has described China as "an economic competitor in the pursuit of technological leadership, and a systemic rival promoting alternative models of governance."[4]

[1]This speech by US President Bill Clinton may be the best example of the optimism felt by many at the time. Of course, in hindsight, some of the President's expectations appear overly optimistic. See Full Text of Clinton's Speech on China Trade Bill, New York Times, 9 March 2000.

[2]The latter is a platitude that has remained popular (also turned into policy, see *Wandel durch Handel*) despite its spectacular failure over a century ago.

[3]Notable examples include the Inflation Reduction Act of 2022 and the CHIPS and Science Act in the US, as well as the European Chips Act, and the European Sovereignty Fund.

[4]See European Commission, Joint Communication to the European Parliament, the European Council, and the Council: EU-China – A strategic outlook. JOIN(2019) 5 final, Strasbourg, 12.03.2019, p. 1. Similarly, the US views China as "the only competitor with both the intent to reshape the international order and, increasingly, the economic, diplomatic, military, and technological power to do it." See 2022 National Security Strategy, October 2022, p. 23.

As a consequence of this shift in attitude towards China, there has also been much discussion about decoupling.[5] While a total decoupling is difficult to imagine, due to the interdependence of the involved economies, decoupling at the level of high-tech is now underway. The competition between China and the West is entering a new and more transparent phase, where regulation makes clear what is expected from the business sector. Business and politics are mixing in this new bowl of legislative steps which seek to curtail business ventures that "might affect national security." While it is not yet clear how the rules of international commerce will be rewritten, the adoption of domestic legislation is encouraged with the purpose of enabling the protection of Western open market values from being taken advantage of any further.[6] The regulatory measures are clearly aimed at China, as outbound direct investment is considered to be an important tool of economic statecraft.[7] Foreign investors can now be barred from entering into deals that may potentially endanger Western essential security interests. How the potential danger is judged, however, is *mostly* left up to the states.

The above attempt at painting a picture of the current atmosphere in international economic relations serves for the understanding of the "*why?*" regarding the proliferation of export controls, investment screening, increases in tariffs, or restrictions in accessing financial markets. Industrial policy aimed at spurring innovation is complemented by measures aimed at slowing down China's technological progress, putting into perspective the scope of the challenges posed by China's activities in the West. In the current atmosphere, politics and business will mix even more intensely, as global business regulation enters into a new stage of evolution. An important part of this new stage of evolution is the proliferation of regulation that allows for unilateral state measures, and the securitization of new areas of international business.

Western economies remain open markets, and the willingness to maintain them as such has not changed. What has changed, is the fact that many aspects of the relationship between China and the West are viewed through the lens of national security. Despite the shift in policy, important economic actors remain highly engaged in China, and Western economies continue to rely heavily on Chinese manufacturing, which is why decoupling seems untenable. Some of the new regulation aims to establish appropriate tools for governments to act with surgical precision,[8] and intervene only when it is deemed necessary. One such instrument is investment screening, which recently underwent reform in the US and has experienced proliferation throughout the European Union (EU). The next section

[5] See Financial Times: Year in a Word: Decoupling, 30 December 2022.

[6] See also: Nettesheim (2020), p. 483.

[7] Wernicke (2020), p. 31.

[8] Not all measures can be characterized in this manner, e.g. export controls recently implemented in the US, which are rather extensive. See the following document published on 13 October 2022: Implementation of Additional Export Controls: Certain Advanced Computing and Semiconductor Manufacturing Items; Supercomputer and Semiconductor End Use; Entity List Modification.

will briefly present the rise to the fore of investment screening as one of the quintessential regulatory measures in the West's competition with Chinese party-state capitalism. The paper will then turn to introducing the EU Regulation on the screening of foreign direct investment (FDI), and some of the lessons held by the first 2 years of its application. This is followed by the presentation of the VIG/AEGON case stemming from Hungary, in which the Commission investigated Hungarian authorities' national security veto of a transaction. This case holds many interesting lessons as to the potential use of investment screening, and the effectiveness of the remedies investors are entitled to. The difficulties faced by investors may prompt them to seek compensation through investment arbitration, as opposed to attempting an overturn of a screening decision through lengthy and risky proceedings. The paper concludes with the author's modest reflections on the potential trajectory that international economic relations might embrace.

2 Regulation for the New Ages: The Screening of FDI

While the discourse concerning the maintenance of open markets has not changed, Western governments are putting a break on *absolute* and *unconditional* openness. China's economic activities, more precisely the CCP's increased presence in Chinese companies' affairs, have been viewed as undermining open market economies. China is accused of obtaining Western technology—through intellectual property theft and forced transfer of technology (asset-stripping)—which is then channeled into heavily subsidized Chinese companies, granting them a massive advantage in global markets.[9] Increased activities of Chinese state-owned enterprises in company acquisitions and takeovers in what are considered strategic economic sectors have prompted legislative responses. One of the regulatory responses by EU Member States is constituted by the introduction of procedures for the screening of FDI on grounds of national security and/or public order. Investment screening is now an important tool of defense against company takeovers that threaten *national security* and/or *public order*. The adoption of investment screening mechanisms (ISMs) by Member States is encouraged via an EU Regulation[10] which aims to ensure that the EU remains an open market, while also providing a tool for protection against national security threats emerging from within the economy, without compromising the fundamental values of the open market.

The United States has prior experience with FDI review, and proceeded to beef up its existing institution, the Committee on Foreign Investment in the United States

[9] See United States Trade Representative (USTR): Findings of the Investigation of China's acts, policies, and practices related to technology transfer, intellectual property, and innovation under Section 301 of the Trade Act of 1974, published 22 March 2018.

[10] Regulation (EU) 2019/452 of the European Parliament and of the Council of 19 March 2019 establishing a framework for the screening of foreign direct investments into the Union.

(CFIUS), via the Foreign Investment Risk Review Modernization Act of 2018 (FIRRMA),[11] and more recently by Executive Order.[12] In the EU, the Commission considered that Member States should coordinate their efforts towards a common approach for the screening of FDI. In a relatively accelerated process, the Regulation proposal for EU-wide investment screening was published in 2017 and subsequently adopted in March 2019. Regulation (EU) 2019/452 of 19 March 2019 establishing a framework for the screening of foreign direct investments into the Union (FDI Screening Regulation) entered into force in October 2020. The main aim of the FDI Screening Regulation is to coordinate Member States' actions on foreign investment and to serve as a guide for establishing national screening mechanisms. The coordinated activity on the FDI screening front establishes a baseline for Member States' collaboration, both through the Commission and directly between them. While maintaining respect for the exclusive competence of Member States to address matters of national security, the Commission encourages all Member States to adopt ISMs in order to safeguard their own national security, and lays down a cooperation mechanism, aiming to harmonize EU-wide investment screening, in order—ultimately—to protect the Single Market. The Regulation comes in the context of a shift in attitude: more emphasis is now being placed on viewing economic security as an integral part of national security. This development will put Member States' security decisions on a collision course with EU law, especially with the fundamental freedom of establishment.

The FDI Screening Regulation has been presented as an instrument that is essential in building EU *strategic autonomy*.[13] A concept associated principally with geopolitics, in addition to defense policy, and the upholding of democratic values, EU strategic autonomy is now also linked to the economy and energy supply, thus taking on a geo-economic dimension.[14] Essentially, strategic autonomy signifies the ability of the EU to decide its own fate and choose its own path. There are a number of challenges to this strategic autonomy, such as Russia's aggression against Ukraine, the strained relationship between the US and China, migration, and the economic fallout from the COVID-19 pandemic as well as the modernized EU industrial policy. These challenges prompted the regulatory responses mentioned herein, most recently with the regulation on foreign subsidies to ensure equal

[11] For more details on the US regulatory endeavors, see Jacobs (2019).

[12] See Executive Order 14083 of September 15, 2022, on Ensuring Robust Consideration of Evolving National Security Risks by the Committee on Foreign Investment in the United States.

[13] EU foreign investment screening mechanism becomes fully operational, Press Release, European Commission, 9 October 2020.

[14] For more on the topic see the briefing prepared by the European Parliament: EU strategic autonomy 2013–2023 – From concept to capacity – July 2022, authored by Mario Damen at the European Parliamentary Research Service.

competition,[15] the national security screening of FDI, and the use of sanctions against individuals, companies, and states.[16]

3 The EU FDI Screening Regulation

The EU is a highly integrated economic union, even though its Member States have different levels of economic development. The existence and functioning of the Single Market depend upon the free movement of goods, services, capital, and persons. In case a company establishes its presence in any of the 27 Member States by exercising the EU fundamental freedom of establishment (Arts. 49–54 TFEU), this has consequences for other Member States and the Single Market as a whole. An important part of the EU common commercial policy (as defined by Article 207(1) TFEU) is that the EU has exclusive competence over FDI. However, the differences in economic development lead to different views and approaches among Member States in terms of their understanding of FDI. Non-economic considerations, such as the protection of critical infrastructure, public order, and national security, have gradually risen in importance. In a global economy where the only certainty is change, complex investment schemes will make it difficult for those interested to discover who the ultimate owner is, who controls a particular investment, and who ultimately benefits from it. Sharing information between Member States, as envisaged by the FDI Screening Regulation, becomes an important tool. It must also be stressed that the FDI Screening Regulation is not intended to discourage foreign investment, but was designed to ensure that foreign investments will not pose a threat to the EU and the Single Market.

Member States are able to derogate from the principle of free movement of capital and establish measures to restrict such movement on grounds of public policy[17] or public security,[18] as per paragraph 4 of the Recital of the FDI Screening Regulation. While FDI falls within the exclusive competence of the EU, safeguarding national security remains the sole responsibility of the Member States, in accordance with the Treaty on the European Union (TEU) and the Treaty on the Functioning of the European Union (TFEU).[19] The drafters of the FDI Screening Regulation rightly recognized that the level of integration reached by the EU mandates cooperation in this area, as an investment may have consequences beyond the borders of the Member State where it is established. In line with this fact, the Regulation provides answers to two important concerns. One is a general concern of the EU, regarding

[15] See Regulation (EU) 2022/2560 of 14 December 2022 on foreign subsidies distorting the internal market.

[16] See EU Sanctions Map, available at https://www.sanctionsmap.eu/#/main.

[17] See Thym (2016).

[18] See Koutrakos (2016).

[19] Also restated in the FDI Screening Regulation Recital paras. (6) and (7).

the security of its Member States and that of the Single Market, the other one pertains to specific areas of interest relating to projects funded from the EU budget. Nonetheless, the Regulation, in line with the provisions of both the TEU and the TFEU, allows for Member States to decide for themselves, whether or not, and ultimately in what shape they are willing to screen foreign investments.

Article 3 of the Regulation contains guidelines for Member States adopting screening mechanisms, such as having relevant timeframes, working in a transparent and non-discriminatory manner, providing recourse against screening decisions, and keeping sensitive business information confidential. The Regulation provides for a cooperation mechanism between Member States on the one hand and the Commission and other Member States on the other hand, basically encouraging convergence in Member States' concepts as to what constitutes a threat to national security when it comes to FDI. Article 4 of the Regulation contains an indicative list of factors that *may* be considered when determining whether an FDI is likely to affect security and public order. It is important to note the *indicative* nature of the factors listed within the Regulation, which ties back to the fact that national security matters belong in the realm of a Member State's sovereign prerogatives, as states themselves are the ones that have to determine what specifically constitutes a national security threat to them.[20] Balancing Member States' interests with the competing interests of other Member States and the Single Market will in all certainty be challenging.

The drafters of the Regulation envisaged the establishment of processes that are proportional, and prefer granting access to investors who make specific commitments, rather than having the investments refused. In addition, the Member States have an obligation to share information and submit a yearly report, which is used by the Commission to issue its own yearly report. The Commission will also have to evaluate the functioning and effectiveness of the Regulation, with the first review coming in October 2023.[21]

While these are important features of the Regulation, it is noteworthy that the establishment of a screening mechanism is left up to the decision of the Member State in its entirety.[22] This means that there is bound to be many variations in how Member States approach this regulatory task. Whether or not an investment is screened and subsequently admitted or rejected is entirely up to the Member State as well. This means that in cases where the Member States' screening mechanisms are similar, or even identical, their application may still be different. There are several reasons why such differences may occur. First, states might not be working with the same information. The Commission already thought of the issue of information asymmetries, making it possible for Member States and the Commission to share opinions and information in the screening process. Of course, whether or not

[20] A matter addressed in para. (7) of the Recital and also in Article 1 Section 2 of the FDI Screening Regulation.

[21] See FDI Screening Regulation Recital para. (34).

[22] Article 3(1) of the Regulation provides that "Member States *may* maintain, amend or adopt mechanisms to screen foreign direct investment..." [emphasis added].

such interventions will be considered is also entirely up to the Member State conducting the screening, although the Commission has its means of pressuring governments.[23] Second, Member States will inevitably have different views regarding what constitutes a threat to their national security and/or public order, just as they will have different opinions on what these concepts mean. Despite the exclusive competence of the Member States, any national security or public order decision that may conflict with Union law will be scrutinized accordingly. Third, differences in economic wants and needs constitute an important factor: countries that are strapped for cash will be less likely to turn away *risky* FDI. Fourth, differences in industrial development, especially regarding key industries and high-tech, will play a major role in the decisions of states: countries, where high-tech development is lagging behind, will be less likely to target FDI in such fields.

From the data gathered by the Commission and subsequently published in its reports on the application of investment screening mechanisms in the EU, we can also get an idea of the magnitude of the task at hand. According to the first Commission's report on the screening of foreign direct investments into the Union,[24] for the year 2020, out of a total of 1793 submissions, 362 cases, or approximately 20% were formally screened, of which 91% were approved. Of the cases screened, 79% were approved without conditions, and 12% with some conditions. 2% of the screened investments were prohibited and 7% were aborted by the parties before any decision was made by the competent authorities. In the second Commission's report on the screening of foreign direct investments into the Union,[25] for the year 2021, out of a total of 1,563 submissions, 29% of cases were formally screened. Of the cases screened, 73% were authorized with no conditions, 23% were authorized with conditions, 1% were prohibited and 3% were withdrawn. What appears as interesting is the growth in the proportion of cases in which screening was actually performed, which, as suggested by the second annual report, is explained by the changes in investment trends, as well as greater attention to what is potentially "critical".[26] Part of the explanation for the growth in the proportion of cases screened is that pursuant to the implementation of screening mechanisms by most EU Member States, many of them reevaluated the scope of their application, pursuant to the serious weaknesses in global supply chains revealed by the global pandemic.

There are a number of considerations that come into play when an instrument as strong as investment screening is adopted. As the case below suggests, these

[23] Indeed, the FDI Screening Regulation was criticized for being limited in its efficiency, as *political pressure* is the only effective tool in the hands of the Commission. See Vig (2020), p. 23.

[24] Report from the Commission to the European Parliament and the Council, First Annual Report on the screening of foreign direct investments into the Union – COM(2021) 714 final, Brussels, 23.11.2021.

[25] Report from the Commission to the European Parliament and the Council, Second Annual Report on the screening of foreign direct investments into the Union – COM(2022) 433 final, Brussels, 1.9.2022.

[26] Id. p. 11.

instruments can be highly effective when it comes to shaping certain economic sectors through intervention.

4 Competition Concerns and National Security

The purpose of this section is to inform the reader about the essential elements of a recent case[27] in which the Commission opened an investigation into the Hungarian authorities' decision to veto an acquisition in an intra-EU setting, invoking national security concerns.

AEGON Group, an insurance company from the Netherlands, was preparing the sale of its subsidiaries in a number of Central and Eastern European countries in September 2020. VIG (Vienna Insurance Group) expressed an interest in acquiring the subsidiaries in Hungary, Poland, Romania, and Turkey. The parties proceeded to sign a sale and purchase agreement on 29 November 2020. VIG, already present in the Hungarian market, would have become a market leader with this acquisition.

Hungarian Government Decree no. 532/2020[28] entered into force on 29 November 2020, widening the applicability of the investment screening regime established by Act LVII of 2018 on controlling foreign investments violating Hungary's security interests, on the day the sale and purchase agreement was signed. The amendment extended the applicability of national security screening in terms of origin, to also include all EU, EEA, and Swiss investors, and in terms of covered industry sectors, to include the insurance industry as well. What is noteworthy in the case of this amendment is that it extended the scope of the ISM beyond what is envisaged by the FDI Screening Regulation, which defines *foreign investor* as meaning "a natural person of a third country or an undertaking of a third country,

[27] Information regarding this case is based on the following sources: European Commission Press release, 21 February 2022, Brussels, "Mergers: Commission finds that Hungary's veto over the acquisition of AEGON's Hungarian subsidiaries by VIG breached Article 21 of the EU Merger Regulation"; European Commission, DG Competition, Case M.10102 – VIG/AEGON CEE, Decision, Brussels, 12.08.2021, C(2021) 6077 final; Vienna Insurance Group and Hungary reach an agreement on the outlines of a cooperation and the further procedure regarding the Hungarian insurance companies AEGON and UNION, 22.12.2021 https://www.vig.com/en/investor-relations/ir-newsinside-information/detail/vienna-insurance-group-and-hungary-reach-an-agreement-on-the-outlines-of-a-cooperation-and-the-further-procedure-regarding-the-hungarian-insurance-companies-aegon-and-union.html; Hungarian FDI veto lifted after pressure from EU Commission – all's well that ends well or dangerous precedent? 14.07.2022, https://www.jdsupra.com/legalnews/hungarian-fdi-veto-lifted-after-3725622/;

Decision in Case no. M.10494 VIG|AEGON CEE, dated 21 February 2022 (hereinafter: the Decision).

[28] Government Decree no. 532/2020 on the economic protection measures to be applied during the emergency, published in the Hungarian Official Journal no. 263 of 28 November 2020, was abrogated one year later via Government Decree no. 647/2021 regulating the application of certain laws in view of the entry into force of Act XCIX of 2021 on transitional rules in relation to emergency situations.

intending to make or having made a foreign direct investment."[29] With the new legal provisions in place, the transaction had to be notified to the Hungarian authorities, which VIG did on 9 December 2020. The authorities performed the national security screening of the investment and decided to prohibit the acquisition on 6 April 2021.

Due to its Union dimension, the acquisition was also notified to the Commission in July 2021, which then conducted its own examination of the transaction. Under its competence pursuant to the EU Merger Regulation,[30] the Commission proceeded to examine whether the acquisition posed any type of competition concern. The Commission examined the transaction under the normal merger review procedure and concluded that it did not raise any competition concern, unconditionally clearing the transaction in August 2021. Subsequently, in October 2021, the Commission launched an investigation into the Hungarian authorities' veto of the transaction.

The parties to the transaction also sought judicial review of the veto of the authorities, but their case was dismissed by the Budapest-Capital Regional Court in September 2021. The parties appealed the decision in front of the Hungarian Supreme Court.

In the meantime, VIG also entered into negotiations with the Hungarian Ministry of Finance reaching an agreement and signing a memorandum of understanding in December 2021. Pursuant to this memorandum of understanding the Hungarian State would gain a 45% participation via Corvinus Nemzetközi Befektetési Zrt., a state-owned investment fund, in UNION Vienna Insurance Group Biztosító Zrt., VIG's Hungarian subsidiary. Basically, in the language of investment screening, the transaction was allowed *with conditions*.

Just as the ink was drying on the paper of the signed deal, the Commission's investigation reached its conclusion and was announced via a press release.[31] The Commission ordered Hungary to withdraw its veto by 18 March 2022, finding that it infringed EU law in a number of ways. It was noted that Hungarian authorities failed to communicate the intended veto to the Commission prior to its implementation. The Commission also retained that Hungary failed to demonstrate that the measure was justified, suitable, and proportionate, which made it incompatible with the EU rule on freedom of establishment and also infringed the legitimate interest rule in Article 21 of the Merger Regulation. The Commission ordered Hungary to withdraw its veto, threatening the possibility of launching an infringement procedure.

---

[29] See Article 2(2) of the FDI Screening Regulation.

[30] Council Regulation (EC) No 139/2004 of 20 January 2004 on the control of concentrations between undertakings.

[31] Mergers: Commission finds that Hungary's veto over the acquisition of AEGON's Hungarian subsidiaries by VIG breached Article 21 of the EU Merger Regulation, Press release, 21 February 2022.

5 The Pandemic, Security, Protectionism, and Competition

The terminology used in investment screening varies from state to state in accordance with the specifics of their legal systems. Even the FDI Screening Regulation uses the terms" security or public order", acknowledging that there are differences specific to Member States' legal traditions in this area that is of their exclusive competence. In the VIG/AEGON case there are a number of elements that are worth exploring in view of the emergency situation mandated by the COVID-19 pandemic, the national security screening of investments, and the competition and freedom of establishment aspects that mix within the case.

Government Decree 532/2020 (GD) was published in Hungarian Official Journal no. 263 on 28 November 2020, accompanied by other legislative measures in response to the COVID-19 pandemic. The GD amended the investment screening mechanism Hungary adopted in 2018 (Act LVII of 2018 on controlling foreign investments violating Hungary's security interests), by expanding its scope of application. Act LVII of 2018 establishes the principal investment screening mechanism in Hungary, aimed at protecting the *security interests* of the State.[32] This is the law that regulates investment screening on grounds of *national security*. The GD, however, extended the applicability of investment screening to include investors from the EU, but only for the duration of the emergency situation mandated by the pandemic.[33]

According to the Commission's Decision, in the veto decision communicated to VIG, the Hungarian authorities only stated the following: "[a]s a result of the review carried out on the basis of this notification, I declare that the notifying party's acquisition of control violates the *national security interest* of Hungary" [emphasis added].[34] In the Press Release of the Commission, dated 21 February 2022, the Commission communicated that the Hungarian authorities argued that the acquisition threatened Hungary's *legitimate interests*. Legitimate interest is the language used in Article 21(4) of the Merger Regulation. This provision allows Member States to assert their legitimate interests in cases of concentrations that have a Union dimension, even against the decision of the Commission. Public security, plurality of the media, and prudential rules are listed as legitimate interests. Measures that are not aimed at protecting either of these three categories, are measures aimed at protecting "any other public interest". Such measures must be submitted to and assessed by the Commission individually before they are implemented, as per the third paragraph of Article 21(4) of the Merger Regulation, referred to as the

[32]There was another screening mechanism adopted as a response to the pandemic, basically aimed at protecting Hungarian state interest and the interest of strategic companies, which is found in Chapter 85 of Law LVIII of 2020 on transitional arrangements and disease preparedness in the event ending the emergency situation.

[33]This should not be confused with the anti-circumvention clause contained in Article 1(1) of Act LVII of 2018.

[34]See para. (15) of the Decision.

communication and standstill obligations. Per a contrario, measures aimed at protecting public security do not have to be communicated to the Commission before they are implemented.

Article 21(2) of the Merger Regulation establishes the sole jurisdiction of the Commission over concentrations having a Union dimension. While Article 21-(4) allows for Member States to adopt measures aimed at protecting their legitimate interests, these are generally assessed to determine if they are in line with Union law. The Commission may assess such measures in order to determine if they are genuinely aimed at protecting a legitimate interest, thus having the ability to ultimately censor *protectionist* measures. Measures adopted in the process of screening FDI on grounds of security or public order are not exempt from such scrutiny. The FDI Screening Regulation's Recital, at Paragraph (36), essentially provides that in case of a screening decision of a Member State which blocks a concentration having a Union dimension, the grounds for screening will be scrutinized in accordance with what may be considered a legitimate interest, as per Article 21(4) Merger Regulation. The Commission's exclusive competence of assessing concentrations having a Union dimension is thus protected even against national security screening decisions. This is reiterated in the present case, the Commission retaining that "public security may be relied on only if there is a genuine and sufficiently serious threat to a fundamental interest of society."[35]

The Commission argued in the Decision that the communication and standstill obligations, in line with the obligation of sincere cooperation, also apply in cases where "there are reasonable doubts as to whether the national measures [...] genuinely aim to protect a 'recognised interest' and/or comply with the principles of proportionality and non-discrimination."[36] The Commission thus recognizes that the Hungarian authorities' veto was based on security concerns, but it expected the same authorities to comply with the communication and standstill obligations, even though there is no such obligation under the Merger Regulation. The Commission basically argues that the Member State's authorities should have been the ones to analyze whether there is any reasonable doubt as to the proportionality and discriminatory nature of their own decision and to reach the same conclusion: that they should comply with the communication and standstill obligations under the Merger Regulation. Failing to do so, the Commission concludes that Hungary's veto amounts to a procedural infringement of Article 21.[37]

According to the Decision, "[t]he third paragraph of Article 21(4) of the Merger Regulation explicitly provides for 'an assessment of [the measure's] compatibility' by the Commission for national measures that do not relate to competition law." The Commission then argues that the Court of Justice upheld its previous finding that "national measures taken to protect interests other than competition" infringed

---

[35] See para. (36) of the Decision.

[36] See para. (32) of the Decision, invoking past practice of the Commission.

[37] See para. (71) of the Decision.

Article 21(4).[38] As an example, the Commission points to a judgment from 2004 in which the Court of Justice upheld its decision that the measures adopted by Portugal infringed Article 21(4). The Decision also underlines the fact that Portugal invoked economic and industrial objectives in said case.[39] Considering that the Hungarian authorities relied on a national security assessment, the case law invoked by the Commission is anything but fitting to this case.

Several arguments presented by the Commission related to the national security risks invoked by Hungary. The Commission states that both VIG and AEGON have been present for decades on the Hungarian market, and no argument has been produced as to the reason why a change in the ownership of AEGON would "entail an increased risk to public security."[40] It also argues that in no other insurance-related case has public security been invoked, stating that such cases are "rare", and that in the present case, neither the Polish nor the Romanian authorities raised public security concerns.[41] There are bound to be differences in the ways in which Member States evaluate national security concerns. The FDI Screening Regulation provides for cooperation between Member States but recognizes that the recommendations made by one Member State are not mandatory to be followed by another Member State. Indeed, a Member State's conclusions regarding a national security concern should not have any bearing on the Commission's assessment of that or another Member State's conclusions either. As to the fact that such cases are "rare", as shown by the statistics in the Commission's reports on the screening of foreign direct investments into the Union, national security vetoes are indeed rare, but this has no bearing on whether or not they are justified. Nevertheless, Hungary did not produce arguments to the satisfaction of the Commission.

In the Commission's view, Hungary has not provided sufficient reasons as to how the acquisition would have affected its *public security*, and sent no documents to justify the veto.[42] Hungary, in turn, invoked national law as precluding it from disclosing classified information.[43] The Commission insists that information should have been made available, at least in a redacted manner, or in the form of a non-confidential summary.[44] It is of the opinion that accepting Hungary's argument that it cannot reveal classified information would frustrate the *effet utile* of Article 21 of the Merger Regulation, and would go against the duty of sincere cooperation.[45] This is applicable to any invocation of national security threats: if their scrutinization is precluded, they can be abused without limits. The Commission adds that while

[38] See para. (44) of the Decision.

[39] Portugal v Commission, Case C-42/01, EU:C:2004:379, see para. (44) of the Decision.

[40] See para. (58) of the Decision.

[41] See para. (59)–(60) of the Decision.

[42] See para. (64)–(65) of the Decision.

[43] See para. (66) of the Decision.

[44] See para. (65) of the Decision.

[45] See paras. (83)–(84) and (88) of the Decision.

Article 346(1)(a) TFEU allows for Member States to withhold classified information, this right is not absolute, and must be interpreted narrowly.[46]

The Decision also states that the veto is an infringement of Article 49 TFEU, which requires the elimination of restrictions on the freedom of establishment. In the Commission's view, the veto is "a form of direct discrimination against VIG on grounds of nationality."[47] While Article 52(1) TFEU allows for restrictions on the freedom of establishment on grounds of public security, such a derogation must be interpreted strictly and can be scrutinized by the institutions.[48] As such, the Commission contends that "the burden is on the national authority to prove that the measure is a suitable and proportionate response to a genuine and sufficiently serious threat to public security", which Hungary failed to meet.[49]

The Commission seems to be careful in making any harsh assessment of the national security veto. While it does express its doubts as to whether or not the veto relies on genuine national security concerns, the Commission concludes that these doubts amount to an infringement of procedural obligations (the communication and standstill obligations) under the Merger Regulation. Furthermore, nowhere in the Decision does the Commission mention the FDI Screening Regulation, relying solely on the Merger Regulation and fundamental legal principles of the EU. The reason for this is that the Hungarian authorities vetoed an intra-EU investment, a transaction that is beyond the scope of the FDI Screening Regulation's focus, *i.e.* foreign direct investments into the Union from *third countries*. Thus, the Commission did not have to address investment screening as a novel tool but only had to rely on previous cases of mergers and acquisitions in which *legitimate interest* considerations were brought up by Member States, in accordance with the Merger Regulation. The Commission basically buttressed the fact that investment and the free flow of capital remain in the European general interest, the Hungarian authorities' decision failing the test for genuine security concern as a legitimate interest.

6 Further Questions Arise

The VIG/AEGON case is a great example of the challenges that the proliferation of investment screening mechanisms will bring. The temptation for states to use this instrument to advance protectionist policies is even greater considering that underlying national security considerations are more difficult to review.

In the above case, the Commission jumped at the opportunity to showcase its competence and assert its exclusive jurisdiction over state measures affecting mergers with a Union dimension. However, it is doubtful that this procedure, despite

[46] See para. (85) of the Decision.
[47] See para. (75) of the Decision.
[48] See para. (76) of the Decision.
[49] See para. (77)–(78) of the Decision.

the apparent swiftness with which the Commission acted, will be sufficient to protect businesses from unilateral state measures grounded in national security considerations. Despite the *security or public order* scope of the screening mechanisms proposed by the FDI Screening Regulation, when it suits them, Member States will not shy away from using this instrument to advance their economic interests. The specific circumstances of the VIG/AEGON case brought it to the attention of the Commission, which had the competence and the willingness to scrutinize the screening decision. The efficacy of the Commission's review of the veto, however, is highly questionable. By the time the Commission reached its conclusions (not to mention, publish its Decision), the investment was allowed with conditions to which the investor adhered. In cases where the investment does not have a Union dimension, it remains to be seen how efficient other avenues for review will prove to be.[50]

The vulnerabilities in the economy brought to the fore by the pandemic have changed states' priorities as to what they consider to be strategic areas that necessitate increased protection. As a result of this, France recently blocked a takeover of hypermarket chain Carrefour by a Canadian company,[51] and Italy blocked the takeover of seed producer Verisem by Chinese-owned Swiss company Syngenta.[52] As opposed to the case coming from Hungary, the French and Italian cases involve investors from outside the EU. In the Italian case, the Commission also pointed to investment screening as a means to avoid the takeover.[53]

While the stated purpose of FDI screening is clear, derailing it in order to advance industrial policy is all but inevitable. This will happen despite the judicial review and other forms of review that are made available. The FDI Screening Regulation prescribes that national legislation should allow for judicial recourse against screening decisions. In the literature, it was noted that recourse is necessary in order to ensure that measures based on national security grounds are proportionate, necessary, and based on genuine security concerns.[54] While Hungarian law does provide for recourse, this judicial review can only extend to matters pertaining to the respect of due process during the screening procedure.[55] It remains to be seen if this level of scrutiny is sufficient in terms of what the Regulation envisaged.

The specific circumstances of the VIG/AEGON case, most notably the fact that the Commission's ruling is obsolete from the viewpoint of the investor's evolving interests, shows that this new avenue of government intervention (i.e. national

[50] In another case stemming from Hungary, the domestic court referred questions to the CJEU for a preliminary ruling, but a ruling has yet to emerge. See Xella Magyarország, Case C-106/22, lodged in February 2022, and the opinion of AG Capeta released in March 2023. There is no ruling as of the closing of this manuscript (15.05.2023).

[51] The Wall Street Journal: France Blocks $20 Billion Takeover of Carrefour by Canada's Couche-Tard, 15 January 2021.

[52] Reuters: Italian court rules veto of Syngenta purchase of seed producer is valid, 13 April 2022.

[53] See Answer given by Mr. Wojciechowski on behalf of the European Commission to Parliamentary question E-003586/2021.

[54] De Kok (2022), p. 86.

[55] Article 6(8) of Act LVII of 2018.

security FDI screening) is able to effectively hinder any deal. In this particular case, we see that even though the Commission intervened, the procedure through which this was done proved to be lengthy. The total duration of this process, however quick it may seem in comparison with other proceedings, is difficult to reconcile with the accelerated nature of business transactions. If a Member State does not immediately implement the decision of the Commission and does not immediately withdraw its veto, the Commission would have to initiate an infringement procedure, which takes even longer and is more cumbersome. In the VIG/AEGON case, the acquisition was ultimately *allowed with conditions*, and the condition was accepted via the agreement reached between the investor and the Hungarian Government. This then begs the interesting question of whether and how the Commission would go about scrutinizing a Member State's decision of *approval with conditions*. For this, a case must emerge in which the conditions put forth are deemed unacceptable by the investor and its target.

The VIG/AEGON case also illustrates the way in which the screening procedure can be used to force the hand of an investor.[56] In line with the aphorism "time is money", delays can effectively kill a deal. Any judicial review and petitioning to the EU institutions will take time and ultimately hold many risks as to their outcome. In the above case, judicial review in front of domestic courts did not produce positive results, and it is evident that the order by the Commission to withdraw the veto had no bearing on the final agreement between the investor and the authorities—especially considering the fact that the agreement was signed on the same day as the Commission reached a decision. In this case, the investigation and subsequent decision by the Commission have arguably been a futile exercise of its competence, or may only have been useful for the investor to gain a degree of leverage. In case Hungary would have chosen to stick to its veto and challenge the Commission's decision, the entire procedure would have been prolonged even further. Lodging an infringement proceeding would also hardly have been a solution for the investor, as such proceedings tend to have a long duration in terms of management and enforcement.[57] Due to the risks posed by the potential derailment of the screening procedure in support of industrial policy objectives, investors will have to calculate their moves with this new layer of risk in mind.

7 National Security Scrutinized

In the current global environment, it is interesting to observe more generally the ways in which international organizations view the national security decisions of states. The more international treaties a country adheres to, the more potential

[56] As has also been noted in professional literature, see de Kok (2022), pp. 102–110.

[57] It is argued that exactly for this reason infringement proceedings are only adequate for addressing systemic issues of the screening mechanisms of Member States. See de Kok (2022), p. 109.

avenues for scrutinizing its decisions. The FDI Screening Regulation recalls that Member States have the "sole responsibility" for safeguarding their national security. Nevertheless, these decisions must be in line with EU law. The Commission will use the tools at its disposal to review decisions that do not meet its criteria in terms of suitability and proportionality. In the above case, the Commission had the Merger Regulation at its disposal for this purpose. Investments that do not fall under the Commission's jurisdiction under the Merger Regulation will have to go through domestic courts, which are also bound to apply EU law. It is noteworthy that the Recital of the FDI Screening Regulation provides that the Regulation's implementation "should comply with the relevant requirements for the imposition of restrictive measures on grounds of security and public order in the WTO agreements [. . .]."[58] It will be interesting to see if recent developments at the WTO will influence how screening decisions will be scrutinized at the level of EU institutions. As it happens, the Commission does not shy away from invoking WTO law when it serves its commercial policy interests.[59]

Regardless of the rules it will choose to invoke, Member States' attitude towards the Commission's decisions may ultimately prove fatal for some transactions, as discussed previously, especially if the domestic authorities do not see eye-to-eye with the Commission. While EU law provides for legal remedies, their effectiveness must also be evaluated in terms of the needs of the business environment. The effects of unilateral state action are swift, and can decisively interfere with the business of even the most well-oiled corporation. Prohibiting an investment can have a number of consequences, and disgruntled investors may ultimately decide that these avenues for reviewing screening decisions are not particularly effective, and instead seek compensation for the losses they suffered. One such avenue for foreign investors is investor-state dispute settlement (ISDS), a dispute resolution mechanism established in essence for the protection of FDI in the face of unreasonable government intervention.

8 From Screening to Arbitration

While it is expected of governments to act in good faith, decisions that are grounded on national security considerations will leave many questions unanswered. The confidential nature of such decisions, their rootedness in political considerations, and their immediate effects on investments are all part of a recipe for much discontent. The limited effectiveness of judicial remedies and EU remedies against national security screening decisions—as argued above—will result in dissatisfied

[58]FDI Screening Regulation, Recital para. (35).

[59]This happened previously, when the Court of Justice of the European Union relied on WTO law, without opening up EU institutions to scrutiny under WTO law, in what was called "confined invokability". For an excellent commentary on the case, see Nagy Cs (2021).

foreign investors looking for ways to recover their losses. One of the best venues for obtaining compensation is international investment arbitration.

There are several limitations to accessing this dispute resolution mechanism,[60] but if an investor is able to bring such a claim on the basis of the applicable international investment agreement (IIA), it will surely want to consider it, especially in view of the *full compensation* it may obtain. Considering the particular context that prompted the proliferation of screening mechanisms—as sketched out in the introductory section of this paper—the IIAs entered into with China, will surely be of interest.[61] Sensitive cases of investment will likely face scrutiny no matter where they come from, as states reassess the importance of certain economic sectors, and economic players, in line with their new strategic priorities.[62]

When considering lodging an arbitration, the investor will have to check for a number of conditions to ensure that its case is arbitrable. First, it will want to check whether its case qualifies for protection under the applicable IIA, making sure that it will be possible to establish jurisdiction. Second, the investor will want to make sure that it is able to reasonably argue that the loss it suffered is connected to the measure adopted by the host state. Third, the investor will have to evaluate whether or not the measure through which the state interfered with the investment is rooted in a genuine national security concern and is necessary for achieving its stated public policy objective, and make a solid argument that it is indeed a disguised restriction, a discriminatory measure, aimed against it. This third part ties into the important matter of whether the applicable IIA includes carve-outs for adopting such measures, or if they have a so-called non-precluded measures (NPM) clause. Not all IIAs contain such a clause, but IIAs which do have an NPM clause, depending on its wording and applicability—i.e. depending on the so-called *nexus requirement* and whether or not it is a *self-judging clause*—may hinder the investor from seeking compensation pursuant to a national security screening measure by which it is affected.

As also noted by Gáspár-Szilágyi, arbitral tribunals are called upon to interpret IIAs in accordance with Article 31 of the Vienna Convention on the Law of Treaties. This means that the text of the treaties will continue to be of the utmost importance, and clauses providing exceptions based on essential security interests will be scrutinized accordingly. He also notes the risks associated with such interpretation, stating that "even relatively straightforward clauses will have a life of their own once interpreted by an arbitral tribunal."

---

[60] Not least of which is the fact that it is not available for intra-EU cases.

[61] An excellent and extensive analysis of all BITs between EU MS and China and some of the non-legal variables regarding Chinese investment in the EU can be found in Gáspár-Szilágyi (2023).

[62] See, for example, the mentioned cases coming from France and Italy. It has also rightly been observed, that the number of Chinese investors that have been affected by the recent proliferation of national security investment screening mechanisms has been relatively low in the EU. See Chaisse (2022).

Furthermore, it is worth mentioning that investment screening is essentially an *ex ante* operation. Consequently, the *attempt to invest*, blocked by state authorities on grounds of national security, may not enjoy the protection of the *average* IIA. However, there are IIAs that grant protection to investments in the pre-establishment phase, on the basis of national treatment, as well as the most-favored-nation treatment. There may also be cases in which an existing FDI is precluded from obtaining further investment on grounds of national security, which ultimately leads to massive losses, prompting the investor to seek compensation for its loss. Some ISMs also provide for *ex post* screening, in which case the investment is already established, but for some reason (*i.e.* spreading its economic activities into covered areas) comes within the purview of the screening mechanism. This is in line with the definition provided in Article 2(3) of the FDI Screening Regulation, according to which screening "means a procedure allowing to assess, investigate, authorize, condition, *prohibit* or *unwind* foreign direct investments" [emphasis added]. In such cases, the host state will have to make sure that its measure resulting in differential treatment, or *the treatment less favorable*, is rooted in genuine national security concerns. The likelihood of claims arising out of measures adopted pursuant to *ex post* screening is evidently higher.

In a nutshell, these are some of the most important considerations regarding the potential for investment treaty protection in cases where national security screening mechanisms may interfere with investors' interests.[63] We will likely see new cases stemming from the use of investment screening, and the wider conflict that is unfolding.[64] For the (potentially) many cases where treaty protection is unavailable to the investor, they will have to turn to other remedies. With the increasing presence of politics in the world of business, it would not be a surprise to see more instances where investors turn to their home states and seek diplomatic protection of their interests.

9 Concluding Remarks

The increase in global economic integration solved many problems but also brought new challenges to light. What is different this time in solving collective action challenges is that the existing international routes are ignored and new, domestic regulation is called upon to answer to these challenges. National security investment screening is part of the legislative measures adopted in Western countries, essentially unilateral, but concerted, that seem to put government decisions on a collision course

[63] There are several new papers addressing this topic extensively. It is also worth exploring a comprehensive research paper published by UNCTAD: The Protection of National Security in IIAs, UNCTAD, New York and Geneva, 2009.

[64] A notable case is the one brought by Huawei against Sweden. See Huawei v Sweden, ICSID Case No. ARB/22/2. See also Du (2022).

with prior international engagements. The word *protectionism* is used frequently regarding the new wave of legislation adopted, as shown in the introductory section. It is not an incorrect term, as some of the measures appear as if the expectations of the most hardline *economic nationalists* have finally been answered.

The US has chosen to frame its response to these challenges outside of the existing international rules system, in a series of domestic regulations. Distrust of the treaties it previously championed has been brewing for some time, and we are now witnessing the results of it. This is something that at least one author predicted years ago: "if WTO or NAFTA panels were to rule against the United States in a series of high-profile cases, it might cause the United States to abandon its support for binding third-party dispute settlement in trade and investment disputes, especially if there was a strong reaction from the US Congress."[65]

We can expect a number of other regulatory measures in addition to the ones briefly mentioned in the introductory section. As the screening of FDI is starting to take shape in Western countries, there is increased talk of outbound investment screening, for example.[66] It is clear that the regulation is aimed at de-risking economic relations. The regulation is pointed mainly at China, in an attempt to stymie its ability to acquire high technology. But these regulations will also have negative effects on companies that are exposed to collaboration with China. It remains to be seen whether these regulatory measures in the West will help de-escalate the situation and possibly bring the parties to the table to devise new agreements between the rivals. The competition with China is now conducted in a transparent manner (prompting references to *Cold War II*) which may ultimately be beneficial in avoiding a military confrontation. Whether or not it will nudge China in a direction where it makes progress on expectations now made even clearer (such as reciprocity in market access), remains to be seen.

References

Answer given by Mr Wojciechowski on behalf of the European Commission to Parliamentary question E-003586/2021. https://www.europarl.europa.eu/doceo/document/E-9-2021-003586-ASW_EN.html

Benson E, Ghiretti F, Elizalde D (2023) Transatlantic approaches to outbound investment screening. Center for Strategic & International Studies. https://www.csis.org/analysis/transatlantic-approaches-outbound-investment-screening

Chaisse J (2022) FDI screening: CFIUS is the benchmark, the EU's is toothless (for now). FDI Intelligence https://www.fdiintelligence.com/content/opinion/fdi-screening-cfius-is-the-benchmark-the-eus-is-toothless-for-now-81790

de Kok J (2022) Legal remedies against investment screening decisions. In: De Jong BJ, Looijestijn-Clearie A, Tans SJ, Veenbrink JM (eds) The rise of public security interests in corporate mergers and acquisitions. Wolf Legal Publisher, Nijmegen, pp 85–111

[65] Murphy (2004), pp. 358–359.

[66] See Benson et al. (2023).

Du M (2022) Huawei strikes Back: challenging national security decisions before investment arbitral tribunals. Emory Int Law Rev 37(1):1–54

European Commission, Joint Communication to the European Parliament, the European Council, and the Council: EU-China – A strategic outlook. JOIN(2019) 5 final, Strasbourg, 12.03.2019. https://eur-lex.europa.eu/legal-content/EN/TXT/?uri=CELEX%3A52019JC0005

European Commission, DG Competition, Case M.10102 – VIG / AEGON CEE, Decision, Brussels, 12.08.2021, C(2021) 6077 final, https://ec.europa.eu/competition/mergers/cases1/202209/M_10102_8196601_401_3.pdf

European Commission Press Release, 21 February 2022, Brussels, "Mergers: Commission finds that Hungary's veto over the acquisition of AEGON's Hungarian subsidiaries by VIG breached Article 21 of the EU Merger Regulation" https://ec.europa.eu/commission/presscorner/detail/en/ip_22_1258

European Parliament: EU strategic autonomy 2013–2023 – From concept to capacity – July 2022, authored by Mario Damen at the European Parliamentary Research Service https://www.europarl.europa.eu/RegData/etudes/BRIE/2022/733589/EPRS_BRI(2022)733589_EN.pdf

Financial Times: Year in a word: Decoupling, 30 December 2022. https://www.ft.com/content/886ed405-37b3-404c-83c7-31d59abb8fec

Gáspár-Szilágyi Sz (2023) When the dragon comes home to roost. Chinese Investments in the EU, National Security, and Investor-State Arbitration (in press at the Journal of International Dispute Settlement)

Hungarian FDI veto lifted after pressure from EU Commission – all's well that ends well or dangerous precedent? 14.07.2022. https://www.jdsupra.com/legalnews/hungarian-fdi-veto-lifted-after-3725622/

Implementation of Additional Export Controls: Certain Advanced Computing and Semiconductor Manufacturing Items; Supercomputer and Semiconductor End Use; Entity List Modification. https://www.federalregister.gov/documents/2022/10/13/2022-21658/implementation-of-additional-export-controls-certain-advanced-computing-and-semiconductor

Jacobs J (2019) Tiptoeing the line between National Security and protectionism: a comparative approach to foreign direct investment screening in the United States and European Union. Int J Leg Inf 47(2):105–117

Koutrakos P (2016) Public security exceptions and EU free movement law. In: Koutrakos P, Shuibhne NN, Syrpis P (eds) Exceptions from EU free movement law. Hart Publishing, pp 190–217

Mergers: Commission finds that Hungary's veto over the acquisition of AEGON's Hungarian subsidiaries by VIG breached Article 21 of the EU Merger Regulation, Press release, 21 February 2022. https://ec.europa.eu/commission/presscorner/detail/en/IP_22_1258

Murphy JF (2004) The United States and the rule of law in international affairs. Cambridge University Press, New York

Nagy Cs I (2021) Case C66/18. Am J Int Law 115(4):700–706

National Security Strategy, October 2022. https://www.whitehouse.gov/wp-content/uploads/2022/11/8-November-Combined-PDF-for-Upload.pdf

Nettesheim M (2020) Screening for what threat: preserving "public order and security", securing reciprocity in international trade, or supporting certain social, environmental, or industrial policies? In: Hindelang S, Moberg A (eds) YSEC yearbook of socio-economic constitutions 2020. Springer, Cham, pp 481–504

Report from the Commission to the European Parliament and the Council, First Annual Report on the screening of foreign direct investments into the Union – COM(2021) 714 final, Brussels, 23.11.2021. https://eur-lex.europa.eu/legal-content/EN/TXT/PDF/?uri=CELEX:52021DC0714

Report from the Commission to the European Parliament and the Council, Second Annual Report on the screening of foreign direct investments into the Union – COM(2022) 433 final, Brussels, 1.9.2022. https://eur-lex.europa.eu/legal-content/EN/TXT/PDF/?uri=CELEX:52022DC0433

Reuters: Italian court rules veto of Syngenta purchase of seed producer is valid, 13 April 2022., https://www.reuters.com/business/italian-court-rules-veto-chinese-purchase-seed-producer-is-valid-sources-2022-04-13/

The Wall Street Journal: France Blocks $20 Billion Takeover of Carrefour by Canada's Couche-Tard, 15 January 2021. https://www.wsj.com/articles/france-blocks-20-billion-takeover-of-carrefour-by-canadas-couche-tard-11610738284

Thym D (2016) The constitutional dimension of public policy justifications. In: Koutrakos P, Shuibhne NN, Syrpis P (eds) . Exceptions from EU free movement law, Hart Publishing, pp 170–189

UNCTAD: The Protection of National Security in IIAs, UNCTAD, New York and Geneva, 2009. https://unctad.org/system/files/official-document/diaeia20085_en.pdf

United States Trade Representative (USTR): Findings of the Investigation of China's acts, policies, and practices related to technology transfer, intellectual property, and innovation under Section 301 of the Trade Act of 1974, published 22 March 2018

Vienna Insurance Group and Hungary reach an agreement on the outlines of a cooperation and the further procedure regarding the Hungarian insurance companies AEGON and UNION, 22.12.2021. https://www.vig.com/en/investor-relations/ir-newsinside-information/detail/vienna-insurance-group-and-hungary-reach-an-agreement-on-the-outlines-of-a-cooperation-and-the-further-procedure-regarding-the-hungarian-insurance-companies-aegon-and-union.html

Vig Z (2020) The regulation of screening of foreign direct investments in the European Union. Pro Futuro 10(4):9–24

Wernicke SF (2020) Investment screening: the return of protectionism? A business perspective. In: Hindelang S, Moberg A (eds) YSEC yearbook of socio-economic constitutions 2020. Springer, Cham, pp 29–41

Toward a Multilevel System of Investment Control Oriented to Crisis Management: Italian Golden Power in the Framework of the EU FDI Screening Mechanism

Sara Pugliese

Contents

Abstract This chapter analyses the 'osmotic' relationship between the parallel evolution of the Italian regulation on special powers and of the EU mechanism on FDI screening to verify the effectiveness of a multilevel system to protect national and EU security. It emerges that—moving on from the 'golden shares', aimed to maintain shares in privatized undertakings—the regulation on golden powers in Italy has assumed an increasingly strategic dimension, until attaining, in line with Regulation 2019/452, a crisis prevention and management function. This trend was accentuated during the Covid-19 emergency, when, to safeguard Italy's ownership of undertakings, the Italian Government significantly strengthened its golden power rules, broadening their range of application to all EU and non-EU investments aiming to gain control over domestic strategic undertakings. In this light, the new golden power rules may be said to work simultaneously with other instruments, such as the 'Patrimonio Rilancio', which supports the 'national champions' or the nationalization of strategic undertakings (as Alitalia). The EU is also coupling FDI screening and direct intervention in the economy, which is increasing its direct

S. Pugliese (✉)
"Parthenope" University Law Department, Naples, Italy
e-mail: sara.pugliese@uniparthenope.it

J. H. Pohl et al. (eds.), *National Security and Investment Controls*,
Springer Studies in Law & Geoeconomics (2024) 3: 231–262,
https://doi.org/10.1007/17280_2024_28, Published online: 21 February 2024

purchase and production role, especially regarding goods essential for emergency response, such as medical countermeasures or semiconductors. This trend appears to have strengthened after Russia's aggression on Ukraine, when blending control over foreign operations and direct public intervention in the economy appears as an effective means of crisis preparedness and management at the EU and Italian levels, one that can assure not only economic stability but also the security and welfare of citizens.

1 Introduction

In the process of liberalization and consequent privatization driven by internal market regulation, since 1994 Italy was one of the first countries to equip itself with a system to exercise special powers over national strategic undertakings. Although it was conceived as an instrument to preserve the government's role in the national economy,[1] the special powers served indirectly as mechanisms to control Foreign Direct Investments (FDI) that put national strategic interests at risk. This system evolved considerably over time, not only due to the influence of European Court of Justice (ECJ) case law[2] but also because it was necessary to include an increasing number of policy goals (national security and protecting the public interest, keeping employment levels up, maintaining the availability and accessibility of goods and services of national interest, and controlling prices and tariffs).[3]

Following the example of Italy and other Member States (MS), in recent years, the European Union (EU) has also built a regulatory framework aimed at strengthening control over FDI in the internal market to protect national and common strategic interests.

In light of the Covid-19 pandemic and the Russian aggression against Ukraine, the need to protect domestic undertakings weakened by the crisis and to assure the security of supply of goods necessary to face emergencies led the EU and the MS, especially Italy, to reform FDI screening mechanisms and seek new ways of monitoring foreign operations.

This chapter examines the evolution of Italian special power regulation, Italian government reforms in light of the recent crises, and their influence on establishing an EU system of control over foreign direct investment and other transactions (FDI). Its ultimate aim is to assess the effectiveness of this system in promptly identifying

[1] See Camera dei Deputati (2005), p. 1 ff.

[2] See, in greater detail, Sect. 2 below.

[3] For an overview of the Italian system, see D'Alberti (2019), p. 83 ff.; Clarich (2019), p. 115 ff.; Napolitano (2019), p. 121 ff.

and countering risks to national and EU strategic interests without disincentivizing foreign investors to enter the domestic and EU internal markets.

2 Italian Golden Shares: Safeguarding General Interests After Privatization

During the 1970s, based on the rules aiming to guarantee the right of establishment,[4] and the freedom to provide services[5] under the 1957 Treaty Establishing the European Economic Community,[6] the European Economic Community (EEC) began liberalizing services. The intent was to ensure foreign service providers could access MS service markets in compliance with the principles of national treatment and non-discrimination.[7] In States such as France, Italy, the United

---

[4]Article 53 of the Treaty Establishing the European Economic Community (TEEC): 'Member States shall not introduce any new restrictions on the right of establishment in their territories of nationals of other Member States, save as otherwise provided in this Treaty'.

[5]Articles 59 TEEC: 'Restrictions on freedom to provide services within the Community shall be progressively abolished during the transitional period in respect of nationals of Member States who are established in a State of the Community other than that of the person for whom the services are intended'.

[6]Treaty Establishing the European Economic Community (TEEC), signed in Rome on 25 March 1957, which entered into force on 1 January 1958.

[7]See, for example, in the financial service sector, First Council Directive 77/780/EEC of 12 December 1977 on the coordination of the laws, regulations and administrative provisions relating to the taking up and pursuit of the business of credit institution, *OJ* L 322, 17.12.1977, p. 30 ff. Directive 2000/12/EC of the European Parliament and of the Council of 20 March 2000 relating to the taking up and pursuit of the business of credit institutions, *OJ* L 126, 26.05. 2000, p. 1 ff. Directive 2006/123/EC of the European Parliament and of the Council of 12 December 2006 on services in the internal market, *OJ* L 376, 27.12.2006, p. 36 ff. Directive 2013/36/EU of the European Parliament and of the Council of 26 June 2013 on access to the activity of credit institutions and the prudential supervision of credit institutions and investment firms, *OJ* L 176, 27.06.2013, p. 338 ff., and its amendments and additions. In the postal service sector, Directive 2002/39/EC of the European Parliament and of the Council of 10 June 2002 amending Directive 97/67/EC with regard to the further opening to competition of Community postal services, *OJ* L 176, 5.07.2002, p. 21 ff. Directive 2008/6/EC of the European Parliament and of the Council of 20 February 2008 amending Directive 97/67/EC with regard to the full accomplishment of the internal market of Community postal services, *OJ* L 52, 27.02.2008, p. 3 ff. In the telecommunication service sector, Commission Directive 88/301/EEC of 16 May 1988 on competition in the markets in telecommunications terminal equipment, *OJ* L 131, 27.05.1988, p. 73 ff. Council Directive of 28 June 1990 on the establishment of the internal market for telecommunications services through the implementation of open network provision, *OJ* L 192, 24.07.1990, p. 1 ff. Directive 2002/21/EC of the European Parliament and of the Council of 7 March 2002 on a common regulatory framework for electronic communications networks and services, *OJ* L 108, 24.04.2002, p. 33 ff. In the energy sector, Directive 96/92/EC of the European Parliament and of the Council of 19 December 1996 concerning common rules for the internal market in electricity, *OJ* L 27, 30 .01.1997, p. 20 ff. Directive 2003/54/EC of the European Parliament and of the Council of 26 June 2003 concerning common rules for the internal market in electricity and

Kingdom, and Belgium, where services were monopolized by State-Owned Enterprises (SOEs) and enterprises in which the State holds a certain number of shares, these rules triggered a privatization process. Nevertheless, to many MS availed themselves of "golden shares"[8] and special powers, allowing governments to maintain control over privatized undertakings and strategic assets.[9]

In Italy, during the 1990s several general and sectoral golden share systems were introduced that often faced scrutiny by the European Commission and by the ECJ. As far as the sectoral rules were concerned, they were subject to infringement procedures by the Commission with the judges of the ECJ affirming their incompatibility with the right of establishment and free movement of capitals.[10] As for the

repealing Directive 96/92/EC, *OJ* L 176, 15.07.2003, p. 37 ff. Directive 2009/72/EC of the European Parliament and of the Council of 13 July 2009 concerning common rules for the internal market in electricity and repealing Directive 2003/54/EC, *OJ* L 211, 14.08. 2009, p. 55 ff. For the railway transport sector, see Council Directive 91/440/EEC of 29 July 1991 on the development of the Community's railways, *OJ* L 237, 24.08.1991, p. 25 ff. Directive 2001/12/EC of the European Parliament and of the Council of 26 February 2001 amending Council Directive 91/440/EEC on the development of the Community's railways, *OJ* L 237, 24.08.1991, p. 25 ff. These regulations are based on the principles of 'Home State control' and 'mutual recognition': service providers authorized in a Member State were allowed to operate in all the internal markets, despite the host MS' opposition for reasons of national interest. These principles were generalized by Directive 2006/123/EC of the European Parliament and of the Council of 12 December 2006 on services in the internal market (the so-called *Bolkestein* Directive), *OJ* L 376, 27.12.2006, p. 36 ff.

[8] A golden share is a type of share that gives its shareholder the power to veto changes to a company's charter. When attributed to a private investor, one golden share should assure control of at least 51% of voting rights. When it is attributed to the Government, it assures special powers that are not proportionate to the share value in terms of profit-sharing rights, equity-participation rights or voting right. The privatization of the British Airport Authority (BAA) is a classic example. The BAA was established by the 1965 Airports Authority Act as a public undertaking aiming to manage some British international airports, such as Heathrow, Stansted, and Gatwick. When it was privatized under the 1986 Airport Act, the Secretary of State was granted the power to adapt the statute of the company that, in 1997, would take over airport management, namely BBA plc. When the company was floated on the London Stock Exchange, a symbolic one-pound share was reserved to the Secretary of State for Transport. Nevertheless, this allowed neither profit sharing rights nor equity participation rights, but subjected numerous decisions concerning airport management (such as transfer or selling) to the Secretary of State's formal consent.

[9] On the possibility to restrict free movement of services, right of establishment, and free movement of capitals, on the grounds of public policy, public security or public health as long as in compliance with the principle of proportionality, see judgement of 14 December 1995, Joined cases C-163/94, C-165/94 and C-250/94, *Criminal proceedings against Lucas Emilio Sanz de Lera, Raimundo Díaz Jiménez and Figen Kapanoglu*, point 23 ff. See also European Commission, *Communication on Certain Legal Aspects Concerning Intra-Eu Investment* (97/C 220/06), C 220, 19 July 1997, p. 15 ff., p. 16.

[10] See judgement of 23 May 2000, case C-58/99, *Commission v. Italian Republic*, point 17 ff., where, according to the Opinion of the Advocate General (AG) J. Mischo, the ECJ considered the Decree Law No 332 of 31 May 1994, converted, after amendment, into Law No 474 of 30 July 1994, providing for acceleration of the procedures for the sale of shareholdings held by the State and public bodies in joint stock companies, and the decrees concerning the "special powers" laid down in the case of the privatisation of ENI SpA and Telecom Italia SpA, incompatible with the Articles 43 TEC concerning the right of establishment, 49 TEC concerning the free movement of services,

general rules, according to the Law Decree n. 332/1994[11] (as modified by Law 481/1995 concerning provisions on the competition and regulation of public services[12]), the President of the Council of Ministers established that some undertakings controlled by the government should, even after privatization, be submitted to special government powers. They consisted of: (a) the authority to prevent private investors from holding important shares or signing agreements and pacts[13] concerning voting rights; (b) authority to veto important strategic decisions (to dissolve the company, transfer the undertaking, authorize mergers, demergers, transfer the company headquarters abroad, or change the corporate purposes); (c) authority to appoint managers. These special powers were not proportional to the shares held by the government, but they were established in the company statute before the sale of the controlling shares. From this point of view, they represented a form of *ex-ante* control of undertakings being privatized since they were reserved to the Government at the moment of undertaking cession independently of any substantial risk to the general interest of the nation, even if the prerogatives they concede to the Government are concretely exercised only afterwards, when necessary (*ex-post*).

Consequently, the Government was left with ample discretion concerning their establishment. To reduce government discretion, Law 488/1999[14] specified that establishing special powers had to be justified by essential reasons of general

and Article 56 TEC concerning free movement of capitals; judgement of 2 June 2005, C-174/04, *Commission v. Italian Republic*, where, according to the Opinion of the AG J. Kokott of 3 March 2005, the ECJ established that the Decree-Law No 192 of 25 May 2001, converted into Law No 301, entitled 'Urgent provisions to ensure the liberalisation and privatisation of specific public service sectors' of 20 July 2001, which provides for the automatic suspension of voting rights attaching to holdings in excess of 2% of the capital of undertakings operating in the electricity and gas sectors, where those holdings are acquired by public undertakings not quoted on regulated financial markets and enjoying a dominant position in their own domestic markets, the Italian Republic has failed to fulfil its obligations under Article 56 TEC. Finally, see judgement of 6 December 2007, joint cases C-463/04 and 464/04, *Federconsumatori and Others (C-463/04) and Associazione Azionariato Diffuso dell'AEM SpA and Others (C-464/04) v Comune di Milano*, where, according to the Opinion of M. Poiares Maduro of 7 September 2006, the ECJ established that Article 56 TEC must be interpreted as precluding a national provision, such as Article 2449 of the Italian Civil Code, under which the articles of association of a company limited by shares may confer on the State or a public body with a shareholding in that company the power to appoint directly one or more directors which, on its own or which grants that State or public body the right to participate in the election on the basis of lists of the directors it has not appointed directly, is such as to enable that State or public body to obtain a power of control which is disproportionate to its shareholding in that company.

[11]Law Decree 332, 31.05.1994 (*G.U.* n. 126, 1.06.1994), converted into Law 474, 30.07.1994 (*G. U.* n. 177, 30.07.1994), to accelerate the elimination of State participation in the ownership of joint stock companies.

[12]*GU* n. 270 del 18.11.1995.

[13]According to the Article 2341 bis of the Italian Civil Code, para-social pacts are agreements stipulated between shareholders outside of the statute.

[14]Law 488, 23.12.1999 on the annual and pluriannual budget (*G.U.* n. 302, 27.12.1999), Article 66, para 3.

interest, especially public order, national security, and defence. Special powers must be suitable and proportionate to the protection of these interests, also in terms of time limits. They should respect the principles of the domestic and European legal order, especially the non-discrimination principle, and comply with the objectives of privatization and the freedom of competition. While Law 350/2003[15] restricted resort to special powers to the State's vital interests, the 2004 Decree of the President of the Council of Ministers[16] further limited their use by specifying that they could be exercised in the event of severe and present danger to the minimum supply of energy resources and goods essential to the public as a whole, in circumstances affecting the continuity of public services, national defence, the protection of public policy and national security, and during health emergencies. Nevertheless, as the Government could decide rather autonomously when risks to the general interest, public order, public policy, national security and defence occur, these criteria did not remove all the uncertainties regarding application and exercise of special powers.

The ECJ case law[17] have already declared—with only one exception[18]—the incompatibility of special powers with Article 56 TEC on free movement of capitals. However, concerning specifically the Italian regulation, in its 2009 European

[15] Law 350, 24.12.2003 on the annual and pluriannual budget (*G.U.* n. 299, 27.12. 2003), Article 4, paras 227 ff.

[16] Decree of the President of the Council of Ministers of 10.06.2004 (*G.U.* n. 139, 16.06.2004).

[17] See Judgment C-367/98 of 4 June 2002, *Commission of the European Communities v. Portuguese Republic*, where, against the position of Advocate General R. H. Colomer, the Court of Justice established that the restrictions on the acquisition of shares based on the nationality of the investors concerned constituted an infringement of Article 56 EC Treaty; 4 June 2002, C-483/99, *Commission of the European Communities v. French Republic*, where, against the position of Advocate General Colomer, the Court of Justice established that Decree No 93-1298 of 13 December 1993 vesting in the State a 'golden share' in Société Nationale Elf-Aquitaine constituted an infringement of Article 56 EC Treaty. The Court arrived at similar conclusions in Judgment C-98/01 of 13 May 2003, *Commission of the European Communities v. United Kingdom*; 13 May 2003, C-463/00, *Commission of the European Communities v. Kingdom of Spain;* 4 March 2005, *Commission of the European Communities v. Federal Republic of Germany* (the so-called "Volkswagen"); 28 September 2006, C-282/04, *Commission of the European Communities v. Kingdom of the Netherlands.* For an analysis, see Fleischer (2003), p. 493 ff.; De Vido (2007), p. 861 ff.; Werlauff (2009), p. 101 ff.; Houet (2015); Van Bekkum (2010), p. 13 ff.; Van Bekkum (2014), p. 811 ff.; Kloosterman and van Bekkum (2008), p. 6 ff.; Papadopoulos (2022), p. 7 ff.

[18] Judgment C-503/99 of 4 June 2002, *Commission of the European Communities v. Kingdom of Belgium,* where the Court acknowledged that the legislation in question was justified by the objective of guaranteeing energy supplies in the event of a crisis, according to Article 56 TEC, providing for a ground of justification based on national security. More recently, see Judgment C-105/12 of 22 October 2013, *Staat der Nederlanden v. Essent NV*, where the Court established that the objectives of combating cross-subsidisation in the broad sense, including exchange of strategic information, in order to achieve transparency in the electricity and gas markets, and to prevent distortions of competition may, as overriding reasons in the public interest, justify restrictions on the free movement of capital caused by provisions of national law. For an analysis of golden share jurisprudence, see Carbone (2009), p. 507 ff.

Commission v. Italy judgment,[19] it found not only a violation of Article 56 TEC (free movement of capital) but also of Article 43 TEC (freedom of establishment). Regarding Article 56, the Court admitted that

> the free movement of capital, as a fundamental principle of the Treaty, may be restricted ...by overriding requirements of the general interest and which are applicable to all persons and undertakings pursuing an activity in the territory of the host Member State. Furthermore, in order to be so justified, the national legislation must be suitable for securing the objective which it pursues and must not go beyond what is necessary in order to attain it, so as to accord with the principle of proportionality.[20]

According to the Court, although the criteria established by the 2004 Decree to exercise Italian special powers represent public interests, Italy provided insufficient guarantees regarding their proportionality as they were not adequately connected to the powers attributed to the Government. As for Article 43 TEC the ECJ found that

> the Decree of 2004 contains no details of the circumstances in which the criteria for the exercise of the power of veto provided by Article 2(1)(c) of Decree-Law No 332/1994 may be applicable. Even if that power may be exercised only in situations of real serious risk or health emergencies...investors do not know, for want of any information as to the actual circumstances permitting the exercise of the power in question, when the power of veto may be applicable. In consequence, it must be considered, as the Commission argues, that the situations allowing the exercise of the power of veto are potentially numerous, undetermined and undeterminable, and that they leave the Italian authorities broad discretion.[21]

---

[19] Judgment of 26 March 2009, C-326/07, *Commission of the European Communities v. Italian Republic.* For an analysis, O'Brian (2010), p. 245 ff.; Colangelo (2009), p. 595 ff.; Papadopoulos (2021), p. 64.

[20] C-367/98, cit., point 49.

[21] C-326/07, point 66. More specifically, the Court accepted, with regard to bodies operating in the oil, telecommunications, and electricity sectors, that the object of ensuring a secure supply of such services in the case of a crisis in the territory of the Member State concerned may constitute a reason of public security and, therefore, justify the restriction of a fundamental freedom (C-463/00, *Commission v. Spain*, above footnote 15, paragraph 71). Nevertheless, the Court ruled that if the Member States remain, in essential respects, free to establish the requirements of public policy and national security as grounds for derogating from a fundamental freedom according to their domestic needs, these requirements must be interpreted strictly, so that their scope cannot be determined unilaterally with no European Community control. Thus, as the Court already stated in its judgments of 9 March 2000, C-355/98, *Commission v. Kingdom of Belgium*, para. 28; 14 March 2000, C-54/99, *Association Eglise de scientologie de Paris and Scientology International Reserves Trust v. The Prime Minister*, para. 17, and C-463/00, *Commission v. Spain*, para. 47, public policy and national security may not be invoked in the absence of a genuine and sufficiently serious threat to a fundamental interest of society. As mentioned above, the Court has applied this analysis to an opposition system within the energy sector in force in Belgium, which covered certain decisions concerning the strategic assets of national companies, notably the energy supply networks and specific management decisions relating to those companies as State intervention are only possible when there is a risk that the objectives of the energy policy might be compromised. The Court considered the Belgian system to be based on objective criteria amenable to judicial review and that the Commission had not shown that less restrictive measures could have been taken to attain the objective pursued (Case C-503/99, *Commission v. Belgium*, above, footnote 15, paragraphs 50 to 53). In the Italian case, according to the Court, the Decree of 2004 contains no details of the actual circumstances in which the power of veto may be exercised, and the criteria it lays down are not,

In conclusion, the Court acknowledged not only the violation of article 56 TEC but, as in C-58/99, also of Article 43 TEC.[22]

The ECJ case law on golden shares moves toward preventing the special powers the MSs keep for themselves from being used to disincentivize private investors, especially foreign ones, from acquiring shares in privatized undertakings, undermining the good functioning of the whole internal market.[23] As these limitations were justified only in cases of necessity, to safeguard national security and the general interest, golden shares may be considered the first FDI-restrictive instruments operating within the MS. Nevertheless, the ECJ jurisprudence appears more attentive to MS compliance with the free movement rules than the risks coming from foreign investors.[24] More specifically, as the judgment concerning Italy shows, the Court stressed the need for a balance between the general interest and government discretion when adopting measures restricting free movement, which must be underpinned by the proportionality principle. This implies applying transparent and clear, rather than indeterminate, criteria.

therefore, based on objective verifiable conditions (C-326/07, above, footnote 18, point 56 ff). See Thym (2016), p. 185 ff.

[22]On the difficulty to replicate the test method adopted in *Commission v. Italy* in other situations, Papadopoulos (2021), p. 70. Indeed, in the following judgement the ECJ returned to apply only one article to verify the compatibility of golden share systems with the Treaty. In the judgment of 17 June 2010, C-105/08, *Commission v. Portugal*, the ECJ excluded the violation of the right of establishment under Article 49 TFEU (formerly 43 TEC), affirming that it is a consequence of the violation of the free movement of capital under Article 63 TFEU (formerly 56 TEC). On the contrary, in its judgment of 8 November 2012, C-244/11, *Commission v. Greece*, the ECJ applied only Article 49 TFEU concerning the right of establishment, disregarding problems relating to the free movement of capital. See, for a more complete analysis, Gallo (2013), p. 917 ff.

[23]De Vido (2007), p. 887 ff.

[24]In reality, in the Italian golden share case, C-326/07, *Commission of the European Communities v. Italian Republic,* AG Colomer in its Opinions underlined that "(. . .) it is worth mentioning that it may be inferred from the events that it was precisely the fear of investments for the purposes of establishment that has led the Italian State to pass the legislation to which the Commission objects. Even if it is not the sole motivation, there is an underlying desire to prevent undertakings in strategic sectors from falling into the hands of financial groups of dubious solvency from outside the Community which may have objectives incompatible with the policies of the Member States" (point 50) and "However, the governments retain some leeway to hold extra-Community investors with dubious objectives in check by limiting their ability to take the actions referred to in Article 4(227)(c) of the Finance Law; in practice, the fact that the right to veto these decisions which are so fundamental to the existence of the undertaking has been dealt with under Article 43 EC means that its incompatibility with the freedom of establishment does not prevent the Member States from using the veto against major shareholders from outside the Community, for such shareholders cannot rely on the fundamental right of establishment" (point 92). Nevertheless, the ECJ did not seem to pay specific attention to this subject, concentrating itself on the impact of golden share systems on free movement rights.

3 Italian Golden Powers: From General to Strategic Interests

The need to reduce Government discretion and increase transparency and proportionality in the rules on special powers, underlined by the Court, together with the EU's intention to apply a broader conception of public interest,[25] induced the Italian Government to reform its regulation in this regard. In 2012, Law Decree n. 21/2012[26] established a new discipline of special powers specifically concerning the corporate structures in the defence and national security sectors, and activities of strategic importance in the energy, transport, and communications sectors. As the special powers no longer consist of the possession of shares by Government but only in public/administrative powers exercised by the Government, independently from any ownership instrument, they are traditionally called 'golden powers'.

The sectors where the golden powers may be applied are clearly specified in the Law Decree rather than being submitted to further decisions, as in the previous golden share regulation. Furthermore, the golden powers are not only applied to privatized undertakings but to all public and private enterprises engaged in strategic activities. According to the Decree, the Italian Government must establish for which assets and activities of strategic interest, in cases of specific defence and national security risk, it may exercise special powers.[27] The new special powers consist in

[25] See, for example, Council Directive 2008/114/EC of 8 December 2008 on the identification and designation of European critical infrastructures and the assessment of the need to improve their protection, *OJ* L 345, 23.12.2008, p. 75 ff., aiming to identify and designate of European critical infrastructures ('ECIs'), and establish a common approach to the assessment of the need to improve the protection of such infrastructures in order to contribute to the protection of people. The Directive induced the MS to focus not only on the "national champions" but also on the critical infrastructures.

[26] Law Decree 21, 15.03.2012 (*GU* n. 63, 15.03.2012). Law Decree n. 21/2012 was converted into Law n. 56, 11.05. 2012 (*G.U.* n. 111, 14.05.2012).

[27] For the procedures and activities of strategic relevance, see Decree of the President of the Council of Ministers n. 253, 30.11.2012 (*GU* n. 29, 04.02.2013) "Regolamento recante individuazione delle attivita' di rilevanza strategica per il sistema di difesa e sicurezza nazionale, a norma del decreto-legge 15 marzo 2012, n. 21, convertito in legge, con modificazioni, dalla legge 11 maggio 2012, n. 56"; Decree of the President of the Council of Ministers 129, 2.10.2013 (*GU* n. 266, 13.11.2013) "Regolamento recante modifiche al decreto del Presidente del Consiglio dei ministri 30 novembre 2012, n. 253, concernente il regolamento recante l'individuazione delle attivita' di rilevanza strategica per il sistema di difesa e sicurezza nazionale, a norma del decreto-legge 15 marzo 2012, n. 21, convertito, con modificazioni, dalla legge 11 maggio 2012, n. 5"; Presidential Decree n. 35, 19.02.2014 (*GU* n. 66, 20.03.2014) "Regolamento per l'individuazione delle procedure per l'attivazione dei poteri speciali nei settori della difesa e della sicurezza nazionale, a norma dell'articolo 1, comma 8, del decreto-legge 15 marzo 2012, n. 21"; Presidential Decree n. 35/2014 (*GU* n. 66, 20 March 2014) "Regolamento per l'individuazione delle procedure per l'attivazione dei poteri speciali nei settori della difesa e della sicurezza nazionale, a norma dell'articolo 1, comma 8, del decreto-legge 15 marzo 2012, n. 21"; Presidential Decree n. 85, 25.03.2014 (*GU* n. 129, 6.06.2014) "Regolamento per l'individuazione degli attivi di rilevanza strategica nei settori dell'energia, dei trasporti e delle comunicazioni, a norma dell'articolo

making the acquisition of shares by private national or foreign investors in undertakings developing activities of strategic relevance for defence and national security interests subject to specific conditions in order to assure supplies, information security, technological transfer, and export control.[28]

In addition to the power to oppose the acquisition of shares by any party other than the Italian State, in case the acquisition of voting rights by the other party is likely to compromise defence and national security, special powers also allow to veto, under the same conditions, decisions concerning mergers, company split-ups, transferring companies abroad, changes to corporate purpose, or dissolution. With regard to investment, the Italian Government considers, in particular, the links between the investor and third-party States that do either not respect human rights principles and the rule of law, international law and thus put the international community at risk; or have relationships with criminal and terrorist organizations. As regards decisions submitted to the power of veto and the acquisition of shares in undertakings of strategic interest for defence and national security, the undertaking that is managing the operation is subject to the notification obligation. It needs to file a complete information report about the decision, the act, or the operation to realize. Government has to exercise the veto in the following forty-five days. Should the undertaking fail to comply with the obligation to notify, it will face administrative pecuniary sanctions that could amount to the double of the operation value. Special powers should be exercised in an objective and non-discriminatory manner.

The notification obligation applies also vis-à-vis strategic decisions and acquisitions of shares to control networks and plants, goods, and relationships of strategic relevance in the energy, transport, and communications sectors. Nevertheless, whereas—in the case of defence and national security—the Italian Government merely needs to establish a sufficiently a serious threat, in the energy, transport, and communications sector there must be an exceptional situation posing an effective threat to the public interests in matters of security, the well-functioning of networks and plants, and the continuity of supply chains. In these sectors, the obligation to notify is imposed only to the non-EU investors acquiring a stable control on the undertaking.[29] Should the Government consider that the acquisition has the potential to undermine the essential State interests, it could submit it to special conditions or, in exceptional cases, oppose it.

As may be inferred from this analysis, the main differences between golden shares and the special powers system and golden powers are that the latter may be

2, comma 1, del decreto-legge 15 marzo 2012, n. 21"; Presidential Decree 86, 15.03.2014 (*GU* n. 129, 6.06.2014) Regolamento per l'individuazione delle procedure per l'attivazione dei poteri speciali nei settori dell'energia, dei trasporti e delle comunicazioni, a norma dell'articolo 2, comma 9, del decreto-legge 15 marzo 2012, n. 21"; Decree of the President of the Council of Ministers n. 108, 6.06.2014 (*GU* n. 176, 31.07.2014) "Regolamento per l'individuazione delle attivita' di rilevanza strategica per il sistema di difesa e sicurezza nazionale, a norma dell'articolo 1, comma 1, del decreto-legge 15 marzo 2012, n. 21, convertito, con modificazioni, dalla legge 11 maggio 2012, n. 56".

[28] See Koutrakos (2016), p. 191 ff.

[29] Non-EU investor is a physical or legal person without registered office or main centre of activity in any Member State of the EU or not established in any Member State.

exercised even if the State has no shares in the undertakings, and they are not established in company statutes as private powers of the public shareholder but can be exercised by the government as a public (high-administrative) power for public purposes. Consequently, they do not constitute an *ex-ante* control but are exercised directly *ex-post* when the government forecasts a serious threat to the national interest. From this perspective, golden powers seem to be totally independent of privatization and represent a form of public control over assets and activities of national strategic interest. Furthermore, golden powers may not only establish "negative" obligations (forbidding some operations) but also "positive" ones (prescribing some operations or conditions useful to ensure the national interests are protected).[30] The discretion conferred upon the government does not pertain to identifying sectors and criteria but only to assessing danger to national security and strategic interests. The logic takes its inspiration from the US system, where control over strategic undertakings does not follow privatization but aims specifically to avoid creeping operations by foreign investors.[31]

Shifting government attention from maintaining *ex-ante* decisional power over privatized undertakings in order to exercise *ex-post* State control over activities undermining national security, the golden power system instead of a "private law" logic of Governmental shareholding to maintain decisional power on the privatized undertakings aims for an "administrative law" logic of screening transactions from the national interest and security point of view. In this perspective, the golden power, promoting a more "strategic" approach, attempted to make the control of undertakings in the fields of national security and essential services more proportional and non-arbitrary. It appeared to respond better to the risks created foreign investors

[30]Bassan (2014), p. 57 ff.; D'Alberti (2019), p. 84.

[31]Control over foreign direct investments in the US is carried out by the Committee on Foreign Investment in the United States (CFIUS) after attempts of foreign investors to enter a strategic domestic undertaking, regardless of its public or private nature. The President makes the final decision. The CFIUS was established in 1975 and has been reformed several times to better specify the CFIUS/Presidential special powers and the notion of national security. The last reform of the US FDI control system was carried out under the 2018 Foreign Investment Risk Review Modernization Act (FIRRMA). Up to now, few cases of operations were submitted to the special powers. In 1990, President Bush, citing grounds of national security, ordered a Chinese government corporation, MAMCO Manufacturing, to sell a Seattle aircraft-parts manufacturer after government investigators reported the Chinese firm could use its new acquisition to gain secret U.S. aircraft engine technology and gain military secrets. In 2012, President Obama prohibited the acquisition and ownership by the Chinese RALLS Corporation of interests in four wind farm project companies in Oregon, which was considered risky for US national interests. Although the Presidential Order based on FIRRMA was generally considered a political act, not submitted to judicial review, the Obama Order against RALLS was considered illegitimate by the US Court of Appeals for the District of Columbia Circuit in *Ralls Corporation v. Committee on Foreign Investment in the United States*, No. 13-5315 (D.C. Cir. July 15, 2014). Since 2016, US Presidents have blocked several Chinese investor operations aimed at acquiring control of US semi-conductor manufacturers, such as the 2016 acquisition of Aixtron, a German-based semiconductor firm holding US assets by Chinese firm Fujian Grand Chip Investment Fund. In 2017 the acquisition of Lattice Semiconductor Corp. by Canyon Bridge Capital Partners, a Chinese investment fund was halted, and in 2018 the acquisition of semiconductor chip maker Qualcomm by Singapore-based Broadcom was blocked. For a general analysis of the US system, see Mann (2019), p. 15 ff.

(mainly sovereign wealth funds and SOE), which appeared particularly aggressive in the Italian (and entire EU) market during the financial crisis.[32] In this regard, the golden powers should be seen as complementary to other measures already in place that aimed to protect Italian strategic undertakings from hostile foreign operations. This includes the "poison pill" introduced in 2006 to oppose hostile takeovers of Special Purpose Entities[33] or the power conferred on the Cassa Depositi e Prestiti (CDP) to acquire shares in companies of significant national interest in terms of strategic activity, employment, revenue, or consequences for the Italian economic and production system.[34]

The first applications of golden power regulations concern the exercise of veto powers by the Italian Government on grounds of national defence and security in relation to the acquisition of shares in undertakings operating in the aeronautical sector—the acquisition of Avio by the General Electric Company through its controlled company Nuova Pignone Holding S.p.a.[35] and the acquisition of shares into Piaggio Aero Industries S.p.a. by Mubadala Development Company, owned by the United Arab Emirates' Government.[36]

Nevertheless, besides the need to protect national defence and security, the necessity to safeguard the technological sectors, especially those connected with communications, from foreign predatory operations grew with the growing power of emergent economies, such as China, in this sector.

More specifically, Decree n. 129/2013[37] inserted telecommunication networks, plants, and broad/ultra-broadband among the infrastructures of strategic relevance, subject to the golden powers.

---

[32] Lamandini (2016), p. 671 ff.

[33] Article 1, paras 381–384 of Law n. 266, 23.12.2005 (*GU* n. 302, 29.12.2005) on the annual and pluriannual budget. A poison pill is a defense tactic used by listed companies to deter activist investors or acquirers from building large stakes or staging a takeover without the board's consent and without paying all shareholders a premium. It consists in specifying the maximum stake a shareholder may amass and diluting the holdings of those who exceed the limit by issuing heavily discounted or free additional shares to the other shareholders. In the Italian case, it consisted of the shareholders' right to request the issue of new financial instruments with voting rights in their favor.

[34] Law Decree n. 34, 31.03.2011 (*GU* n.74 del 31.03.2011), Article 7, converted by Law n. 75, 26.05.2011 (*GU* n. 122, 27.5.2011), and the Decree of the Ministry of Economics of 3.05.2011, establishing the definition of undertakings that might be acquired by the CDP. Regarding these instruments and competition regulations, see Arnaudo (2017), p. 435 ff.

[35] See the Decree of the President of the Council of Ministers of 6.06.2013, "Esercizio dei poteri speciali per il sistema di difesa e di sicurezza nazionale in relazione alla cessione di ramo d'azienda della societa' AVIO S.p.a." (*GU* n.193 del 19-08-2013). The main Government-imposed conditions concern supply security, information security, technology transfer, control over the export of strategic activities; assuring continuity in the production and logistic activities Avio provides for the Italian Military Forces and the Italian Public Authorities; avoiding any decisions likely to reduce technological and industrial capabilities; appointing an Italian citizen to be in charge of the transfer and export of weapons, and employing Italian nationals in strategic activities.

[36] The Decree was not published. For an analysis, Comino (2014), p. 1019 ff.

[37] Presidential Decree n. 129, 2.10.2013 modifying Presidential Decree n. 253, 30.11.2012 concerning the individuation of activities of strategic relevance for national security and defence *ex* Decree 21/2012 (*GU* n. 266 13.11.2013).

Law Decree n. 148/2017[38] extended government control to intensive high-technological infrastructures.[39] As for the energy, transport, communication, and intensive high-technological sectors, if the buyer comes from a country outside the EU, the Government could bear in mind that it may be controlled by the government of a non-EU country and that it receives substantial government funding. The Decree also introduced heavy sanctions for failure to declare relevant share acquisition in the defence and national security sectors.

4 The Italian Golden Power System in the Context of the EU FDI Mechanism: Toward a Risk Prevention and Management Perspective

Given the growing fears surrounding foreign investments, particularly those operated by Sovereign Wealth Funds and SOEs,[40] and following the example of Member States and third countries,[41] the EU decided to equip itself with a FDI screening

[38] Law Decree n. 148, 1.08.2017, concerning urgent financial measures (*G.U.* n. 242, 16.10.2017) converted into Law n. 172, 4.12. 2017 (*G.U.* n. 284, 5.12. 2017). On 16 October 2017, a Decree of the President of Council of Ministers was adopted, aimed to impose specific conditions and requirements for the acquisition of Telecom shares by the French company Vivendi. These consisted in the creation of a body (*Organizzazioine di sicurezza*) to ensure the protection of essential national security and defence interests. See also the Decree of 2 November 2017, which, in the light of the changes to TIM's governance, granted Vivendi control of and access to TIM's strategic assets, making it a requirement to adopt development, investment, and maintenance plans to guarantee the continuity of the overall service, as well as the obligation to adopt technical and organizational risk management measures. In the same period, the Italian Government exercised its first power to oppose to prevent French company Altran acquiring Next Ast S.r.l., an Italian company producing software for the aerospace and defence and sectors.

[39] Article 14. They include critical and sensitive infrastructures, comprising data storage and management; financial infrastructures; critical technologies, comprising artificial intelligence, robotics, semiconductors, dual-use technologies, network security, space and nuclear technology; supply chain security in critical inputs; access to critical information, and the ability to control sensitive information.

[40] MS expressed these fears also as a justification to maintain golden share systems. See judgement of 10 November 2011, C-212/09, *Commission v. Portuguese Republic*, point 84 ZP 'the Portuguese Republic points out, inter alia, that at the present time concerns exist about certain investments made particularly by sovereign wealth funds, or investments that might be linked to terrorist organisations, in undertakings in strategic sectors, which constitute a threat of that nature in relation to energy supply. Given that a Member State is under an obligation to guarantee the security of a regular and uninterrupted supply of oil and natural gas, that State can legitimately equip itself with the means required to guarantee the fundamental interest of security of supply in the event of a crisis and it is the duty of the State concerned to ensure that adequate mechanisms are put in place which will enable it to react rapidly and effectively to guarantee that the security of that supply is not interrupted'. On the risks to national security coming from Sovereign Wealth Funds, see De Luca (2015), p. 178 ff., 180 ff.

[41] For the other MS, in addition to the Italian golden power regulation, see also the case of France, where the FDI screening mechanism is based on freedom limited by the need for prior approval by

mechanism. As a consequence, Regulation 2019/452[42] established a framework whereby the MS screen FDIs within the Union on the grounds of national security or public order; it also set up a mechanism for cooperation among the MSs and between the MS and the European Commission[43] regarding FDIs likely to affect national security or public order. It includes the possibility for the Commission to issue opinions on such investments.[44]

---

the Ministry of Economy vis-à-vis all foreign investments that affect the exercise of public authority or involve an activity that may affect public policy. See Law n. 99-1071, 16 December 1999 "Code Monétaire et Finanicer" modified by Decree n. 2005-1739, 30 December 2005, Decree n. 2012-691, 7 May 2012, Law n. 2013-100, 28 January 2013, Law n. 2013-1117, 6 December 2013, Ordinance n. 2014-158, 20 February 2014, Law n. 2016-731, 3 June 2016, Decree n. 2017-932, 10 May 2017, Decree n. 2018-1057, 29 November 2018, Law n. 2019-486, 22 May 2019. For an analysis, see Perroud (2019), p. 71 ff., b) Spain, where Royal Decree n. 664/1999 established a liberalized system for foreign investments, which had to produce only an *ex-ante* declaration except with regard to investments in national defense-related activities, which must be authorized. Other special regimes have been created through the introduction of further rules. See Navarro and Ventoso (2018), p. 182 ff., c) Germany, where, due to fear of Chinese acquisitions of domestic technology leaders and critical infrastructures, the material scope of sector-specific review, applicable to defense and certain IT security industries, was extended in 2018, and a notification obligation concerning foreign investments in critical civilian infrastructures was introduced. See the Foreign Trade and Payments Ordinance (Außenwirtschaftsverordnung – AWV) of 2 August 2013, modified by the Ordinance of 19 December 2018. Also see von Andreae (2019), p. 77 ff., c) Hungary, where the general FDI screening mechanism was established by Act no. LVII of 2018 on the Control of Foreign Investments Detrimental to the National Security Interests of Hungary (the Hungarian Act), providing for a notification obligation. Outside the EU, several States have a specific regulation on investment screening: a) Australia, where, since 1975, investments in sensitive sectors are submitted to the Foreign Investment Review Board; b) Canada, where the 1985 Investment Act submits any transactions that might threaten national security to national security review; c) China, where, despite the policy of foreign investment attraction introduced in the 1980s, the 2008 Anti-Monopoly Law introduced a national security review on acquisitions and mergers endangering national security. The 2019 New Foreign Investment Law reinforced the protection of national interests. See Carrai (2019), p. 23 ff., d) Republic of Korea where, in 2011, FDI screening was introduced when targeted companies are in possession of national core technologies classed as being of high technological and economic value in the Korean and overseas markets or bringing high growth potential to their relative industries., e) Japan, where, as of 2017, foreign acquisitions of shares and equity in all corporations belonging to selected sectors, whose number was extended in 2019, are submitted to review. f) The Russian Federation, where, as of 2017, any foreign investor acquiring 5 per cent or more of the share capital of a company without undergoing obligatory screening has its voting rights in the company suspended. g) The US, see above, footnote 27. For an overall overview, see Karl et al. (2019), p. 1 ff.

[42] Regulation (EU) 2019/452 of the European Parliament and of the Council of 19 March 2019 establishing a framework for screening foreign direct investments withing the Union, *OJ* L 79I, 21.3.2019, p. 1 ff.

[43] The cooperative mechanism was preferred to the initial European parliament proposal of establishing a European Committee on Foreign Investments. See Di Benedetto (2017), p. 572 ff.

[44] See Pettinato (2019), p. 57 ff.; Vellucci (2019), p. 123 ff.; Hindelang and Moberg (2020), p. 1427 ff.; Zwartkruis and de Jong (2020), p. 447 ff.; Verellen (2021), p. 19 ff. For the purposes of Regulation, 'foreign direct investment' means 'an investment of any kind by a foreign investor aiming to establish or to maintain lasting and direct links between the foreign investor and the entrepreneur to whom or the undertaking to which the capital is made available in order to carry on

Among the factors determining whether a FDI is likely to affect national security or public order, MS and the European Commission may consider its potential effects on critical physical and virtual infrastructures,[45] critical technologies and dual-use items,[46] supply of critical inputs,[47] access to sensitive information,[48] and the freedom and pluralism of the media.[49]

The screening mechanism is based on four tracks: (1) the creation of a domestic screening mechanism; (2) investments undergoing screening; (3) screening on investments already planned or completed; (4) screening on investments able to affect projects or programs of EU interest.[50]

The screening mechanism established by Regulation 2019/452 applies as of 11 October 2020. Imposing coordination with the other MS and the European Commission, it reduces MS autonomy in establishing their foreign investment screening mechanisms, with an indirect effect also on the attraction strategies. Nevertheless, the Commission could adopt only a non-binding opinion, and the final decision concerning FDI authorization is up to the State. Unlike the national systems, which appear more oriented to avoiding foreign predatory acquisitions of "national champions", Regulation 2019/452 is inspired more by a logic of prevention and management of risks undermining EU strategic autonomy in administrating critical infrastructures, technologies, supply chains, raw materials, and semi-finished products,[51] as well as to have a greater negotiating power vis-à-vis third countries.[52]

---

an economic activity in a Member State, including investments which enable effective participation in the management or control of a company carrying out an economic activity'. Portfolio investments should be considered excluded from this definition (see Recital 9).

[45] Article 4, §1. They include energy, transport, water, health, communications, media, data processing or storage, aerospace, defence, electoral or financial infrastructure, and sensitive facilities, as well as land and real estate crucial for the use of such infrastructure.

[46] These include artificial intelligence, robotics, semiconductors, cybersecurity, aerospace, defence, energy storage, quantum and nuclear technologies as well as nanotechnologies and biotechnologies.

[47] These include energy or raw materials, as well as food security.

[48] These include personal data, or the ability to control such information.

[49] For a detailed analysis, see Pugliese (2020a), p. 15 ff.; Pugliese (2022a), p. 215 ff. The projects and programmes of EU interest are listed in the Annex to the Regulation, modified by Commission Delegated Regulation (EU) 2020/1298 of 13 July 2020 amending the Annex to Regulation (EU) 2019/452 of the European Parliament and of the Council establishing a framework for screening foreign direct investments into the Union, *OJ* L 304, 18.9.2020, p. 1 ff., and by Commission Delegated Regulation (EU) 2021/2126 of 29 September 2021 amending the Annex to Regulation (EU) 2019/452 of the European Parliament and of the Council establishing a framework for the screening of foreign direct investments within the Union, *OJ* L 432, 3.12.2021, p. 1 ff.

[50] For further details, see Pugliese (2022a), p. 216 ff.

[51] See Regulation 2019/452, Recitals 8 "The framework for the screening of foreign direct investments and for cooperation should provide Member States and the Commission with the means to address risks to security or public order in a comprehensive manner, and to adapt to changing circumstances..." and 11 "It should be possible for Member States to assess risks to security or public order arising from significant changes to the ownership structure or key characteristics of a foreign investor".

[52] On the limits of its application by the European Commission, mainly of the monitoring system, Hillebrand Pohl (2022a), p. 1 ff.

After adopting Regulation 2019/452, the Italian golden power system was updated several times to comply with EU FDI screening mechanism's logic and to extend FDI control to the sectors indicated by the Regulation 2019/452. In line with the significant attention devoted to communication technologies in Regulation 2019/452, but also with regard to the EU Directive 2016/1148 concerning measures for a high standard level of network and information system security across the Union[53] Italy introduced two new Law Decrees.

Law Decree n. 22/2019[54] included electronic communications through 5G broadband services among activities of strategic importance for defence and national security. Specifically, contracts and agreements for purchasing goods and services relating to 5G broadband realized by non-EU investors have to be notified to allow the Government to exercise its power of veto or impose prohibitions and conditions.

Law Decree n. 105/2019,[55] establishing the "Cybersecurity national perimeter", imposed that the exercise of the special powers in the Information and Communication Technology (ICT) sector has to be preceded by the assessment of vulnerability factors, such as the risk that the transaction could undermine the integrity and security of data. The Law Decree mandated the President of the Council of Ministers to identify the goods and relationship between undertaking that are of strategic relevance in all the sectors listed in Article 4 of Regulation 2019/452 to be assessed in terms of danger to national security and public order, including risks to networks and plant security, as well as to supply continuity.

These reforms slowly led the Italian golden power system away from the objective of strictly maintaining national ownership of strategic undertakings towards that of risk prevention and management pursued at EU level through Regulation 2019/452. They thus strengthened the strategic dimension of exercising golden power. Nevertheless, mandating the Government to identify the goods and networks of strategic relevance in the sectors mentioned in Regulation 2019/452, and also to identify other sectors of strategic relevance—as the Regulation list is not exhaustive—, the reform preserved Italy's autonomy to identify the national interests, i.e., sectors where controls should be strengthened and, if necessary, special power exercised.

[53]Directive (EU) 2016/1148 of the European Parliament and of the Council of 6 July 2016 concerning measures for a high common level of security of network and information systems across the Union, *OJ* L 194, 19.7.2016, p. 1 ff.

[54]Law Decree n. 22, 25.03.2019, *GU* n. 71, 25.03.2019, concerning urgent measures to assure security, financial stability, and market integration in the event of Brexit, converted into Law 41, 20.05.2019 (*GU* n. 120, 24.05.2019).

[55]Law Decree n. 105, 21.09.2019 (*GU* n. 222, 21.09.2019), converted into Law 133, 18.11.2019 (*GU* n. 272, 20.11.2019). For an analysis, see Scarchillo (2020), p. 659 ff.

5 EU FDI Screening and Italian Golden Power During the Covid-19 Pandemic: Increasing FDI Screening During Emergencies

After the outbreak of the Covid-19 pandemic, the European Commission adopted 'Guidance to the Member States concerning foreign direct investment and free movement of capital from third countries, and the protection of Europe's strategic assets, ahead of the application of Regulation (EU) 2019/452'.[56] Underlining 'an increased risk of attempts to acquire healthcare capacities (for example for the production of medical or protective equipment) or related industries such as research establishments (for instance developing vaccines) via foreign direct investment',[57] the European Commission calls upon MS for a sort of 'early application' of the Regulation. More specifically, the European Commission clarifies that the 'threat to their security or public order', required by Regulation 2019/452 in order to exercise FDI screening, includes situations where such threats are linked to a public health emergency and that the notion of 'all relevant factors', that must be considered when determining whether a FDI may affect security or public order, also refers to risks for critical health infrastructures and the supply of critical input. Lastly, the European Commission recalls that, according to the above-mentioned case law on 'golden shares', the exception of 'public policy or public security' provided for in Article 65 TFEU[58] may justify restrictive measures to ensure the security of supply or the provision of essential public services. Consequently, they could also be adopted to safeguard public health, which the Court of Justice has recognized as an overriding reason in the general interest.[59] The European Commission underlines, in particular, that the MS could introduce restrictions on foreign investment in companies with valuations on the capital market considered well below their true or intrinsic value. This would safeguard the public interest by assessing, for instance, whether these undervalued investments might lead to over-reliance on third-country foreign investors for the provision of essential supplies or essential services.[60] In practice, the pandemic emergency justifies restrictions on foreign investments.

---

[56] COM (2020) 1981 final, 25.3.2020.

[57] COM (2020) 1981 final, p. 1. On the balance between health emergency and investor interests, see Levashova (2022), p. 109 ff.; Cristani (2022), p. 61 ff; Accaoui Lorfing (2022), p. 31 ff.

[58] According to article 65 TFEU, "the provisions of Article 63 shall be without prejudice to the right of Member States: ...(b) to take all requisite measures to prevent infringements of national law and regulations, in particular in the field of taxation and the prudential supervision of financial institutions, or to lay down procedures for the declaration of capital movements for purposes of administrative or statistical information, or to take measures which are justified on grounds of public policy or public security".

[59] C-54/99, *Église de Scientologie*, point 17; C-503/99, *Commission v Belgium*, point 47, C-463/00, *Commission v Spain*, point. 72.

[60] As an example of undertakings of essential facilities object of transactions during the health crisis, see, for example, the selling, since 2020, of several assets of Condotte d'Acqua spa that attracted attention of foreign investors, as, for example, the Australian Macquarie or the China State

In compliance with the EU Guidelines, the Italian Government adopted temporary golden power rules to be applied during the Covid-19 emergency. More specifically, Article 15 of Law Decree n. 23/2020[61] (the so-called Liquidity Decree) enabled a significant reinforcement of the golden power system. Firstly, it extended the obligation to notify to the purchase of shares in the financial, credit, and insurance sectors. Furthermore, going beyond Law Decree n. 105/2019, it extended the obligation to notify to all the sectors listed in Article 4 of Regulation 2019/452.[62] Secondly, with the specific aim of combating the Covid-19 emergency, the obligation to notify was extended to all share purchases by foreign investors relating to Italian undertakings. These obligations, in force until 31 December 2021 but being repeatedly extended afterwards,[63] should also be applied to EU investors, especially those controlled by the Public Authorities of a Member State, when they ensure the assumption of stable control over an Italian undertaking.[64] The reasoning behind this rule lies in the focus of the new golden power regulations. They are not only aimed at avoiding the acquisition of stable control over national assets by investors connected

---

Construction Engineering Corp. (CSCEC), a Chinese SOE. To avoid the loss of national ownership of principal Condotte assets, in 2021 Fincantieri, controlled by the Italian Government, acquired INSO – Sistemi per le Infrastrutture Sociali S.p.A., operating in field of health infrastructures, and its controlled SOF, operating in the field of facility management and medical equipment.

[61] Law Decree n. 23, 8.04.2020 containing urgent measures to face the Covid-19 emergency (*GU* n. 94, 8.04.2020).

[62] The risk of overlapping with other control mechanisms, e.g., antitrust or financial prudential supervision, is high. On this last issue, Lener (2020), p. 545 ff.

[63] Law Decree n. 34, 19.05.2020 (*GU* n.128, 19.05.2020) established that the special FDI screening regime concerning control over strategic assets would be in force until 31 December 2020, but Law 176, 18.12.2020 (*G.U.* n. 319, 24.12.2020) extended the period of application to 30 June 2021. More recently, Law Decree n. 56, 30.04.2021 (*G.U.* n. 103, 30.04.2021) extended application to 31 December 2021, while Law Decree n. 228, 30.12.2021 (*GU* n. 309, 30.12.2021) established a further extension until 31 December 2022. For details of the sectors of strategic relevance and related assets, see Presidential Decrees 179, 18.12.2020 and 180, 23.12.2020 (*GU* n. 322, 30.12.2020).

[64] More specifically, share acquisition in strategic undertakings by EU operators must be notified when they lead to a position of control, while third-country investor purchases must be notified when they allow voting or capital rights amounting to at least 10% with an investment of at least 1,000,000 euro. In reality, this is not the first time that Italy has exercised control over EU investments. In addition to the above-mentioned Vivendi and Altran cases, the Italian Government intervened in the mergers between *Wind Acquisition Holding Finance Spa* in *3 Italia S.p.a.* and *Wind Telecomunicazioni S.p.a.* in *H3G S.p.a.*, where the government made some recommendations, mainly to assure transparency in investments and to protect employment. Other countries too exercised special powers over investments by Italian undertakings in their countries. Of note is the *Atlantia-Abertis* case, where the Spanish Government opposed the Italian Atlantia bid to acquire Abertis Infraestructuras due to concern that the deal could put the country's most important roads under full foreign control. As a consequence, Atlantia withdrew its offer and arranged a joint acquisition with Hochtief (a German subsidiary of the Spanish company Actividades de Construccion y Servicios SA-- ACS). European Commission Decision of 6 July 2018, pursuant to Article 6(1)(b) of Council Regulation No 139/2004 and Article 57 of the Agreement on the European Economic Area Case M. 8894 – *ACS / HOCHTIEF / ATLANTIA / ABERTIS INFRAESTRUCTURAS*.

with hostile countries but also at ensuring that the appropriate levels of essential goods and services are provided essentially by national investors.[65] Nevertheless, the new regulations had the effect to strengthen the control procedures regarding foreign investments in strategic assets, employing extremely general expressions that lend themselves to very broad and discretionary interpretations, with a potentially disincentivizing effect for foreign investors to enter the Italian market.[66]

Conversion Law 40/2020[67] extended the obligation to notify to the health sector, with particular regard to the production, import, and wholesale distribution of medical, surgical, and individual protection devices, as well as to the agri-food and steel sectors to protect employment levels.

The extension of the sectors with the obligation to notify and the screening of even EU investors are symptomatic of a new approach to foreign investors on the part of the Italian Government. While Law Decree n. 21/2012 and its modifications sought to maintain government control over the relevant decisions concerning national strategic undertakings in a framework of liberalization and privatization, Law Decree n. 23/2020 and its subsequent modifications show the underlying intent to safeguard the national ownership of undertakings, especially those highly sensitive to emerging from the crisis (e.g., the financial and health sectors).[68]

From this perspective, despite not being a measure of industrial policy, the emergency golden power system appears to be complementary to other instruments adopted in the same period to strengthen State action in economics. The reference is to *Patrimonio Rilancio* established by Article 27 of Law Decree n. 34/2020 (the so-called Relaunch Decree).[69] It is an 'earmarked asset' created and managed by Cassa Depositi e Prestiti (CDP) Spa,[70] consisting of goods and titles owned by the Ministry of Economics and devolved, by Decree of the Ministry of Economics, to interventions and operations geared to kickstarting and supporting the Italian economic and production system after the Covid-19 emergency.[71] As for attribution of the 'earmarked asset', the CDP issues participating instruments in favour of the Ministry of Economics, whose returns are based on the asset's economic

---

[65] Vasques (2020), p. 124 ff., raising some doubts concerning the proportionality and effectivity of the system established by the Decree. See also Marra (2021), p. 312 ff., p. 317.

[66] Marra (2021), p. 323. Pugliese (2022a), p. 234 ff.

[67] Law 40, 5.06.2020, *G.U.* n. 143, 6.06.2020.

[68] On how golden power changed from being an exception to an ordinary economic policy measure involving all foreign investment to protect the ownership of Italian undertakings, see Rescigno and Rimini (2020), p. 528 ff.

[69] Law Decree n. 34, 19.05.2020 (*GU* n. 128, 19.5.2020), concerning urgent measures connected to the Covid-19 emergency, converted into Law n. 77, 17.07.2020 (*G.U.* n. 180, 18.07.2020).

[70] CPD is a financial institution controlled by the Ministry of Economics.

[71] "Earmarked Assets" can be devolved to undertakings with their registered office in Italy, not operating in the financial, credit, and insurance sectors, and with a revenue greater than 50,000,000 euro. They are compliant with liquidity recapitalization interventions disciplined by the Temporary Framework and its modifications, and, when necessary, they are notified to the European Commission, in accordance with article 108 TFEU.

performance.[72] When deciding how to intervene, the Ministry of Economics considers the importance of the undertaking for technological development, critical and strategic infrastructures, environmental sustainability, logistics and supply chains, employment, and the job market. Corporate restructuring could benefit undertakings which, despite temporary capital and financial imbalances, have adequate revenue perspectives. The instrument's specificity is its double public-private character: the CDP operates through instruments of private law to realize, using public resources, the public objective of avoiding the failure of Italian strategic undertakings or becoming victims of predatory activities by foreign investors.[73]

The Italian effort to strengthen public interventions in the capital of strategic undertakings is also clearly evident in the provisions concerning specific sectors being severely jeopardized by the health emergency and considered strategic for the national economy. By way of example, Article 202 of Decree 34/2020 establishes that a State-owned undertaking must provide air transport. On this basis, the Government planned to nationalize the "Alitalia" airline company to avoid a foreign incursion that would deprive Italy of its flagship carrier.[74] Other nationalizations of key businesses for the national economy have taken place outside the framework of Decree 34/2020, such as the entry of Invitalia, a State-owned development agency, into Arcelor Mittal InvestCo, which currently manages the former ILVA steel plant in Taranto,[75] and the CDP's participation in Autostrade.[76]

[72]The preferred type of "Earmarked asset" interventions are convertible bond loans, shares in capital growth, and the acquisition of shares listed on the secondary market.

[73]Minervini (2021), p. 230 ff. According to Ministry of Economics Decree n. 26 of 3 February 2021 the 'Patrimonio Rilancio' may carry out transactions in the context of the EU Temporary Framework on State Aid and operate at market conditions. In the first case, operations consist in equity investments and loans to strategic undertakings. They serve to ensure commercial continuity. In the second case, the operations are carried out in compliance with the principle of the private investor and may consist in capital restructuring operations. The 'Patrimonio Rilancio' has been operative since 2 July 2021.

[74]The company has been in serious difficulty since 2017 when control passed from the administrators of Ethiad, which held little less than half the stock, to an external administration appointed by the Government and shored up thanks to three bridging loans. Due to the suspension of flights during the pandemic, the company suffered further serious losses and risked collapse. On 11 November 2020, the Italian Ministry of the Economy created ITA, a newco devoted to buying or leasing Alitalia activities. The transfer of Alitalia assets to ITA was submitted to European Commission State aid authorization procedure. The European Commission and Italy reached an agreement on 27 May 2021.

[75]On 14 April 2021, Invitalia and Arcelor-Mittal stipulated an agreement to create a public-private partnership in the steel sector, Acciaierie d'Italia Holding (AdI). Initial public equity amounts to 38%, but this will increase to 60%. As the undertaking is facing a severe crisis, on 18 January 2024 the Italian Government has adopted the Law Decree 4/2024 (*GU* n. 14, 18.01.2024) facilitating the extraordinary administration for strategic undertakings. This measure could lead to the complete AdI nationalization.

[76]On 31 May 2021, Atlantia sold its participation in Autostrade (88%) to CDP. On 7 August 2021, Government approved the selling on the basis of the golden power rules (see above Law Decree n. 23/2020, in this paragraph).

Even if the complementarity between special power reform and the instruments to sustain strategic undertakings in difficulty represents a path toward a more 'defensive' system for screening foreign investments, it must be underlined that they were designed to be temporary and exceptional measures, strictly justified by the difficult situation caused by the Covid-19 emergency and being completely in the scope of the European Commission's State Aid Temporary Framework.

Italian Government intervention in the framework of Law Decree n. 23/2020 confirmed the intensification of golden power control[77] and its focus on new sectors particularly exposed to the risk of predatory investments after the Covid-19 emergency, especially the medical,[78] financial,[79] technology,[80]

---

[77] Secretary of State to the Presidency of the Council of Ministers, *Relazione concernente l'attività svolta sulla base dei poteri speciali sugli assetti societari nei settori della difesa e della sicurezza nazionale, nonché per le attività di rilevanza strategica nei settori dell'energia, dei trasporti e delle comunicazioni (Anno 2021)*, 30.06.2022, p. 24, remarking that, out of 496 notifications, the power to oppose had been exercised on two occasions, and the power of veto had been used once; in twenty-six cases the special powers have been exercised (eleven in the 5G sector); in one hundred and sixteen, the special powers were not used, even if in eight occasions, recommendations were made to the undertakings involved. The other notifications concerned cases where golden powers were not applicable, notifications that had been withdrawn by the proponent or else were incomplete or faulty, and the exercise of an advisory power (a sort of "early application" of the pre-notification). The EU was notified about 96 operations in accordance with Regulation 2019/452, Article 6; in thirty-seven cases, the European Commission and other MS expressed their intention to issue an opinion or comments, and in twenty-nine instances, they asked for further information, but no negative opinion was expressed. For a list of the operations notified to the EU by Italy, see *Relazione*, op. cit., p. 226 ff. Trend of increasing notifications is confirmed by the Reoprt 2022 (Secretay of State to the Presidency of the Council of Ministers, *Relazione concernente l'attività svolta dal Governo in materia di poteri speciali ("Golden powers") relativa all'anno 2022*, 13 July 2023. The veto power has been exetercited in a sole case (licenising concession for robot from ROBOX to the chinese Effort Intelligence Equipment), the opposition power three times (against an Hong Kong and two russian investors) and in eight cases some conditions were imposed.

[78] DPCM 6.7.2020 ANC Inc. (acquisition of Molmed through ANC Biologicss Italy); DPCM 3.03.2021, Pagac Iii Nemo Holding (Hk) Ltd (acquisition of shareholding and voting rights in Hefei SARI Oborgen Biopharma Co. Ltd and, indirectly, in NMS Group S.p.A). See also Sottosegretario di Stato alla Presidenza del Consiglio dei Ministri, *Relazione,* op.cit., p. 23, observing the growing involvement of the Health Ministry in golden power assessment procedures.

[79] DPCM 6.7.2020, Banca Farmafactoring S.p.A. And Banca Depositaria Italiana S.p.A., DPCM 21.05.2021, Castor S.r.l. (voluntary takeover bid on the Cerved Group).

[80] DPCM 10.03.2022 Alpi Aviation S.r.l. (acquisition by Mars (HK) lnformation Technology Co., object of a veto power).; DPCM 9.09.2021, Incorporated and Bain Capital Investors LLC (acquisition, through Watson Merger Sub Inc., of Coherent Inc. and Coherent Italia s.r.l); DPCM 23.09.2021, Moog Italiana S.r.l.; DPCM 10.12.2021, Modis Investment Bve Modis International Ag (acquisition of Akka Italia S.r.l. e Bertone Digital Mobility S.r.l), object of a request of further information by European Commission and Austria.; DPCM 11.11.2021, Applied Materials Italia S. r.l.., Applied Materials Hong Kong Limited, Zhejiang Kesheng Intelligent Equipment Company Limited, Zhejiang Jingsheng Mechanical & Electrical Co (sale of business of applied materials by Zhejiang Kesheng Intelligent Equipment Company Limited), where the Government exercised its opposing power; DPCM 7.06.2022, Robox (acquisition by Chinese Efort Intelligent Equipment of shares with the aim to realize technology transfer). On these cases, see Sabatino (2021), p. 192 ff.

cybersecurity,[81] 5g,[82] agri-food,[83] raw materials,[84] and critical semi-finished product sectors.[85] This underlines that the objective of strengthening national security and cybersecurity—already pursued before the Covid-19 emergency but subsequently more urgent[86]—was coupled with the need to safeguard the national production of some ICT products (in particular semiconductors) critical to national production chains, such as the automotive industry, and that, due to the rising demand for high consumption electronic products during the pandemic, are running out.

6 EU FDI Screening and Italian Golden Power Between Health Emergency and Russian Aggression on Ukraine: From Emergency to the Structural Regulation of Crisis Preparedness

After the acute phase of the Covid-19 emergency, the need to strengthen the protection of the EU industrial system from predatory operations not only by foreign private investors but also by foreign Governments through SOEs or subsidized undertakings became a matter of real urgency for the European Commission. With

[81] DPCM 14.7.2021 Ontario Teachers' Pension Plan Board (acquisition of RSA Security LLC); DPCM 30.06.2021, Selta S.r.l.; DPCM 18.11.2021, Digitalplatform (acquisition of Selta); DPCM 12.05.2021, Libra Holdco S.à.r.l. (acquisition of OEP 14 LP); DPCM 28.05.2021, Ruby Investment Holdings, Lp (acquisition of RSA Security Italy S.r.l.).

[82] See DPCM 25.03.2021 Linkem (purchase of hardware and software by Huawei Technologies Italia S.r.l., the ZTE Corporation,); DPCM 09.09.2021 Linkem (contract with Gemtec Technology); Vodafone Italia Spa, DPCM 20.05.2021, 21.01.2021 (Huawei software update); DPCM 30.06.2021 and 8.07.2021, Fastweb Italia Spa (buying a software compatible with 5G standalone from Huawei); DPCM 5.08.2021 Fastweb (modifying software by Huawei, ZTE, and Askey); DPCM 11.02.2022, (buying the licence from Anritsu Corporation); DPCM 24.02.2022, Wind Tre (Frame Agreement Wind Tre Italia-Zirc ZTE); DPCM 17.03.2022, Wind Tre Spa (renegotiation of contracts with an intra-EU supplier, Sirti Spa).

[83] DPCM 21.10.2021, Syngenta Crop Protection Ag and Psp Verisem Luxembourg Holdings S.a.r.l. (acquisition by Sygenta of Verisem's entire capital), where the Government exercised its powers to oppose; DPCM 14.12.2021, Mitsui & Co., Ltd. (acquisition of control over Isi Sementi S. p.a.).

[84] DPCM 24.04.2021, Montanstahl SA (acquisition of Siderval's entire capital); DPCM 13.07.2021 Taiwan Cement Corporation and Engie Eps S.A. (acquisition of shareholding in Engie EPS SA).

[85] See DPCM 26.02.2021, Zephyr German Bidco Gmb (acquisition of Flender GmbH); DPCM 31.03.2021 Shenzhen Invenland Holdings Co. Ltd (Acquisition in LPE S.p.a.); DPCM 23.11.2021, Zhejiang Jingsheng Mechanical; DPCM 8.09.2022, Asm International N.V. (specific prescriptions about the acquisition of LPA S.p.a.).

[86] Aware that the highly intensive use of new technologies during the pandemic increased the risks of cyberattacks, mainly against the Public Administration, Law Decree n. 82 of 14.06.2021 strengthened the role of the National Agency for cybersecurity and its involvement in decision-making concerning golden power in the technological sector.

its White Paper of 17 June 2020 on foreign subsidies,[87] the European Commission emphasized the need, as the text reads, to 'pursue a model of open strategic autonomy. This will mean shaping the new system of global economic governance and developing mutually beneficial bilateral relations while protecting ourselves from unfair and abusive practices'.[88] So, while continuing its efforts to strengthen relations with trade partners by stipulating bilateral agreements,[89] it also indicated instruments to protect EU strategic interests, both by reinforcing trade defence and strengthening the EU's role in ensuring the proper functioning of the strategic value chains. With regard to trade defence, the reference is principally to the Regulation (EU) 2022/2560 of the European Parliament and of the Council of 14 December 2022 on foreign subsidies distorting the internal market.[90] There is also a reference to other acts, as the Regulation on International Procurement Instrument, which allows the Commission to restrict access to the procurement procedures of MS for undertakings from countries that do not open their public procurement markets to EU undertakings or the Anti Coercition Instrument, aimed at detect and respond to economic coercitions.[91] One should also read the proposals geared toward improving the resilience of critical assets and cybersecurity according to the same logic of strengthening the security of strategic assets,[92] as well as the Proposed Directive on Corporate Sustainability Due Diligence.[93]

On the other hand, with regard to the functioning of the strategic value chains, one needs to consider the significant role that the European Commission is carving out

[87] COM (2020) 253 final, 17.06.2020.

[88] COM (2020) 253 final, p. 4. On the 'open strategic autonomy' Hillebrand Pohl (2022b), p. 1 ff., Casolari (2023), p. 323 ff.

[89] See the EU-China Comprehensive agreement concluded on 30.12.2020 and the EU-UK Trade and Cooperation agreement of 31.12.2020; the progress made during 2021 and 2022 in negotiations with Australia (see the 11th and 12th Round Reports) and Indonesia (see 13th Round Report); the re-launch of negotiations with India (See, European Commission, EU, and India's ambitious kick-start trade agenda, News Article, 17.06.2022); the conclusion of negotiations with New Zealand on 30.06.2022, with Chile on 9 December 2022, with Kenya on 19 June 2023.

[90] *OJ* L 330, 23.12.2022, p. 1 ff.

[91] Regulation (EU) 2022/1031 on the access of third-country economic operators, goods, and services to the Union's public procurement and concession markets and procedures supporting negotiations on the access of Union economic operators, goods and services to the public procurement and concession markets of third countries (International Procurement Instrument – IPI), *OJ* L 173, 30.6.2022, p. 1 ff.; Regulation 2023/2675 of the European Parliament and of the Council of 22 November 2023 on the protection of the Union and it Memeber States from economic coercion by thord countries, OJ L, 7.12.2023.

[92] COM (2020) 823, 16.12.2020, Proposal for a Directive of the European Parliament and of the Council on measures for a high common level of cybersecurity across the Union, repealing Directive (EU) 2016/1148, COM (2020) 829, 16.12.2020, Proposal for a Directive of the European Parliament and of the Council on the resilience of critical entities; COM (2023) 160, 16 March 2023, Proposal for a Regulation of the European Parliament and of the Council estabilsihing a framework for a secure and sustainable supply of critical raw naterials.

[93] COM (2022) 71 final, 23 February 2022, Proposal for a Directive of the European Parliament and of the Council on Corporate Sustainability Due Diligence and amending Directive (EU) 2019/1937.

for itself not only as a market supervisor and regulator but also, especially during the crises, as a pivotal actor in the phases of purchasing, storage, and even production of critical goods. This concerns, in particular, purchasing procedures, such as the joint procurement procedures,[94] and the setting up of industrial facilities to guarantee the proper and primary supply of raw materials and semi-finished products necessary to secure continued production in the EU industrial system, also in situations of shortage.[95] Thus, like the Italian system, the EU mechanism for reacting to crises is also based on the correspondence between the enhancement of foreign operation control and the direct intervention of public actors in the economy.[96]

In the wake of the Russian aggression on Ukraine, the need to monitor foreign operations in the internal market more closely[97] and the call for more incisive EU intervention to centralize the purchase and storage phases of energy sources in particular, have become crucial. Consequently, the Repower EU strategy,[98] establishing a common storage mechanism and mechanisms of joint procurement, also developed a new investment control mechanism: the certification for storage system operators. This procedure obliges MS to verify whether a storage system owner or operator might jeopardize the security of the energy supply or the essential security interests of the Union (or any Member State) and requires them to dispose of

[94] Joint procurement procedures were employed during the Covid-19 emergency to procure medical countermeasures on the basis of the Joint Procurement Agreement on medical countermeasures signed on 2014. They were also the basis for the stipulation of the so-called Advance Purchase Agreements with the vaccine manufacturers. Pugliese (2020b); Pugliese (2021), p. 251 ff.; Pugliese (2022b); Petti (2022), p. 1333 ff.

[95] The reference is to Article 8, §8 of Council Regulation (EU) 2022/2372 of 24 October 2022 on a framework of measures for ensuring the supply of crisis-relevant medical countermeasures in the event of a public health emergency at Union level, *OJ* L 314, 6.12.2022, p. 64 ff., allowing the Commission to provide financing for the production and/or development of crisis-relevant medical countermeasures through the so-called "EU-FAB facilities". The reference is also to the Integrated Production facilities and Open EU Foundries, designed to assure, in the event of shortage, the supply of semiconductors established by Regulation (EU) 2023/1781 of the E£uropean Parliament and of the Council of 13 September 2023 establishing a framework of measures for strenghtening Europe's semiconductor ecosystem (Chips Act) Articles 13-14. See Pugliese (2022b).

[96] The same method appears to be applied in the US. As for FDI screening, cfr. the Executive Order on Ensuring Robust Consideration of Evolving National Security Risks by the Committee on Foreign Investment in the United States, 15.09.2022. Regarding trade defence, see Executive Order n. 14005, 25.01.2021 on Ensuring the Future is Made in All of America by All of America's Workers. See Chaisse (2022), p. 8. On US Government intervention in the economy, see the *Build Back Better Framework*, the plan to fund social, environmental, health, and immigration investments. The Infrastructure Investment and Jobs Act (Public Law No: 117-58, 15.1.2021) and Inflation Reduction Act (Public Law No: 117-169, 16.08.2022) are included within the Framework.

[97] Guidance for the Member States concerning FDI from Russia and Belarus in view of the military aggression against Ukraine and the restrictive measures laid down in recent Council Regulations on sanctions C (2022) 2316, *OJ* C 151I, 6.4.2022, p. 1 ff.

[98] COM (2022) 108 final, 8.3.2022, REPowerEU: Joint European Action for more affordable, secure and sustainable energy; Regulation (EU) 2022/1032 of the European Parliament and of the Council of 29 June 2022 amending Regulations (EU) 2017/1938 and (EC) No 715/2009 with regard to gas storage, *OJ* L 173, 30.6.2022, p. 17 ff, Article 2.

their shareholding or rights. Even if this procedure is intended to control both the EU and the foreign investors, it is a way of blocking predatory operations vis-à-vis EU energy infrastructures.

Following the example of the EU Institutions, the Italian Government also decided to reinforce investment screening. Nevertheless, although the reform is included in Decree 21/2022,[99] containing urgent measures to contrast the economic and humanitarian effects of the Ukrainian crisis, golden power regulation seeks to overcome the emergency regulation and make permanent modifications to Law Decree n. 21/2012 established by the Decree 23/2020 and Law 40/2020. Indeed, differently from the modifications established by the 2020 Decrees, these modifications are not subject to a deadline. The principal changes consist in the imposition of obligation to notify the establishment of new undertakings developing activities of strategic relevance for national security and defence, the simplification of the notification procedure (principally through joint notification by the investor and the strategic undertaking involved), and the introduction of the pre-notification system rendering a preventive assessment on the applicability of golden powers to the planned operation possible. The Decree confirms the obligation to notify on EU investors assuming a controlling stake in Italian undertakings, albeit only in some specific sectors,[100] and also requires third-country investors assuming even a minority shareholding to give notice. It establishes an Assessment and Strategic Analysis Body and new regulations concerning special powers in the cybersecurity sector, extending them to cloud technology and applying the obligation to notify to the entire annual purchasing plan.[101] Lastly, it establishes a regulatory framework regarding the supply of critical raw materials, whose export outside the EU is subjected to the obligation to notify. It is up to the Government to identify the critical materials based on the national interest and the requirements of critical supply chains.[102]

Conversion Law n. 51/2022[103] brought several amendments to Law Decree n. 21/ 2022, the most important of which are the introduction of a "greenfield clause", imposing the obligation to notify on all national and foreign investors setting up undertakings on Italian territory exercising activities or holding assets of strategic

[99] Law Decree n. 21, 21.03.2022 (*GU* n. 67, 21.03.2022), Articles 24–28.

[100] The sectors in question are: communications, energy, transports, health, agri-food, and finance.

[101] See DPCM 28.09.2022 on the exercise of special powers on Tim and Vodafone annual plans.

[102] In reality, ferrous scraps are the only raw materials explicitly mentioned within the Decree. The possibility to apply investment screening mechanisms to critical materials was the object of a restrictive interpretation in Court of Justice 13 July 2023, cause 160/22, *Xella*.

[103] Law 51, 20.5.2022 (*GU* n. 117, 20.05.2022). See also DPCM n. 133, 1.08.2022 (*GU* n. 211, 9.09.2022), "Regolamento recante disciplina delle attività di coordinamento della Presidenza del Consiglio dei ministri propedeutiche all'esercizio dei poteri speciali di cui al decreto-legge 15 marzo 2012, n. 21, e successive modificazioni ed integrazioni, della pre-notifica e misure di semplificazione dei procedimenti".

importance, the extension of special powers to the operations on assets covered by public concession, and the definition of entities external to the EU.[104]

The consolidated golden power system, by submitting all foreign investments in strategic sectors under scrutiny, pursues the protection of national strategic interests by attributing veto powers to the Italian Government aimed to strictly maintain Italian ownership of strategic undertakings. If, on the one hand, it assures robust protection of Italian national security and the notification to the Commission and other countries regarding operations constituting a risk for the EU interest, it could also disincentivize all EU and non-EU investors, completely stopping the flow of foreign capitals toward the Italian system. Although a fall in foreign capital may be balanced by high public investment in sustaining national undertakings, the complete closure of the Italian economy to FDI would deprive it not only of indispensable financial, technological, and employment opportunities but also of the innovative effects that openness to FDI alone can trigger. These perils can only be avoided through use of golden power that is geared toward the principle of proportionality and transparency,[105] following the case law of the ECJ.[106] Further, it is necessary to apply a more strategic approach, based on a logic of crisis preparedness, not seeking to safeguard Italian ownership of national champions but to identify significant risks in terms of national security, public services, continuity of supply, and the protection of fundamental individual rights and freedom, as well as to adopt all the measures necessary to ensure Italian economy resilience.

7 Conclusions

The evolution of the Italian special power regulation seems to have become intertwined with the parallel process of creating an EU foreign operation screening mechanism in a sort of "osmotic" relationship, where objectives, methods, procedures, and tools have influenced each other with the intent to realize a fully integrated multilevel system to protect national and EU strategic security.

Despite adapting to EU principles and logic, Italian golden power maintains its original characteristic of focusing specifically on operations to acquire the ownership of strategic undertakings, ignoring the other risks highlighted by the European Commission in its 2020 White paper, and specifically, participation in public procurement procedures and calls to obtain EU funding. In reality, the rules the Decree 21/2022 for monitoring raw material exports represent a turning point

[104] More specifically, it has been extended to the entities that, although having the EU nationality, have their main business center and their usual residence abroad.

[105] In *Tar Lazio*, I, 13.04.2022 n. 4484, the administrative judge acknowledged the character of "high administration" of golden power decisions. As a consequence, they are the object of a judicial review in terms of their manifest illogicality.

[106] Chieppa (2022), p. 27 f.

leading toward the diversification of the targets of control, cresting a linkage between FDI screening and export control,[107] which presupposes a gradual transition from a "patrimonial" logic, of protecting ownership, to a "strategic" one, of protecting assets and value chains. This change in perspective, more evident after the launch of the European Economic Security Strategy,[108] the adoption of the proposal aimed at reforming the investment screening mechanism,[109] and the opening of a consultation to assess risks coming from outbound investments,[110] has important implications for the meaning of golden power, which should not yet be seen as an instrument of "reason of State" but as a means of directly safeguarding the citizens' needs and demands, their access to essential goods and services, the maintenance of their welfare and way of life, their resilience to severe global emergencies, their fundamental rights (especially to health, security, privacy, freedom of expression, communication, and information). In this perspective, during privatization of undertakings of general interest, golden powers could be intertwined with other instruments, as, for example, tender specifications governing the conditions to choose the buyers.[111] In Italy, this should be taken into account especially in operations of re-privatization as, for example, the ITA case.[112]

---

[107] European Commission - Press release, EU investment screening and export control rules effectively safeguard EU Security, Brussels, 2 September 2022.

[108] JOINT (2023) 20, 20.06.2023 European Commission and High Representative of The Union for Foreign Affairs and Security Policy, *Joint Communication to the European Parliament, The European Council and The Council On "European Economic Security Strategy"*.

[109] COM (2024) 23, 24.01.2024, *Proposal for a Regulation of the European Parliament and of the Council on the screening of foreign investments in the Union and repealing Regulation (EU) 2019/452 of the European Parliament and of the Council.*

[110] COM(2024) 24 final, 24.01.2024, *White Paper on Outbound Investments.*

[111] In the judgement of 27 February 2019, C-563/17, *Associação Peço a Palavra and Others v Conselho de Ministros*, referring to a case of re-privatization of an air carrier company, the ECJ, according to the Opinion of AG M. Campos Sánchez-Bordona, established that 'Article 49 TFEU must be interpreted as not precluding tender specifications governing the conditions to which a reprivatisation process of an air carrier company is subject from including: – a requirement that the purchaser of the shares subject to the reprivatisation process has the capacity to fulfil the performance of the public service obligations on that air carrier company, and – a requirement that the purchaser maintain that air carrier company's headquarters and effective management in the Member State concerned, in so far as the transfer of that company's principal place of business outside of that Member State would mean that company losing the air traffic rights conferred on it under bilateral agreements between that Member State and third countries with which that Member State has particular historical, cultural and social ties, which is for the referring court to ascertain. Article 49 TFEU must be interpreted as precluding those tender specifications from including a requirement that the purchaser of those shares ensure that the existing national hub is maintained and developed'. On the possibility, coming from this judgement, to use the tender considerations to promote Corporate Social Responsibility, see Papadopoulos (2022), p. 38 ff.

[112] Since 2022 Italian Government launched a negotiation with Lufthansa for the acquisition of a minority share in ITA. The Presidential Decree of 22 December 2022 'Procedura di dismissione della partecipazione del Ministero dell'economia e delle finanze in ITA S.p.a.' (*GU* n.1, 02-01-2023) establishes the condition that the buyer has to be an airline company and has to assure the compliance with the business plan elaborated in accord with the Government, the access into

So, in an "osmotic" cycle, the new Italian perspective constitutes a model for the EU, which is learning to match investment screening with direct intervention in the economy, but the Italian vision looks, in turn, toward a new concept of why the State has to intervene in the economy, following the EU's example: no longer to pursue the strengthening of political consensus, like the Italian welfare schemes of the sixties, but to address permanent crisis preparedness and management. As recent emergencies have shown, when economic stability is undermined by external dynamics (epidemics, wars), only State intervention, in terms of risk prevention—by controlling predatory operations—and risk correction, through the acquisition of direct production and supply functions, can correct distortions and external influences so as to allow private actors to operate in an efficient, fair, and well-functioning economic environment.

References

Accaoui Lorfing P (2022) Tools of international investment agreements and investment contracts: national security interest and force Majeure. In: Levashova Y, Accaoui Lorfing P (eds) Balancing the protection of foreign investors and states responses in the post-pandemic world. Kluwer, Alphen aan den Rijn, pp 31–60

Arnaudo L (2017) À l'économie comme à la guerre. Note su golden power, concorrenza e geo-economia. Mercato Concorrenza regole:435–450

Bassan F (2014) Dalla golden share al golden power: il cambio di paradigma europeo nell'intervento dello Stato sull'economia. IX Studi sull'integrazione europea:57–80

Camera dei Deputati, La golden share, Roma, 2005

Carbone SM (2009) Golden Shares e fondi sovrani. Diritto del commercio internazionale:503–545, 507 ff.

Carrai MA (2019) China's foreign direct investment screening and the future of global investment. In: Napolitano G (ed) Foreign direct investment screening. il Mulino, Bologna, pp 23–38

Casolari F (2023) Supranational security and national security in light of the EU strategic autonomy doctrine: the EU-member states security nexus revisited. Eur Foreign Aff Rev:323–340

Chaisse J (2022) Is the US going to screen outbound FDI? FDiIntelligence 14.10.2022

Chieppa R (2022) La nuova disciplina del golden power dopo le modifiche del decreto-legge n. 21 del 2022 e della legge di conversione 20 maggio 2022, n. 51. Federalismi: 1–28

Clarich M (2019) La disciplina del golden power in Italia e l'estensione dei poteri speciali alle reti 5G. In: Napolitano G (ed) Foreign direct investment screening. il Mulino, Bologna, pp 115–120

Colangelo M (2009) Regole comunitarie e golden share italiana. Mercato Concorrenza Regole: 595–601

---

strategic markets, and the increasing of long-haul routes. No reference to public service obligations is contained in the decree. Taking into account the importance of the airline service in assuring logistic connections between the different Italian zones, crucial for workers and families, as well as the need to serve a role of international hub for the principal Italian airport infrastructures, the interest of service users should to take into account in the re-privatization decision. On 24 January 2024, the European Commission opened an indepth investigation into proposed acquisition at stake in ITA Airways by Luftanhsa.

Comino A (2014) Golden powers per dimenticare la golden share: le nuove forme di intervento pubblico sugli assetti societari nei settori della difesa, della sicurezza nazionale, dell'energia, dei trasporti e delle comunicazioni. Rivista Italiana di Diritto Pubblico Comunitario: 1019–1053
Cristani F (2022) How pandemics (may) affect state defenses: invoking necessity in COVID-19-related international investment arbitration cases. In: Levashova Y, Accaoui Lorfing P (eds) Balancing the protection of foreign investors and states responses in the post-pandemic world. Kluwer, Alphen aan den Rijn, pp 61–74
D'Alberti M (2019) Il golden power in Italia: norme ed equilibri. In: Napolitano G (ed) Foreign direct investment screening. il Mulino, Bologna, pp 83–90
De Luca A (2015) The EU and Member States: FDI, portfolio investments, golden powers and SWFs'. In: Bassan F (ed) Research handbook on sovereign wealth funds and international investment law. Elgar, Cheltenham, pp 178–205
De Vido S (2007) La recente giurisprudenza comunitaria in materia di golden shares: violazione delle norme sulla libera circolazione dei capitali o sul diritto di stabilimento? Diritto del commercio internazionale:861–893
Di Benedetto F (2017) Reciprocity in international trade and investment law and the establishment of a European Committee on Foreign Investment. In Diritto del Commercio Internazionale:572–602
Fleischer H (2003) Case C-367/98, Commission of the European Communities v. Portuguese Republic (Golden shares); C-483/99, Commission of the European Communities v. French Republic (Golden shares). Common Mark Law Rev:493–501
Gallo D (2013) Corte di giustizia UE, golden shares e fondi sovrani. Diritto del commercio internazionale:917–949
Hillebrand Pohl J (2022a) Open strategic autonomy and the new geoeconomics: consequences for EU trade policy. The University of Adelaide Policy Brief 18, November 2022, pp 1–8
Hillebrand Pohl J (2022b) Monitoring the impact of the EU's new foreign investment screening mechanism. The University of Adelaide Policy Brief 19, January 2023, pp 1–5
Hindelang S, Moberg A (2020) The art of casting political dissent in law: the EU's framework for the screening of foreign direct investment. Common Mark Law Rev 57:1427–1460
Houet J (2015) Les Golden Shares en droit de l'Union européenne. Editions Larcier, Brussels
Karl J et al (2019) National security-related screening mechanisms for foreign investment. An analysis of recent policy developments, UNCTAD Investment Policy Monitor: Special Issues, December 2019
Kloosterman J, Van Bekkum J (2008) Golden shares and European company law: the implications of *Volkswagen*. Eur Company Law:6–12
Koutrakos P (2016) Public security exceptions and EU free movement law. In: Koutrakos P, Shuibhne NN, Syrpis P (eds) Exceptions from EU free movement law. Hart, Oxford, pp 190–217
Lamandini M (2016) Golden share e libera circolazione dei capitali in Europa e in Italia. Giurisprudenza commerciale:671–689
Lener R (2020) Brevi note sul golden power nel settore finanziario alla luce del Decreto Liquidità. Analisi giuridica dell'economia:545–555
Levashova Y (2022) The legitimate expectations of investors under the fair and equitable treatment in times of pandemic and aftermath. In: Levashova Y, Accaoui Lorfing P (eds) Balancing the protection of foreign investors and states responses in the post-pandemic world. Kluwer, Alphen aan den Rijn, pp 109–130
Mann C (2019) The global rush toward foreign direct investment screening: lessons from the United States. In: Napolitano G (ed) Foreign direct investment screening. il Mulino, Bologna, pp 15–22
Marra G (2021) L'assetto dei poteri speciali per il controllo degli investimenti dal 1994 al d.l. liquidità n. 23/2020. Giurisprudenza Commerciale:312–323
Minervini V (2021) L'improvvisa «accelerazione» (post COVID) dell'azionariato di Stato. Il patrimonio destinato di cui all'art. 27 D.L. Rilancio. Giurisprudenza Commerciale:230–270

Napolitano G (2019) I golden powers italiani alla prova del Regolamento europeo. In: Napolitano G (ed) Foreign direct investment screening. il Mulino, Bologna, pp 121–140
Navarro E, Ventoso A (2018) Spain. Foreign Invest Regul Rev:182–194
O'Brian M (2010) Case C-326/07, Commission of European Communities v. Italian Republic, Judgement of the Court of Justice (Third Chamber) of 26 March 2009, not yet reported. Common Mark Law Rev:245–261
Papadopoulos T (2021) COVID-19 crisis and screening of foreign direct investments in EU privatised companies: Commission of the European Communities v Italy (C-326/07). Int Trade Law Regul:54–75
Papadopoulos T (2022) Privatizations of State-owned companies and justifications for restrictions on EU fundamental freedoms: past, present and future perspectives. In: Chaisse J, Górski J, Sejko D (eds) Regulation of state-controlled enterprises: an interdisciplinary and comparative examination. Springer, Berlin, Heidelberg, pp 223–270
Perroud T (2019) The screening on foreign direct investment in France. In: Napolitano G (ed) Foreign direct investment screening. il Mulino, Bologna, pp 71–76
Petti A (2022) Eu Covid-19 purchase and export mechanism: a framework for EU operational autonomy. Common Mark Law Rev:1333–1370
Pettinato C (2019) The new EU regulation on foreign direct investment screening: rational and main elements. In: Napolitano G (ed) Foreign direct investment screening. il Mulino, Bologna, pp 57–61
Pugliese S (2020a) Special Economic Zones (SEZs) in EU port infrastructures as a means of attracting foreign investment. How to manage risks to EU strategic interests? Transnational Dispute Management Journal, Special Issue "The Interaction Between International Investment Law and Special Economic Zones (SEZs)": 1–24
Pugliese S (2020b) L'efficacia del Joint Procurement Agreement dell'UE nell'emergenza COVD 19 e la sua compatibilità con il diritto OMC, SIDIBlog, 14 novembre 2020
Pugliese S (2021) Appalti di aggiudicazione congiunta nell'emergenza Co-vid-19 e sistema Omc: un esperimento regionale per una risposta globale. Quaderni di SIDI BLOG, 2020/7: 251–280
Pugliese S (2022a) The EU investment screening mechanism as a means of reacting to the COVID-19 emergency: the example of Italy. In: Levashova Y, Accaoui Lorfing P (eds) Balancing the protection of foreign investors and states responses in the post-pandemic world. Kluwer, Alphen aan den Rijn, pp 203–243
Pugliese S (2022b) Toward a new EU strategic dimension: common purchase and investment screening mechanisms as a means of crisis preparedness and management. Il Diritto dell'Unione europea:391–424
Rescigno M, Rimini E (2020) Golden power e coronavirus: regole per l'emergenza o per il futuro. Analisi Giuridica dell'Economia:517–544
Sabatino G (2021) The 'golden power' on foreign investments in EU law in the light of covid crisis. Eur Company law:189–195
Scarchillo G (2020) Golden Powers e settori strategici nella prospettiva europea: il caso Huawei. Un primo commento al Regolamento (Ue) 2019/452 sul controllo degli Investimenti Esteri Diretti. Il Commercio internazionale:569–601
Thym D (2016) The constitutional dimension of public policy justifications. In: Koutrakos P, Shuibhne NN, Syrpis P (eds) Exceptions from EU free movement law. Hart Publishing, Oxford, pp 170–189
Van Bekkum J (2010) Golden shares: a new approach. Eur Company Law:13–19
Van Bekkum J (2014) Cross-border investments in undertakings and the future of EU company law. Eur Bus Law Rev:811–844
Vasques L (2020) Golden Power. Alcune note a margine della disciplina emergenziale del controllo governativo sulle acquisizioni in Italia. Mercato Concorrenza Regole:119–137
Vellucci S (2019) The new regulation on the screening of FDI: the quest for a balance to protect EU's essential interests. Diritto del Commercio Internazionale:123–155

Verellen T (2021) When integration by stealth meets public security: the EU foreign direct investment screening regulation. Leg Issues Econ Integr 48:19–42

von Andreae J (2019) Challenges in a new reality: German foreign investment control in times of change. In: Napolitano G (ed) Foreign direct investment screening. il Mulino, Bologna, pp 77–82

Werlauff E (2009) Safeguards against takeover after Volkswagen – on the lawfulness of such safeguards under company law after the European Court's Decision in "Volkswagen". Eur Bus Law Rev 2009:101–117

Zwartkruis W, de Jong BJ (2020) The EU regulation on screening of foreign direct investment: a game changer? Eur Bus Law Rev 31:447–474

Negotiating Mitigation Agreements: Prenup-Agreements for a Future Ménage à Trois?

Dominik Eisenhut

Contents

Abstract This piece gives an overview of agreements to mitigate national security concerns between the concerned state on the one hand and the acquiring company and the target company on the other hand. Through such mitigation arrangements, states seek to alleviate their national security concerns. The acquiring and target companies, in turn, are willing to make certain undertakings to obtain an—albeit conditional—clearance of the transaction. Mitigation actions have become increasingly popular with screening authorities, allowing them to preserve at the same time the security interests of the state and a general investor-friendly business environment, important to attract foreign capital. The article will look at typical types of security undertakings and at the different legal means to implement these undertakings.

The views expressed in this article are the authors only and do not reflect those of its employer.

D. Eisenhut
Airbus, Toulouse, France
e-mail: dominik.eisenhut@airbus.com

J. H. Pohl et al. (eds.), *National Security and Investment Controls*,
Springer Studies in Law & Geoeconomics (2024) 3: 263–276,
https://doi.org/10.1007/17280_2024_23, Published online: 1 March 2024

1 Background and Context: Security Undertakings as the Golden Middle Way?

Security undertakings can strike a balance between an outright prohibition of a transaction due to security concerns and the State's alternative option to clear and allow the transaction despite these concerns. Such undertakings, often also referred to as mitigation actions or simply "conditions", allow for a more tailored approach: The concerns can be mitigated with specific undertakings of the investor and the target company, thereby respecting the state's right to intervene in private business dealings and preserving a (foreign) investor-friendly economic policy.

It is therefore not surprising that the clearing of investments under conditions has become a widely used and increasingly popular tool. While in 2020, when reporting obligations of EU member states on screening decisions started, 12 percent of all screening decisions in the EU were approved under such conditions, the percentage already rose to 23 percent in 2021.[1] It seems that Member States, many of which have only very recently established investment screening laws, become increasingly aware and fond of the possibilities such undertakings offer them.

Before entering subsequently into the "how" and "what" of security undertakings, a general comment on the mitigation of security concerns seems warranted. It has been pointed out elsewhere that one of the biggest legal challenges in the law of investment screening is the opaqueness of the notion of "national security" and of its standard of judicial review.[2] In the context of mitigation actions, this opaqueness also constitutes the principal difficulty in negotiating security undertakings: As difficult it is to assess potential security concerns of the target company's host state upfront when contemplating an investment in the first place, as difficult and unpredictable it is to objectively determine which mitigation actions might be sufficient to alleviate the security concerns of the host state. In addition to the subjectivity of the security concerns themselves, the determination of the measures that the State may consider sufficient to address these security concerns is equally subjective and often unilaterally determined by the State—despite its obligation to respect the proportionality principle that is applicable both under national administrative and European law. The investor, therefore, is negotiating against an evasive standard, without the possibility to objectively determine at what point the raised security concerns of the State have been sufficiently addressed through its security undertakings.

As the title of this piece suggests, this difficult negotiation environment involves usually three parties—the State, the investor, and the target company—who have to anticipate not only the possible future threats to the host State's national security, but also how these can be proactively remedied upfront. The complexity of this task may

[1] Commission Annual Report 2022 on Investment Screening in the EU, COM (2022) 433 final.

[2] Nettesheim (2020).

therefore withstand the comparison with a prenuptial agreement in which the fears and future needs of not only two, but three have to be addressed.

The article will first look at the legal means available to implement agreed mitigation actions (Sect. 2), and then examine some general considerations for the mitigation of security concerns (Sect. 3), such as negotiation strategies (Sect. 3.1), challenges of multijurisdictional filings (Sect. 3.2), and the drastic solution to carve-out specific business areas from the transaction (Sect. 3.3). Subsequently, it will describe typical mitigation actions (Sect. 4), grouped around types of security concerns such as the fear of technology drain (Sect. 4.1), the fear of foreign state influence (Sect. 4.2), and the fear of loss of autonomy (Sect. 4.3).

2 Legal Means of Fixing Mitigation Actions

In regard to the "how" of implementing security undertakings of the target and/or the acquiring company, the administrative laws of EU Member States with screening mechanisms in place provide for a large variety of legal instruments. Usually, the national screening laws leave it open to the screening authorities by which legal means they deem the security interests at stake best protected.

For example, the German Foreign Trade Regulation[3] mentions the possibility of imposing "instructions" as a condition precedent to clearing investments without giving further guidance on the content or legal form of such instructions.[4] The relevant provision (Section 59 AWV) stipulates only that the parties involved in the transaction and affiliated companies may be subject to instructions "in order to uphold essential security interests of the Federal Republic of Germany, of another Member State of the European Union or in relation to projects or programmes of Union interest within the meaning of Article 8 of Regulation (EU) 2019/452." Unsurprisingly and in line with the Member States' and EU's general practice, it does not further specify the security interests that justify such instructions.

What is more surprising is that the provision does not further specify the legal character of the instructions. The term instruction (*Anordnung*) is not a defined legal term and may comprise different unilateral state measures or bilateral agreements between the state and the investor(s) and/or the target company. Other EU Member States' regimes for imposed mitigation measures also mostly refrain from prescribing concrete legal tools by which security concerns are to be mitigated.[5] In practice, it seems that the following legal tools are most commonly used across EU Member

[3] Außenwirtschaftsverordnung (AWV) of 2 August 2013, last amendment dated 25 April 2022 (BGBl. I S. 2865; 2021 I S. 4304).

[4] Section 59 (1) AWV for investments in all industry sectors, and Section 62 AWV for the so-called "sector-specific" investments in the area of security and defence.

[5] For an overview on Italy, Spain, Portugal and Greece (by Paolo Vargiu, p. 117), Germany and France (by Philipp Stompfe, p. 79), Poland, Lithuania and Latvia (by Marek Jaskowski/Szymon Pawlowski, p. 139), Hungary and Romania (by Szilard Gaspar-Szilagyi, p. 187), Finland, Norway,

States to impose instructions as condition precedent to the clearance of an investment:[6]

- Remittal of an administrative act that is clearing the investment with specific conditions;[7]
- Issue of a legal decree fixing the specific obligations of the involved companies and the rights of the state;[8]
- Conclusion of a public–private agreement between the investor(s) and/or the target company that fixes the conditions to be fulfilled to obtain and maintain the clearance;
- Inclusion of certain State rights and representations into the Articles of Association of the target company, e.g., with regard to board representation, preemption rights, or reserved matters;
- Lawful golden shares in case of privatizations, where a foreign investor acquires a controlling stake in a privatized company and the state remains as a minority shareholder.[9]

Irrespective of their legal nature, all these forms of instructions are usually the result of lengthy and in-depth discussions between the investor and the screening authorities, often also with the direct involvement of the target company's management and advisors. While the screening authority has to determine where its security concerns would be sufficiently alleviated through specific undertakings and measures, the investor has to decide up to where he is willing and able to enter into such arrangements without compromising the business case of the transaction. The subsequent section intends to give an overview of key aspects of these discussions and on typical instruments with which specific recurring security concerns could be alleviated.

3 Mitigating Security Concerns

3.1 General Remarks on Negotiating Security Undertakings

The most fundamental challenge of negotiating security undertakings has already been addressed above: The notion of "security interests" and the related standard of

Sweden and Demark (by Jonas Hallberg, p. 209) see Part II in: Hindelang/Moberg (Eds.), YSEC Yearbook of Socio-Economic Constitutions, Springer 2021, pp. 79 et seq.

[6] For a more specific tool to control investments in the context of privatisations of state-owned companies through tender specifications see Case C-563/17 *Associação Peço a Palavra* ECLI:EU: C:2019:144. For an analysis of this case, see: Papadopoulos (2022), pp. 223–270.

[7] See for example Article R. 153-9 French Financial and Monetary Code.

[8] Such as the "Golden Powers"-regime in Italy, Decreto Legge 21/2012 of 15 March 2012, Gazzetta Ufficiale n. 63.

[9] Papadopoulos (2020).

review of whether these interests are legitimately concerned remains opaque, and the legal boundaries against which a company is negotiating mitigation actions for these security interests also remain unclear. As it is already difficult to objectively establish whether an alleged security interest is actually truly at stake or not in the first place, it is equally difficult to objectively "prove" that a certain required mitigation action is sufficient or unjustified because it goes beyond what can be reasonably requested, taking into account the proportionality principle.

In light of these difficulties for the investor, it is of utmost importance to build a trustful relationship with the involved authorities and ensure transparency in the discussions from the outset. The investor is well advised to provide all potentially relevant information on the transaction from the beginning and to avoid (multiple) further requests for additional information. A staggered information exchange not only delays the review process,[10] but it can also create the impression on the side of the authorities that the parties are not willing to fully cooperate in the screening process or are even trying to hide certain aspects of the deal from them.

Therefore, it is advisable to provide an as-complete-as-possible set of information with the initial application, accompanied by the offer to explain and discuss the nature and stakes of the transaction. During these discussions, it can be very useful to involve dedicated subject-matter experts for areas such as IT, export control, or research and development activities and thus move from the legal-conceptual level to discussing the concrete security concerns of the State with regard to the transaction. If national security and confidentiality limitations allow, an external mediator may also facilitate the negotiations.

3.2 *Specific Aspects of Multijurisdictional Filings*

If the target company comprises legal entities in more than one state, additional complexity comes from the fact that the transaction will have to be cleared for each of these affiliated companies separately and according to the national screening laws—if any—of the respective host state. These proceedings may vary both in their procedures (timelines, information to be provided, etc.), and in their material standard of review. In addition, and although each State makes the screening decision on its own, the States do exchange and coordinate between them in case of multijurisdictional filings. Between EU Member States, the EU Screening Regulation[11] lays out a dedicated coordination and consultation mechanism for the Member States to share information and concerns with regard to a transaction having

[10]Most national screening procedures foresee that the deadlines to take a screening decision only start once the investor has provided all requested information, see for example Section 14a German Foreign Trade Law (Außenwirtschaftsgesetz of 6 June 2013, BGBl. I p. 1482).

[11]Regulation (EU) 2019/452 of the European Parliament and of the Council of 19 March 2019 establishing a framework for the screening of foreign direct investments into the Union, OJ L 79I, 21.3.2019.

effect in multiple jurisdictions. Beyond the EU, informal exchanges between screening authorities are also common. When negotiating mitigation actions, this coordination on the side of governmental interlocutors needs to be duly taken into account by the investor.

First, an investor may negotiate to alleviate security concerns in one country that are not even those of the respective state itself but those of another state that has expressed these concerns during the intergovernmental consultation process. In particular, in the EU regime, Member States are explicitly requested to take these concerns of another Member State—or the EU itself—into account.[12] In practice, it is very difficult to convince a governmental counterpart that a feared security concern is unfounded or can be mitigated through certain measures if these concerns are not its own. A meaningful way to mitigate this additional obstacle is to directly and in parallel engage with the respective third State (or the EU Commission) to convince it of your proposed solution. This is, however, not always possible, as the investor, due to the strict confidentiality of the exchanges between EU Member States via the Commission's coordination mechanism, does not have the right to know which other State has raised the concern. In practice, however, it may often be possible to determine where a concern is coming from and to proactively reach out to the concerned state.[13]

A second risk of multijurisdictional filings may come from the side of the investor. In practice, it can be difficult to maintain the same level of information and identical proposals for mitigation in parallel discussions with several screening authorities. The complexities in particular of large groups of companies and the fact that the discussions are often led by different teams of in-house counsel or law firms in different countries make it very difficult to ensure fully aligned communication and negotiation tactics in practice. Because on the governmental side, the information exchange between screening authorities is well established, diverging information or proposed mitigation undertakings will be laid open between them and can lead to annoyance and mistrust. This risk can, however, be mitigated through a tight and detailed harmonization of the investor's different negotiation teams.

3.3 The "Bazooka" of Mitigation Actions: Carving Out Security-Critical Business Perimeters

Before turning to the most common mitigation actions in more detail, one generic measure that is as efficient as it is painful for the investor needs to be mentioned: as the most drastic measure before abandoning the transaction that is facing

[12] See Article 6 of the Screening Regulation 2019/452.

[13] Note that the Commission might propose changes to remedy this practical problem in a future amendment of the Investment Screening Regulation, see Commission Annual Report 2022 on Investment Screening in the EU, COM (2022) 433 final, pp. 14 et seq.

insurmountable security concerns, the parties may contemplate carving out certain business areas from the transaction that are specifically sensitive. This, of course, only makes sense if the to-be carved out perimeter would cover all business areas that raise concerns and thus would mitigate the reservations of the concerned State and—from the investor's perspective—if the business case of the transaction is still valid for the post carve out target company. Depending on the specificities of the transaction, the carved-out, security-relevant business could then either stay with the seller or be sold separately to an intra-EU bidder.

However, before resorting to such limitation of the scope of the contemplated transaction, practice has established a variety of less onerous measures that can be agreed upon with the screening authorities to obtain investment clearance. The subsequent section will describe different common undertakings to address some recurring concerns.

4 Typical Mitigation Actions

Looking at the different mitigation actions often agreed upon to enable a transaction, they can be structured around the related security concerns they usually address. The concerns raised by states during the discussion of a transaction very often fall into three categories: the fear of "technology drain"; the fear of foreign influence on key industry sectors; and the fear of losing critical domestic technology or production capabilities and thus autonomy in the respective area.

4.1 The Fear of "Technology Drain"

In the current geo-economic context, the most relevant fear is certainly that of a foreign investor being mainly interested in obtaining access to certain critical technologies and not so much in the (financial or strategic) business case of the investment as such. The real aim of the transaction is suspected to be obtaining technological competitive advantages for the acquiring company or the state behind it. For that aim, the relevant technology and know-how would be "stripped" off the target company and transferred to other companies controlled by the investor—often competitors—who benefit from the additional advantage of improving their market position towards the target company. This fear is certainly most prominent in regard to investors from China, particularly if the investor is directly or indirectly controlled by the Chinese State.[14]

The most formalistic arguments to counter this fear are limitations set by the **export control** laws of the target's home country. Today, the combination of

[14] See Prud'homme and Von Zedtwitz (2019); Prud'homme et al. (2018).

European and national export control laws covers a significant part of those technologies that raise the fear of losing them to another state. While the EU Dual-Use-Regulation[15] or US Export Administration Regulations (EAR)[16] cover the majority of high-tech products and intellectual property and subjects them to a regime that allows customs agencies to control and prohibit their export abroad, national export control laws in the EU cover technology that has a defense and security nexus. Because today's technological advances are very often useable in parallel for both civil and security purposes, the boundaries between the two regimes are increasingly blurred, with technology spill-overs in both directions. Irrespective of whether the national defence and security or the dual-use export regime applies, the export of almost all critical technologies outside the EU or the US can be prevented through the refusal of the necessary export clearance. With this in mind, the home state of the target company may take the investor by its word and clear the investment under the assumption that its aim is the strategic and commercial interest in the target company's business itself. If it turns out that the real aim was or has become the "stripping" of the target's technology, this can be prevented through the refusal of export authorizations. Compared to an interdiction of the investment at the outset, this ex post supervision through export control is certainly the less invasive and more investor-friendly approach.

However, in practice, screening authorities often counter this "export control argument" by claiming—to make a blunt summary—that export control often does not work in practice. While in their view, export control usually works for tangible assets being shipped abroad, where processes and controls can be more or less easily applied and monitored, to the contrary and even though the export control regime also covers intangible assets such as intellectual property and know-how, the transfer of intangible assets is much more difficult to control in practice. The transfer of documentation (as hard-copy or electronic files) and of software code (requiring some form of tangible data storage) may still be traceable. This becomes much more difficult in regard to "mere" know-how", which, however, often contains truly valuable technological knowledge. How, to cite an example of a European screening authority, would technology transfer be prevented by export control if the acquired company sends key engineers abroad to work with their colleagues in an affiliated company, thereby de facto transferring their knowledge on processes, methods, and simply experience with what works and what does not work in certain research areas, to their colleagues abroad. To use the example of software again, a company does not have to transfer the source code as such to create technology transfer; it may often be sufficient to discuss the software architecture and features with capable software engineers abroad, who will save months if not years of time in coding a similar software. Even though such "training" and "know-how" transfer would

[15] Regulation (EU) 2021/821 of the European Parliament and of the Council of 20 May 2021 setting up a Union regime for the control of exports, brokering, technical assistance, transit and transfer of dual-use items, OJ L 206, 11.6.2021, p. 1.

[16] See https://www.bis.doc.gov/index.php/regulations/export-administration-regulations-ear.

under many export control regimes[17] also be subject to export clearance, the tracing and monitoring of these activities is practically very difficult.

To address these concerns, it may be advisable for the investor and the target company to offer certain **information rights and reporting obligations** to complement the protection through export control and create additional comfort and trust on the side of the State. Such information rights and obligations may be agreed upon in various forms and intervals: They may be submitted annually or each quarter, in writing or in a meeting supported by a presentation. The content may be at the discretion of the target company or follow a pre-agreed structure or template. Often, it will contain information such as a description of the main areas of research, financial expenditure on R&D activities, newly registered patents or other intellectual property rights, expiry or transfer of such intellectual property rights, or of technology areas where for obsolescence or strategic reasons the company intends to cease its activities.

In particular, in the context of the "export control" argument, the target company and the investor may agree to share information on business dealings of the target company with the affiliated companies of the investor in its home country, e.g., whether delivery or technology transfer agreements have been concluded, which common R&D projects are being conducted, which goods or services were traded between these entities, etc.[18] Obviously, this type of information may often contain commercially or technologically sensitive information that a company usually has no intention or obligation to disclose to third parties, including states. Additionally, they entail significant effort time and cost for the target company, which has to compile information that may not be systematically tracked and captured during its usual business processes. Such commitments therefore have to be carefully contemplated. They may sometimes nevertheless be necessary to convince investment screening authorities to clear a bespoke transaction.

As a further measure to alleviate concerns about technology-"theft", investors may be willing to **undertake not moving R&D capabilities and resources out of the target entity**. Such an undertaking may take the form of a commitment to maintain the head count and budgets of the target's research departments at the same level for several years. Obviously, this is a stark commitment of the investor, significantly impacting its freedom to take strategic and business decisions autonomously. In extreme but not unprecedented scenarios, this may lead to an obligation to maintain resources and financial expenditure for technologies or production activities that are no longer in the scope of a company, in its strategy, or that are even obsolete. It is thus strongly advisable to agree on a fixed period for which such an undertaking shall be valid.

---

[17]The most categorical regime certainly being US - International Traffic in Arms Regulations (ITAR), which even comprise the mere nationality or the fact that someone has worked or lived in the USA in its field of application and thus require US export clearance for any activity of that person outside the USA.

[18]For related transparency obligations under European company law (Art. 9c (1) of the Shareholders Rights Directive II) see Papadopoulos (2020), pp. 707–709.

Finally, it should be mentioned that similar to mitigation through export control limitations, but narrower in scope, **security and classification laws** in the respective target state can alleviate concerns with technology drain. In particular, in the area of defence and security, states have established a system of classification of information (notably including information comprising or related to technology) that entails certain specific legal obligations on the companies handling such information.[19] These may be obligations to store classified information in separated and locally hosted IT environments, to only transfer it via secured or encrypted e–mails or other tools, and—particularly relevant in our context—not to transfer it abroad without specific authorization. Similar to export control, these obligations under security laws are sanctioned under criminal law and can entail significant administrative fines for companies. In the limited area where they are applicable, these restrictions provide for an additional convincing argument against the fear that the target company could transfer such information to its new shareholders abroad.

4.2 *The Fear of Foreign (State) Influence*

The second common fear of states towards foreign investors is that of losing control over certain critical industry sectors. Over the last years, with the COVID-19 pandemic, the Ukraine war, and supply chain disruptions, notably from Asia to Europe and North America, states have become aware that domestic production capabilities in industries such as energy production and distribution, pharmaceuticals, semiconductors and microchips, or ammunition are critical to preserving a state's sovereignty. As a consequence, they are much more sensitive today to foreign state influence in these sectors than they were only a few years ago, at the height of economic interdependencies over the last decades of globalization. The consequence of this development is tighter control of foreign investments overall; with specific regard to mitigation actions, these concerns have also gained importance. They are frequently raised when undertakings are discussed to allow for a transaction to be cleared.

The fear of foreign influence can be addressed with agreements on various measures to limit and/or supervise the investor's influence on the target company. Practically, these measures can be enshrined in the target company's corporate governance via dedicated public–private agreements between the target company, the investor, and the State. More rarely, they are implemented through the target company's statutes or through shareholder agreements.

One of these undertakings can be the granting of the **right to** the State to **propose, nominate, or appoint members of the company's corporate bodies, usually the**

[19] See for example the German Security Act (Sicherheitsüberprüfungsgesetz of 20 April 1994, BGBl I p. 867), or the French Defence Law (Code de la Défense of 21 December 2004, Section 1 – Informations Classifiés).

supervisory board, or to consent to their nomination. To preserve the investor's operative control over the target company, these rights usually only apply to outside supervisory board members and not to executive management.

The right to *appoint* members of the board is certainly the furthest reaching one, with significant impact on the economic freedom of the company's shareholder(s), and therefore rather exceptional and only used in specific, particularly security-relevant companies in the defence and security sector, or in companies that operate critical infrastructure.[20]

It is more common to agree on a right of the State to *nominate or propose* certain candidates to the board, which then nevertheless have to be elected by the shareholder assembly. Additionally, the selection can be left entirely to the company, but with a right of the State to "veto" individual appointments. All these measures, however, constitute significant limitations to the fundamental freedom of the company's owners to steer its activities and therefore will only be agreed upon in specific, particularly sensitive contexts.

An additional legal issue related to such appointments arises when the State intends to appoint public servants and other government officials for these board positions. Under most national laws, public servants are obliged to solely act in the interest of the State employing them and have the duty to follow instructions of the public entity to which they are assigned.[21] When appointing public servants to the board, this obligation is in conflict with the corporate laws on director's duties of most states, which determine that the board members of a company have to be independent from outside instructions and at all times have to solely act in the interest of the company.[22] In addition, as part of their mandate, the board members are obliged to keep confidential all matters discussed in their role as a board member and not to share it with third parties. However, the states may occasionally appoint government officials precisely because they intend to obtain both insight into the company's dealings through them and sometimes also to exert influence. It is submitted that this conflict of legal obligations as directors under corporate law and as public servants cannot be satisfactorily resolved and therefore inherently creates legal risk for these board members being public servants to breach either of the two conflicting legal obligations. It seems therefore advisable to abstain from granting the State a right to appoint public servants as board members.

Below the outright right to appoint or nominate board members, security undertakings sometimes contain the **obligation to respect certain nationality requirements with regard to the executive and/or supervisory management of the target company**. The State may, for example, oblige the new shareholders of the

---

[20] In addition, where the rights of the appointed board members indirectly lead to powers of the State that are similar to those of golden shares, the respective limitations under the case law of the ECJ need to be respected, see Papadopoulos (2020).

[21] See for example Section 62 para 1 German Federal Public Servants Law (*Bundesbeamtengesetz*, BBG).

[22] See for example Principle 20 of the German Corporate Governance Code, https://www.dcgk.de/en/code/current-version/e-conflicts-of-interest.html.

target company to appoint the majority of board members holding the nationality of the State in which the target company has its seat. If not the majority, it could also be agreed that a certain percentage of board members need to hold a certain nationality. Within the EU, the nationality requirement is often substituted by the requirement to appoint EU nationals. This is particularly advisable because the strict nationality requirement faces legal obstacles within the EU under the Treaty on the Functioning of the European Union (TFEU). In its *Schiebel* case, the European Court of Justice found an Austrian law[23] incompatible with the free movement of workers and the freedom of establishment, which stipulated that the Managing Directors of Austrian companies in the sector of security and defence needed to be Austrian nationals.[24] The Court held that this outright nationality requirement was not proportional to the aim of protecting Austria's national security interests,[25] as there would have less restrictive means to achieve the aim: The Court eluded to possibilities such as an obligation to have permanent residence in Austria or to undergo a background security check before the appointment.[26] Indeed, nationality requirements are a rather unsuited tool to preserve security interests in the target company; they are, however, not entirely uncommon. As also indicated by the Court in *Schiebel*, permanent residence, background and security checks on the nominees or regular exchanges with them on security-relevant topics are probably more suited undertakings.

Another, more straightforward means of control after the acquisition of a company would be the **establishment of reserved matters, in which the State has to be consulted or in which it might have a veto right**. These reserved matters can be made subject to agreement of the State directly, or, in case the state has appointed care-takers in the company's management or supervisory board, via the board. Such reserved matters may concern matters of fundamental importance for the future of the acquired company, such as moving the legal seat abroad, mergers involving the target company, or its liquidation or significant changes to the company statutes. They may also concern less fundamental but still critical business decisions, such as entering into joint ventures or other forms of cooperation abroad, the sale and transfer of business areas or intellectual property rights, or the decision to invest in new activities outside of the home country. Obviously, the agreement on reserved matters by the investor significantly impacts its economic freedom to steer the acquired company and therefore needs to be carefully contemplated by the acquirer.

A less restrictive and therefore more acceptable undertaking could be the **granting of certain preemption rights** to the State for the event that the shareholders of the target company should later decide to cease or sell certain activities,

---

[23] Section 141 of the Austrian Trade Code 1994 (Gewerbeordnung 1994).

[24] ECJ Case C-474/12 (Schiebel Aircraft GmbH v Bundesminister für Wirtschaft, Familie und Jugend), 4 September 2014, ECLI:EU:C:2014:2139.

[25] The Court ruled on the deviations from the fundamental freedoms permitted under the exceptions due to national security considerations under Articles 52 and 62, and 346 (1) (b) TFEU.

[26] See Schiebel Case (above Fn 24), at para. 38.

assets, or subsidiaries in which they are no longer interested or if the shareholders would decide to move these activities abroad. In this case, the State may then have the right to acquire the to-be-divested activities. The details of such preemption rights very much depend on the individual investment case and on the parties involved. Often, the preemption right is defined in a way to exclude share or asset transfers within the acquiring group of companies, as long as the ultimate shareholding remains the same and thus the State's interests are preserved despite the group-internal restructuring.

Additionally, such **preemption rights** may also be used **to sanction violations of other security undertakings** the investor has entered into with regard to the target company but failed to fulfil. To address this scenario, the State may request the right to purchase the shares of the target company. Such a "punitive" preemption right ensures the compliance of the investor with its obligation under agreed security undertakings and in addition provides the State with an effective tool to ultimately preserve its security interests if the contractual undertakings are violated.

Similar to the typical mitigation actions to counter the State's fear of technology drain summarized above under Sect. 1, the measures aimed at alleviating concerns regarding the loss of control over critical companies are very often accompanied by **information rights** of the State, allowing it to supervise the business dealings of the company and to exert rights such as veto or preemption rights in a timely manner and based on first-hand information. Regarding the possible formats and extent of such information rights, reference can be made to Sect. 4.1 above.

4.3 The Fear of Loss of Autonomy

The third fear, which is often evoked by screening authorities, is closely related to the fears mentioned above. Loss of technological competence and loss of control over the domestic industry in critical sectors may also lead to the ensuing loss of autonomy to produce or more generally provide certain goods or services in the country, thus remaining independent from imports of these goods. The unavailability of face masks at the beginning of the COVID-pandemic is one example, and the lack of domestic production capabilities for semiconductors, microchips, and energy are more topical and dramatic today. Although foreign investment in principle does not usually result in local industrial capacities and capabilities being moved abroad, foreign owners of critical industry companies admittedly may have business interests and strategies that are not in line with the home state's striving for autonomy in the respective industry sector.

To counter these concerns, the same tools described above for "technology theft" and "foreign control" are commonly used. In particular, undertakings to maintain domestic production and research capacities and reporting obligations to demonstrate respect for these commitments may be warranted to address this third typical fear of investment authorities.

5 Conclusion

The above chapter has illustrated that there are means to address the security concerns of a state vis-à-vis foreign investors that can efficiently alleviate these fears without jeopardizing the investment. The concrete measures and the method of their implementation very much depend on the individual case and on the parties involved. Both for economic and political reasons, it makes good sense to resort to mitigation actions rather than to block foreign investment. Therefore, if security undertakings are not used to deter foreign investment but are only used where they are effective and proportional to the national security concern at the state, they are a legitimate and important tool in the investment screening tool box of the states. Finally, a prenup-agreement for this "ménage à trois" may indeed be the tool of choice in this complex environment.

References

Nettesheim M (2020) Screening for what threat: preserving "public order and security", securing reciprocity in international trade, or supporting certain social, environmental, or industrial policies? In: Hindelang S, Moberg A (eds) YSEC Yearbook of Socio-Economic Constitutions 2020. Springer, Cham. https://doi.org/10.1007/16495_2020_8

Papadopoulos T (2020) Screening of foreign direct investments through European company law. In: Hindelang S, Moberg A (eds) YSEC Yearbook of Socio-Economic Constitutions 2020. Springer, Cham. https://doi.org/10.1007/16495_2020_9

Papadopoulos T (2022) Privatizations of state-owned companies and justifications for restrictions on EU fundamental freedoms: past, present and future perspectives. In: Chaisse J, Górski J, Sejko D (eds) Regulation of state-controlled enterprises: an interdisciplinary and comparative examination. Springer, pp 223–270. https://doi.org/10.1007/978-981-19-1368-6_10

Prud'homme D, Von Zedtwitz M (2019) Managing "forced" technology transfer in emerging markets: the case of China. J Int Manage

Prud'homme D, Von Zedtwitz M, Jan Thraen J, Bader M (2018) "Forced technology transfer" policies: workings in China and strategic implications. Technol Forecast Soc Change 134:150–168

International Coordination of National Screening Procedures: The Case of the EU Cooperation Mechanism

Fabien Gehl

Contents

Abstract This chapter identifies the main challenges at the crossroads of international cooperation and investment screening, which are confidentiality, reconciling international cooperation with national interest, ensuring efficiency and adding value. The chapter then argues that the EU cooperation mechanism has addressed those challenges successfully, even if not perfectly. Finally, the chapter offers a glimpse into the flagship international cooperation initiative at the European level: the EU-US Trade and Technology Council Working Group on investment screening.

F. Gehl (✉)
European Commission, Brussels, Belgium
e-mail: Fabien.Gehl@ec.europa.eu

J. H. Pohl et al. (eds.), *National Security and Investment Controls*,
Springer Studies in Law & Geoeconomics (2024) 3: 277–290,
https://doi.org/10.1007/17280_2024_32, Published online: 24 February 2024

1 Introduction

Today, there is hardly an aspect of public policy that does not have an international dimension and the related cooperation with third countries. From phytosanitary measures to semiconductors, every policy-making field comes with its international dialogue or cooperation. This is less straightforward for the screening of foreign direct investment, which for long has remained a domestic matter. With national security at its heart, this policy area has rarely been international, beyond punctual and ad hoc contact between national authorities.

This chapter will discuss the challenges posed by international cooperation in the field of investment screening (Sect. 2) and show how the EU cooperation mechanism set up by Regulation (EU) 2019/452[1] on investment screening ("the Regulation") has addressed some of them (Sect. 3). Finally, the chapter will briefly explore one of the international cooperation initiatives led at the EU level, namely, the EU-US Trade and Technology Council (Sect. 4).

2 The Tensions at the Intersection of International Cooperation and National Screening

Due to the very nature of investment screening, it is not a policy that lends itself easily to international cooperation. Challenges are numerous, and one can identify four main tensions that countries will face when developing cooperation on investment screening: first, the need to reconcile the confidentiality requirements with the need to exchange information; second, finding ways to reconcile the objectives of international cooperation with the national interests of the countries involved; third, the necessity to address the calls for less red tape while adding new processes; and fourth, determining how to add value through international cooperation.

2.1 *Exchange of Information Vs. Confidentiality*

Investment screening by national authorities requires a high level of confidentiality. On the one hand, the information submitted by the investors and target companies is, in most cases, business confidential. Any leaks could harm the parties to the deal and, in certain cases, have ramifications for the stock market. On the other hand, the risk assessment run by national screening authorities involves national security matters, with occasional input from the intelligence community. The information and analysis underpinning any risk assessment must largely remain unknown to

[1] Regulation (EU) 2019/452 of the European Parliament and of the Council of 19 March 2019 establishing a framework for the screening of foreign direct investments into the Union.

actors outside of the government to avoid risking countries' national security. However, engaging in international cooperation necessarily means engaging in some level of information exchange with other screening authorities or government actors. In some cases, this cooperation can have a public dimension with outreach activities vis-à-vis stakeholders, such as industry or civil society.[2]

Against this backdrop, international cooperation will need to comply with the confidentiality requirements intrinsic to investment screening activities while defining a set of information that can be shared to make this cooperation meaningful. Furthermore, countries might wish to engage in specific agreements to ensure the confidentiality of the shared information.

2.2 International Cooperation Vs. National Interest

Cooperating internationally on investment screening inevitably brings a new dimension into the national screening arena, i.e., the perspective of a third country. In a policy that is essentially devised to protect the national interest and in an environment where countries compete globally for attracting foreign direct investment, considering the view of a third country is not evident.

2.3 Additional Red Tape Vs. Calls for an Efficient Process

At the national level, much attention is given to reducing the impact of investment authorisation schemes in terms of time, costs and procedures. National screening authorities are keen to not unnecessarily delay their authorisation decisions and not to be perceived as a stumbling block to the openness of their foreign investment regimes. As a consequence, any initiative to inject an international cooperation dimension into investment screening will need to take this into account. Any additional delays or additional forms to fill would need to be scrupulously examined before being put into place, with the objective of remaining as efficient and business friendly as possible.

2.4 The Need to Create Added Value

The legitimacy of international cooperation in the field of investment screening and its broad acceptance by the authorities and stakeholders involved will derive from its

[2]See for example the stakeholders meetings taking place in the context of the EU-US Trade and Technology Council: https://futurium.ec.europa.eu/en/EU-US-TTC/wg8/news/summary-2nd-us-eu-stakeholder-event-ttc-investment-screening-working-group-13-december-2022.

added value. Without a well-defined purpose and identified benefits, any such initiative is condemned to fail. With the tensions listed above, international cooperation will need to bring gains not available otherwise to authorities and stakeholders in the form of new information (investment patterns, information on investors or threats, etc.), discovering new best practices, or ad hoc cooperation on specific cases.

3 How Does the EU Regulation Address Those Challenges?

As indicated above, international cooperation can only take place if it manages to overcome and address the described tensions. The EU cooperation mechanism is far from being the most advanced example of international cooperation on investment screening, while remaining a very specific and *sui generis* form of international cooperation as it takes place in the very particular context of the EU internal market. It is in this respect interesting to note that the notion of a cooperationmechanism has been proposed by the Commssion from the outset in its legislative proposal.[3] After more than two years of application, one can establish that it has successfully addressed many of the challenges it faced.

3.1 The Confidentiality Issue

Mindful of the critical importance of this issue, the legislators have injected a set of robust confidentiality requirements into the Regulation. As recognised by the Commission, "*Appropriate handling and protection of any information submitted* [. . .] *is vital to ensure the necessary trust between all parties involved, i.e. the parties to a transaction, the notifying Member State, the 26 other Member States and the European Commission*".[4]

Those requirements start at the very beginning of the screening process by imposing the following on Member States' national screening mechanism: "*confidential information, including commercially sensitive information, made available to the Member State undertaking the screening shall be protected*". This first confidentiality requirement frames the Member States obligation in their operations under their national mechanism. It is a clear signal and guarantee to stakeholders, investors in particular, that the information provided to screening authorities will be protected.

[3]See Article 8 of Proposal for a Regulation of the European Parliament and of the Council establishing a framework for screening of foreign direct investments into the European Union, COM(2017) 487 final.

[4]Second Annual Report on the screening of foreign direct investment, COM(2022) 433 final, p. 20.

As the natural follow-up to this obligation, the EU cooperation mechanism is subject to a similar requirement: "*Member States and the Commission shall ensure the protection of confidential information acquired in application of this Regulation in accordance with Union and the respective national law*".[5] This requirement is to be combined with the obligation for Member States to "*ensure that classified information provided or exchanged under this Regulation is not downgraded or declassified without the prior written consent of the originator*".[6] In this set up, not only the information provided to the EU cooperation mechanism should be protected by default, but the will of the party from which the information is originating has to be respected. This corresponds to the usual practice for the handling of classified information at the European level.[7] To this end, the Commission has developed new, secured IT tools for the exchange of information with Member States at different levels of classification.[8]

A third aspect of the confidentiality requirement is that the information received in the context of the application of the Regulation shall only be used for the purpose for which it was requested,[9] i.e., for screening a given transaction. As a consequence, the information exchanged within the EU cooperation mechanism cannot be used for other objectives, such as competition or industrial policies. The information is to be used solely for the screening of the case at hand.

This approach is topped up by a very strict principle of "*need to know*", including within the European institutions themselves. Only individuals directly participating in the risk assessment and related decision-making process have access to the information exchanges among the Member States and the Commission.

The outcome has been rather satisfactory thus far, and processes put into place have been "*reliable, with no reported leaks regarding notifications, opinions or other action under the Regulation.*"[10]

---

[5] Article 10(2) of Regulation (EU) 2019/452 of the European Parliament and of the Council of 19 March 2019 establishing a framework for the screening of foreign direct investments into the Union.

[6] Article 10(3) of Regulation (EU) 2019/452 of the European Parliament and of the Council of 19 March 2019 establishing a framework for the screening of foreign direct investments into the Union.

[7] See for example: Article 3 (2) of Council Decision of 23 September 2013 on the security rules for protecting EU classified information (2013/488/EU): "[EU Classified Information] *shall not be downgraded or declassified nor shall any of the markings referred to in Article 2(3) be modified or removed without the prior written consent of the originator*". See also: Commission Decision (EU, Euratom) 2015/444 of 13 March 2015 on the security rules for protecting EU classified information.

[8] As notably required by Article 11(2) of Regulation (EU) 2019/452 of the European Parliament and of the Council of 19 March 2019 establishing a framework for the screening of foreign direct investments into the Union.: "*A secure and encrypted system shall be provided by the Commission to support direct cooperation and exchange of information between the contact points.*"

[9] Article 10(1) of the Regulation (EU) 2019/452 of the European Parliament and of the Council of 19 March 2019 establishing a framework for the screening of foreign direct investments into the Union.

[10] First Annual Report on the screening of foreign direct investment, COM(2021) 714 final, p. 19.

3.2 Balancing International Cooperation with National Interest

A very delicate balance between European and national interest has been achieved through the establishment of the EU cooperation mechanism by the Regulation. Essentially, the screening of foreign investment at the European level complements and does not replace screening at the national level. Indeed, the Regulation complements the national screening mechanisms currently maintained by 18 EU Member States[11] by establishing a mandatory cooperation mechanism designed to allow all Member States and the Commission to collectively assess potential threats to security and public order deriving from Foreign Direct Investment ("FDI"), regardless of where in the EU the investment in question takes place or whether it is subject to screening. This mandatory cooperation mechanism is considered to be essential in the context of the internal market, where FDI materialised in the national market of one Member State could have an impact on the national markets of other Member States. Although the final decision on any FDI remains with the Member State where the investment takes place, the cooperation on screening will allow for the exchange of relevant information and inform the decision-making at Member States' level. Under the EU cooperation mechanism, Member States and the Commission have the possibility to comment or issue an opinion on FDI taking place in one Member State. Comments by Member States and Commission's opinions are neither binding nor public.

For FDI undergoing screening at the national level, cooperation is launched by a notification from the screening Member State to other Member States and the Commission.[12] This notification shall include a basic set of information on the foreign investor and the undertaking concerned, such as their ownership structure, participation of the foreign investor in the capital, information related to their business operations, approximate value of the investment, the Member States in which they conduct relevant business operations, the funding of the investment and its source, and the date when the FDI is planned to be completed or has been completed.[13] Following this notification, other Member States and the Commission have 15 days to indicate their intention to provide a comment or an opinion and to ask for additional information. The screening Member State has to endeavour to provide the additional information requested. This obligation entails, if necessary, requesting information directly from the investor or the undertaking concerned

[11] Austria, Czechia, Germany, Denmark, Finland, France, Hungary, Italy, Lithuania, Latvia, Malta, Netherlands, Poland, Portugal, Spain, Romania, Slovenia, Slovakia.

[12] Article 6(1) of Regulation (EU) 2019/452 of the European Parliament and of the Council of 19 March 2019 establishing a framework for the screening of foreign direct investments into the Union.

[13] Article 9(2) of Regulation (EU) 2019/452 of the European Parliament and of the Council of 19 March 2019 establishing a framework for the screening of foreign direct investments into the Union.

(other Member States or the Commission have no legal grounds to establish direct contact with the investor or the undertaking concerned). Upon receipt of the additional information, other Member States and the Commission have another 20 days to issue a duly justified comment or opinion to the screening Member State. Comments by Member States and opinions issued by the Commission are legally non-binding. However, the recipient Member State shall give due consideration to them.[14] In certain circumstances, the Commission's opinion relates to an investment affecting a project or programme of EU interest on grounds of security or public order, such as Galileo, Horizon 2020 or the Trans-European Transport Network projects, the recipient Member State shall take utmost account of it and provide an explanation to the Commission if its opinion is not followed.

As indicated in the EU's second Annual Report, the Commission has issued opinions in less than 3% of the cases submitted to the EU cooperation mechanism.[15] This translates into a very considerate approach on the EU side based on which concerns are only raised in well-founded cases. In addition, it shows the EU's will to balance the objectives of being open to foreign direct investment while at the same time being able to act when necessary to protect security or public order in the EU.

In the balancing act between European and national interests, the Regulation has made a clear choice in regard to the ultimate decision-making level, namely, the Member State where the investment shall take place. At the same time, it is opening up the assessment of the transaction to input from the Commission and other Member States.

3.3 Keeping up with the Efficiency Requirement

The EU cooperation mechanism has been built with efficiency in mind. The process is straightforward, with only a few steps and excessively short deadlines.

In regard to the process itself, the Member State authorities remain the investor's one stop shop. All information is transmitted via the national authority, and it is not necessary for the investor to set up any additional level of communication with the European level. The communication among Member States and the Commission takes place through a network of contact points, in accordance with the requirements of the Regulation.[16] Notifications, requests for additional information as well as

[14] Article 6(9) of Regulation (EU) 2019/452 of the European Parliament and of the Council of 19 March 2019 establishing a framework for the screening of foreign direct investments into the Union.

[15] Second Annual Report on the screening of foreign direct investment, COM(2022) 433 final.

[16] "*Each Member State and the Commission shall establish a contact point for the implementation of this Regulation. Member States and the Commission shall involve those contact points on all issues relating to the implementation of this Regulation.*" Article 11(1) of Regulation (EU) 2019/452 of the European Parliament and of the Council of 19 March 2019 establishing a framework for the screening of foreign direct investments into the Union.

opinions and comments will be shared through this single channel of communication among contact points in a system that will be mostly invisible and inaccessible for the investor and the parties to the transaction.

Regarding timelines, as indicated in Sect. 3.2, the Regulation has set out tight and strict deadlines. The screening at the European level is articulated around two phases of 15 and 20 calendar days. While there is no option to extend those timelines, the final time dedicated to a case may vary, depending on how much time will be necessary to collect the additional information requested at the end of the first phase (the end of the 15 calendar days) and the beginning of the second phase (for a duration of 20 calendar days). In its first Annual Report, the Commission established that the average duration for Member States to provide additional information was 31 calendar days, while varying from two to 101 calendar days.[17]

For the process to remain meaningful, the Regulation has set out simple but fundamental requirements for the Member States' national screening mechanisms. Indeed, while the Regulation is rather shy in regard to the harmonisation of national screening mechanisms, it has clearly required a minimum of synchronisation from the Member States: "*Member States shall apply timeframes under their screening mechanisms. The screening mechanisms shall allow Member States to take into account the comments of other Member States referred to in Articles 6 and 7 and the opinions of the Commission referred to in Articles 6, 7 and 8*".[18] This obligation is paramount to the effectiveness of the EU cooperation mechanism. It is essential that all Member States having set up a national screening mechanism comply with it and anticipate sufficient time to take into account opinions by the Commission and comments by Member States without jeopardising the effectiveness of the system.

In concrete terms, the most recent numbers show that the EU cooperation mechanism is functioning well. Of the 414 cases notified in 2021, the vast majority (86%) were closed in phase 1, i.e., very quickly, with only 11% of the notified cases (compared to 14% in the period covered by the previous report) closed in phase 2, and less than 3% of cases resulted in a Commission opinion. While most cases are assessed rapidly, within the prescribed 15 calendar days in phase 1, the duration of cases entering phase 2 continues to show significant variation. This is due to the time needed by Member States to provide answers to a Commission request for additional information, with national authorities often depending on the investor for the requested information.[19]

While the evidence points toward a satisfactory modus operandi in regard to process and timelines, shortcomings have also been identified. First, the current timelines do not address multijurisdiction cases in a consolidated manner, since their notification in the various Member States might be submitted at different moments

[17] First Annual Report on the screening of foreign direct investment, COM(2021) 714 final, p. 13.

[18] Article 3(3) of Regulation (EU) 2019/452 of the European Parliament and of the Council of 19 March 2019 establishing a framework for the screening of foreign direct investments into the Union.

[19] Second Annual Report on the screening of foreign direct investment, COM(2022) 433 final, p. 16.

and hence trigger the legal timelines in an unsynchronised fashion. Second, another concern emerges from the fact that the 20-day period of the second phase is of the same length for both the Member States and the Commission. This can sometimes mean that the Commission would have to issue an opinion before or at the same time as a Member State issuing a comment, whereas the opinion could have benefitted from this additional input of a Member State.

3.4 A Clear and Well-Defined Added Value

The EU cooperation mechanism is built in a way that the risk assessment carried out by the Commission and the other Member States on a given transaction does not impede or affect the national security assessment by the Member States where the investment shall take place, but it rather adds a clear additional dimension. In this respect, the room of manoeuvre of the Commission is well defined. The Regulation enables the Commission to issue opinions on specific foreign direct investments in three instances: first, if it considers that such investments are likely to affect the security or public order of more than one Member State; second, if it considers that such investments are likely to affect projects or programmes of Union interest on grounds of security or public order; and third if it has relevant information in relation to that foreign direct investment.[20]

The first scenario, where the security and/or public order of more than one Member State is likely to be affected, points towards a notion of collective security where the EU as a whole is likely to face the negative consequences of a potential investment. Although the Regulation does not define 'security' and 'public order', it provides a non-exhaustive list of factors that may be considered by the Member States and the Commission when screening FDI. Those factors are articulated around two main aspects of the risk assessment. First, they relate to the effects of an investment on critical infrastructures (with a number of examples ranging from energy, transport, health to defence and financial infrastructures), critical technologies (examples include dual use, artificial intelligence, robotics, cybersecurity and many more), supply of critical inputs, access to sensitive information, freedom and pluralism of media.[21] Second, the Regulation lists certain features of a foreign investor, such as whether it is controlled by a foreign government, whether it has already been involved in activities affecting security or public order or whether there

[20] Article 6(3) of Regulation (EU) 2019/452 of the European Parliament and of the Council of 19 March 2019 establishing a framework for the screening of foreign direct investments into the Union.

[21] Article 4(1) of Regulation (EU) 2019/452 of the European Parliament and of the Council of 19 March 2019 establishing a framework for the screening of foreign direct investments into the Union.

is a serious risk that it engages in illegal or criminal activities.[22] Those features will be part of the threat analysis that is carried out by Commission services when examining a transaction.

The second scenario, which relates to risks affecting programmes and projects of Union interest, is a key feature of the EUcooperation mechanism, as it gears towards the protection of European critical assets, which were not necessarily protected before the Regulation was applied. Projects and programmes of Union interest include "*those projects and programmes which involve a substantial amount or a significant share of Union funding, or which are covered by Union law regarding critical infrastructure, critical technologies or critical inputs which are essential for security or public order*".[23] More concretely, the Regulation in its dedicated Annex offers a list of such programmes. This Annex can be regularly updated by the Commission and notably includes programmes such as:[24] European GNSS programmes (Galileo and EGNOS), Copernicus, Union Space Programme, Horizon Europe, the Trans-European Networks for Transport, Energy, Telecommunication, the Connecting Europe Facility, the Digital Europe Programme, or various defence programmes. When those programmes are likely to be affected on grounds of security and/or public order by a transaction, the Commission might issue an opinion on the basis of Article 8 of the Regulation. This legal basis will trigger one specificity in the sense that Member States "*where the foreign direct investment is planned or has been completed shall take utmost account of the Commission's opinion and provide an explanation to the Commission if its opinion is not followed*",[25] whereas opinions usually only require Member States to "*give due consideration*" to the recommendations of the Commission.[26] The risks to projects and programmes of Union interest therefore confer a slightly stronger status to the Commission's opinions, indicative of the importance given by the European legislator to these

[22] Article 4(2) of Regulation (EU) 2019/452 of the European Parliament and of the Council of 19 March 2019 establishing a framework for the screening of foreign direct investments into the Union.

[23] Article 8(3) of of Regulation (EU) 2019/452 of the European Parliament and of the Council of 19 March 2019 establishing a framework for the screening of foreign direct investments into the Union.

[24] Commission Delegated Regulation (EU) 2021/2126 of 29 September 2021 amending the Annex to Regulation (EU) 2019/452 of the European Parliament and of the Council establishing a framework for the screening of foreign direct investments into the Union. OJ L 432, 3.12.2021, pp. 1–6.

[25] Article 8(2)(c) of of Regulation (EU) 2019/452 of the European Parliament and of the Council of 19 March 2019 establishing a framework for the screening of foreign direct investments into the Union.

[26] See Article 6 (9) of Regulation (EU) 2019/452 of the European Parliament and of the Council of 19 March 2019 establishing a framework for the screening of foreign direct investments into the Union.

programmes and of the added value of the Commission's input into the cooperation mechanism.

4 Beyond the EU: The EU Cooperation Mechanism and International Cooperation

The EU cooperation mechanism is not limited to the boundaries of the EU, and the "*Member States and the Commission may cooperate with the responsible authorities of third countries on issues relating to the screening of foreign direct investments on grounds of security and public order*."[27] This provision of the Regulation has opened the door to international activities around EU cooperation. At this juncture, the flagship initiative in this area is the Working Group on Investment Screening established in the context of the EU-US Trade and Technology Council (TTC).

The TTC indeed features a Working Group dedicated specifically to Investment Screening, which has to date held three meetings and organised two stakeholder events.[28] Those meetings confirmed a high level of interest and engagement from each side in cooperating further in this field. It also resulted in the adoption of a work programme aimed at improving the understanding of shared and individual risks related to investments and how the respective screening regimes of the US and the EU identify and mitigate such risks. At the Trade and Technology Council ministerial meeting of 16 May 2022, the EU and US reaffirmed the importance of investment screening while remaining open to foreign investment. Both sides also agreed to continue sharing information and experiences on investment screening and to use the Trade and Technology Council to develop a holistic view of the security risks related to specific sensitive technologies and the policy tools addressing them.[29]

Thus far, the EU and the US have exchanged analysis regarding investment trends of foreign investors over time and exchanged information, including data, trends, origins of investors or sectors of interest. In addition, the EU and the US have

[27] Article 13 of of Regulation (EU) 2019/452 of the European Parliament and of the Council of 19 March 2019 establishing a framework for the screening of foreign direct investments into the Union.

[28] Situation on 15 December 2022.

[29] At the ministerial meeting in Paris-Saclay (May 2022), the US and the EU agreed on the following actions: "*a. continue to share information and experience, which can help to broaden perspectives within the respective screening systems, including through practical exercises and case studies, involving thematic experts; b. start developing a holistic view of the security risks related to specific sensitive technologies and the policy tools addressing them, including in particular export controls and investment screening; c. continue conducting joint virtual outreach events for stakeholders as appropriate; and d. explore conducting a practical "tabletop" exercise in the later part of 2022 to continue to facilitate the exchange of best practices on a more technical and practical level*" (https://ec.europa.eu/commission/presscorner/detail/en/IP_22_3034).

exchanged on best practices regarding their respective screening regimes (procedures, methodologies, understanding of technology-specific risks, handling of complex ownership structures) and on how the EU and the US understand and identify security risks related to specific sensitive technologies. In the future, the Working Group will continue to discuss security risks posed by certain investments to specific sensitive technologies and to more holistically assess the use of different policy tools available to address these risks. This cooperation does not extend to individual cases.

The objective of this transatlantic cooperation is clear: it allows the EU and the US to deepen their collective understanding of shared and individual risks, emphasises the importance of investment screening as one of the key tools to address national security and public order risks, and explores potential opportunities for deeper technical exchanges for an increasingly efficient future collaboration. As the EU cooperation mechanism develops and matures, the TTC represents a formidable opportunity to build transatlantic links on the basis of this policy, which is growing in importance.

5 Conclusion

As so very often in the EU, the EU cooperation mechanism is a *sui generis* tool that responds to the particularities of the European construction and of its internal market. In its current version, the EU cooperation mechanism has managed to address the main tensions at the crossroads of international cooperation and investment screening. By developing its own international agenda, the EU cooperation mechanism is allowing itself to exchange views with like-minded partners on shared risks and investors or countries of concern. This has become particularly critical in the current geopolitical context.

Going further and as shortcomings become increasingly blatant, the system will evolve, and the EU cooperation mechanism will probably take a different shape. As a next step, the Commission is mandated to evaluate the functioning and effectiveness of the Regulation by October 2023.[30] This exercise will be a useful occasion to have a fresh look at all aspects of European cooperation on investment screening.

References

Commission Decision (EU, Euratom) 2015/444 of 13 March 2015 on the security rules for protecting EU classified information

[30] See Article 15 of of Regulation (EU) 2019/452 of the European Parliament and of the Council of 19 March 2019 establishing a framework for the screening of foreign direct investments into the Union.

Commission Delegated Regulation (EU) 2021/2126 of 29 September 2021 amending the Annex to Regulation (EU) 2019/452 of the European Parliament and of the Council establishing a framework for the screening of foreign direct investments into the Union
Council Decision of 23 September 2013 on the security rules for protecting EU classified information (2013/488/EU)
First Annual Report on the screening of foreign direct investment, COM(2021) 714 final
Press release of the EU-US ministerial meeting in Paris-Saclay (May 2022), (https://ec.europa.eu/commission/presscorner/detail/en/IP_22_3034)
Proposal for a Regulation of the European Parliament and of the Council establishing a framework for screening of foreign direct investments into the European Union, COM(2017) 487 final
Regulation (EU) 2019/452 of the European Parliament and of the Council of 19 March 2019 establishing a framework for the screening of foreign direct investments into the Union
Reports of stakeholders meetings taking place in the context of the EU-US Trade and Technology Council: https://futurium.ec.europa.eu/en/EU-US-TTC/wg8/news/summary-2nd-us-eu-stakeholder-event-ttc-investment-screening-working-group-13-december-2022
Second Annual Report on the screening of foreign direct investment, COM(2022) 433 final

MIX
Papier aus verantwortungsvollen Quellen
Paper from responsible sources
FSC® C105338

If you have any concerns about our products,
you can contact us on
ProductSafety@springernature.com

In case Publisher is established outside the EU,
the EU authorized representative is:
Springer Nature Customer Service Center GmbH
Europaplatz 3, 69115 Heidelberg, Germany

Printed by Libri Plureos GmbH
in Hamburg, Germany